Fifth Edition

Materials and Components
of
Interior Architecture

J. Rosemary Riggs, *Allied member ASID*

Brigham Young University, Emeritus

R. F. Brown

DESIGN ELEMENTS.

Prentice Hall, Upper Saddle River, New Jersey 07458

Library of Congress Cataloging-in-Publication Data

Riggs, J. Rosemary.
     Materials and components of interior architecture / J. Rosemary
Riggs. —5th ed.
        p.   cm.
     Includes bibliographical references and index.
     ISBN 0–13–923228–1
     1. Building materials.   2. Household appliances.   3. Plumbing—
Equipment and supplies.   4. Interior decoration.   I. Title.
TA403.R525   1999
698—dc21
                                                                    98-4590
                                                                    CIP

Acquisition Editor: Elizabeth Sugg
Editorial Assistant: Maria Krall
Managing Editor: Mary Carnis
Project Manager: Linda B. Pawelchak
Prepress and Manufacturing Buyer: Ed O'Dougherty
Cover Director: Jayne Conte
Cover Design: Liz Nemeth
Electronic Art Creation: Asterisk Group, Inc.
Marketing Manager: Danny Hoyt
Copy Editing: Patricia M. Daly
Proofreading: Nancy Menges
Color insert design: Warren Fischbach

Cover art: Amtico resilient vinyl special design floor at the
famous Winter Gardens, Blackpool, U.K. More than 2,500
individually cut pieces make up this highly intricate floor
design, which was put together like a vast jigsaw with every
piece fitting together perfectly. (Photo Courtesy of Amtico
International Inc.)

This book was set in 10/12 Palatino by Pine Tree
Composition, Inc., and was printed and bound by
Banta Company. The cover was printed by Banta Company.

© 1999. 1996, 1989, 1985 by Prentice-Hall, Inc.
Upper Saddle River, New Jersey 07458

Previously published as *Materials and Components of Interior Design*

Printed in the United States of America
10   9   8   7   6   5   4   3

ISBN 0-13-923228-1

PRENTICE-HALL INTERNATIONAL (UK) LIMITED, *LONDON*
PRENTICE-HALL OF AUSTRALIA PTY. LIMITED, *SYDNEY*
PRENTICE-HALL CANADA INC., *TORONTO*
PRENTICE-HALL HISPANOAMERICANA, S.A., *MEXICO*
PRENTICE-HALL OF INDIA PRIVATE LIMITED, *NEW DELHI*
PRENTICE-HALL OF JAPAN, INC., *TOKYO*
PEARSON EDUCATION ASIA PTE. LTD., *SINGAPORE*
EDITORA PRENTICE-HALL DO BRASIL, LTDA., *RIO DE JANEIRO*

Contents

6
Ceilings 131

7
Other Components 139

8
Cabinet Construction 159

9
Kitchens 169

10
Bathrooms 189

Foreword

Interior design and architecture are an extraordinary combination of science and art. Few other professions require both areas of expertise.

With the tremendous advances in today's materials and technologies it can be a daunting task to achieve successful results within the limitations of time, financial resources, and material constraints. At best, design can be an outstandingly uplifting process, a reward within itself.

To maximize the opportunity for "besting" the design result, knowledge of the product and material resources as well as synergistic thinking are essential. The most innovative solutions are sabotaged by the details.

I think back to my firm's CEO Buckminster Fuller—how he challenged designers to think "outside the box"; to think of the interior systematically instead of as a random arbitrary compilation of products and materials. He would say, "If the invention, the materials, the object doesn't work, then it isn't beautiful; and if it isn't beautiful, then it doesn't work!"

Many of us are familiar with Leonardo da Vinci's sketch design of a man or a proposed flying machine that looked somewhat like a bicycle with wings. Though brilliantly conceived, the design did not work because the materials were too heavy and not strong enough to perform as envisioned. Three hundred years later, high-grade carbon filament (mylar) was invented and could withstand pressure greater than 100,000 pounds per square inch (psi). Mylar is extremely light and is often used to make sails. As a result, in 1980, Paul MacAlready crossed the English Channel on the *Gossamer Albatros*, a light plane covered with a high-carbon mylar filament. Suddenly, da Vinci's idea had become a reality.

We all know how new materials have changed our world in recent history (for example, plastic and fiberglass). J. Rosemary Riggs's book, *Materials and Components of Interior Architecture*, takes into account the dramatic advances made available to the design professional.

Those who use this book must seek connections among the individual elements discussed herein and relate them, by ecological, operational, and aesthetic reasoning, to the design and goals of those who will use the final facilities. What a wonderful time to be in the design profession

Joyce Burke-Jones, FASID
1997–1998 National President of ASID and
Principal in the firm of Buckminster Fuller,
Sadao & Zung Architects

Preface

While teaching an introductory class in interior design, I noticed that the students usually chose paint or wallpaper for the walls and always used carpet on the floor, as though these were the only suitable treatments for walls and floors. I felt a need to break the cycle by exposing students to the fascinating world of materials—and so this book started to take shape.

I was unable to find a book that fully covered the exciting nonstructural materials available to the interior designer. Some authors concentrated on historical aspects of the home, both in architecture and furniture. Some emphasized upholstered furniture, draperies, and carpets; whereas still others stressed the principles and elements of design and color and the aesthetic values that make up a home. No one, however, concentrated on the "nuts and bolts" of interior design. Some books purporting to cover all types of flooring did not even mention wood floors, whereas others had only one or two paragraphs on the subject. In the fourth edition of this book, a chapter on environmental concerns was added, and this fifth edition contains updated information on products that are environmentally stable. Throughout this edition, for those particularly interested in environmental concerns, products and manufacturers are mentioned that are participating in some way in the recycling processes. (See Chapter 1, "Environmental Concerns.") Chapter 1 should be of prime interest to those designers (most of us) who believe that the environment is precious and worth saving. Environmental responsibility and recycling are also ways to help cope with the growing landfill problem.

In the past, the interior design profession has dealt mainly with the more decorative aspects of design. Today it has become increasingly necessary for interior designers to be knowledgeable not only about the finishing materials used in the design field, but about some structural materials as well. Many interior designers are working for or with architects, so it is important that they understand the properties and uses of all materials. Thus, the *raison d'être* of this textbook.

Most sales representatives realize that the interior design student of today is the customer of tomorrow, but there are still some who do not understand the scope of the interior design field. Many interior designers are women, and I have found that the ability to talk knowledgeably about materials earns the respect of a man in the profession.

Installation methods are discussed in this book because there are some contractors (luckily only a few) who will use the cheapest method of installation, one that may not be the best for that particular job. Installation methods have been taken from information provided by manufacturers, associations, and institutions involved with that product. Knowledge of the correct installation procedures ensures a properly installed project. The instructor's manual provides many real-world examples of problems with products that have been improperly installed, and some installation problems are mentioned in this fifth edition. In researching material for this edition, I read in technical journals of various problems, such as yellowing in carpet, moisture in concrete slabs, and discolorations in vinyl flooring. Awareness of a potential problem before it occurs can prevent headaches in the future.

Maintenance information on many materials has also been included, because the cost of maintenance should be one of the deciding factors in product selection. What may be an inexpensive material at first may be the most expensive over time because of high maintenance costs.

Most of the world uses the metric system, and the U.S. government has stressed the importance of a transition to the metric system, so designers will find increasing use of millimeters, meters, grams, and kilograms as measurements for length and weight. The wallcovering industry has already converted to metric or European measurements. Some manufacturers, particularly those who sell to Canada and other foreign countries, now list their products in two systems, inches and metric. Thus Appendix A contains handy conversion tables of most of the measurements used in interior design.

In doing my research and talking to many manufacturers, I have found a growing awareness of customers' needs and wishes. Dependability is one thing the consumer requires, whether for a private home or a large commercial installation. Thus many manufacturers offer warranties (one manufacturer offers a lifetime structural guarantee on the wood floor).

All disciplines have their own jargon. To communicate properly with contractors and architects, a designer must understand their jargon. Designers or prospective builders who have read and studied *Materials and Components of Interior Architecture* will be able to talk knowledgeably with architects and contractors about the uses of materials and their methods of installation. This understanding will also enable designers to decide for themselves which materials and methods are best for a given installation and avoid being influenced by the bias of salespeople.

One word about the spelling of *moulding*: The Architectural Woodwork Institute uses this spelling, and the term is spelled this way in Canada, where this textbook is also used. The dictionary I consulted has both spellings. To be consistent I have used *moulding* throughout this book.

This book can serve as a reference for designers who are already practicing, because it brings to their attention new materials on the market and improvements in current ones, many of which won awards in 1997. The appendices are useful reminders of manu-

facturers and their products. When a product is unique to one manufacturer, that manufacturer's product has been mentioned. Wherever possible, generic information has been used. A contractor who read this book told me that contractors would also benefit from using it as a reference tool.

In arranging the subject matter, I placed the chapter on environmental concerns first, because all chapters on materials stress environmental concerns. The chapter on paint follows because all types of surfaces—floors, walls, and ceilings—may be painted. Then, starting from the bottom, the logical progression was a chapter on carpets, Chapter 3 (carpet is the most common floor covering). (The Carpet and Rug Institute provided invaluable assistance in writing Chapter 3.) Chapter 4 deals with all the other types of materials for floors.

Many of the same materials used for flooring are also discussed in Chapter 5, but this time they are used on walls; the installation, finish, and maintenance vary of course. Chapter 6 covers ceilings, areas that are usually either painted or ignored. Chapter 7 discusses all the other components that make up a well-designed room, including mouldings, doors, hardware, and hinges.

Chapter 8 explains the construction, structure, and design of fine cabinetry and could not have been written without the assistance of the Architectural Woodwork Institute. (The information presented in Chapter 8 will come in handy for inspecting ready-made furniture because cabinets and furniture are constructed similarly.) Study of Chapter 8 will enable designers to provide rough drawings of cabinetry that is as economical as possible to construct. *Architectural Woodwork Quality Standards,* 7th edition, version 1.0, 1997 should be consulted for precise drawings.

Chapter 9 discusses kitchens. With the background of the previous chapter, Chapter 9 enables a designer to make an intelligent selection of the appropriate cabinetry. Chapter 9 also covers the various appliances and the newest innovations in kitchen design. Chapter 10 describes bathrooms, both residential and institutional. Chapters 9 and 10 were included because designers will be called on frequently to assist in the renovation of homes—including the very expensive areas of kitchens and bathrooms. These remodeling jobs will probably cost about 10 to 15 percent of the house value. A full bath added to an older three-bedroom, one-bath house will not only guarantee recouping the cost of the improvements, but will increase resale value.

A glossary of words boldfaced in the text appears at the end of each chapter. It can be used as an aid for students studying for exams. Appendix A lists manufacturers and associations that sell or represent the products mentioned in the chapters. Appendix B lists the names and addresses of the manufacturers named in Appendix A. Every effort has been made to make this list as up to date as possible, but businesses do change names and locations. For this fifth edition, I have added Web sites, where available, so students and designers can immediately access product information.

While compiling the index for this book, I realized that it can also be an aid in preparing for comprehensive exams, such as a final or the National Council for Interior Design Qualification (NCIDQ) exam. Thus in the index I have listed, in parentheses, all the words in the glossaries; I have done this for two reasons: First, the page number enables users to find the word (the usual purpose of an index). Second, students can test themselves on whether they are familiar with the word and its meaning.

If one manufacturer seems to be given more emphasis than another, it is not necessarily because its product is better than others on the market, but because the manufacturer has been extremely helpful (providing information and brochures, checking sections for accuracy, and, most important, providing photographs with which to illustrate the various sections). This is why the products of Kentucky Wood Floors, Kohler Company, and Wilsonart International are featured in photographs more frequently than other manufacturers.

I am indebted to the many manufacturers and trade organizations that have so willingly sent me technical information and brochures, from which I have compiled up-to-date data. As mentioned previously, I am grateful to the Carpet and Rug Institute for providing extensive information and for granting permission to quote from its informative book, *Specifier's Handbook*. This handbook has been the basis for much of the information contained in Chapter 3.

I have found the trade organizations to be very helpful and would like to thank in particular the Architectural Woodwork Institute for the many drawings and technical information found not only in Chapter 5, "Walls," but also Chapter 8, "Cabinet Construction." The Oak Flooring Manufacturers Association provides industry-wide standards for wood flooring installation. The Marble Institute of America reviewed the section on marble floors and walls, while the Tile Council of America, the authority for all types of hard materials for floors and walls, provided the installation information for those materials. Each of these associations is the recognized authority in its field.

Many professionals helped me ensure the accuracy and relevance of information presented in this text. Robert Hanks of Bridgepoint Corporation realized that proper maintenance is vital to the durability of carpet. Sherwin-Williams was a great help in making sure that the information in Chapter 2 was current. (There have been many technical changes in that field).

Most of all, I would like to thank my husband, sculptor Frank Riggs, for serving as house husband and for offering his support and encouragement. He has also helped with many of the line drawings in the text. I am also grateful to him for not complaining about meals served at odd times during the writing of this new edition. Once I get on the computer, time is irrelevant.

J. Rosemary Riggs

Introduction

For too many years, the fields of architecture and interior design have been treated as two separate disciplines involved in creating a pleasant living environment. The architect planned the exterior and interior of the home, often with little attention to where the furniture was to be placed. The interior designer had to contend with such things as walls that were not long enough to allow placement of furniture, or heating vents placed directly under the bed or some other piece of furniture. On the other hand, designers would often ruin the architect's design by using the incorrect style of furniture, thereby spoiling the whole concept of the building.

Today, these problems are being resolved. Many architects have interior designers on their staff, as is the case with Joyce Burke-Jones, the author of the Foreword. The result is that both disciplines cooperate from the beginning of a project.

From the interior designer's point of view, this cooperation involves learning and appreciating the language and problems associated with architecture. The American Institute of Architects (AIA) is the professional organization for architects; the American Society of Interior Designers (ASID) and the International Interior Design Association (IIDA) are the professional organizations for interior designers. It is because of the professionalism of these organizations that the fields of architecture and interior design have gradually become aware of the need for closer cooperation. This book is dedicated to fostering that cooperation.

Trademarks

Envirosense is a registered trademark of the Envirosense Consortium

TOPsiders is a registered trademark of TOPsiders

Gridset is a registered trademark of Rockland React Rite

Intersept is a registered trademark of Porter Paints

Antron is a registered trademark of E.I DuPont de Nemours Co. Inc.

Syndecrete is a registered trademark of Syndesis

Eurostone is a trademark of Chicago Metallic

ER^3 and Powerbond are registered trademarks of Collins & Aikman Floorcoverings

Clean Air Choice and ICI Lifemaster are trademarks of the Glidden Corp.

Spred 2000 is a registered trademark of the Glidden Corp.

Koroseal and Vicrtex are registered trademarks of Koroseal Wallcoverings

Essentials Inspirations are trademarks of Mannington Commercial Flooring

Trus Joist MacMillan and Parallam are registered trademarks of Trus Joist MacMillan, Ltd.

Sherwin-Williams is a registered trademark of Sherwin-Williams

EverClean is a trademark of Sherwin-Williams

PermaWhite is a registered trademark of Wm. Zinsser & Co. Inc.

Portersept is a registered trademark of Porter Paints

Flame Control is a registered trademark of Flame Control Coatings Inc.

OMNIPLEX is a registered trademark of Seagrave Coatings Corp.

Aquafleck is a registered trademark of California Products Corp.

Polomyx is a trademark of Surface Protection Industries

Zolatone is a registered trademark of Surface Protection Industries

Duroplex is a registered trademark of Triarch Industries

Chroma Spec and Scuff Master are trademarks of Master Coating Technology

DuPont, Antron, DuraTech, Antron Lumena are registered trademarks of E.I. DuPont de Nemours Co. Inc.

Scotchguard is a registered trademark of the 3M Company

Teflon is a registered trademark of E.I. DuPont de Nemours Co. Inc.

SpillBlock is a trademark of E.I DuPont de Nemours Co. Inc.

Wear-Dated is a registered trademark of Solutia Co.

Traffic Control is a trademark of Solutia Co.

TacFast is a registered trademark of TacFast Carpet Systems

UltraBrite is a trademark of Harris-Tarkett, Inc.

PermaGrain is a registered trademark of PermaGrain Corp.

Hartco and HartWood are registered trademarks of Hartco, Inc.

Aged Woods is a registered trademark of Aged Woods Inc.

Hydroment is a registered trademark of Bostik

Street Shoe is a registered trademark of Basic Coatings

Glitsa is a registered trademark of Glitsa Corp.

Formica is a registered trademark of Formica Corp.

Pergo is a registered trademark of Pergo Inc.

Wilsonart is a registered trademark of Wilsonart International

Intarsia is a registered trademark of Intarsia Inc.

Hardibacker is a registered trademark of James Hardie Building Products

Crossville Ceramics, Cross-Colors and Custom Color are registered trademarks of Crossville Ceramics

Cross-Sheen, Crosstyle, Geostyle, Cross-Quilt and Crossborder are trademarks of Crossville Ceramics

Frenchquarter is a registered trademark of Daltile

Laura Ashley is a trademark of Laura Ashley Co.

Plaza is a registered trademark of Johnson Wax Co.

DELPHI and VISTABRIK are registered trademarks of Pittsburgh Corning

Marmoleum is a registered trademark of Forbo Industries

Linosom is a registered trademark of Azrock Products

Inspirations and Essentials are trademarks of Mannington Commercial

Johnsonite and Permalight are registered trademarks of Johnsonite Corp.

ComfortTech, Safe-T-First, and Optix are trademarks of Johnsonite Corp.

Clorox is a registered trademark of The Chlorox Company

BioSpec is a registered trademark of Mannington Commercial Flooring

Medintech and Step Master are registered trademarks of Armstrong World Industries

Masonite is a registered trademark of Masonite Corp.

Natural CORK and Planks Plus are trademarks of Natural CORK Ltd. Co.

VUE, VISTABRIK and PC are registered trademarks of Pittsburgh Corning

ENDURA and SPYRA are trademarks of Pittsburgh Corning

KWiK'N EZ is a registered trademark of Pittsburgh Corning

LITHOTEX and CHROMIX are registered trademarks of L.M. Scofield Company

Sheetrock is a registered trademark of the U.S. Gypsum Company

Portersept Surface Sealer is a registered trademark of Porter Paints

Gold Bond, National Gypsum, Durasan and Uni-Kal are registered trademarks of the National Gypsum Company

Tough Kote and Hi-Impact are trademarks of the National Gypsum Company

Anaglypta and Lincrusta are registered trademarks of Mile High Crown

ESSCAPE is a trademark of Essex

Quantex is a trademark of MDC Wallcoverings

Koroseal, Vicrtex and Gossamer Steel are registered trademarks of Koroseal Wallcoverings

Gossamer Basics is a trademark of Koroseal Wallcoverings

Sasso is a registered trademark of Koroseal Wallcoverings

Tassoglas and Novaglass are trademarks of TASSO USA

Velcro is a registered trademark of Velcro USA Inc.

Tedlar is a registered trademark of E.I DuPont de Nemours Co. Inc.

PreFixx is a trademark of Divers Tech General, Wallcovering Division

Marlite and Displawall are registered trademarks of Commercial and Architectural Products, Inc.

Peg-Board is a registered trademark of The Masonite Corp.

Formica is a registered trademark of Formica Corporation

SOLICOR is a registered trademark of Wilsonart International

COLORCORE is a registered trademark of Formica corporation

Formula 409 is a registered trademark of The Chlorox Co.

Glass Plus is a registered trademark of Dow Brands

Mr. Clean is a registered trademark of Proctor & Gamble

Fill 'n Glaze is a trademark of 3M Company

Restoration Glass is a trademark of Bendheim Corp.

Viracon Privacy Glass is a trademark of Viracon Inc.

3M is a trademark of the 3M Corp.

VITRICOR is a registered trademark of Nevamar

QuarryCast is a registered trademark of Formglas Inc.

Parallam is a registered trademark of Trus Joist MacMillan

Cirrus Borders and Cirrus Themes are trademarks of Armstrong World Industries

Rotunda and Quadradome are registered trademarks of USG Interiors

Skylight and Transparencies are trademarks of USG Interiors

PLANAR and Interfinish are registered trademarks of Interfinish, a division of Chicago Metallic Corp.

Chicago Metallic is a registered trademark of Chicago Metallic Corp.

MAGNA T-CELL is a trademark of Chicago Metallic Corp.

Compásso is a trademark of USG Interiors

AutoCAD is a registered trademark of Autodesk

Corian is a registered trademark of E.I. DuPont de Nemours Co. Inc.

Gibraltar is a registered trademark of Wilsonart International

Focal Point and The Frank Lloyd Wright Collection are registered trademarks of Focal Point Inc.

Specicast is a trademark of Focal Point Inc.

LustrMetl and Kaylien are registered trademarks of Kaylien

Soss is a registered trademark of Universal Industrial Products

Schlage is a registered trademark of Schlage Lock Company

ULTIMA is a trademark of Schlage Lock Company

Weiser Lock is a registered trademark of Weiser Lock

Blue Creek is a trademark of Jenn-Air Company

Ultra Quick-Start is a trademark of Jenn-Air Company

LightTouch is a registered trademark of GE Company

PureSource and UltraStyle are trademarks of Frigidaire

Frigi-Foam is a registered trademark of Frigidaire

Excalibur is a registered trademark of Whitford Corp.

Plus Steam is a trademark of Russell Range

Spacemaker Plus is a trademark of GE Company

GE Monogram is a registered trademark of GE Company

Hidavent is a trademark of Thermado Corp.

Life in the Country and Revival are trademarks of Kohler

Precision Wash System is a trademark of Frigidaire

BodySpa is a trademark of Kohler

Kohler and Duostrainer are registered trademarks of Kohler

Pforever Warranty is a trademark of Price Pfister

Assure, Coralais, and Kohler Coordinates are trademarks of Kohler

Moen and Chateau are registered trademarks of Moen Inc.

Canac is a registered trademark of Canac

Perma-Edge is a registered trademark of Wilsonart International

Wood-Mode is a registered trademark of Wood-Mode

Scotch-Brite is a registered trademark of 3M Company

Avonite is a registered trademark of Avonite Inc.

Swanstone is a registered trademark of Swan

Nuvel is a registered trademark of Formica Corporation

Re-Bath is a registered trademark of Re-Bath

Heritage is a registered trademark of American Standard

J-Dream and J-Allure are trademarks of Jacuzzi Corp.

Jacuzzi and PowerPro are registered trademarks of Jacuzzi Corp.

Taboret is a registered trademark of Kohler Co.

Precedence, Freewill, BodySpa, Rite-Temp, MasterShower, Memoirs and Vessels are trademarks of Kohler Co.

Brilliance is a trademark of Delta Faucet Co.

Signature and Innovations are registered trade marks of Delta Faucet Co.

Solitaire and Eclipse are registered trademarks of Broan Manufacturing Company Inc.

Ultra Silent is a trademark of Broan Manufacturing Company Inc.

Maximum-Security Accessories is a trademark of Bobrick

Eagle Eye and MICROFLO are trademarks of Speakman Co.

SENSORFLO and Anystream are registered trademarks of Speakman Co.

Marblestal and Georgia Marble are registered trademarks of the Georgia Marble Co.

James Hardie and Hardibacker 500 are trademarks of James Hardie Interior Products

Powerbolt is a trademark of Weiser Lock

Grohe is a registered trademark of Grohe America Inc.

Tarkett is a registered trademark of Tarkett Inc.

Naturelle is a trademark of Tarkett Inc.

Lightwise Window and Mystique are trademarks of Pittsburgh Corning

Decora is a registered trademark of Pittsburgh Corning

Will-Trim is a registered trademark of Willamette Industries Inc.

Flex Trim is a trademark of Flex Trim Inc.

Powerbolt 3000 and Powerbolt are trademarks of Weiser Lock

Wave Oven is a trademark of Amana Home Appliances Inc.

Pure Touch, MicroTech are trademarks of Moen Inc.

Culligan is a registered trademark of Culligan Inc.

Best and Solitaire are registered trademarks of Broan Manufacturing Company Inc.

Septic Disposer and Bio-Charge are registered trademarks of In-Sink-Erator

In-Sink-Erator is a registered trademark of In-Sink-Erator

Ulta Silent is a trademark of Broan Manufacturing Company Inc.

Push-Clean and Touch-Clean are registered trademarks of Delta Faucet

Power-Lite and Briolette are trademarks of Kohler

1

Environmental Concerns

The Center for Environmental Study states,

> We stand at a crossroads. For the first time in history, we face the prospect of irreversible changes in our planet's life support systems. The growing human population and the by-products of our industrial and technological society threaten our planet's air, water, climate and biodiversity. These threats present a challenge to our society—to learn to live in harmony with our planet.

Members of the design community and the manufacturers they work with can, if they wish to, lead the way in helping to save this country from overburdened landfills. This can be achieved in both the manufacturing process itself and in the disposal of the product after it is no longer needed. An example would be using linoleum instead of vinyl flooring. Linoleum is a product manufactured from natural materials and will, at the end of its use, gradually biodegrade.

On July 28, 1992, the Federal Trade Commission (FTC) announced guidelines for environmental marketing claims. The guidelines are recommendations, not enforceable regulations. They are intended to reduce consumer confusion and prevent false or misleading use of common environmental terms. The FTC defines "recycled content" as materials recovered or diverted from the solid waste stream, either during the manufacturing process (preconsumer) or after use (postconsumer). Scrap produced from manufacturing processes in which the end product is not for consumer use is commonly referred to as "postindustrial."

AIR QUALITY ISSUES

The increasing awareness of indoor air quality issues and the growing incidence of Sick Building Syndrome (SBS) affecting worker comfort, well-being, and productivity highlight the vital need for improved workplace air quality worldwide.

Probably the best-known examples of environmental concern are the precautions taken when dealing with any form of asbestos. Before the mid-1980s, one of the ingredients used in the resilient flooring industry and in acoustical ceiling tiles was asbestos. This mineral has been proven injurious to health; therefore, the Resilient Floor Covering Institute (RFCI), a trade association of resilient flooring manufacturers, has developed a set of recommended work practices for the removal of resilient flooring, regardless of whether or not it contains asbestos. Following the RFCI's recommendations will ensure that the removal of an older resilient floor complies with Environmental Protection Agency (EPA) and Occupational

Safety and Health Administration **(OSHA)** regulations regarding the handling of asbestos-containing materials, should it be determined that removal is necessary.

Asbestos is hazardous to health when it becomes "friable," or free floating and airborne, as in a dust form. However, asbestos used in resilient flooring manufactured prior to the mid-1980s is firmly encapsulated in the product because of the manufacturing process. The EPA has determined that encapsulated, or nonfriable, asbestos-containing products are not subject to extensive regulatory requirements as long as they remain in that state. Resilient flooring, either vinyl composition tile or sheet vinyl, is nonfriable provided that it is not sanded, sawed, or reduced to a powder by hand pressure.

To ensure that any asbestos present in resilient flooring does not become dislodged and friable, the RFCI has recommended work practices that specifically prohibit sanding, dry scraping, mechanically pulverizing, or beadblasting the resilient flooring or felt backing. In other words, workers should refrain from any procedure that produces dust.

Common substrates used today in kitchen cabinet and furniture applications are particleboard and Medium Density Fiberboard (MDF). Particleboard is a generic term for a panel primarily composed of **cellulosic** materials (usually wood), generally in the form of discrete pieces or particles, as distinguished from fibers. The cellulosic material is combined with a synthetic resin or other suitable bonding system by a process in which the interparticle bond is created by the bonding system under heat and pressure. Additives, when introduced during the manufacturing process, modify certain panel properties. MDF is a generic term for a panel primarily composed of lignocellulosic fibers combined with a synthetic resin or other suitable bonding system and bonded together under heat and pressure. Additives may be introduced during manufacturing to improve certain properties.

Because products manufactured with these materials have the potential to emit minute quantities of formaldehyde, the following information is supplied by the Composite Panel Association: "Urea Formaldehyde (UF) adhesives are used in most particleboard and MDF products worldwide. . . . UF resins are easy to work with, and provide strong and cost effective bonding systems. Acting as a cross link or 'polymerizer' in UF resins, formaldehyde enables the adhesive to bond the wood particles and fibers together."[1]

The particleboard industry, primarily through new resin technology and better process control techniques, has dramatically reduced formaldehyde emissions from its products since the early 1980s. Levels dictated for formaldehyde emission by current U.S. standards are among the lowest in the world. Today's product standards (ANSI A208.1 Particleboard, A208.2 MDF) limit formaldehyde emissions to levels many times lower than those common in the past.

There are, however, a number of ways that formaldehyde emissions from particleboard can be reduced even further. Some occur naturally, some are brought about by the manufacturer, and some can be carried out by the end user. Several of the more common include

Aging: Emissions are always highest when the product is new. Emission levels begin to "decay" immediately after production and are usually at half the initial amount in about 6 months or less. Within a year, these levels have usually "decayed" to approximate equilibrium with background ambient levels.

Low-emission resin technology: New resin technology developed in the last 10 years has allowed manufacturers to produce high-quality particleboard with "low-mol ratio" resins. These resins have fewer excess molecules of formaldehyde and consequently yield less free formaldehyde.

Formaldehyde scavengers: Manufacturers may add formaldehyde scavengers to the wood and resin mix before pressing, or apply them to the surface of the panel after pressing. Scavengers combine with the free formaldehyde to form stable chemical compounds.

Coatings and laminates: Formaldehyde emissions from particleboard can be reduced by as much as 95% with a sealing finish. Commercial grain prints, high- and low-pressure laminates, veneers, and good paint coatings all make good vapor barriers for formaldehyde. These methods are much more effective when the edges are also sealed by banding, foil finishing, or applying one or more coats of paint or sealer. For maximum reduction of emissions, small parts, such as drawer fronts, backs, and sides, should be coated both on the faces and on the edges even though they are not normally visible. This also applies to the underside of the tops, drawer bottoms, and so forth. Wet coatings may be applied by dipping, rolling, brushing, or spraying. Heavy single coats should be avoided when possible; two thin coats are better than one thick coat. Sand the edges well before sealing or between coats to prevent **wicking-in** of the wet coating.

The effectiveness of any application depends on the thickness of the material applied. Referring to paints, sealers, and so forth, a one mil (.001″) mil, applied to all surfaces, is considered necessary for effective control, but any sealer thickness is better than none at all.[2]

The Envirosense® Consortium is a nonprofit membership organization that promotes a proactive approach to indoor air quality issues. Members of the Consortium include interior product manufacturers, architectural and design firms, environmental law firms, energy and utility companies, and research and development firms and laboratories.

Members of the Consortium promote a three-part "Total Systems Approach" to indoor air quality: building systems, product systems, and maintenance systems. In addition, members of the Consortium meet twice yearly to present case studies, updates, and research results to one another so they can assure the most up-to-date answers for customers who call for assistance. Through its comprehensive Web site, Envirosense offers online newsletters, product updates, **IAQ** (indoor air quality) discussion areas, IAQ product profiles, e-mail directories, and access to the latest technical papers and case studies. A wealth of information is available on control of microbial sources and volatile organic compound emissions. Twenty-four Consortium members lend their knowledge to provide a site where interested parties can "one-stop-shop" on the Internet (the Consortium's e-mail address is iaq@mindspring.com and its Web site address is http://www.envirosense.org).

Systems Approach

The Envirosense Consortium represents the first complementary "systems approach" to solving IAQ problems using coordinated solutions that satisfy, and in some cases pioneer, environmental standards while maintaining energy efficiency. Based on a "design-to-disposal" perspective, the concept encompasses three major sectors which, while seemingly distinct, are inextricably interwoven:

Building systems: design/construction/operation/monitoring

Product systems: manufacture/installation/performance

Maintenance systems: cleaning/approved products/training.

Building Systems

This section is in the architects and construction province, and as such is not something with which interior designers are involved directly.

Comprehensive pre-building IAQ consulting concepts and proactive IAQ inspection and monitoring programs have been developed. These services, when integrated with innovative electronic monitoring systems, provide property owners with unparalleled safeguards concerning the well-being of their buildings.

Product Systems—Manufacture/Installation/Performance

Independent researchers have implicated bacterial or fungal contamination in over 40 percent of SBS cases and virtually all building-related illness (**BRI**) problems. Also of primary concern to the Consortium are unwanted emissions from a variety of sources. Therefore, two major contributors to poor indoor air quality—microbial contamination and volatile organic compounds (**VOCs**) emissions—were selected as solution priorities.

The challenge was the apparent paradox that most products used for treating microbial contaminants were themselves toxic; some contained heavy metals, and most used carriers or aerosols to dispense the active ingredients. High concentrations of such products can expose the product applicators and/or building occupants to risks, and possibly create long-term problems with respect to the ultimate disposal of the treated products.

Since bacteria and fungi routinely settle and multiply on exposed interior surfaces, Consortium members aimed research at creating an effective, environmentally friendly antimicrobial shield which could be incorporated into fabrics, carpets, plastics, paints, adhesives, wall coverings, lacquers, floor and ceiling surfaces, and air filters. The agent had to be very low in toxicity to animals, plants, and humans during manufacture; biologically active throughout the life of the products; and easily neutralized for safe disposal.

Results of this research produced an ideal, versatile antimicrobial complex providing a protective, durable "inhibitory zone," or germ barrier, that can be added in the manufacturing process to a wide variety of interior finishing and furnishing materials.

Even a building utilizing proper design and superior interior products must be maintained by well-trained and adequately equipped staff.

A "green list" of environmentally friendly cleaning materials has been identified. Products have been certified as environmentally safe, biodegradable, and water soluble, and they not only meet, but exceed, current standards. Cleaning service operatives receive training in the proper use of these specially formulated materials to ensure that optimum cleaning is accomplished while minimizing the risks of exposure from residues of these compounds. Alternatively, the approved cleaning products and training in their use are offered to building owners with in-house cleaning staffs.

Conclusion

Envirosense embraces a Total Systems Approach which includes the building design, operation, environmental control and monitoring, product specifications and performance and a well-thought-out maintenance program. This coordinated solution is the key to helping building owners and users . . . positively impact the quality of their indoor environment.

It is anticipated that buildings adopting the Envirosense concepts will be recognized as environmentally friendly structures. Occupiers and tenants will progressively be more selective about their choice of buildings, and investors have already started to appreciate the value of incorporating environmental concerns in their property portfolios.[3]

Other Approaches to Environmental Issues

Many contemporary buildings are sealed environments to increase **HVAC** (heating, ventilating, and air conditioning) efficiency. This means that pollutants derived from such manufactured materials as synthetic fabrics, plywood, carpets, and paints are not cleared from the building. A NASA-funded study directed by Dr. B. C. Wolverton, a 20-year veteran in horticultural research, proved that the plants commonly used in interior plantscaping cleanse the air of many harmful pollutants, such as formaldehyde, benzene, and trichloroethylene. Golden pothos, philoden-

dron, corn plants, and bamboo palms are particularly effective in cleansing the air of formaldehyde. Spathifhyllum (peace lily), dracena warneckei, and dracena "Janet Craig" remove quantities of benzene, such as tobacco smoke. Marginata, warneckei, and spathiphyllum work well in removing trichloroethylene. The Plants for Clean Air Council recommends one potted plant for each 100 square feet of floor space.

When the air is too dry, people are susceptible to colds and flu. When the humidity is too high, people can develop other ailments. Through their natural processes of transpiration and evaporation, office plants add moisture to the dry, overheated air often found in sealed office environments. At the same time, studies show that plants do not add moisture in significant amounts when the air is already moist. A study conducted at Washington State suggested that plants help regulate humidity. When plants were added to an office environment, the relative humidity stabilized within the recommended "healthy" range of 30 to 60 percent.

By using a professional plantscaping service, offices will have design uniformity throughout the workplace, plants in peak condition, and plants for correct light levels and HVAC conditions found in a particular workplace. TOPsiders® Panel Mount Planters are aesthetically correct, measure 6″ × 6″ × 24″ or 30″ (this size provides proper scale and proportion for open plan systems), and are easily installed and taken down. TOPsiders have brackets for mounting on tops or sides of partitions and are available in metal or marble finishes and 13 colors. Matching ROUNDZ are also available (Figure 1–1).

Companies may need to alter their HVAC systems. According to Joseph Milam of Environmental Design International, Ltd.,

> New cost cutting concepts of hoteling, telecommuting, and teaming are driving businesses to change how they configure their office space. In many cases these changes result in fitting the same number of people into less space. Older HVAC systems were designed for one person per 150 to 200 usable square feet, and a PC on every third or fourth desk. In a modern office with higher-occupant densities, the HVAC system needs to accommodate personal computers on every desk as well as more people in less space. Most mechanical systems that are seven or more years old generally provide 5 to 7-1/2 cubic feet per minute (cfm) of outside air per person. Today's standards ASHRAE 62-1989 require 20 cfm per person.[4]

Figure 1–1
TOPsiders Panel Mount Planters provide proper scale and proportion for open plan systems and are easily installed and taken down. The TOPsiders shown fit on top of the partitions. (Photo courtesy of TOPsiders.)

The following information from Interface, a member of Envirosense, shows what a responsible company can do in setting standards for other manufacturers to follow:

Interface is dedicated to offering alternatives which ensure that we do not contribute to the environmental problem, but that we contribute to the solution. Interface's environmental efforts are focused on three critical areas:

Materials, Processes, and Programs

Interface Flooring Systems (IFS) is committed to conforming to the spirit and to the letter of sound environmental practices. Prior to any process or material change, we undertake an evaluation of the environmental impact the change may have on any area of our business, including product quality, commercial use, or Mother Earth.

Our commitment to this environmental effort is evidenced by the investment in a state of the art testing laboratory at our Interface Research Corporation facility. We are able to test for VOCs and **off-gassing** as well as other critical factors related to the environment. An example of our commitment is the development of Gridset® adhesive

which is manufactured by our subsidiary Rockland React Rite. Gridset establishes new industry standards for VOC and off-gassing emissions of adhesives which have historically been a major source of VOCs. Gridset produces less than half the VOCs in proposed EPA standard for VOC emissions.

In addition to Gridset, all of the recommended chemicals used in the Interface Service Management (ISM) maintenance program have been thoroughly tested and certified as environmentally responsible. Interface invites and welcomes comparison of its environmental efforts (and investment therein) with those of any other companies in the field.

Proactive Solutions to Indoor Air Quality Problems Through the Envirosense Consortium

Indoor Air Quality, Sick Building Syndrome, and Building Related Illness are all real issues of growing concern and importance in today's work place. Interface offers real solutions today through its Envirosense Consortium.

The Interface led, Envirosense Consortium delivers a family of products, ranging from interior fabrics, plastic components, wall coverings, upholstery fabric, paints, coatings, and laminates, to flooring, ceiling tile, and HVAC components, which, collectively, demonstrably inhibit the growth of microorganisms, and thereby offer an enhanced interior environment for today's commercial building.

Intersept®, an EPA-registered antimicrobial, the active agent incorporated into all Envirosense products, is a durable, environmentally friendly, broad spectrum antimicrobial which inhibits the growth of microorganisms and controls bacteria and fungi—major sources of indoor air quality contamination.

Recycle/Reuse— A Continuing Process

Interface has created a worldwide multi-disciplinary task force which is dedicated to identifying and implementing programs and processes to reduce waste generation, increase the percentage of materials recycled, and increase the proportion reused in the manufacture of products and other applications. Our thrust goes beyond this internal effort, to include our customers in recycling and selective replacement programs, reducing the impact on land fills.

At present, Interface recycles up to 50 percent of the waste from manufacturing. Throughout the world, we are aggressively seeking additional opportunities to reduce the waste generated, as well as to find methods of increasing the percentage of materials recycled.

During 1992, Interface introduced a new packaging system which employs a two piece box containing a high percentage of recycled materials. This new box configuration allows our customers to pack used carpet tiles in the boxes in which they receive new tiles, so the tiles can be returned to Interface for recycling.

Once the carpet life has been exhausted, Interface recycles the material in an environmentally sound manner. At present, two methods exist:

1. Closed loop reuse of the material, by separating components and using these in the manufacturing of new carpet or other industrial products. Projects are currently under way to recycle nylon polymers by depolymerizing type 6 nylon fiber to **caprolactam,** and extruding first quality fiber from it. This initiative differs from more commonly known recycling efforts as it is a "closed loop" process which ensures the new polymer is the same as the original.
2. Environmentally friendly disposal; several initiatives are under way, in conjunction with the major fiber suppliers, to turn old carpet materials (broadloom or tile) into recyclable materials, used outside the carpet industry.[5]

Most fiber manufacturers are recycling old carpeting, but with restrictions. Some require that both the old and new carpet be of their fiber. Others merely require that the new carpet be made from their fiber. Almost all require that the freight on the old carpet be paid by the new buyer. However, if there is a large quantity of old carpet to be disposed of in a landfill, the disposal cost may be offset by returning the old carpet. Returning old carpet eliminates that many more landfill problems.

Following is a list of those manufacturers of products covered in this textbook who are members of Envirosense Consortium, Inc.: Bentley Mills, carpet; General Polymers Corp., epoxy and terrazzo flooring systems; Interface Flooring Systems Inc./Huega USA,

carpet systems for commercial, institutional, health care, retail, hospitality, and residential markets; Interface Research Corp., Intersept antimicrobial compound, licensing of Envirosense program; Interface Service Management, carpet maintenance and appearance retention programs; Porter Paints (Division of Courtaulds Coatings, Inc.), paints, coatings, and adhesives for wall coverings; and USG Interiors, Inc., ceiling tile systems.

According to the Carpet and Rug Institute,

Carpet manufacturers are striving to minimize the quantities of natural and energy resources used in day-to-day operations. They are reducing waste, reusing and recycling raw materials, packaging materials, waste, and by-products. Individual companies are pursuing environmental efforts at different points in the manufacturing process. . . .

Advanced monitoring systems and processes in the mills help conserve water, electricity and other fuels. As an example, new developments in dyeing techniques require less water. Dye materials are removed from waste water; the waste water is monitored, reprocessed, and then reintroduced into the manufacturing system. New systems recycle thermal energy, capturing, condensing, and then re-heating the water for use in the finishing of carpet. Oil waste is sold to recycling companies or is used as a boiler fuel. . . .

Although more efficient manufacturing is reducing excess carpet waste, such as selvedges, trimmings, and shearings, the industry has found creative uses for carpet by-products, to avoid the use of local landfills. Individual companies are engaged in recycling efforts, including the following.

Fiber and yarn that cannot be reused in manufacturing are often sent to yarn vendors that sell them for crafts and other end uses.

Excess carpet is cut into mats and sold.[6]

Similarly, "DuPont offers the Carpet Reclamation program as a service to ensure that the old carpet you remove does not go into a landfill. DuPont will take anything back regardless of origin when you purchase a new carpet of DuPont Antron®. Because of the importance of this issue, we have developed reclamation guidelines."[7]

Syndecrete® is a restorative product, reconstituting materials extracted from society's waste stream to create a new, high-valued product. Syndecrete was developed by Syndesis as an alternative to limited or nonrenewable natural materials, such as wood or stone, and synthetic petroleum-based solid and laminating materials. Like standard concrete, Syndecrete is chemically inert and is not subject to out-gassing. Syndecrete can incorporate 41 percent recycled or recovered materials from industry and postconsumer goods. Fly ash, a powder residue that results from the combustion of pulverized coal in electric power-generating plants, is added by 15 percent to displace the cement base. Polypropylene fiber, a recovered off-fall scrap with a three-dimensional reinforced matrix, increases the tensile strength of the product and gives it a physical property akin to wood.

Aggregates, added to vary the texture and appearance of Syndecrete, have included recycled materials such as metal shavings, postconsumer plastic regrinds, recycled glass chips, and scrap wood chips, creating a contemporary interpretation of the Italian tradition of terrazzo. Scrap materials are actively sourced from local businesses and curbside recycling centers.

Syndecrete is certified as a recycled product by the Californians Against Waste Foundation, and environmental consultants recommend it for use by chemically sensitive persons. Products discussed in this textbook and manufactured by Syndesis include countertops, tiles, sinks, bathtubs, and showers. Figure 1–2 shows a bathtub made of Syndecrete.

Gensler and Associates Architects, one of the world's largest architectural and interior design firms, is taking a stand for environmentally sound design. One example is the design of the Los Angeles offices of HBO (Home Box Office). Gensler recycled all demolished materials, including wood, paper, glass, plastics, copper, and aluminum. Recycling bins were placed on each floor of the construction area. The carpeting was laid with low-toxicity carpet adhesive, and special solution-dyed, nontoxic carpeting was installed (carpet manufacturers accelerated the off-gassing process before installation). The carpeting was shipped off-site and was ventilated for 48 hours with massive amounts of fresh air. Linoleum, while more expensive, was used instead of vinyl composition flooring, and low-biocide, low-fungicide paints were also used. Where possible, existing furniture and ceiling tiles were reused and repainted with **nonbridging** paint.

Green Seal is an independent, nonprofit organization dedicated to protecting the environment by promoting the manufacture and sale of environmentally responsible consumer products and the implementation of environmentally responsible practices. It sets environmental standards and allows the use of its certification mark on products found to meet them. Green Seal also educates consumers on how to use their buying decision to help the environment. Underwriters Laboratories Inc. (UL) is one of the main testing contractors for Green Seal. The seal is granted after studying how a product was manufactured, packaged, used by the consumer, recycled, and what will be left as waste when the product finally makes its way to the dump. Standards are periodically reviewed and updated to incorporate advances in technology and industry practices.

Products are Green Seal certified only after rigorous testing and evaluation, including plant visits. To date, more than 300 products have been awarded the Green Seal. These include many manufacturers of products covered in this textbook (Figure 1–3).

In the public interest, the Carpet and Rug Institute (CRI) has developed three IAQ testing programs that will minimize the potential of emissions from new carpet installations. The programs cover carpet, carpet cushion, and floor covering adhesive products. The goal for the programs is to help consumers with their buying decisions by identifying products that have been tested and meet stringent IAQ requirements:

In the testing programs for carpet, separate carpet cushion, and floor covering adhesives for carpet installations, samples are collected from the manufacturer's production process. Each sample is tested individually for chemical emissions by an independent laboratory, using highly sophisticated, dynamic, environmental chamber technology.

Figure 1–2
This bathtub was made from Syndecrete, a restorative product reconstituting materials extracted from society's waste stream in the creation of a new, high-valued product. (Photo courtesy of Syndesis.)

Figure 1–3
Green Seal emblem. (Emblem courtesy of Green Seal.)

The test procedure follows an approved methodology recognized by the Environmental Protection Agency (EPA) and the American Society for Testing and Materials (ASTM D-5116). The VOC emissions are identified and quantified as though the products were in a real building situation. Products are retested on an on-going basis to ensure that the required emission levels are not exceeded.

Carpet products are tested for total VOC, formaldehyde (to show it is not used in manufacturing), 4-PC (4-phenylcyclohexene), and styrene. Separate cushion products are tested for total VOC, BHT (butylated hydroxtoluene), formaldehyde, and 4-PC. The carpet floor covering adhesive program is a test that is similar to the carpet and cushion tests. The criteria take into account that adhesives are a wet substrate when applied during the installation process. Adhesives are tested for total VOC, formaldehyde, and 2-ethyl-1-hexanol. This program covers floor covering adhesives, as well as accessory adhesive products such as seam sealers.

The products that meet the emission criteria are allowed to display the [CRI] label (Figure 1–4). If the products exceed the emission criteria, the manufacturer is so advised and is requested to make process or formulation changes in order to reduce the emissions. After the appropriate product modification, the manufacturer may resubmit the product for additional testing. Products that do not meet the test criteria will not thereafter be

allowed to affix the label until they meet the test program criteria. . . .

In each of these programs the authorized label displayed on the product contains an identification number assigned specifically to the individual manufacturer for each product that meets the criteria.

It is also important to know that with most products, adequate ventilation can lower concentrations and minimize the impact on indoor air quality. Regular and effective cleaning also adds to good air quality.[8]

The CRI serves the industry and consumers with practical, technical, educational, and issue-related information. The CRI only deals with three carpet installation products. See the CRI's Web site, at www.carpet-rug.com, for more detailed information.

The carpet industry has taken many steps to ensure carpet's positive role in the indoor environment. The CRI's *Indoor Air Quality Testing and Labeling Program* is one step. The following information, not previously covered, is condensed from *Covering the Future*, a CRI brochure: Installation guidelines for consumers and installers have been developed to maintain good indoor air quality during the installation of new carpet. With adequate air ventilation, the minimal emissions from carpet will dissipate within the first 48 to 72 hours of installation. Formaldehyde is *not* used in the manufacturing of carpet, contrary to popular belief. The industry emphasizes consistent guidelines for preventive, daily, and restorative carpet maintenance to ensure good indoor air quality.

The following companies, manufacturers of products covered in this textbook, are all involved in recycling or preserving our planet in some way. It is probably true that manufacturers of similar products are also working on environmental concerns. Specifiers who are concerned about the environment should check with other manufacturers as well. The list is alphabetical.

1. Chicago Metallic manufactures Eurostone™, an all-environment ceiling panel, manufactured from expanded volcanic perlite, ceramic clay, and an inorganic binder. These panels are impervious to heat, moisture, and microorganisms. Because they will not support the growth of bacteria or fungus, they cannot contribute to problems with IAQ. This makes them ideal for use in schools, medical facilities, and hospitals. Eurostone is environmentally safe and recyclable and contains no synthetic mineral fibers.

Figure 1–4
The three labels of the CRI Indoor Air Quality Testing Programs. Color is white on an emerald green background. (Labels courtesy of the Carpet and Rug Institute, Dalton, GA.)

2. Collins & Aikman Floorcoverings is now turning used carpet into new carpet backing and estimates that it will potentially be able to reclaim 75 million pounds of vinyl-backed carpet per year from customer installation sites. Currently, 3.5 billion pounds of carpet end up in landfills each year. The Collins & Aikman process, under the Infinity Initiative, allows 100 percent of the reclaimed carpet to be returned to the manufacturing process, closing the loop, so to speak, in the recycling process. Previously, Collins & Aikman was recycling used carpet into other industrial goods, such as parking curbs and industrial flooring blocks. Collins & Aikman Floorcoverings is the only company in the industry to provide a written guarantee to customers certifying that any floorcovering it reclaims, even a competitor's, will never be introduced into a landfill or incinerated.

The backing, ER³® (Environmentally Redesigned, Reused, Recycled), made in this process contains 100 percent recycled material, cutting the need for virgin material to be taken from the earth. Last, but by no means least, the recycled product carries the same 15-year warranty as the original non-recycled Powerbond® backing.

3. ICI Paints North America/Glidden created a wash-water management program to help eliminate plant waste at its manufacturing facility in Carrollton, Texas. ICI realized it could reduce waste by reusing wash water, which, in turn, would reduce landfill sludge generated by wash-water treatment. The program saved the Carrollton facility more than $400,000 in raw material recovery and wash-water treatment avoidance in 1997 alone. ICI/Glidden's technological and environmental breakthrough in paints is the first latex paint without petroleum-based solvents. The Clean Air Choice™ paints—Spred® 2000 and its companion brand for professional painters, ICI Lifemaster™ 2000—use a unique resin that allows

the petroleum-based solvent to be eliminated in the formula.

4. All carpet tiles and performance broadloom products manufactured by Interface have Intersept permanently incorporated into the molecular structure of their backing systems. Intersept works by attacking the cellular walls of bacteria and fungi. Upon contact, the organism loses its ability to multiply and colonize. Intersept is warranted to provide long-term protection against microbial growth. Interface products are recommended for use in health care facilities.

5. Methods used to control emissions at the manufacturing source for Koroseal® and Vicrtex® wallcoverings are solvent recovery, incineration, and the use of the water-based inks, instead of the organic solvent–based inks (high VOC). Solvent recovery is where organic solvent vapors are collected and, through a condensing operation, converted back to a liquid for use or sale. In incineration, the organic emissions are incinerated in a catalytic process, thereby reducing emissions to acceptable levels. The printing inks and coatings are converted from organic solvent-based to water-based systems. Also, cadmium-containing chemicals have been used in the production of vinyl wallcovering for many years, both as a heat stabilizer and as a color pigment. Through research, all cadmium-containing color pigments have been eliminated from use in Vicrtex wallcoverings. All Vicrtex wallcoverings are produced containing mildew- and staph-resistant additives in the vinyl and plastisol. The Vicrtex wallcovering using the ASTM D-21-90 method received a rating of 0, which means that there was no surface fungal growth on the tested samples.

6. Mannington Commercial is the only manufacturer to include recycled vinyl content (postconsumer and industrial recycled vinyl) in the manufacture of all Essentials™ and Inspirations™ vinyl composition tile (VCT) products. Recycling vinyl does not affect the color or cost of the final product. Mannington uses 5 percent or greater postconsumer and industrial recycled vinyl products in the organic binder (plastics) portion of their VCT. This percentage represents hundreds of thousands of tons of vinyl scrap that would otherwise go to a landfill.

7. The National Paint and Coating Association's Pollution Prevention awards in 1996 were given to Engineered Polymer Solutions, Inc., ICI Paint North America/Glidden, and PPG Industries, Inc. Engineered Polymer Solutions, Inc. (EPS) was given the award for designing and building its new plant in Marengo, Illinois, with a vapor recovery unit rather than the more commonly used incinerator or oxidizing fume scrubber system. By using the vapor recovery unit, EPS was able to recover and reuse approximately 10,000 pounds of monomer and save thousands of dollars annually. Environmental responsibility can pay off.

From 1988 to 1995, PPG's coatings and resins achieved a 57 percent reduction in the hazardous waste rate and a 61 percent reduction in the total waste rate. Actual hazardous waste volumes were reduced by almost 29,000 tons per year and total waste volumes were reduced by more than 38,000 tons per year in that same period. This volume reduction has been accompanied by a decrease in the toxicity of the waste generated. During this period, production at coatings and resin facilities increased by 26 percent. In previous years, many other paint companies were honored with Pollution Prevention awards.

8. Sponge Cushion Inc. (SCI) has won approval from the Carpet and Rug Institute for its carpet cushion product line to carry a "Green" Indoor Air Quality label of certification and compliance. Sponge cushion is the first full-line rubber cushion manufacturer to be approved and is among only three cushion producers to be certified under the program to date. SCI's products contain "zero" emission of three specified chemicals, and substantially lower VOC emissions than the test criteria call for. Shaw Industries also won approval for three cushion products: mechanically frothed, rubberized polyurethane, and synthetic fiber. Bretlin Inc. and Dixie Manufacturing received approval for their synthetic fiber cushions.

Lists of approved carpet manufacturers and adhesive manufacturers can be obtained from CRI (see Appendix B).

9. Trus Joist MacMillan® converts 64 percent of a log into Parallam® PSL, whereas traditional sawmill methods convert only 40 percent of a log into lumber. Ordinary sawmilling bores rectangular timber out of the center of round logs, squandering the outermost layers of the tree on lesser-grade products like wood chips and fuel. Parallam PSL can capture this valuable wood fiber and use its natural strength and parallel grain to create massive beams, posts, and headers.

GLOSSARY

BRI. Building-related illness. A variety of illnesses that have been attributed to toxic fumes inside a building.

Caprolactam. The white crystalline cyclic amide that is one of the components from which nylon is made.

Cellulosic. Containing cellulose material, the chief substance composing the cell walls of trees and plants.

EPA. Environmental Protection Agency.

HVAC. Heating, ventilating and air conditioning, almost always written using initials.

IAQ. Indoor air quality. The result of measuring the air inside a building for toxic emissions.

Mildew. Discoloration caused by fungi.

Nonbridging. A paint that will not cover the small holes in an acoustical tiled ceiling. See Chapter 6, page 133.

Off-gassing. The process by which toxic fumes are emitted from carpet when it is newly laid.

OSHA. Occupational Safety and Health Administration.

SBS. Sick Building Syndrome. The symptoms of an illness caused by toxic emissions inside a building.

VOC. Volatile organic compound. Toxic emissions from solvents in paints and other ingredients used in manufacturing.

Wicking in. Absorption of liquids into a material; in this case the absorption of paint into the substrate.

NOTES

[1]Composite Panel Association, *Particleboard from Start to Finish.* Gaithersburg, MD: Composite Panel Association, 1997, p. 32.

[2]Ibid., pp. 126–128.

[3]Envirosense, *A "Total Systems" Approach,* Envirosense Consortium, pp. 1–3.

[4]Joseph Milam, Principal at EDI, Ltd. Consulting Engineers.

[5]Interface, *Environmental Responsibilities,* pp. 14–17 (boldface added).

[6]Carpet and Rug Institute, *Covering the Future: Environmental Stewardship of the Carpet and Rug Industry.* Dalton, GA: CRI, 1995.

[7]*The Questions Kit for Retail Professionals,* DuPont Flooring Systems, 1996.

[8]Carpet and Rug Institute, *Indoor Air Quality Testing Programs.* Dalton, GA: CRI, 1997.

2 Paints and Finishes

The earliest known paintings were found in the Lascaux caves in France and in the Altamira cave in Spain and date from as early as 15,000 B.C. A thousand years later the Egyptians were making colors from soil and importing dyes such as indigo and madder. To this they added materials that are sometimes found in paints that artists use: gum arabic, egg white, gelatin, and beeswax. The Egyptians also developed varnish from gum arabic about 1000 B.C.

It is only since 1867 that prepared paints have been available on the American market. Originally, paint was used merely to decorate a home, as in the frescoes at Pompeii, and it is still used for that purpose today. Modern technology, however, has now made paint both a decorative and a protective finish.

The colors used are also of great psychological importance. A study by Johns Hopkins University showed that planned color environments greatly improved scholastic achievement. Many major paint companies now have color consultants who can work with designers on selection of colors for schools, hospitals, and other commercial and industrial buildings. Today, paint is the most inexpensive method of changing the environment.

Paint is commonly defined as a substance that can be put on a surface to make a film, whether white, black, or colored. This definition has now been expanded to include clear films.

COMPONENTS OF PAINTS

Most paints are classified according to their **binders**—for example, whether the contents of the vehicle or liquid portion are water or **solvent** based.

Solvents

Solvents, when used in paints, are liquids that dissolve the **resins, gums,** or other binder constituents. These liquids are mineral spirits for **alkyds,** water for latex emulsions, alcohol for shellac, and lacquer thinner for lacquers. These solvents are used as thinners and are also used to clean the paint equipment and clean up any spills. Turpentine was used as a solvent before mineral spirits came on the market, but it is not used today due to volatile organic compound (VOC) compliance, toxicity, high cost, and strong odors. VOCs react with sunlight to form smog.

According to the NAHB Research Center, the function of the solvent is to carry the other ingredients over the surface. The solvent then evaporates, leaving the binder, **pigment,** and additives to form a film on the surface. The solvent is the "wet" in wet solvent-based paint. Common solvents include mineral spirits, alcohol, xylene, and/or naptha [boldface added].[1]

Solvent-containing coatings can be used safely if overexposure is avoided and proper protective equipment is used. The disposal of all types of coating materials is controlled by government regulations. Leftover paint can always be donated to community groups.

Binders

Binders are liquid adhesives that form a surface film. These adhesives bind the pigments to the surface, creating a strong and durable bond. The quality of the binder is an important factor in the useful life of a coating. Both natural and synthetic substances are used as binders in solvent-based coatings. Natural substances include shellac, rosin, linseed oil, soybean oil, sunflower oil, tung oil, and manila gum. Synthetic substances include alkyd, **epoxy,** and **urethane.** . . . Binders used in water-based paints include styrene butadiene **acrylic,** 100% acrylic and vinyl acrylic latexes. Natural resins are not used as binders in water-based paints. . . . Water-based coatings are usually called latex coatings [boldface added].[2]

Pigments

Pigments are fine particles or powders used in paint to confer the following properties: color, **hiding power** or opacity, and protection and corrosion repression on iron and steel. Different pigments have different purposes. **Titanium dioxide** is the best white pigment for hiding power. Other pigments, whether organic or inorganic, merely add color to the paint. The third type, **extender** pigments such as **calcium carbonates,** are inert.

Their [extender pigments] functions include influencing the flow, leveling, settling, and application characteristics of paint. Although they are not hiding pigments, they can contribute to hiding by improving the efficiency of the primary pigments.

In flat paint, extenders improve sheen, uniformity, and touch-up capability. In "eggshell" and semi-gloss paints, they affect **gloss.** In exterior paints, they promote durability and resistance to staining, and help to prevent dimensional cracking of the paint film.

Specialty additives, usually present as minor paint components, provide most other features. The specialty additive zinc oxide is used in both alkyd and latex coating to resist mildew, preventing its growth and spread over the paint film. In alkyd paints, zinc oxide reacts with the oils and alkyds to increase consistency, harden the film, and lessen yellowing in aging. Zinc phosphate, another specialty additive, inhibits the conversion of iron into rust [boldface added].[3]

Additives

Additives are special-purpose ingredients that provide extra performance features. Common additives include thickeners and mildewcides. Thickeners minimize pigment settling and enhance the application qualities of coatings, and mildewcides alleviate mildew problems.[4]

To comply with the VOC emissions laws, more **solids** are being added, which makes the paint heavier bodied; and, therefore, it may take longer to dry. In many areas of the United States, the amount of VOC, expressed in pounds of VOC per gallon, is restricted (Figure 2–1). According to a publication by the paint manufacturer Sherwin-Williams®, "a National VOC Regulation is expected to become effective January 1, 1998. This National Regulation will not automatically replace existing State/Local regulations unless those areas specifically repeal the local regulations. Some areas may maintain their existing, more stringent, VOC regulations."[5] Both OSHA and the EPA have strict rules governing not only the manufacture of paint, but also its application. Check the appropriate regulatory agency for the VOC limits in your area. Paint companies often sell specially manufactured paints in California, which has the strictest VOC regulations. The effects of the aforementioned national regulation on the coatings industry will be extensive. Under these regulations, alkyd/oil paints will still be available, but will be a higher solid material than presently sold. Most paint companies will be discontinuing products that do not meet the new regulation and replacing them with VOC-compliant coatings.

Several paint companies have developed very durable latex paints. Sherwin-Williams has produced EverClean™, a new stain-resistant interior latex wall paint, available in flat, satin, and semigloss that gives the washability and durability performance usually found in glossy **enamel** finishes. The paint dries to a virtually nonporous film, preventing absorption of stains into the paint finish. EverClean Semi-Gloss provides mildew resistance and exceptional moisture resistance. Perma White® mildew-proof bathroom wall and ceiling paint from Wm. Zinsser & Co., Inc. features a five-year mildew-proof guarantee. It is also scrubbable and blister- and peel-proof. In Chapter 1,

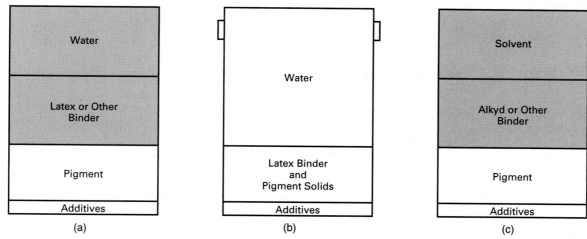

Figure 2–1

Components of paint. Ingredients in (a) quality latex paint, (b) low-cost latex paint, and (c) quality alkyd paint. (Drawings courtesy of Builders Guide to Paints and Coatings, *NAHB Research Center.)*

Clean Air Choice™ paints from The Glidden Company were described.

According to the NAHB Research Center,

The glossiness of a paint is a function of a measurement called pigment volume concentration (PVC). PVC is the percentage by volume of pigment in the total volume of a dried paint film. (The term pigment as used here includes both pigments and extenders. Note that PVC is *not* a measure of the proportions of pigment to **vehicle,** but rather to binder.) Where the PVC is low, the particles of pigment are relatively widely dispersed in the vehicle. The resultant film is glossy, reflecting the predominance of the smooth vehicle in the dried mixture. As PVC increases, a greater number of particles of the pigment protrude above the surface of the more crowded mixture, deflecting light and reducing the gloss. In "flat" paint, the pigment content far exceeds the concentration of the vehicle [boldface and italic added].[6]

Figure 2–2 shows how the PVC affects light reflectance.

Several finishes, or **lusters,** are available in both alkyds and latex:

Flat. These paints, with the highest PVC, provide a velvety appearance and a rich, soft-looking surface on walls where less glare is desired and little washing is required. Examples of rooms for which flat paint might be appropriate

include the den, library, or adult or guest bedrooms.

"Eggshell," "Pearl," or "Satin." These terms are used by various manufacturers to denote a paint formulation of slightly lower PVC than flat paint, providing slightly higher light reflections. They combine this characteristic with moderate scrubability. Such paints can be used in areas of the home where finger marks must from time to time be removed, but where frequent heavy-duty scrubbing will not occur.

Semi-gloss. This is the next step down in PVC. Semi-glosses provide a mid-range sheen, and semi-glosses have good scrubability. They can be used in kitchens, bathrooms, and children's rooms. Where a significant amount of scrubbing can be anticipated, it is important to choose a good quality semi-gloss.

Gloss or High Gloss. These low-PVC paints provide a very shiny surface with easy washability. It should be noted that higher gloss paints, with their low PVC count, are more likely to show surface imperfections. [This is true with both walls and woodwork and explains the importance of proper surface preparation.][7]

The classification of paints according to gloss ratings depends on the ability of the surface to bounce back varying amounts of light beamed on it. These readings show the relative reflectance of the coated surface as compared with a smooth, flat mirror (Table

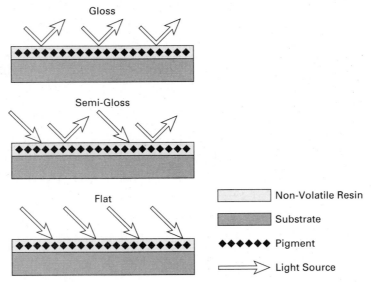

Figure 2–2
An illustration of how pigment volume concentration affects light reflectance. (Drawings courtesy of Builders Guide to Paints and Coatings, *NAHB Research Center.)*

2–1). The ratings in Table 2–1 measure the light reflectance of the surface only. Table 2–2 shows the percentage of light reflected by different hues and their different values.

Enamel is a term whose meaning has become increasingly imprecise over time. It originally designated a hard, durable, high-gloss interior paint. However, some flat paints are now called "flat enamels." While enamel formulations run toward gloss or semi-gloss, a flat appearance can be produced through the use of appropriate additives. Enamels include both alkyd and latex paints.

TABLE 2–1
Standard Gloss Range for Architectural and Special Coatings

NAME	GLOSS RANGE	TEST METHOD (ASTM D-523)
Flat	Below 15	85° meter*
Eggshell	5–20	60° meter
Satin	15–35	60° meter
Semi-Gloss	30–65	60° meter
Gloss	Over 65	60° meter

*Angle at which light is reflected.

Source: Consumerism Subcommittee of the NPCA Scientific Committee acting with the Subcommittee D01.13 of the American Society for Testing and Materials (ASTM).

TABLE 2–2
Percentage of Light Reflected by Colors

COLOR	PERCENTAGE OF LIGHT REFLECTED
White	89
Ivory	77
Canary yellow	77
Cream	77
Orchid	67
Cream gray	66
Sky blue	65
Buff	63
Pale green	59
Shell pink	55
Olive tan	43
Forest green	22
Coconut brown	16
Black	2

Today, manufacturers generally use the term "enamel" to indicate a higher quality paint with greater durability and smoother finish.[8]

Enamels and other paints should be applied to a properly prepared surface. A glossy surface will not have **tooth** and should be sanded with sandpaper or a liquid sanding material before application of another coat of paint.

Because of the VOC laws, latex enamels have been greatly improved, and one advantage is that latex enamels do not yellow.

PRIMERS

A primer is the first coat applied to the **substrate** to prepare for subsequent finishing coats and may have an alkyd or latex base. Some primers also serve as sealers and function on porous substrates such as some woods, and particularly on the paper used on **gypsum board.** These nonpenetrating sealers prevent the waste of paint caused by absorption of the porous materials and provide a good base for the final coats. Other primers are specially formulated for use on wood surfaces, on which the natural dyes in the wood might cause unsightly stains. Some finish coats are self-priming, whereas others require a separate primer. The manufacturers' specifications will provide this information:

> Manufacturers often formulate primers and finish coats that are intended to be used together as a system. Where such systems are offered, it is good practice to use them rather than choosing one manufacturer's primer and another manufacturer's topcoat.[9]

Portersept® with surface sealer can be used as a sealer under wallcoverings, reducing damage to drywall during removal, and as a premium-quality primer under paints for plaster, wood, drywall, and metal. The Intersept controls the growth of microorganisms on the paint film.

FLAME-RETARDANT PAINTS

Products from Flame Control® Coatings Inc. comply with federal, state, and local building and fire code requirements. They retard flame spread and penetration of heat, through their **intumescent**-sublimative-ablative and synergistic flame-suppressing action. On contact with flame or excessive heat, Flame Control intumescent **fire-retardant** coatings decompose and puff up (intumesce) forming a thick, dense, spongy foam layer that checks flame spread and retards heat penetration. These paints are for use in schools, hospitals, offices, factories, warehouses, homes, farms, or wherever there is a need for greater fire protection and lasting beauty. Flame Control Coatings Inc.'s Flame Control No. 320A is a VOC compliant flat latex,

intumescent, fire-retardant paint, and therefore equipment is cleaned with water.

Flame-retardant paints are specified for public buildings, especially offices and hotels. After the tragic hotel fires of the early 1980s, it has become necessary to consider these paints seriously. Although they are not fireproof, they do reduce the flammability of the substrate.

For many commercial painting contracts, a Class A fire rating, defined as a **0–25 flame spread,** is required by law. Included in some technical data are the amounts of smoke developed and fuel contributed. More people die in fires from smoke inhalation than from the flames, so perhaps the smoke development figure is more important than the flame spread figure.

A great deal of misunderstanding exists about fire ratings and flame-retardant paints. The fire ratings are based on paints applied to a wood surface (e.g., fir) or a noncombustible surface (e.g., cement-asbestos board). A paint applied to a cement-asbestos board will have a lower flame spread rating than the same one applied in the same manner to the wood surface because of the difference in combustibility of the substrate materials.

STAINS

Stains are pigments applied to bare or sealed wood and may be transparent or opaque, depending on requirements. Medium to light hues enhance the wood surface. Stains differ from paints in that they do not mask the inherent texture of the substrate. There are several different types of stains. Probably the most common for interior use is the solvent-based type, in which the oil penetrates to a measurable depth, thereby giving a more durable colored base. The solvent-based stains should be covered with a urethane varnish when used on doors, window sills, and cabinetry to provide a protective, durable surface for the wood. Because of the higher cost of urethane varnish, other wood surfaces not subject to heavy traffic or abuse may be coated with an alkyd varnish.

Water-based stains have a water vehicle and have a tendency to penetrate the surface rapidly, but not always evenly. Because water raises the grain of the wood, sanding is necessary, whereas it is not needed with oil-based stains. Alcohol stains have an alcohol base and dry extremely quickly because of the rapid evaporation of the solvent. They are mainly used under lacquer and are applied by spraying.

Non–grain-raising **(NGR)** stains are more of a surface type of stain than a penetrating one, but they do not require sanding before application of the final coat. Both alcohol stains and NGRs are used industrially because of ease of application and fast-drying qualities.

Stain waxes do the staining and waxing in one process, penetrating the pores of the wood and allowing the natural grain to show, while providing the protective finish of wax. Real wood paneling may be finished with a stain wax provided that the surface of the wood will not be soiled.

VARNISH

Varnish is a transparent or pigmentless film applied to stained or unstained wood. Varnish dries and hardens by evaporation of the volatile solvents, **oxidation** of the oil, or both.

Where a hard, glossy finish that is impervious to moisture is needed, spar varnish is recommended for both outdoor and indoor use. In areas where moisture is not present, an alkyd varnish provides a slightly longer-lasting finish. Polyurethane is a synthetic resin used to make varnish resistant to both water and alcohol, thus making it usable as a finish on wood floors and tabletops. This type of varnish does not yellow or change color as much as conventional varnishes. The moisture-cured urethane varnishes are more durable but are also more expensive. **Humidity** must be rigidly controlled, because less than 30 percent humidity will cause too slow a curing time, and too high humidity will cause too fast a curing time, resulting in a bubbly surface.

Where a satin finish is needed, the gloss varnish surface may be rubbed down with steel wool, or a satin varnish may be used. Names of finishes do not seem to vary as much in opaque paints as they do in varnishes. One manufacturer will label varnish "dull" and another will call it "flat." Semigloss may also be called "satin" or "medium-rubbed-effect," and high gloss may be called "gloss." Remember that the paired names are synonymous.

Flame Control Coatings Inc. has a Class B water-based fire-retardant varnish for new or previously coated wood surfaces (except floors). The varnish does not leach or turn white on aging or washing.

Varnish stains are pigmented and give a very superficial-colored protective surface to the wood. They are used when a cheap, fast finish is wanted, but they never have the depth of color obtained with other stains. When the surface of a varnish stain is scratched, the natural wood color may show through.

SHELLAC

Shellac is a resinous substance secreted by the lac bug and dissolved in alcohol. It is available in clear, orange, and pigmented white. Shellac was the original glossy, transparent surface finish for furniture and was the finish used on what are now considered antiques. The urethane and oil varnishes have replaced shellac because they are not as quickly affected by heat and water. On a piece of furniture, shellac will turn white when exposed to water and/or heat. Shellac is an inexpensive finish and is seldom used today. Old shellac should never be used because the surface will not dry thoroughly. When there is any doubt about the age of a particular shellac, it should be tested before it is used on a project. If the surface remains tacky, the shellac should be discarded in the proper manner because it will never harden.

LACQUER

Lacquer is a paint that dries by solvent evaporation only and is applied by a spray gun. Lacquer may or may not contain pigments and is used commercially in the finishing of wood furniture and cabinets. A fine built-up finish may be achieved by many coats of lacquer, each of which is finely sanded before the subsequent coats.

DANISH OIL

Danish oil finish, either clear or with a stain, is used on wood. The clear gives a natural finish whereas the stained contains a wood stain to achieve the colored effect. Danish oil finish has as its main components tung oil and boiled linseed oil, and it gives the wood a rich, penetrating oil surface while sealing the pores.

NOVELTY FINISHES

Several companies now manufacture multicolored wall coatings that give the surface a **faux** finish—stone, fabric, or texture. The finish consists of separate and distinct pigmented enamel particles suspended in an aqueous solution; the vehicle is a modified acrylate. These nonflammable coatings are sprayed over a special basecoat, with a two-step final coat.

Aquafleck® Acrylic Latex Multi-Color is a decorative, durable, seamless wall finish ideal for new or existing space. Aquafleck is water based, virtually odorless, nontoxic, VOC/VOS compliant, USDA approved, Class I fire rated, scrubbable, requires no evacuation during application, generates no hazardous waste, and is easy to clean up with water. Available in 48 standard colors, Aquafleck also offers custom color-matching capabilities; an acrylic polyurethane clear glaze coat is available in a gloss or satin finish for maximum protection.

Duroplex® coatings are tough finishes applied exclusively by factory-trained installers who are in the painting trade. Depending on the desired finish, Duroplex can be applied by spray or roller methods and cures to a surface hardness that is 80 percent as hard as mild steel. It is as tough as concrete and provides an improved performance dimension to drywall.

Chroma Spec™ and Scuff Master™, from Master Coating Technology, are applied using a different method than the two types mentioned previously. The mixture is a combination of polyurethane and acrylic, but it has a catalyst that is added just before application. The catalyst adds a great deal of strength but is also VOC compliant. Instead of one container of paint, Chroma Spec uses a different container for each color. By adjusting the pressure in the three nozzles, the flow can vary from speckles to strings.

COLOR

Color is the least expensive way to dramatize, stylize, or personalize a home. Colors affect us psychologically, and they should be selected with this in mind. When studying paint chips, be sure to mask other colors on the same paint card. Otherwise, the eye will tend to blend all the colors rather than see them individually. Another point to remember is that when matching a color, select a hue several shades lighter. **Chroma** is the degree of saturation of a hue. A color at its full intensity has maximum chroma.

APPLICATION METHODS

The four most common methods of applying paints are brush, roller, pad, and airless spray. Pads and rollers are do-it-yourself tools, although the roller may be used in remodeling if removal of furniture is impossible. The best available equipment should be used, since poor-quality tools will result in a poor-quality paint job.

Whatever the material used for the bristles (hog hair or synthetic), brushes should have **flagged bristles** that help load the brush with more paint while helping the paint flow more smoothly. Cheap brushes have almost no flagging, which causes the paint to flow unevenly. Brushes are used for woodwork and for uneven surfaces, whereas rollers are used for walls and flat areas.

Spraying is used to cover large areas, such as walls and ceilings in new homes, but especially for commercial interiors. Airless spraying uses fluid pressure. Most airless spraying uses undiluted paint, which provides better coverage but also uses more paint. All surrounding areas must be covered or masked to avoid overspray, and this masking time is always included in the painting contractor's estimates.

Spraying is eight to ten times faster than other methods of application. These figures refer to flat walls, but spraying is an easier and more economical method of coating uneven or irregular surfaces than brushing, since it enables the paint to penetrate into the crevices. When spraying walls, the use of a roller immediately after spraying evens out the coat of paint.

Spraying is also the method used for finishing furniture and kitchen cabinets. For a clear finish on furniture and cabinets, heated lacquer is used, which dries quickly, cures to a hard film with heat, and produces fewer toxic emissions. Heated lacquer is formulated to be used without **reduction,** thus giving a better finished surface.

Because OMNIPLEX® is sprayed, it is discussed in this chapter. It is a lightweight, nonporous polyester material that is applied to simulate the colors and patterns of granite, onyx, and other natural stone. OMNIPLEX is available in 12 stone finishes and can be custom blended, textured or sanded smooth, matte finished, or polished to a glossy luster like real stone. A clear topcoat is available for added protection or higher gloss. OMNIPLEX is EPA compliant and may be used on all surfaces, walls, counters, or furniture.

Other faux finishes are obtained by using paints but applying them by methods other than those described previously—including stippling with a sponge, swirling (to imitate marble), and using other methods that will achieve the desired effect. Some people add sand to the paint to give a stucco appearance.

SURFACE PREPARATION

Surface preparation is the most important procedure to achieve a good paint finish. According to Sherwin-Williams, "as high as 80% of all coatings failures can be directly attributed to inadequate surface preparation that affects coating adhesion. Selection and implementation of proper surface preparation ensure coating adhesion to the substrate and prolong the service life of the coating system."[10]

Mildew is also a major cause of paint failure. It is not produced by the paint itself; rather, it is a fungus whose spores will thrive in any damp, warm place—exterior or interior. Several mildew-cleaning solutions are available, the simplest of which is bleach and water. Other remedies have additional ingredients and may be purchased premixed, but caution should be used with these products because they are extremely irritating to the eyes and skin. Instructions should be read and followed carefully.

Until the late 1950s, lead-based paints were used. Renovation of buildings painted before the late 1950s must be done by a professional contractor trained in proper handling of lead-based paints. In 1978 the U.S. government banned the use of lead in any consumer paints.

Wood

Moisture is the major problem when painting wood. Five to 10 percent moisture content is the proper range. Today most wood is **kiln dried,** but exposure to high humidity may change that moisture content. While knots in the wood are not technically a moisture problem, they also cause difficulties when the surface is to be painted, because the resin in the knots may **bleed** through the surface of the paint; therefore, a special knot sealer must be used.

All cracks and nail holes must be filled with a suitable wood putty or filler, which may be applied before or after priming according to instructions on the can or in the paint guides. Some woods with open pores require the use of a paste wood filler (Table 2–3). If a natural or painted finish is desired, the filler is diluted with a thinner; if the surface is to be stained, the filler is diluted with the stain.

If coarse sanding is required, it may be done at an angle to the grain; medium or fine sanding grits should always be used with the grain. Awkward places should never be sanded across the grain because the sanding marks will show up when the surface is stained.

Plaster

When preparing a plaster wall for painting, it is necessary to ensure that the plaster is solid, has no cracks, and is smooth and level, since paint will only emphasize any problems. Badly cracked or loose plaster should be removed and repaired. *All* cracks, even if hairlines, must be repaired, since they will only enlarge with time. To achieve a smooth and level wall,

the surface must be sanded with a fine sandpaper and, before the paint is applied, the fine dust must be brushed from the wall surface. Plaster is extremely porous, so a primer-sealer is required, which may be latex or alkyd.

Gypsum Board

On gypsum board, all seams must be taped, and nail or screw holes must be filled with spackling compound or joint cement; these filled areas should then be sanded. Care should be taken not to sand the paper areas too much because doing so causes the surface to be **abraded.** The abrasion may still be visible after the final coat has dried, particularly if the final coat has any gloss. Gypsum board may also have a texture applied (as described in Chapter 5, p. 98), and the luster selected will be governed by the type of texture. Gypsum board must also be brushed clean of all fine dust particles before the primer is applied.

Metal

Metals must have all loose rust, **mill scale,** and loose paint removed before a primer is applied. There are many methods of accomplishing this removal. One of the most common and effective is sandblasting, in which fine silica particles are blown under pressure onto the surface of the metal. Small areas may be sanded by hand. For metals other than galvanized metal, the primer should be rust inhibitive and specially formulated for that specific metal.

Masonry

Masonry usually has a porous surface and will not give a smooth topcoat unless a block filler is used. Product analysis of a block filler shows a much larger percentage of calcium carbonate than titanium dioxide. A gallon of masonry paint does not cover as large an area as a gallon of other types of paint, because the heavier calcium carbonate content acts as a filler. One problem encountered with a masonry surface is **efflorescence,** which is a white powdery substance caused by an alkaline chemical reaction with water. An alkaline-resistant primer is necessary if this condition is present. However, the efflorescence must be removed before the primer is applied.

WRITING PAINTING SPECIFICATIONS

The specifier should learn how to read the technical part of the product guide, or find the same information on the label of the can. Some manufacturers state

TABLE 2–3
Wood Classification According
to Openness of Pores

NAME	SOFT	HARD	OPEN PORE	CLOSED PORE	NOTES
Ash		X	X		Needs filler
Alder	X			X	Stains well
Aspen		X		X	Paints well
Basswood		X		X	Paints well
Beech		X		X	Varnishes well, paints poorly
Birch		X		X	Paints and varnishes well
Cedar	X			X	Paints and varnishes well
Cherry		X		X	Varnishes well
Chestnut		X	X		Requires filler, paints poorly
Cottonwood		X		X	Paints well
Cypress		X		X	Paints well and varnishes well
Elm		X	X		Requires filler, paints poorly
Fir	X			X	Paints poorly
Gum		X		X	Varnishes well
Hemlock	X			X	Paints fairly well
Hickory		X	X		Needs filler
Mahogany		X	X		Needs filler
Maple		X		X	Varnishes well
Oak		X	X		Needs filler
Pine	X			X	Variable
Redwood	X			X	Paints well
Teak		X	X		Needs filler
Walnut		X	X		Needs filler

Source: Abel Banov, *Paintings and Coatings Handbook.* Torstar Corporation, 1973, p. 127.

in the product description that it is a short-, medium-, or long-oil coating. A long-oil paint has a longer drying period and is usually more expensive. One property of a long-oil product is that it coats the surface better than a short-oil product because of its wetting ability.

The volume of solids is expressed as a percentage per gallon of paint. This percentage can vary from as much as 90 percent in some industrial coatings and from 40 percent to the high teens in architectural paints. If, for the sake of comparison, a uniform thickness of 1 1/2 **mils** is used, the higher percentage volume paint would cover 453 square feet and the lower percentage only 199 square feet. This, of course, means that more than twice as much paint of the lower volume would have to be purchased when compared with the higher volume. Thus, the paint that may be a bargain may turn out to cost more if the same result is to be achieved.

Painting specifications are a way of legally covering both parties in the contract between the client and the painting contractor. There will be no misunderstanding of responsibility if the scope of the paint job is clearly spelled out, and most major paint companies include in their catalogs sample painting specifications covering terms of the contract. Some of these are more detailed than others. Tables 2–4 and 2–5 will aid the designer in calculating the approximate time required to complete the painting contract.

A time limit and a penalty clause should be written into the contract. This time requirement is most important, because painting is the first finishing step in a project and, if it is delayed, the completion date is in jeopardy. The penalty clause provides for a deduction of a specific amount of money or a percentage for every day the contract is over the time limit.

TABLE 2–4
Coverage According to Method of Application

METHOD	COVERAGE PER HOUR
Brush	50–200 sq ft
Roller	100–300 sq ft
Spray	300–500 sq ft

TABLE 2–5
Average Coat Requirements for Interior Surfaces

SURFACE	VEHICLE	NUMBER OF COATS
Woodwork	Oil gloss paint	2–3 coats
	Semi-gloss paint	2–3 coats
Plaster	Alkyd flat	2–3 coats
Drywall	Alkyd flat	2–3 coats
	Vinyl latex	3 coats
Masonry	Vinyl latex	3 coats
Wood floor	Enamel	3 coats

Information on surface preparation may be obtained from the individual paint companies. The problems created by incorrect surface treatment, priming, and finishing are *never* corrected by simply applying another coat of paint.

High-performance paints should be selected if budget restrictions permit, because high-performance paints last several times longer than regular paints. This longer durability means that business or commercial operations will not have to be shut down as frequently. Therefore, the increase in cost will more than offset the loss of business. The words *high performance* should be included in the product description.

The method of application should be specified: brush, roller, or spray. The method must suit the material to be covered and the type of paint to be used. Moreover, primers or base coats must be compatible with both the surface to be covered and the final or topcoat. When writing painting specifications, items to be excluded are just as important as items to be included. If other contractors are present at the site, their work and materials must be protected from damage. One area should be designated as a storage for all paint and equipment, and this area should have a temperature at or near 70°F, the ideal temperature for application of paints. The painting subcontractor should remove daily all combustible material from the premises.

The specifier should make certain that inspections are made before the application of each coat, because these inspections will properly cover both client and contractor. If some revisions or corrections are to be made, they should also be put in writing and an inspection should be made before proceeding.

Cleanup is the responsibility of the painting contractor. All windows and glass areas must be free of paint streaks or spatters. The area should be left ready for the succeeding contractor to begin work without any further cleaning.

Some states do not permit interior designers to sign a contract for clients, whereas other states do allow this. The designer should check state laws to see whether he or she or the client must be the contractual party.

USING THE MANUFACTURER'S PAINTING SPECIFICATION INFORMATION

All paint companies have different methods of presenting their descriptive literature, but a designer with the background material this chapter provides will soon be able to find the information needed. For example, first the material to be covered is listed, then the use of that material, and then the finish desired. Let us use wood as an example: The material is wood, but is it going to be used for exterior or interior work? If interior, is it to be used on walls, ceilings, or floors? Each different use will require a product suitable for that purpose. Floors will obviously need a more durable finish than walls or ceilings.

Another category will be the final finish or luster—flat, semi-gloss, or gloss? Will you need an alkyd, a latex, or, for floor use, a urethane? This category is sometimes classified as the vehicle or generic type. The schedule then explains which primer or sealer is to be used for compatibility with the final coat. After the primer, the first coat is applied. This coat may also be used for the final coat, or another product may be suggested. Drying time for the different methods of application may also be found in the descriptive literature. Two different times may be mentioned, one "dust free" or "tack free," meaning the length of time it takes before dust will not adhere to the freshly painted surface. Sometimes a quick-drying paint will have to be specified because of possible contaminants in the air. The second is recoat time; this is important so that the application of the following coat can be scheduled.

The spreading rate per gallon will enable a specifier to calculate approximately how many gallons are needed for the job, thereby estimating material costs. Sometimes, in the more technical specifications, an analysis of the contents of the paint is included both by weight and by volume. The most important percentage, however, is the volume amount, because weight of solids can be manipulated whereas volume cannot. This is the only way to compare one paint with another. The type and percentage of these ingredients make paints differ in durability, application, and coverage. Some paint companies now have these percentages printed on the label of paint cans, similar to the manner in which percentages of the daily requirements of vitamins and minerals are printed on food packages.

If paint is to be sprayed, there will be information on lowering the **viscosity** and, for other methods of application, the maximum reduction permitted without spoiling the paint job. Most catalogs also include a recommended thickness of film when dry, which is expressed as so many mils **DFT** (dry film thickness). This film may be checked with specially made gauges. The DFT cannot be specified by the number of coats. The film thickness of the total paint system is the important factor and not the film thickness per coat.

PROBLEMS WITH PAINT AND VARNISH AND HOW TO SOLVE THEM

The ideal temperature for application of paints and varnishes is 70°F, but effective application can be achieved at temperatures ranging from 50°F to 70°F. Cold affects viscosity, causing slower evaporation of the solvents, which results in sags and runs. High temperature lowers viscosity, also causing runs and sags. High humidity may cause less evaporation of the solvent, giving lower gloss and allowing dirt and dust to settle and adhere to the film. Ventilation must be provided when paints are being applied, but strong drafts will affect the uniformity of luster.

Today, most paint starts with a base, and the pigments are added according to charts provided to the store by the manufacturer. Sometimes it is necessary to change the hue of the mixed paint, and this can be done by judicious addition of certain pigments. It is vital that the designer be aware of the changes made by these additions. Any hue can now be matched by using a **spectrophotometer** hooked up to a computer, which can provide the necessary formula.

BIBLIOGRAPHY

Builders Guide to Paints and Coatings. Upper Marlboro, MD: NAHB Research Center in cooperation with Sherwin-Williams.

"50,000 Years of Protection and Decoration," History of *Paint and Color.* Pittsburgh, PA: Pittsburgh Plate Glass Company.

Innes, Jacosta. *Paint Magic.* New York: Pantheon, 1986.

Morgans, W. M. *Outlines of Paint Technology.* Vol. 1—*Materials,* 2nd ed. London and High Wycombe: Charles Griffin & Co. Ltd., 1982.

Painting and Coating Systems for Specifiers and Applicators. Cleveland, OH: Sherwin-Williams, 1994.

Rose, A. R. "With Paint . . . It's the Dry Film That Counts." *Decorative Products World,* November 1981, pp. 58–59. New York: Time-Life Books, 1976.

GLOSSARY

Abrade. To scrape or rub off a surface layer.

Acrylic. A synthetic resin used in high-performance, water-based coatings.

Alkyd. Synthetic resin modified with oil.

Binder. Solid ingredients in a coating that hold the pigment particles in suspension and attach them to the substrate. Consists of resins (e.g., oils, alkyd, latex). The nature and amount of binder determines many of the paint's performance properties—washability, toughness, adhesion, color retention, and so on.

Bleed. Color penetrates through another coat of paint.

Calcium carbonate. An extender pigment.

Chroma. A measurement of color; the degree of saturation of a hue.

DFT. Dry film thickness. The mil thickness when coating has dried.

Efflorescence. A white alkaline powder deposited on the surface of stone, brick, plaster, or mortar and caused by leaching.

Enamel. Broad classification of paints that dry to a hard, usually glossy finish.

Epoxy. Extremely tough and durable synthetic resin used in some coatings.

Extenders. Ingredients added to paint to increase coverage, reduce cost, achieve durability, and alter appearance. Less expensive than prime hiding pigments such as titanium dioxide.

Faux. French for "fake" or "false." Includes marbling or other imitation finishes.

Fire retardant. A coating that (1) reduces flame spread, (2) resists ignition when exposed to high temperature, or (3) insulates the substrate and delays damage to the substrate.

Flagged bristles. Split ends.

Gloss. Luster. The ability of a surface to reflect light. Measured by determining the percentage of light reflected from a surface at certain angles (see Table 2–1).

Gum. A solid resinous material that can be dissolved and that will form a film when the solution is spread on a surface and the solvent is allowed to evaporate. Usually a yellow, amber, or clear solid.

Gypsum board. Thin slabs of plaster covered with a heavyweight 100 percent recycled paper covering.

Hiding power. The ability of paint film to obscure the substrate to which it is applied. Measured by determining the minimum thickness at which film will completely obscure a black and white pattern.

Humidity. The amount of water vapor in the atmosphere.

Intumescent. A mechanism whereby fire-retardant paints protect the substrates to which they are applied. An intumescent paint puffs up when exposed to high temperatures, forming an insulating, protective layer over the substrate.

Kiln dried. Lumber dried in an oven to a specific moisture content.

Luster. Same as gloss.

Mill scale. An almost invisible surface scale of oxide formed when iron is heated.

Mils. Measurement of thickness of film. One one-thousandth of an inch. One mil equals 25.4 microns (micrometers).

NGR. Non-grain-raising: a type of stain.

Oxidation. Chemical reaction upon exposure to oxygen.

Pigments. Insoluble, finely ground materials that give paint its properties of color.

Reduction. Lowering the viscosity of a paint by the addition of solvent or thinner.

Resin. A solid or semisolid material that deposits a film and is the actual film-forming ingredient in paint. May be natural or synthetic. See *Gum.*

Solid. The part of the coating that remains on a surface after the vehicle has evaporated. The dried paint film.

Solvent. Any liquid that can dissolve a resin. Generally refers to the liquid portion of paints and coatings that evaporates as the coating dries.

Spectrophotometer. An instrument used for comparing the color intensities of different spectra.

Substrate. Any surface to which a coating is applied.

Titanium dioxide. A white pigment providing the greatest hiding power of all white pigments. Non-toxic and nonreactive.

Tooth. The slight texture of a surface that provides good adhesion for subsequent coats of paint.

Urethane. An important resin in the coatings industry.

Vehicle. Portion of a coating that includes all liquids and the binder.

Viscosity. The resistance to flow in a liquid. The fluidity of a liquid such as water has a low viscosity and molasses a very high viscosity.

0–25 flame spread. Lowest acceptable flame-retardant rating for commercial and public buildings.

NOTES

[1] *Builders Guide to Paints and Coatings,* NAHB Research Center, 1993, p. 5.

[2] Ibid., pp. 5 and 6.

[3] Ibid., pp. 8 and 10.

[4] Ibid., p. 6.

[5] *Painting & Coating Systems 1997–1998.* Cleveland, OH: Sherwin-Williams, 1997, p. 11.

[6] *Builders Guide to Paints and Coatings,* p. 10.

[7] Ibid., pp. 10 and 12.

[8] Ibid., p. 12.

[9] Ibid., p. 13.

[10] *Paintings & Coatings Systems,* p. 5.

3

Carpet

HISTORY OF CARPET

The origins of carpet weaving have been lost in antiquity. The first wool carpet may have been crudely handwoven in Ninevah or Babylon around 5000 B.C. An Egyptian fresco, depicting workers at a loom, provides concrete evidence of skillful weaving as far back as 3000 B.C. The most ancient records, including the Bible, mention the use of carpets. Nomadic tribes of central Asia were known to have woven hand-knotted rugs—not only to cover the cold ground in their tents, but for saddle blankets and tent flaps as well. As treasures were brought back from Eastern conquests by the Greeks and Romans, Persian rugs were among the most sought after and valued possessions. Exactly when hand-knotted Oriental rugs were first woven is uncertain. Marco Polo, however, brought the news of their incredible beauty with him on his return to Italy from the Orient in 1295. The Saracens had been weaving carpets in France as early as the 8th century.

No royal support for carpet weaving was given until Henry IV set up a workroom for weaving in the Louvre in 1604. Royal support not only meant the development of carpets that reflected courtly taste, but also ensured the protection and growth of the industry. The Spanish were the first Euro-peans to make hand-tied pile rugs. Often credited with the "invention" of the weaving industry is Englishman Thomas Whitty of Axminster, who, in the 1700s, developed the first machine loom that could weave carpets, which resulted in Axminster carpets. The Frenchman Joseph-Marie Jacquard devised a mechanism for figured weaving or patterning in 1800, and it was first used in Wilton, England.

In Colonial America, the first floor coverings were herbs, rushes, or sand spread on the floor. Later, rag rugs made from clothing scraps and hooked or braided mats were used. Affluent settlers, however, introduced America to prized Oriental rugs, which they brought with them to the New World. Oriental rugs may have as many as 500 to 600 knots per square inch and are named for the pattern and district where they are woven. It is interesting to note that whereas Europeans buy old Oriental rugs, Americans prefer to buy new ones.

The first U.S. carpet mill was started in Philadelphia in 1791. America's most important historical contribution to the industry was the invention of the power loom by Erastus Bigelow in 1841. Years later, the first Brussels (looped-pile carpet) was made here, utilizing the **Jacquard** method of color pattern control, and with further modification the first **Wilton** carpets were also woven in the United States. By the later 19th century, a great deal of machinery and skilled labor found its way to the United States, and the roots of many of today's major carpet manufacturing firms were established.

For centuries, a hand-made wool rug has been a status symbol. In the past, the high price of a wool rug or carpet was probably due to the tremendous labor involved; an ancient weaver needed 900 days to complete an Oriental carpet.[1]

Thus, carpets were originally for the wealthy. Today, because of modern technology, carpet is one product that gives more value for the money than in the past.

This chapter deals with carpet, defined as fabric used as a floor covering, rather than rugs (carpet cut into room or area dimensions and loose laid). Area rugs also include Oriental rugs, **kilims, rya** rugs, **dhurries,** and American Indian rugs. (It is interesting to note that, according to historians, American Indians developed weaving traditions independently from other civilizations.) Much of the information on weaves, pile, and so on may also apply to area rugs.

Area rugs are gaining in popularity because of the mobility of our population. Rugs can be used in many ways: as accents over existing carpet, to highlight a wood floor, or to spotlight area groupings.

Some carpet manufacturers offer helpful data on their products and on carpets in general. For example, designers can receive updated information from DuPont's Flooring Systems Design Consultants. This information will include comparative specification analysis of similar carpets, advice on selecting a carpet that will perform best in a given setting, news on current carpet styles and trends as well as color trends in commercial interiors, information about carpet backing systems, and information on the new DuPont Flooring Systems, products, and services (a valuable resource for any problems that may arise). (See Color Plate 1, a 1997 DuPont Commercial Carpeting Award winner.)

Much of the information presented in this chapter is taken, with permission, from the Carpet and Rug Institute's *Specifier's Handbook*, a detailed and informative book available from the CRI. All interior designers should have a copy in their design library.

FUNCTIONS OF CARPET

According to the Carpet and Rug Institute, the following are the primary functions of carpet:

Acoustical. Carpet absorbs ten times more airborne noise than any other flooring material and as much as most other types of standard acoustical materials. It virtually eliminates floor impact noises at the source. . . .

Beauty. Carpet provides a tremendous choice of colors, textures, and designs to suit every taste. Custom-designed carpet for commercial installation is also available at reasonable prices. Carpet has a way of framing the furnishings in a room or office that makes them look more important and distinctive.

Atmosphere. Carpet dramatically enhances the feeling of quality in interior design—a major consideration in hotels and motels. Carpet also has the ability to "de-institutionalize" a building—a significant factor in improved patient morale in hospitals, and in student attitudes in school.

Thermal Insulation. Physically, the pile construction of carpet is a highly efficient thermal insulator. Mechanical demonstrations have shown that over a cold cement slab, carpet's surface temperature is substantially higher than that of hard surface tile. Thus, carpet relieves coldness at foot and ankle levels and lends a psychological warmth as well. . . .

Safety. The National Safety Council reports that falls cause most indoor injuries. . . . Carpet's ability to cushion falls and prevent serious injuries means savings in medical costs, and man-hours to businessmen.

Comfort. Carpet reduces "floor fatigue". . . . This characteristic is important to salespeople, teachers, nurses, waiters—all those who spend many hours on their feet during the course of their work.[2]

Collins & Aikman have added another dimension to the function of carpet with their Imaginations floor-covering, a map of the United States and a circle that introduces numbers as in a clock face, with the alphabet on the outside for letter recognition. (See Color Plate 2.) Imaginations' colorful and informative Activity cards provide a quick guide for teaching with Imaginations floor covering learning aids. Each card outlines activities incorporating bright colors and shapes that will help students understand important concepts, such as letter and sound recognition, telling time, and math. The Activity cards provide clear, easy-to-follow instructions for leading a class in fun, educational exercises using these two patterns. Imaginations is a wonderful carpet for kindergartens and early primary grades.

The three C's—Color, Comfort, and Cost—are probably the major factors in residential carpet choice, whereas in commercial and institutional projects durability, traffic, cost, and ease of maintenance are more important features. The properties considered in carpet selection also include type of fiber, density of pile, depth of pile, method of construction, and cleanability.

FIBERS

Fiber type is the major decision in selecting a carpet. Each fiber has its own characteristics, and modern technology has greatly improved the features of synthetic fibers. The cost and characteristics of the fiber need to be considered together so the final selection will fulfill the client's needs.

The most prevalent natural fiber used in carpet is wool, but in some rare instances silk, linen, and cotton may be used. Other natural fibers gaining in popularity are sisal and coir. Synthetic fibers are always more colorfast than natural fibers because to produce colored fibers, the dye can be introduced while the fiber is in its liquid state, and integral dyes are more colorfast than surface dyes. Wool, in its natural state, is limited to off white, black/gray, and various shades in between.

Carpet manufacturers do not produce the actual fibers described in this section, but rather buy the fibers from various chemical companies.

Nylon. Nylon was introduced by DuPont in 1938 and accounts for nearly 90 percent of all carpet sold today.

There are numerous types of nylon; however the two used to produce carpet fibers are type 6,6 and type 6. . . . Since 1947, the carpet industry has moved through five generations of nylon carpet fibers; however, all, to some degree, are still found in carpet manufactured today. The generation can best be distinguished by technical advances in the performance of the nylon fiber.

The first generation nylon fibers were round, clear, and readily showed soil. Being round and clear, the fibers actually magnified the soil. Inherent **static** build-up was, and still is, a disadvantage of this type of fiber.

The second generation of nylon fibers effectively reduced soil magnification by changing the fiber shape or cross section from round to noncircular configuration. . . . These second generation nylon fibers are sometimes referred to as soil-hiding types.

The third generation nylons are characterized by improved soil-hiding properties and built-in static protection. The soil-hiding characteristics were improved, in some cases, by further modifying the cross sections and by adding a delustering agent to the fiber. The anti-static properties can be brought about by the use of conductive **filaments** (metallic, or carbon based) incorporated within the nylon fibers.

The fourth generation nylons go one step further by adding carpet protectors to the fiber to make them "soil resistant." Some fiber producers have also included anti-microbial treatments in or on the fiber.

Technical developments have provided improved stain release properties to some advanced generation nylon fibers; some of which are promoted as "fifth generation" nylons.[3]

Antron® Legacy nylon from DuPont has a square 4-hole hollow **filament** shape, which diffuses light to create an appealing luster. Ideal for heavy traffic/soiling areas, it has DuPont's patented fluorochemical treatment, DuraTech®, which is applied only to Antron nylon fibers during the carpet manufacturing process. DuPont Antron Lumena® has antimicrobial properties, as does DuraTech. Both Antron products are antistatic and suitable for office environments with electronic information systems.

As a synthetic fiber, nylon absorbs little water; therefore, stains remain on the surface rather than penetrate the fiber itself. Dirt and soil are trapped between the filaments and are removed by proper cleaning methods. In addition, nylon has excellent abrasion resistance. The reason for worn or thin spots is that the yarn has been damaged physically by grit and soil ground into the carpet. This problem can be taken care of with proper maintenance.

Wool. Wool has, for many years, represented the standard of quality against which all other carpet fibers are measured; this is still the case today to some degree. Most important are the aesthetics and inherent resilience of wool. The best wool for carpet comes from sheep that are raised in colder climates, such as New Zealand (domestic wools are too soft and fine for carpets). Although wool has a propensity for high static generation, treatments are available to impart static-protection properties. Wool retains color for the life of the carpet despite wear and cleaning. It has good soil resistance because of its naturally high moisture content and has excellent pile resilience.

When price is no object, the best carpet fiber is wool. Wool blends, usually 80 percent wool and 20 percent nylon, have a larger market segment than a decade ago. Wool will stain or bleach in reaction to some spills, however, and is not as easy to clean as nylon. "Wool is naturally flame resistant, forming a char that will neither melt nor drip."[4]

Acrylic. Acrylic is the synthetic fiber that most feels like wool. Acrylic carpets have a low soiling rate, clean well, are highly static resistant, and have very good to excellent abrasion resistance and excellent colorfastness. In properly constructed carpets, pile resilience is good. "Acrylics are always used in **staple** form, and sometimes can be found in blends with other fibers."[5]

In the 1960s and early 1970s, acrylic was a popular fiber for commercial and residential carpet because of its good performance. New dyeing processes introduced in the 1970s, however, favored nylon due to its high dyeing rate and resistance to deformation under hot and wet conditions. Now producer-dyed acrylic is being offered, which should again make acrylic a viable fiber for commercial and residential installations.

Polyester. "Polyester has excellent color clarity and retains its color and luster. It is resistant to water soluble stains, and is noted for a luxurious 'hand' when used in thick cut pile textures. Polyester is offered for carpet in staple form only. Polyester is an important carpet fiber, but more in residential styles than for commercial carpet applications."[6] Polyester is a soft fiber with good soil and wear resistance, but it has a tendency to crush with wear.

The Carpet and Rug Institute also states that

> **Polypropylene** is classified as an olefin . . . and is the lightest commercial carpet fiber, with a density of 0.905. It has excellent strength, toughness, and chemical resistance. The fiber is offered as both **continuous filament** and a staple. It is sold as a **solution dyed** fiber or yarn. Because of its very low moisture absorbency and the fact that the color is sealed into the fiber, olefin has excellent resistance to stains. It has resistance to sunlight fading, and generates low levels of static electricity.[7]

Olefins do, however, have fair to poor resilience of pile. Polypropylene should not be used outdoors unless specifically recommended by the carpet manufacturer.

Cotton. Cotton is an expensive natural fiber most often used for flat woven rugs such as Indian dhurries.

Sisal. Sisal, the world's strongest natural fiber, is made from yarns spun from the sisal fibers extracted from the long, spike-shaped leaves of the tropical sisal plant. Coir is also a natural fiber taken from the tough fibrous husk that surrounds the coconut. Because sisal and coir are natural fibers, there will be color variations when left undyed; however, several companies are dyeing, painting, or stenciling these fibers.

CONSTRUCTION METHODS

In the beginning, carpet looms were only 27 inches wide. That width is still available, but most carpet is usually 12 feet wide, although some carpets come in 15-foot widths and carpet may be custom sized for large installations. Another method of production is the **carpet module,** available in 12-inch × 12-inch and 18-inch × 18-inch sizes, although 24-inch × 24-inch is occasionally used. Tiles 36 inches × 36 inches are rarely used. Should severe damage occur, modules (Figures 3–1 and 3–2) are easier to remove and replace than 12- or 15-foot widths.

The main manufacturing processes in order of quantity of carpet produced are tufting, weaving, needle punch, and others, some of which are shown in Figure 3–3.

Tufting

In a tufted piece of carpet, the back is woven first and then the face is tufted into it and backed with additional material. Tufting is a much faster process than

Figure 3–1
Installation and removal of carpet modules is easy, as shown in this photograph. (Photo courtesy of Interface Flooring Systems, Inc.)

Figure 3–2
Tatami Tile in gray and tan were used in this office. The texture of the tiles simulates the texture of a Tatami mat. (Photo © Jonathan Hillyer Photography Inc.; photo courtesy of Interface Flooring Systems, Inc.)

Tufted

Wilton Weave

Velvet Weave

Axminster Weave

Knitted

Figure 3–3
Construction methods.

the traditional weaving method and has greatly reduced the cost of carpet, thereby making it available to more buyers. The technique is fast, efficient, and simple. More than 90 percent of all carpet sold in the United States is tufted.

Weaving

Weaving is a fabric formation process used for manufacturing carpet in which **yarns** are interlaced to form cloth. The weaving loom interlaces lengthwise (warp) and widthwise (filling) yarns. **Pitch** is measured by the number of lengthwise warp yarns; in a 27-inch width, the higher the number, the finer the weave. Carpet weaves are complex, often involving several sets of warps and filling yarns. The back and the face are produced simultaneously and as one unit. When describing an area rug, the term *tapestry weave* is sometimes used. Coir and sisal are always woven.

According to the DuPont company, "When a woven carpet backing is used, specify 100% moisture-resistant warp, filling and stuffer yarns for this construction to eliminate shrinkage during wet cleaning or where installation is on or below grade."[8]

Velvet carpets are the simplest of carpets to weave. They are made on a velvet loom that is not unlike the Wilton loom without the Jacquard unit. The rich appearance of velvets is due to their high pile density. Velvets can be cut or looped pile.

Knitted

Knitted carpets were not made by machine until 1940. Their quality is generally high, depending on the

yarns used and their density. Knitting a carpet involves at least three different facing yarns and perhaps a fourth for backing. Face yarns are knitted in with warp chains and weft-forming yarns in a simple knitting process. Variations of colors, yarns, and pile treatment (cut or looped, high or low) create design choices for knitted carpets. Knitting today is a speedy process that produces fine-quality carpet:

> Most knitted carpet is solid colored or tweed, although some machines have pattern devices. Both loop and cut pile surfaces are available.

Needle Punching

> Needle-punched carpet is a durable, felt-like product manufactured by entangling a fiber fleece with barbed needles. . . . A latex coating or attached padding is applied to the back. . . . Technological advances in machinery now allow a diverse range of designs, including ribs, sculptured designs, and patterns. Needle punched carpet is almost always glued down when installed.[9]

Aubusson

Aubussons are flatly woven tapestries and carpets in silk or wool, named for the French town where they originated (circa 1500). Tapestries bear narratives or portraits, whereas carpets feature architectural designs in rich colors or flowers in muted pastels.

Axminster and Wilton

Although the appearance of Axminster and Wilton carpets may be similar, the construction is very different. In an Axminster, pile tufts are individually inserted from colored yarns arranged on spools, making possible an enormous variety of colors and patterns (Figure 3–4). The Wilton looms have Jacquard pattern mechanisms that use punched cards to select pile height and yarn color. In a Wilton, unwanted yarn colors are buried under the surface of the carpet, limiting the color selection to five or six colors. The carpets are often patterned or have multilevel surfaces. The traditional fiber in Axminster and Wilton construction is wool, but a blend of 80 percent wool and 20 percent nylon is sometimes used. One way to distinguish between the two types is to roll them across the warp and weft. A Wilton will fold in both directions, an Axminster only in one (see Figure 3–4).

Figure 3–4
A woven wool Axminster from Stark shows Stark's custom version of the pattern Dalkeith, with a border of a custom version of Basketweave. This carpet was installed in the prestigious Porto Vecchio luxury condominiums in Alexandria, Virginia. (Photo courtesy of Stark Carpet.)

DYEING

Color is the most important aesthetic property of carpet. Designers should be familiar with the major methods of color application to carpet. This increases their ability to specify the most appropriate carpet for a given application.

Solution-dyed yarns and fibers are pre-colored by the fiber manufacturer, who introduces pigments into the molten polymer before extrusion into fiber. Solution-dyed fibers have outstanding fade resistance and wet fastness. Stabilized with ultraviolet inhibitors, they are excellent for outdoor applications. The most common solution-dyed carpet fiber is polypropylene, but polyester and nylon are also available.

Stock Dyeing

Stock dyeing is the application of color to fibers before conversion into **spun yarn.** This method of dyeing is probably the oldest method of coloring yarns and is still important today for dyeing wool. Other fibers, such as acrylic, polyester, and some nylon, can also be dyed in this manner.

In stock dyeing, bulk staple fiber is placed in a large drum-like kettle where a prepared dye liquor is forced through the fiber. By controlling the temperature and, in some cases, the pressure, the dyeing is continued until the dyestuff has been completely exhausted from the bath onto the fiber. The kettle is then drained, and the fiber is rinsed, followed by centrifuging to remove excess water. It [the fiber] is then dried and ready for spinning. Fiber blending during the spinning operation produces uniform color throughout the yarn lot.

Stock dyeing is a valuable styling device for contract carpet designers. Heather blends and **Berber** effects are produced by combining stock-dyed fibers of various colors. . . .

Skein Dyeing

Skein dyeing is a technique that applies color to yarn. . . . Almost any yarn and fiber may be dyed this way if the yarn has sufficient strength and scuff resistance to withstand skein winding and back winding onto tufting cones. The method is applicable to spun yarns, **bulked continuous filament yarns** (BCF), heat-set yarns, and nonheat-set yarns of many fiber types. Although a high labor cost is involved, skein dyeing is especially suited to small volume production of custom colorations.[10]

Helios is well known for its extensive use of skein-dyed wool and is able to achieve beautiful rich colors through its advanced skein-dyeing techniques. This method produces a depth and richness of color that cannot be achieved in any other dyeing process.

Piece Dyeing

Piece dyeing is the application of color from an aqueous dyebath onto unfinished carpet consisting only of primary backing and undyed yarns. . . . Piece dyeing is generally for solid colors. However, two or more colors can be produced in tweed, Moresque, or stripe patterns in the same carpet from a single dyebath. This is achieved by using fibers of modified and/or altered dye affinity.[11]

Most residential carpet today is dyed using the piece-dyeing method, since manufacturers can store the plain or undyed carpet until a particular color is needed.

Carpet Printing

Carpet printing is accomplished with machinery that is essentially enlarged, modified textile printing equipment. . . . Printed carpet is available in a wide variety of patterns or textures ranging from low-level loop carpet to **Saxony,** cut-loop, and

shag. Printed carpets can simulate woven patterns at much lower cost.

Jet printing machinery consists of rows of color jets arranged across the width of the carpet. The jets are closely spaced, about an eighth to a tenth of an inch apart. Each jet may be opened or closed by computer-controlled valves as the carpet moves under the row of jets. Controlled patterns are produced without screens or physical contact of machinery against carpet. Each row of jets applies a different color. Pattern changes are rapid, requiring only computer program modifications. The jets squirt color onto the carpet surface, but unlike screens, do not crush the pile, resulting in superior texture. . . . The machinery is costly, but the obvious advantages suggest that various types of the jet printing technology may gain importance in the carpet industry.[12]

A printed patterned carpet is shown in Figure 3–5.

Although floorcloths are mentioned in the section on wood floors in Chapter 4, the manner in which they are designed and constructed is appropriate for discussion here. In the past, heavy canvas was stretched and cut to size, then primed and stenciled or hand painted in a variety of patterns, and then sealed with oil. Today, extra-heavy canvas up to 12 feet wide is used and treated with a custom-developed flexible, nonyellowing protective coating to ensure longevity and prevent cracking. There are several contemporary companies and designers who have stock patterns but who also make floorcloths on commission.

Fabric Protectors

Fabric protectors can be introduced after the dyeing process. According to the Bridgepoint Corporation, there are three basic types of fabric protectors:

Colloidal silica, which fill pores, thus preventing soil from becoming embedded.

Silicones, which provide a water-repellent coating; and fluorochemicals, which form an invisible shield on the fibers that helps prevent soil and stains from sticking.

Fluorine is very inert and wants nothing oily, watery, solid, or liquid to adhere to it. Colloidal silicas were first introduced in the early 1950s, and usually show good dry soil performance over short periods of time but have no oil or water repellency at all. In addition, colloidal silica finishes generally detract from the luster of carpet and may give a harsh hand to the fiber.

Figure 3–5
A patterned carpet of DuPont Antron nylon was used in the Richfield Retirement Community, Salem, Virginia. (Photo courtesy of DuPont Flooring Systems.)

Products based upon silicones form a water-repellent coating on the fiber. But even though they are good water repellents, silicone finishes have no resistance to oily substances and, consequently, they frequently show poor dry soil performance. In fact, they often attract some types of soil resulting in a carpet that appears dirtier than one without a protective finish. The silicone products are formulated in organic solvents that are usually flammable and sometimes odor causing. The product should be used only in well-ventilated areas and never used around an open flame or while smoking. Silicone products offer a viable alternative to fluorochemical products when cost is the main concern.

Fluorochemical products form a protective coating on the carpet fibers that helps keep dirt from lodging itself within the fibers. These unique products are characterized by outstanding dry soil resistance and resistance to wet soil. They provide very good resistance to both water- and oil-based liquids. Dirt or soil tends to remain on top of fabrics treated with fluorochemicals and can usually be vacuumed away. The fluorochemicals will work in basically two ways. When a fluorochemical product is applied, it will disperse and **wick** to cover all of the fiber surfaces as long as it is applied properly. The coverage is spread throughout the fabric and the dirt and stain repellency will work even at the base of a carpet as long as the product is there. The fluorochemicals also impart a high degree of surface tension. This surface tension is created by an electrical charge that will hold a liquid on the surface of the fiber. The surface tension can be broken easily by physically forcing the liquid into the fabric. If the liquid is dropped onto the surface from a distance, it will usually break the surface tension. When this surface tension is broken, the liquid is being forced into the air spaces rather than being absorbed into the fiber protected with a fluorochemical.

Fluorochemical protectors fall into two categories; water-based and solvent-based. The two main manufacturers of the water-based fluorochemicals are 3M with Scotchgard®, and DuPont with Teflon® and DuraTech®. (See Color Plate 4.)

The 3M Company sells the Scotchgard® product while DuPont allows for the private labeling of their products. Therefore, many products containing DuPont Teflon® have appeared in the marketplace. Make sure the recommended concentration of Teflon is being used.[13]

DuPont now offers SpillBlock™ in its residential carpets. This carpet-backing system is available only on DuPont-approved brands, and it works to help keep spills above the backing, where they are easier to get to. Although not completely impervious, it makes cleaning faster and helps keep spills from soaking through and hiding and then wicking to the surface later.

Another factor to consider for computer rooms and electronic offices is a backing engineered for control of electrostatic discharge (**ESD**).

Fire-retardant products are also used, especially in commercial installations where fire codes require such products. Wool self-extinguishes when the source of ignition is removed and merely chars, leaving only a cold ash, which can be easily brushed away with no permanent scars; in contrast, synthetic fibers melt.

FLAMMABILITY TESTING

It is extremely important for designers to realize the legal ramifications of flammability specifications because of possible damage and liability lawsuits. Designers should require carpet suppliers to submit written documentation of fire code compliance.

Monsanto Contract Fibers has prepared a special report on flammability resistance, part of which follows:

> With the Federal regulations which govern the manufacturing of all carpet, it is now against the law to make or sell any carpet which does not pass the Methenamine Tablet Test (DOC FF 1-70).
>
> All fires have three distinct stages: ignition, flashover, and expansion. In the ignition stage, the fire has started but is contained in a small area of one room. Flashover occurs when the fire spreads beyond its point of origin and everything in the room is burning. In the expansion stage, the fire leaves the room and spreads over into other rooms or down a corridor. If the fire can be contained during the ignition stage, minimal damage will occur.
>
> This is the rationale behind the Methenamine Tablet Test, or pill test, as it is more commonly known. In this test, eight identical carpet specimens are placed in a draft-free environment. A methenamine tablet is positioned in the center of each specimen and ignited. If two or more of the specimens burn for three inches in any direction, the carpet fails the test and cannot be sold in the United States.
>
> Another method for testing the flame resistance of carpet is the Steiner Tunnel Test (ASTM E-84). Here, a carpet sample 20-inches wide and 25-feet

long is placed on the ceiling of the test tunnel with its pile facing down. The carpet is exposed to a gas jet flame in a temperature range of 1,600°F to 1,800°F for 10 minutes or until the carpet has been completely burned. The flame-spread is observed every 15 seconds, and the longest distance of flame-spread is measured. This distance is then used to determine a flame-spread rating. This test is being replaced by the Radiant Panel Flooring Test in most states because of its greater accuracy.

The Chamber Test (UL-992) is a variation of the Tunnel Test. Here, the carpet sample and any padding or other underlayment are placed on the floor of the test tunnel and exposed to a high heat burner and a draft of air. This test is not widely accepted, because its results are inconclusive.

A more accurate test is the Radiant Panel Flooring Test (ASTM E-648), which simulates conditions that could cause flame-spread in a carpet system, but applies only to carpet installed in corridors. In this test, the carpet sample and underlayment are positioned inside a test chamber. A radiating heat panel, not a direct flame, is placed at a 30° angle above one end of the sample. This panel generates heat at the carpet surface ranging from 1.1 watts/cm^2 directly beneath the panel to about 0.1 watts/cm^2 at the far end of the sample. The total distance the sample burns is measured and then converted to watts/cm^2. This number is called the critical radiant flux **(CRF)**. Each sample is tested three times and an average CRF is derived. The higher the CRF, the more resistant a carpet system is to flame-spread. For example, oak flooring has a CRF of about 0.35 to 0.40 in comparison to carpet, which may have a CRF above 1.1.

As relates to smoke generation by solid materials, the latest edition of the *Life Safety Code* states that it is neither necessary nor practical to regulate interior floor finishes on the basis of smoke development. However, if a smoke requirement is deemed necessary, it is recommended that floor covering of all occupancies have a maximum specific optical density of 450 (flaming) when tested in accordance with the NFPA Standard no. 258 (ASTM E-662-79).[14]

TYPES OF PILE

Today's carpets feature any of several types of pile:

Loop pile has a surface consisting of uncut loops. Variations include high and low loops, colors, and highly twisted yarns.

Cut pile (plush) may be made from unset yarns (frizzy ends) for an even velvety texture or from set yarns (firm ended) to give a velour texture with tuft definition. These carpets look more luxurious than loop, but they also tend to show footsteps or flaws more readily. Patterned wovens or printed tufteds will offset such characteristics. Area rugs, particularly those with borders or a colored pattern, often use a **sculptured** cut pile. Where two colors meet, the pile is cut in a V shape to delineate the pattern and produce a three-dimensional effect. Plain carpet may also be carved in any design.

Frieze (hard twist) is cut pile from a highly twisted yarn set in a snarled configuration. It will hide footsteps, **shedding,** and **shading,** which occurs when pile lays in opposite directions.

Semishag (plush) is soft, cut pile with shorter piles than shags. Ends of yarn stand up so the carpet has a pebbled look.

Shag is soft carpet with long pile. An example is the Scandinavian rya rug, in which different yarns may be used, but always with the side of the yarn exposed to give a shaggy look.

Tip sheared is loop pile carpet with some loops sheared on the surface to create areas of cut pile and a luxurious, sculpted look.

Berber was named after the original hand-woven wool squares made by the North African tribes. It is now made by machine but features a country, homespun effect and natural colors. Usually coarse loop pile but also made in cut pile, shags, and a variety of designs, Berber is most often used in contemporary rooms. The Berber weaving system is the oldest in the history of rugmaking—it may be as old as the second millennium B.C. Flat, hand-loomed woven rugs are still being produced by the American Indians, as well as in India, China, Iran, and elsewhere (Figure 3–6).

Along with the quality of the fiber, the amount of fiber is crucial to a carpet's durability. The depth of pile is not as important as its **face weight** (i.e., the density of fiber in the pile). If asked, sales staff will disclose (if sometimes reluctantly) the face weight of a carpet. In terms of durability, carpets are often divided into four grades:

1. Grade One is intended for residential or domestic use;
2. Grade Two is for normal contract (commercial) use;

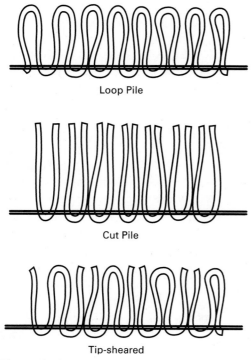

Loop Pile

Cut Pile

Tip-sheared

Figure 3–6
Piles.

3. Grade Three is for such public areas as lobbies where face weight is especially important;
4. Grade Four is for stairs, offices containing chairs with casters, and institutions. Many Grade Four carpets have uncut loop pile for greater resilience.[15]

CARPET CUSHIONING

The padding or cushioning is the "unseen" but indispensable element of a carpet installation. Cushioning makes the carpet feel better and look better longer. Carpet is seldom replaced because it "wears" out. It is usually changed because it "uglies" out—or loses its fresh, new appearance. By reducing pile height loss and pile crushing, cushion can help keep a carpet "new looking"—and therefore stretch its usable life span.

According to the Carpet Cushion Council (CCC),

Carpet cushioning can significantly improve a carpet's acoustical properties. . . . In floor sound absorption tests, a carpet laid directly on concrete floor, with no cushion, measured a **Noise Reduction Coefficient (NRC)** of 0.25. In a like test, the same carpet with a cushion on a concrete floor measured a Noise Reduction Coefficient of 0.65, a

considerably better performance. . . . Carpet cushion also improves the overall thermal insulation properties of a floor covering. . . .

There are five types of carpet cushion: fiber, sponge rubber, prime urethane foam, bonded urethane foam, and mechanically frothed urethane foam [Table 3–1]. . . .

There are three basic types of fiber carpet cushion: natural fiber (such as animal hair and jute), synthetic carpet fiber (like nylon, polypropylene, and polyester), and resinated recycled textile fiber (synthetic fibers recycled from textile manufacturing processes). The grade of fiber cushion is determined by its weight in ounces per square yard. Fiber cushions tend to have a firm "walk" or "feel" [see Table 3–1 for type selection].

There are two specific types of sponge rubber carpet cushion: flat sponge (smooth or flat surface) and rippled sponge (rippled or waffled surface). Flat sponge offers a firm feel; rippled sponge is softer. Grades are measured by weight in ounces per square yard.

There are three types of prime urethane foam carpet cushion: conventional prime, grafted prime, and densified prime cushion. Conventional prime and grafted prime urethane cushion are manufactured by a chemical mixing reaction process. There are many types of prime urethane available today with a variety of density and firmness. The best products are those that combine the right balance of properties for comfort and durability. In densified prime, the chemical structure is modified during the manufacturing process to produce a product with specific performance characteristics. Grades of densified prime urethane are determined by the foam density, or weight of the material per cubic foot.

Bonded foam cushions are made by combining shredded pieces of urethane through a fusion process into a single sheet of material. Bonded foam grades are also measured by density.

Mechanically frothed urethane foam cushions are made from a process originally developed to apply cushioned backings to carpet. The urethane foam cushioning is applied to a sheet of nonwoven material, forming a carpet cushion product with a typically higher density and firmer feel. . . .

The Carpet Cushion Council has the following suggestions about the selection of cushioning for particular areas: the heavier the traffic, the thinner the cushion. In heavy traffic areas like hallways, stairs, rooms with lots of activity, and rooms with heavy furniture such as dining rooms, choose thinner (3/8 inch or less) and heavier cushion to protect the carpet. For bedrooms, dens, and areas where a more luxurious feel is desired, thicker and more resilient cushion can be used. But again, it is best to go with higher weight or higher density products to help make the carpet last longer.[16]

As can be seen from Table 3–1, the Carpet Cushion Council has established recommended minimum contract cushion criteria for three levels of traffic. Any cushion type and grade certified as meeting the CCC's guidelines can be expected to perform satisfactorily at that level under normal conditions, when used with a carpet made for the same specified traffic.[17] To make proper selection easier, the various categories of cushioning have color-coded labels: red label—commercial, moderate traffic; green label—heavy traffic; blue label—commercial, extra heavy traffic.

WRITING CARPET SPECIFICATIONS

Construction

Carpet construction specification prescribes how a carpet is to be manufactured without reference to its end use or performance. There are many factors in construction that help define the finished quality of carpet. Those most frequently written into construction specifications are as follows:

1. Construction type (tufted, woven, knitted, etc.)
2. **Gauge** (pitch)
3. Stitches per inch (**wires** per inch)
4. Pile height (wire height)
5. Pile fiber (generic type nylon, polypropylene, polyester, wool)
6. Yarn ply, count, and heat set
7. Pile yarn weight (ounces per square yard)
8. Backing material:
   a. In woven carpet—type and weight per square yard
   b. In tufted carpet—types and weights per square yard for both primary and secondary backs
9. Back coating type and weight per square yard
10. Finished total weight per square yard.

Construction specifications can be proprietary, identifying a specific carpet by grade, name, and manufacturer. An "or equal" specification could also identify a specific grade, listing its construction factors so other manufacturers can bid for the order competitively. In this case, the usual procedure is to approve "or equals" in advance of the actual bidding. Full attention can then be given to price and delivery information when bid documents are analyzed.

Performance

To clarify the difference between performance and construction specifications, performance specifications define what characteristics the carpet must deliver in use. . . . In other words, performance specifications tell the manufacturer what the carpet must do without detailing how it must be made. By contrast, a construction specification tells the manufacturer, in very precise terms, how the carpet is to be manufactured without stipulating performance needs.

Specifying performance rather than construction can also take other important pressures off the specifier. For example, if the specifier does not regularly deal with carpet products, the latest technology and materials may be overlooked. The best, most economical product to ensure the desired performance may not be chosen. . . .

Whether written for construction or performance, most carpet specifications also incorporate requirements governing the following items:

1. Type of installation (tackless or glue-down)
2. Cushion type and grade, if required
3. Installation procedures and accessories
4. Certification that materials meet federal, state, and local government ordinances (particularly for flammability[18])
5. Delivery and installation schedules
6. Carpet maintenance (Request maintenance instructions from the manufacturer.)

Special requirements for different types of installation sites can be very complex and technical. For example, in window-wall architecture, fade resistance could be a matter of primary concern. In a hospital medical dispensary, stain resistance might be placed high on the list of performance priorities. Special static protection properties may be necessary for computer and data-processing areas. . . .

The following concerns should be addressed:

1. Budget
2. Surface texture, pattern or design [see Color Plate 3]

TABLE 3–1
Minimum Recommended Criteria for Satisfactory Carpet Cushion Performance in Contract Installations

TYPES OF CUSHION	CLASS I *MODERATE TRAFFIC*

Commercial Application

Office Buildings: Executive or private offices, conference rooms
Health Care: Executive, administrative
Schools: Administration
Airports: Administration
Retail: Windows and display areas
Banks: Executive areas
Hotels/Motels: Sleeping rooms
Libraries/Museums: Administration

Minimum recommended criteria for satisfactory carpet cushion performance in contract installations

---

Fiber

Rubberized Hair	Wt. 40 oz.	Th: .27″	D = 12.3
Rubberized Jute	Wt. 32 oz.	Th: .25″	D = 12.3
Synthetic Fibers	Wt. 22 oz.	Th: .25″	D = 7.3
Resinated Recycled Textile Fiber	Wt. 24 oz.	Th: .25″	D = 7.3

Rubber

Flat Rubber	Wt. 62 oz.	Th: .150″	CR @ 25% = 3.0 psi min.	D = 21
Rippled Waffle	Wt. 56 oz.	Th: .270″	CR @ 25% = 0.7 psi min.	D = 15
Textured Flat Rubber	Wt. 56 oz.	Th: .220″	CR @ 25% = 1.0 psi min.	D = 18
Reinforced Rubber	Wt. 64 oz.	Th: .235″	CR @ 25% = 2.0 psi min.	D = 22
			CR @ 65% = 50.0 psi min.	

Polyurethane Foam

Grafted Prime Polyurethane*	D = 2.7	Th: .25″	CFD @ 65% = 2.5 psi min.
Densified Polyurethane*	D = 2.7	Th: .25″	CFD @ 65% = 2.4 psi min.
Bonded Polyurethane**	D = 5.0	Th: .375″	CFD @ 65% = 5.0 psi min.
Mechanically Frothed Polyurethane***	D = 13.0	Th: .30″	CFD @ 65% = 9.7 psi min.

CLASS II *HEAVY TRAFFIC*	CLASS III *EXTRA HEAVY TRAFFIC*

Office Buildings: Clerical areas, corridors (moderate traffic)
Health Care: Patients' rooms, lounges
Schools: Dormitories and classrooms
Retail: Minor aisles, boutiques, specialty
Banks: Lobbies, corridors (moderate traffic)
Hotels/Motels: Corridors
Libraries/Museums: Public areas (moderate traffic)
Convention Centers: Auditoriums

Office Buildings: Corridors (heavy traffic), cafeterias
Health Care: Lobbies, corridors, nurses' stations
Schools: Corridors, cafeterias
Airports: Corridors, public areas, ticketing areas
Retail: Major aisles, check outs, supermarkets
Banks: Corridors (heavy traffic), teller windows
Hotels/Motels: Lobbies and public areas
Libraries/Museums: Public areas
Country Clubs: Locker rooms, pro shops, dining areas
Convention Centers: Corridors and lobbies
Restaurants: Dining areas and lobbies

Wt. 40 oz.	Th: .3125"	D = 12.3		Wt. 50 oz.	Th: .375"	D = 11.1
Wt. 40 oz.	Th: .25"	D = 12.3		Wt. 40 oz.	Th: .34"	D = 11.1
Wt. 28 oz.	Th: .3125"	D = 7.3		Wt. 36 oz.	Th: .35"	D = 8.0
Wt. 30 oz.	Th: .30"	D = 7.3		Wt. 38 oz.	Th: .375"	D = 8.0

Wt. 62 oz. Th: .150" CR @ 25% = 3.0 psi min. D = 21
NOT RECOMMENDED FOR USE IN THIS CLASS
Wt. 64 oz. Th: .235" CR @ 25% = 1.5 psi min. D = 22
Wt. 64 oz. Th: .235" CR @ 25% = 2.0 psi min. D = 22
                          CR @ 65% = 50.0 psi min.

Wt. 62 oz. Th: .150" CR @ 25% = 4.0 psi min. D = 26
NOT RECOMMENDED FOR USE IN THIS CLASS
Wt. 80 oz. Th: .250" CR @ 25% = 1.75 psi min. D = 26
Wt. 54 oz. Th: .200" CR @ 25% = 2.0 psi min. D = 22
                          CR @ 65% = 50.0 psi min.

D = 3.2 Th: .25" CFD @ 65% = 3.5 psi min.
D = 3.5 Th: .25" CFD @ 65% = 3.3 psi min.
D = 6.5 Th: .25" CFD @ 65% = 10.0 psi min.
D = 15.0 Th: .223" CFD @ 65% = 49.9 psi min.

D = 4.0 Th: .25" CFD @ 65% = 5.0 psi min.
D = 4.5 Th: .25" CFD @ 65% = 4.8 psi min.
D = 8.0 Th: .25" CFD @ 65% = 8.0 psi min.
D = 19.0 Th: .183" CFD @ 65% = 30.5 psi min.

Maximum thickness for any product is 3/8"
   D—Denotes Density in lbs./cu.ft.
   Oz.—Denotes weight in ounces/sq. yd.
   CR—Denotes Compression Resistance in lbs./sq. in. as measured by ASTM D-3676
   CFD—Denotes Compression Force Deflection as measured by ASTM D-3574

All thicknesses, weights and densities allow a −5% manufacturing tolerance
   *   = Polymer densities
   **   = Particle size not to exceed 1/2"

3. Color—solid, tweed, figured
4. Traffic load—light, medium, heavy
5. Maintenance levels that will be sustained—good, better, best
6. Minimum life expectancy
7. Installation requirements. . . .

**Performance Factors
to Consider:**

1. Ease of maintenance
2. Stain resistance
3. Resistance to cigarette burns
4. Resistance to excessive wear
5. Very firm—for ease of rolling objects
6. Superior sound absorption
7. Superior impact insulation
8. Superior static control
9. Low moisture absorbency
10. Luxurious appearance
11. Superior dimensional stability
12. Superior resistance to sunlight
13. Flammability requirements.[19]

RECYCLING

Carpet manufacturers and the companies who make the chemicals from which fibers are made have united in an effort to recycle both used fibers and factory waste. In the past, these two types of discards were added to landfills in great quantities, but manufacturers have become increasingly aware that dumping is not the responsible solution (see Chapter 1).

MEASURING

Before estimating the amount of carpet needed for a particular job, there are several points that the designer needs to remember. First, if carpet is available in widths other than the usual 12 feet, then all the carpet must be of that width. DO NOT COMBINE DIFFERENT WIDTHS because of differences in dye lots. Second, the **nap** or pile of the carpet must be considered, and all pieces must have the nap running in the same direction (toward the entrance unless otherwise specified) or the seams will be obvious. Third, seaming and nap direction must be shown on all carpet seaming plans. Placement of furniture will often decide where seams should

be placed. Seams should never be in the middle of high-traffic areas, such as at right angles to a doorway, across a hallway, or in front of often used office machines such as copiers and drinking fountains. In residential seaming layouts, seams must not be placed directly in front of seating areas.

Carpets that have to be seamed at right angles will also have an obvious seam; however, seams placed under a door are often necessary. The nap on stairs should run downward. The warp (nap) should always run in the longer direction.

The precise measuring of the carpet should be done by the installer on site, and a carpet seaming diagram should be submitted to the designer for approval. Nonetheless, the designer should understand how carpet measuring is done.

Carpet usually comes in 12-foot widths, but 6-foot, 9-foot, and 15-foot widths are sometimes available. Whatever width is selected, it will be necessary to piece or seam the carpet. This may entail purchasing slightly more yardage, because the fewer the seams, the better the appearance will be.

Although carpet comes in widths measured in feet, the amount ordered is always in square yards, so a square foot answer must be divided by 9 to arrive at the square yardage needed. (From experience, the author finds that when taking exams design students commonly make this error and, as a result, specify an order of far too much carpet.) However, the CRI has proposed a change to square feet in order to make comparisons with other types of flooring materials easier.

All measurers seem to have their own method of calculation. Some suggest using templates; others have complicated formulas. Some answers are very close with little waste, and others have few seams and much waste. The number of seams does depend on each job. A master bedroom may have a seam 1 foot in from a wall where a dresser, bed, or other piece of furniture is to be placed, because there the seam will not be visible, but in an art gallery the same seam placement would be unacceptable. Whichever method is used, the installer is responsible for the accuracy of the measurements.

In today's computerized design offices, programs are available to assist the designer in producing an economical yet viable plan. Some programs actually produce a floor plan with measurements, nap directions, and seam placements. The program can provide an estimate, with the 12-foot width going across the room or at right angles. A pattern repeat can be programmed so the repeat is considered. Some programs do the calculation but do not provide a line drawing of the seams and cuts, but rather a summary of how many pieces are needed.

PROBLEMS

Sprouting. Occasionally, a tuft will rise above the pile surface of a carpet. Just snip off these tufts level with other tufts. *Do not pull them out* (if you do, you will create a hole).

Ripples. Ripples in carpet are usually the result of improper stretching during installation, stretching of the back yarns after the carpet was installed, or elongation of the backing fibers from moisture. With a jute-backed carpet, it is not uncommon to have ripples during periods of high humidity that disappear during periods of low humidity. A dehumidifier may help to eliminate this problem. Using waffled sponge cushioning under a woven carpet will also cause this problem.

Mildew. Mildew can be a problem on carpet and rugs, but it does not have to be. If a carpet is going to be used where mildew or other bacteria-growing conditions are present some or all of the time, then a carpet with all synthetic fibers (both front and back) should be used.

Indentations. When a heavy object, such as a piano or piece of furniture, is allowed to remain for an extended period of time in one spot on a carpet, indentation or crush marks will develop. In most cases, the crushed areas can be either restored or greatly improved. The crushed pile can be lifted by working it gently with a coin. The yarn should be lifted to its original appearance without fuzzing or distorting the yarn. After the yarn has been raised, the area should be moistened with a steam iron held at least 4 inches above the pile. The procedure can be repeated if the original appearance was not obtained the first time. Moving furniture a few inches will help prevent permanent indentations. Moving the furniture will also help prevent damage to the back of the carpet from small furniture legs and rollers.

To help prevent matting, Monsanto Company has created Wear-dated® carpet. Its new Traffic Control™ fiber system employs a unique dual fiber design. By taking tough nylon fibers and interweaving them with acrylic fibers, Monsanto has built in a new type of resilience.

Corn Rowing. Corn rowing is a characteristic that should be expected in carpet with higher tufts and lower density pile. Corn rowing develops in the traffic areas or those areas subjected to mechanical action, such as in front of chairs and television sets. Vac-uuming alone will not raise the fallen yarns. Specially designed carpet rakes will lift the yarns but will not keep them erect—the yarns will be crushed again when subjected to foot traffic.

Shedding or Fluffing. When a newly installed carpet is vacuumed, a large amount of fiber may be found in the vacuum. This is a normal process. A carpet made with staple fibers will not have all the fibers anchored into the back or tightly held in the yarns. Mechanical action will work some of the fibers loose. As the carpet is vacuumed, some of the loose fibers will be removed. Many styles of carpet are sheared as one of the final steps in manufacturing. Most fibers are removed at the factory, but some of these sheared fibers will fall into the carpet pile. The shorter the fiber and the longer the tuft, the greater the number of loose fibers in the yarns will be. The yarns with less twist will not hold the loose fibers as tightly. Therefore, they are easier to remove. A deep brushing action produces the maximum removal.

Static Electricity. Static electricity is caused by the rubbing together of two different types of materials, which results in a transfer and a build-up of electrical charges. Most carpets have some type of treatments built into them that will eliminate the static electricity problem. Moisture in the air will help the problem but may produce condensation on window glass in colder climates.

Shading. Shading, sometimes called watermarking, is a natural characteristic of cut pile carpet and should be expected to develop. It is not something that is due to neglect during manufacturing; nor is it something that the manufacturer can eliminate in a plush or velvet type of construction. Shading helps to break up the plainness or sameness in solid color, dense, cut pile carpet. It is a characteristic that occurs in good-quality carpet, and it should be enjoyed; but the client should be made aware of this characteristic. When the carpet is manufactured and rolled, the ends of the face yarns will all lean toward the end of the roll. After the carpet is installed and vacuumed, the pile will have a uniform appearance. This uniformity is a result of the light being reflected from a uniform surface.

Some changes can be expected after the carpet is used. The traffic areas will appear a little different from the adjacent, unwalked-on areas. This difference is because the carpet pile has been compressed by the pressure from footsteps. Vacuuming and brushing will help raise the crushed pile. An occasional vacuuming, however, cannot equalize the continual compressing of the carpet. The end user will have to work to keep the pile erect. Sometimes these shaded spots will occur even in areas with little or no traffic and may be called shading, watermarking, pooling, high-lighting, or pile reversal. Vacuuming and brushing the pile all in one direction, or professional cleaning, may temporarily improve the condition. This changes only the top portion of the pile, however, and shading will soon redevelop. With some plush carpet, vacuum cleaner marks and footsteps may show after the carpet has been freshly cleaned.

Carpet Yellowing. Carpet yellowing, under certain conditions, can occur on the surface of light-colored carpets. This phenomenon is one of the most perplexing problems in recent memory mainly because of the large variety of possible causes and the difficulty of determining the exact cause in a particular situation.

Carpet yellowing can be attributed to any one of the following:

Nitrous oxide—Some combinations of fuels (e.g., the furnace in a home or office) give off nitrous oxide. In areas with restricted air flow and/or lack of direct sunlight, nitrogen may build up on the fibers and create a light yellow color effect.

BHT—BHT is a nonpoisonous, odorless preservative that is often added to products such as food stuffs, bread, cereal, candy, beverages, plastics, nylons, shoe soles, some carpet cushions, and some types of carpet.

Ozone fading—High levels of ozone in the air can cause carpet dyes to fade and exhibit a yellow cast.

Heating trends—Many houses have fireplaces, wood stoves, or kerosene heaters. If these are not vented properly, they may cause high concentrations of nitrous oxide.

Improper cleaning solutions—If the carpet has been cleaned using cleaning solutions with a high pH, it may become susceptible to yellowing.

It is difficult to determine exact causes of yellowing. With so many factors contributing to the problem, the potential for yellowing always exists. The problem can occur on all types of fibers and may not be limited to specific areas. It does seem to be more prevalent in coastal areas with high humidity and in colder climates, when homes are sealed up for the winter and air flow is restricted.

According to the Carpet Cushion Council, yellowing can be corrected by

- Increasing sunlight or light source.
- Increasing air circulation and ventilation (opening windows).
- Spraying the affected areas with a 10% solution of pharmaceutical grade citric acid and allowing it to dry thoroughly. The residue is then thoroughly vacuumed up to remove the crystals. (Test application should always be made in a small area before performing general application.)
- Cleaning the affected area with a mild acidic detergent (it is highly recommended that cleaning only be done by a certified cleaner where references have been checked).[20]

INSTALLATION

The International Certified Floorcovering Installers Association is an organization that certifies carpet installers. The certification covers five different categories.

Residential I (R-1)—Minimum two years experience. Construct seams in entry-level carpet.

Residential II (R-2)—Minimum four years experience. Construct seams in Berber patterned and dense cut pile carpets.

Commercial I (C-1)—Minimum two years experience. Construct glue-direct seams in base-grade carpet. Work with entry-level carpets.

Commercial II (C-2)—Minimum four years experience. Construct seams in patterned carpet, double-glue, attached backings.

Master Installer—Minimum seven years experience. Hand sew bull-nose stair. A master installer has complete understanding and skills in all categories of certification.

The Association's certification test also covers written OSHA, EPA, and CRI-104 and CRI-105 knowledge. Oral tests are given concerning job layout, pattern matching, power stretching, installation procedures, reading blueprints, and estimating jobs. Certification will assist the designer in choosing a qualified installer.

The Carpet and Rug Institute (CRI) provides standard industry reference guides for the installation of both residential and commercial textile floor-covering materials. CRI-105 gives the residential installation standards, and CRI-104 gives the commercial installation standards. If there is a dispute or problem with a job, these documents will determine how an installation will be judged. The best carpet installer available should always be used.

There are three principal methods of commercial carpet installation. These are stretch-in, direct glue-down (including attached cushion), and double glue-down. Stretch-in installations are stretched in over a separate cushion using **tackless strips** to hold the carpet in place. These installations are best suited to areas which must have maximum underfoot comfort and luxury.

The most important aspects of stretched-in tackless strip installations are: (1) sufficient stretching of carpet; (2) proper selection of cushion; (3) correct environmental conditions before, during, and after installation.[21]

Tackless strips are narrow pieces of wood with two to four rows of pins, set at a 60 degree angle and long enough to penetrate the backing. The strips are nailed or glued down around the perimeter of the room a slight distance from the wall. When installing carpet over a cement floor, two rows are used. For stairs, the strips are placed at the base of the riser and the back of the tread. After the tackless strip is nailed down, the padding is cut to fit inside the strips. The principle of the tackless installation is that the carpet is stretched by means of a knee kicker or power stretcher so it hooks over the pins in the wooden strip. Knee kickers are permissible only in areas so small that power stretchers do not fit, such as closets. The excess carpet is cut off and the small amount remaining is tucked into the slight gap between the strip and the wall. The base is then installed to cover this area.

The revolutionary TacFast® Carpet System utilizes the mechanical bond of hook and loop technology. The carpet is manufactured with a loop fabric that covers the entire underside of the carpet. A specially engineered 3M hook tape then bonds with the carpet to hold it in place.

The hook tape, utilizing a pressure-sensitive adhesive, is applied directly to the floor around the perimeter of the room and at seams. During carpet installation, the hook tape cover is removed, allowing the loops on the carpet to "catch-on" to the hooks on the tape and thus creating the mechanical bond. The powerful bond is strong yet forgiving. It is easy to replace or reinstall the carpet; this allows for adjustments so the installer can align the seams to get the job done right.

The hook tape is warranted to stay on the floor for 15 years. This means that for future retrofits, whether replacing the entire carpet or just worn sections, there is no need to replace the hook tape (this saves both time and money). Because no liquid adhesives are required, there are no adhesive odors during or after installation.

TacFast's unique manufacturing and installation process provides design opportunities that are restricted only by imagination. From functional borders and inserts to intensive creative design, TacFast provides unlimited possibilities (Figure 3–7).

The Carpet and Rug Institute finds that most complaints about wrinkling or buckling in tackless installations result from inadequate stretch during initial installation or from cushion that does not provide adequate support for the carpet. Guidelines for proper stretch for various carpet constructions are contained in *CRI 104, Standards for Installation of Commercial Textile Floorcovering Materials*. Adequate stretch can only be obtained by the use of power stretchers. Additional information concerning the amount of stretch for each carpet can be obtained from either the carpet manufacturer or the secondary backing manufacturer.

Construction and density of the cushion are equal in importance to adequate stretch. Firm, low-profile cushion with minimal deflections should be used in commercial traffic areas. Cushions that are too thick and soft will permit carpet backings to stretch and eventually wrinkle. Recommendations from both cushion and carpet manufacturers should be considered prior to tackless stretch-in installations.

Regardless of the method of installation chosen, seams are always of utmost importance for a quality installation. Most modern installations employ hot-melt tape seams, which are generally adequate. Follow the carpet manufacturer's recommendations for seaming. Woven carpet constructions may require hand sewing or other specialized seaming techniques. In all cases, cut edges must be buttered with appropriate seam sealer prior to seaming. All carpet, with or without cushion, may be glued down. These installations are well suited to heavy traffic and to rolling traffic.

Double glue-down installations combine cushion and carpet in a floor-covering system by first gluing the cushion to the floor and then the carpet to the cushion. This method, often referred to as double-stick, has grown in popularity due to combining the stability of direct glue-down of carpet with the cushioning benefits of separate cushion.

Figure 3–7
The Hyatt Regency, Dearborn, used the TacFast Carpet System in its Great Lake Convention Center. Over 2400 square yards featuring a custom design pattern were used because of TacFast's design capabilities and ability to stay in place during the constant set-ups and tear-downs of convention displays. The small photo shows a design section of the TacFast carpet that has been lifted off the hook tape positioned on the floor. The large photo shows the finished installation. (Photo courtesy of 3M and TacFast Systems International.)

The cushion materials must be designed specifically for this method of installation in order to achieve a successful installation.

Direct glue-down and double glue-down installations can be made on many subfloors, including wood, concrete, metal, terrazzo, ceramic tile, and other suitable surfaces. Generally, most are on concrete; therefore, proper preparation of the sub-

floor is needed for adequate adhesion. Testing concrete for moisture and alkalinity is necessary for best results.

The specified amounts of adhesives must be applied to floors to obtain the required 100 percent adhesive transfer into the carpet back. The quantity applied is controlled by the size of the notches in the installers' floor adhesive trowels. If too little is used, carpet will not adequately adhere to the floor. Adequate open time for adhesives to develop **tack** (to partially set) prior to laying carpet into the adhesives is also very important for many of today's carpet backing systems. For the purpose of improved indoor air quality, low-VOC adhesives are available from most adhesive manufacturers.

Carpet with an attached cushion, secondary, unitary, or woven backing may be adhered to floors; whereas separate cushion stretch-in installations are usually limited to woven construction or tufted carpet with secondary backings. For heavy and rolling traffic or other severe conditions, direct glue-down of carpet with secondary, unitary, woven, or attached cushion backing is recommended.[22]

The Carpet and Rug Institute finds that the major cause of separation from the floor in a glue-down installation is an insufficient amount of carpet floor adhesive.

The glue-down method may also be used for **carpet modules.** Because of their heavy backing, carpet tiles may also be loose laid. Carpet modules can be freely rotated and/or replaced without detracting from overall like-new appearance of the installation, particularly in the health care, institutional, retail, and hospitality areas, with their heavy use and traffic. This type of installation also eliminates restretching problems, with no movement of pattern-type carpet or bordering. It is also useful in furnishing the upper floors of tall buildings, where delivering heavy, cumbersome rolls of broadloom may present a problem. (This is particularly true in the case of refurbishing when construction cranes and elevators used to lift the original carpets are no longer available.)

Coir and sisal are highly absorbent, and therefore, for at least 24 hours prior to installation, they should be allowed to acclimate to the humidity and temperature of the room in which they will be placed. The direct glue-down procedure is the best method of wall-to-wall installation for coir and sisal if there are no great fluctuations in humidity or temperature. If these conditions exist, then loose laying is suggested.

The following should be included in installation contracts:

1. Scope, including description of area involved as well as details on measurements, seam locations, diagrams, etc.
2. Qualifications required of contractor and installation specialists and references for similar jobs. . . .
3. The installation contractor must perform work in strict compliance with all local, state, and federal regulations. The Occupational Safety and Health Administration Hazard Communication standard must also be followed where applicable.
4. Storage and delivery responsibilities.
5. Preparatory work responsibilities (installer, general contractor, or owner) including:
   — inspection and cleaning of subfloors;
   — vertical transportation;
   — removal and replacement of furniture;
   — removal and disposition of existing floor-covering.
6. Submittal and approval of materials to include moldings, base materials, cushions, adhesives, etc. *Note:* The selection of an appropriate adhesive is essential to a successful installation. The use of low VOC emitting adhesives should be considered for improved indoor air quality.
7. Method of installation:
   a. Stretch-in with separate cushion
   b. Direct glue-down
      without cushion
      with attached cushion
   c. Double glue-down.
8. Specify that installation should be in accordance with *CRI 104, Standard for Installation of Commercial Textile Floorcovering Materials* for all aspects not specifically covered by manufacturers' recommendations.
9. Adequate ventilation must be provided during and after the installation by the general contractor or owner to eliminate or minimize lingering odors.
10. Responsibility for cleanup.
11. Disposition of excess carpet.
12. Details of guarantee.
13. Time of installation, completion date, final acceptance inspection by specifier and installer prior to acceptance.[23]

One type of finished floor not previously mentioned is raised access flooring. This type of flooring consists of removable steel or concrete panels that sit on pedestals 3 to 18 inches above the existing concrete slab subflooring. Raised access flooring products from InterfaceAR create an underfloor cavity so voice, data, and power cabling can be perfectly routed and easily accessible. The raised flooring also works as an air

plenum, allowing the cool, fresh, rising air to push the warm, contaminated air up and out of breathing range. The floor panels can be covered in a number of finishes, including carpet tiles. The result is an underfloor cavity that can shave less than 3 inches off the floor-to-ceiling height but generate significantly more flexible and productive floor space (Figure 3–8).

MAINTENANCE

Carpet is the only textile product on which people walk. This is why carpet construction, or performance, and installation specifications are so critical. Also critical is the specification of maintenance. Specification of any one of these three elements without knowledge or consideration of the other two increases the risk that the carpet will not perform up to potential or expectation.

Even properly specified carpet can wear out or appear to be worn out if it is not maintained adequately. Dirt is unsightly but it can also be abrasive. As foot traffic deposits soil and causes the pile yarns to flex, embedded grit cuts the face fibers. The carpet begins to lose density and resilience. Threadbare spots appear, and the carpet wears out. Moreover, allowing soil to build up and to spread may give the carpet a worn-out appearance even if the face fibers are essentially intact.

If carpet is not vacuum cleaned regularly, the dirt builds up and begins to spread. To guard against build-up, a well-planned program is essential in commercial installations with high traffic loads. Planned maintenance is the key to extending the life expectancy of carpet. The maintenance plan is no less important than the initial carpet specification and installation.

Planning the Maintenance Program

The maintenance plan should be developed as the carpet specifications are being considered. (In fact, a plan should be prepared in case the carpet is installed prior to completion of construction.)

When preparing the maintenance plan, keep in mind that one of the advantages of carpet compared to hard floors is that carpet localizes soil. Carpet tends to catch and hold soil and spills where they occur instead of allowing them to spread quickly. This feature of carpet suggests that the best maintenance plan will identify in

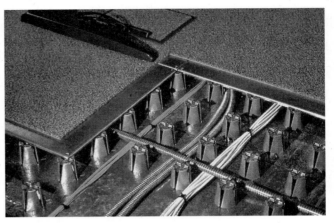

Figure 3–8
InterfaceAR raised access flooring systems organize voice, data, and power cabling with as little as 3 inches shaved off floor-to-ceiling height. (Photo courtesy of InterfaceAR.)

advance the most likely areas for soiling and spilling. The plan will specify maintenance schedules and procedures for these areas, as well as the remainder of the carpet.

Specifically, heavy traffic areas, like entrances and lobbies, will not only require the most substantial carpet, they will probably have to be vacuumed once a day. In some instances, greasy motor oil from parking lots should be anticipated.

Kitchen smoke in restaurants and cafeterias will contribute heavily to overall soiling. Stains and spills in restaurants and hospitals will be common. Routine procedures for attending to these as quickly as possible are necessary.

Whatever the nature of the installation, it is wise to anticipate dealing with soil from the very first day the carpet is installed. Otherwise, abrasive dirt may build up faster than it can be handled.

Daily and Periodic Procedures

Two elements essential to an efficient maintenance program include daily procedures encompassing both regular vacuuming and spot cleaning, and scheduled overall cleaning to remove discoloring grime and to refresh the pile.

Overall grime not only causes discoloration, but it presents another undesirable quality: Carpet that is not cleaned and reconditioned regularly, no matter how faithfully it is vacuumed, will tend to permanently crush and mat down. As greases present in smoke or pollutants in the air settle on the carpet, pile yarns may become gummy enough to stick to each other and flatten in use. Matted carpet appears to be worn out even if there is no real pile loss. Obviously, carpet that must be replaced because it *looks* worn out is no less costly than carpet that must be replaced because it *is* worn out.

Color as a Maintenance Factor

The color of the carpet can contribute significantly to minimizing the appearance of dirt, particularly for entrances and lobbies, which get the bulk of tracked-in soil. If possible, colors should be chosen that blend with the color of the dirt brought in from outside.

Since the most common dirt colors are greys, beiges, browns, and reds, carpet colors for entrances should be chosen from these tones. The best choice would be a tweed coloration combining two or more of the colors.

Another choice might be a multicolored, patterned carpet which would add visual interest while helping camouflage dirt and spills until they can be removed. Such highly patterned carpet is a popular choice for hotel lobbies and restaurants [see Figure 3-5].

Lighter, more delicate colors are best reserved for inside spaces—offices, guest rooms, lounges—where soiling rates are obviously lower and danger of accidental spills is more remote.

Walk-Off Mats

As a matter of preventative maintenance, **walk-off** mats should be installed in all entrances to collect dirt before it reaches the carpet inside. Walk-off mats can be constructed of stiff bristles or pieces of the carpet used inside; or they can be one of a variety of types specially made for commercial use. Some have aluminum strips between the carpet. (Sometimes pieces of carpet used as walk-off mats can, if the backing is rough enough, cause as much wear as walking on the carpet itself.)

Elevators should also be carpeted, even if the entrance lobby is not. It is wiser to have soil wiped off on the elevator carpet rather than having it tracked over the carpet elsewhere.

It is common to have two sets of walk-off mats and removable carpets available. Because the mats take such heavy abuse, one set is kept in place while the other is being cleaned.[24]

Another method of dirt control is to use a recessed mat or grating inside exterior doors. These gratings feature a system of self-cleaning recessed treads that are closely spaced to prevent the smallest heel from catching, yet allow dirt and sand to collect below the surface. The grate removes easily for cleaning.

In the residential carpet industry, soiling problems may occur related to products used by family members. For example, in a teenager's room acne medicine may spill on the carpet; in another room, aerosols or furniture polish may be the culprit. In bathrooms a toilet bowl cleaner or a dandruff shampoo can cause a dark brown stain, often with a blue fringe. Urine is also a culprit in small area discoloration. These spots begin at the backing and progress upward over a period of time. They may be dull yellow or even red. The characteristic ammonialike odor will be present for only a few hours, and it is replaced by a musty odor. Bleach can be a problem in the laundry area, or it may be tracked in from the swimming pool. Dimethylsulfoxide, otherwise known as DMSO, is widely used for relief of pain from arthritis, back problems, athletic injuries, and other muscular aches. It is a clear liquid with an odor similar to garlic and causes rapid loss of color on carpet due to its solvent action.

Vacuuming Schedules

According to the Carpet and Rug Institute,

> Of all the carpet maintenance procedures, vacuuming takes the most time and attention . . . yet is the most cost effective. The carpet should be inspected for spots during vacuuming. Spots should be removed as soon as possible. The longer they are allowed to set, the more permanent they may become.

The following is a normal vacuuming schedule:

High Traffic—Vacuum daily

Medium Traffic—Vacuum twice weekly

Light Traffic—Vacuum weekly

This broad guide recommends minimum schedules only. To reduce this general rule to specifics, some definitions will be useful. Track-off areas are where a carpet collects foot soil tracked in from the outdoors or from hard surfaced floors indoors. . . . Funnel areas are where foot traffic is squeezed into or through a concentrated area, such as a doorway, stairwell, in front of drinking fountain, vending machine, etc. . . . These areas can be identified in advance of soiling. Planned vacuuming in these areas, *even when soil is not visible,* will help prevent soil build-up. Also it will help focus maintenance attention on the places where it is known that soil will be tracked.

In the final analysis, an adequate schedule must be based on the individual installation and its own traffic load and soiling rate. For example, soil may accumulate so rapidly at entrances (track-off areas) that carpet at those locations will have to be vacuumed several times a day. In another instance, rooms may be entered directly from an uncarpeted corridor. Under those circumstances, even light traffic may cause heavy soiling, and the carpet may have to be vacuumed several times a week. Only experience will tell whether more frequent vacuuming is indicated.

Vacuum cleaning equipment for implementing a maintenance program with the maximum efficiency is a basic necessity. Two types of machines may be required. The first of these, a heavy-duty wide track machine, is recommended for large open areas. Because of its size, maintenance time can be measurably reduced with commensurate savings in labor costs. Such large industrial vacuums should be equipped with a cylindrical brush, or a beater-bar, to whip embedded dirt to the surface, and also with a powerful suction.

A second machine, an industrialized version of the domestic upright vacuum cleaner, belongs in every maintenance program. It, too, should have a good brushing action or a beater-bar and powerful suction. If possible, it should also have a hose and wand attachment for cleaning under heavy furniture not normally moved. Otherwise, a canister vacuum, preferably with a power head, may also be needed for hard-to-reach places.

Spot Removal

Identification and immediate action are the keys to effective spot removal procedures. To minimize time and effort, it is helpful to know what causes a spot so that treatment can begin without guesswork. In most installations, spot identification may not be difficult because the possibilities are limited. In others, it could be a real problem.

A drug-dispensing area in hospitals, for example, is susceptible to hundreds of spotting and staining agents. Employees must be instructed to report spills as they occur and to identify the spilled material.

It is also important to clean up spills as quickly as possible. The longer a spot sets, the more difficult it may be to remove. If it sets too long, it might react with the carpet dyes and cause permanent discoloration. Hence, an alert staff and a well-stocked spot removal kit are important to a good carpet maintenance program. . . . Always test a cleaning agent to determine its effect upon the carpet dye, fibers, and the spot before applying larger amounts. . . .

Detergent Solutions

Specifically, detergent solutions to be used on wool should have a neutral pH. Natural fibers absorb moisture and are apt to be somewhat more vulnerable to chemical damage from acids or alkalis.

Man-made fibers, on the other hand, absorb less moisture. Detergents which are alkaline in nature, between 7.0 and 10.0 pH, cut grease and suspend soil better and can be used satisfactorily on man-made fibers but should be tested on each color.

Whether neutral or alkaline, some detergents may leave a sticky residue that will cause rapid resoiling on the face of the carpet. The better detergents will dry to a crisp flake, which can then be removed by vacuuming. . . .

There are many factors that will influence the frequency of cleaning, but a maintenance plan should be in effect before the traffic areas start to show discoloration. If the traffic areas are allowed to become excessively soiled, on-location cleaning may not remove sufficient soil to restore them to an acceptable level. The high-use areas must be cleaned more frequently in order to maintain a satisfactory overall appearance.

Five major methods are used in the maintenance and cleaning of carpet: These methods are absorbent compound; absorbent pad or bonnet (dry); dry foam cleaning; shampoo cleaning; and steam cleaning (hot water extraction). . . .

Cleaning Methods

ABSORBENT COMPOUND is the lowest moisture system that can be used on carpet. In heavily soiled areas, a preconditioner may be applied prior to the application of the absorbent compound. . . .

ABSORBENT PAD or BONNET (DRY) is another minimum moisture system, which can be used on nearly all carpet. Deeply soiled traffic areas are normally treated prior to cleaning with a preconditioner. . . . The drying time is normally one to three hours, after which the carpet should be thoroughly vacuumed to further remove any cleaning agent and loosened soil.

DRY FOAM CLEANING uses a detergent solution, which can be aerated before it is applied to the carpet. This method adds only a minimum amount of moisture to the carpet and, therefore, can be used on most carpets. Normally, in the heavily soiled traffic areas, a preconditioner is used to loosen the soil before cleaning with the dry foam method. . . . Drying normally takes place within one to three hours, unless multiple passes have been made over the carpet.

SHAMPOO CLEANING can be employed on nearly all types of carpet, if properly used. Heavily soiled traffic areas are usually treated with a preconditioner prior to overall cleaning. . . . The drying time will be determined by the amount of moisture allowed to remain in the carpet and may vary from one to twelve hours, and, in extreme cases, as long as twenty-four hours.

STEAM CLEANING (hot water extraction) applies the largest amount of cleaning solution, and when operated by a skilled operator, can be used on most carpets. In heavily soiled areas, a preconditioner may be applied as the first step. . . . The maximum drying time should not be longer than twenty-four hours.

The above methods illustrate the various systems available. They may be used separately or in combination. Some may be used for maintaining traffic areas, while others may be used for overall cleaning. Some methods may not be suitable for all types of carpet construction, such as certain cut pile construction; therefore, it is always advisable to obtain the carpet manufacturer's recommendations for the preferred methods to be used in order to prevent invalidation of applicable warranties. Again, the important points are to develop a regularly scheduled maintenance program and to have qualified, skilled individuals perform the cleaning.[25]

Beware of the bargain carpet cleaning companies that will clean a whole house for a ridiculously low price. They often hire untrained people and, in the case of water extraction, may soak the carpet so it takes a long time to dry completely, especially in high-humidity areas. The time invested in developing a plan for carpet maintenance will pay off in longer use from the carpet. *Cleaning should be done before the carpet shows signs of soil.* It is essential that the manufacturer's recommendations be followed, especially if guarantees and liabilities are involved.

BIBLIOGRAPHY

Bridgepoint Corporation, *Protector Course.* Salt Lake City, UT: Bridgepoint Corporation, 1990.

Burlington Industries, Inc., *Carpet Maintenance Guide for Hospitals and Health Care Facilities.* King of Prussia, PA: Burlington Industries, Inc., Carpet Division, 1987.

Carpet and Rug Institute, *Carpet Specifier's Handbook.* Dalton, GA: Carpet and Rug Institute, 1987.

Monsanto Contract Fibers, *Concepts Ideas for Specifiers.* Atlanta, GA: Monsanto Fiber and Intermediates Co.

Revere, Glen, *All About Carpets.* Blue Ridge Summit, PA: TAB Books, 1988.

Reznikoff, C. S., *Specifications for Commercial Interiors.* New York: Whitney Library of Design, an imprint of Watson-Guptill Publications, a division of Billboard Publications, 1989.

The Wool Bureau, New York, NY.

GLOSSARY

BCF. Bulked continuous filament. The name given to continuous strands of synthetic fiber that are first spun into yarn and then texturized to increase bulk and cover.

Berber. A looped pile rug from North Africa. May be patterned or natural colored. Today, Berbers are mostly textured natural earth tones.

Carpet modules. Carpet precut into 18- or 24-inch squares or other suitable dimensions.

Carpet yellowing. An unwanted change of color.

Continuous filaments. Continuous strand of synthetic fiber extruded in yarn form without the need for spinning that all natural fibers require.

Corn rowing. A characteristic that should be expected in carpet with higher tufts and lower density pile, resulting in the pile laying flat.

CRF. Critical radiant flux.

Dhurrie. A reversible tapestry woven, flat rug with no pile. Originally from India; today it comes mostly in pastel colors.

ESD. Electrostatic discharge to be considered around computers.

Face weight. Density of fiber in the pile.

Filaments. A single continuous strand of natural or synthetic fiber.

Gauge. The distance between needles in tufted carpets as measured in fractions of an inch. Gauge is also the number of yarn ends across the width of the carpet.

Indentations. Marks left in the carpet from heavy pieces of furniture remaining in one place.

Jacquard. An apparatus on a carpet weaving loom that produces patterns from colored yarns. The pattern information is contained on perforated cards. The holes in the cards activate the mechanism that selects the color to be raised to the pile surface.

Kilim. A flat-woven or pileless rug.

Mildew. A discoloration caused by fungi.

Nap. Carpet or rug pile surface.

Noise reduction coefficient (NRC). The average percentage of sound reduction at various Hertz levels.

Pitch. Number of lengthwise warp yarns in a 27-inch width.

Plenum. An air compartment maintained under pressure and connected to one or more distributing ducts.

Ripples. Waves caused by either improper stretching or humidity.

Rya. A Scandinavian hand-woven rug with a deep, resilient, comparatively flat pile. Usually of abstract design.

Saxony. A cut-pile carpet texture consisting of heat-set plied yarns in a relatively dense, erect configuration, with well-defined individual tuft tips. Saxonies' tip definition is more pronounced than in single plush.

Sculpturing. A patterned carpet made by using high and low area.

Set yarns. Straight yarns.

Shading. Apparent color difference between areas of the same carpet. The physical cause is the difference between cut end luster and side luster of fibers.

Shedding. Normal process of excess yarns coming to the surface in a freshly installed carpet.

Solution dye. In synthetic fibers, the dye is part of the liquid chemical that forms the filament, resulting in a colorfast fiber.

Sprouting. Protrusion of individual tuft or yarn ends above pile surface. May be clipped with scissors.

Spun yarns. Yarns produced by drawing out and twisting of numerous staple fibers into yarn.

Staple fiber. Short lengths of fiber that may be converted into spun yarns by textile yarn spinning processes.

Static electricity. Shoe friction against carpet fiber causes production of electrostatic charge that is discharged from carpet to person to conductive ground (e.g., a doorknob).

Tack. Partially set.

Tackless strip. Narrow lengths of wood or metal containing either two or three rows of angled pins on which carpet is stretched and secured in a stretch-in installation.

Walk-off. Mats on which most of the exterior soil is deposited.

Wick. To carry moisture by capillary action.

Wilton. Carpet woven on a loom with a Jacquard mechanism, which utilizes a series of punched cards to select pile height and yarn color.

Wires. Stitches per inch.

Yarns. A continuous strand composed of fibers or filaments and used in the production of carpet and other fabrics.

NOTES

[1]Adapted from Wool Bureau Library, Volume 6, *Rugs and Carpets* (boldface added).

[2]Carpet and Rug Institute, *Specifier's Handbook,* 5th ed. Dalton, GA: Carpet and Rug Institute, 1992, pp. 17–18. All quotes from *Specifier's Handbook* reproduced with permission.

[3]Ibid., p. 50 (boldface added).

[4]Ibid., p. 51.

[5]Ibid., p. 49 (boldface added).

[6]Ibid., p. 51.

[7]Ibid., p. 51 (boldface added).

[8]*Carpet Specification and Appearance Guide,* DuPont Flooring Systems, p. 7.

[9]CRI, *Specifier's Handbook,* p. 47.

[10]Ibid., p. 52 (boldface added).

[11]Ibid., p. 53.

[12]Ibid., p. 53 (boldface added).

[13]Bridgepoint Corporation, "Protector Course." Salt Lake City, UT: Bridgepoint Corporation, 1990 (boldface added).

[14]*Concepts, Ideas for Specifiers,* Monsanto Fiber and Intermediates Co., p. 11 (boldface added).

[15]Jack Lenor Larsen, *Material Wealth, Living with Luxurious Fabrics,* New York: Abbeville Press, 1989, pp. 195 and 197. Permission to reprint granted by John Calman & King Ltd., London, England.

[16]Carpet Cushion Council, *The Supporting Facts About Carpet Cushion.* Riverside, CT: Carpet Cushion Council, January 1997.

[17]Carpet Cushion Council, *Commercial Carpet Cushion Guidelines.* Riverside, CT: Carpet Cushion Council, January 1997.

[18]Carpet and Rug Institute, *Specifier's Handbook,* p. 60.

[19]Ibid., pp. 61–62.

[20]Carpet Cushion Council, Fact Sheet, 1994.

[21]Carpet and Rug Institute, *Specifier's Handbook,* p. 56.

[22]Ibid., pp. 56 and 57.

[23]Ibid., p. 56.

[24]Ibid., p. 64.

[25]Ibid., pp. 65–67.

4

Floors

WOOD

Wood was used in ancient times for flooring. According to the Bible, Solomon's Temple had a floor of fir, whereas the Romans used wood on only the upper floors of their buildings and used stone on the main floor. These stone floors persisted throughout the Dark Ages. In peasant homes, of course, a dirt floor was spread with straw; however, heavy, wide oak planks predominated in larger domestic structures.

The first wood floors were called puncheon floors, made of split logs, flat side up, fitted edge to edge, and smoothed with an ax or an adz. When saws became available to cut the wood into planks, white pine plank flooring of great widths was used in the Colonial period in the United States and was pegged in place.

In 18th- and early 19th-century America, sand was frequently spread over the wood floor to absorb dirt and moisture. Later, these floors were stained and then covered by Oriental rugs in wealthy homes; in more modest homes, they were left either bare or covered by homemade rugs. When renovating an old pine plank floor, the knots, which are much harder than the surrounding wood, have a tendency to protrude above the level of the worn floor and must be sanded to give a smoother surface. In some early floors that have not been renovated, it is possible to trip over these knots because they extend so far above the level of the floors. In the early 19th century, **stenciling** was done directly on the floor in imitation of rugs, parquet floors, marble, and tile. Painted floors and **floorcloths** came to be highly regarded until the carpet industry spelled the decline of floor cloths in the 1830s and 1840s. These floorcloths are now making a comeback.

Parquetry and **marquetry** were used in France from the early 1700s; one of the most famous examples of this period is the beautiful parquet floor at the Palace of Versailles. In 1885, the invention of a machine capable of making a **tongue and groove** in the edge of the wood and the use of **kilns** combined to produce a draft-proof hardwood floor.

In the Victorian era, inlaid border patterns using contrasting light and dark wood were put together in an intricate manner (Figure 4–1). End-grain wood was even used to pave streets at the beginning of the 20th century. In the early 1920s, unit block flooring was introduced, which made parquet floors more reasonably priced because each piece did not have to be laid down individually, but more easily in one block.

Wood, as a material for floors, has made a comeback in recent years, particularly in contemporary homes. This is due in part to the use of polyurethane and urethane varnishes, which give an almost maintenance-free finish. Previously, a wood floor had to be

Figure 4–1
Buckingham, the border pattern from Kentucky Wood Floors, is shown in quartered oak and walnut. This pattern is 5/16 inches thick and 12 inches wide. (Photo courtesy of Kentucky Wood Floors.)

kept waxed, then frequently stripped of wax build-up, resanded, and refinished. Also contributing to the popularity of wood floors are manufacturers' warranties, which extend from 5 to 25 years.

Wood is divided into two broad categories: the hardwoods from deciduous trees, which lose their leaves in winter, and the softwoods from conifers or evergreens. In reality, there is an overlapping of hardness because some woods from evergreens are harder than those from broad-leafed trees. The harder woods will, of course, be more durable. This durability, together with color and texture, must be considered in both flooring and furniture construction. Ease of finish should also be considered when the wood will have an applied finish.

According to the National Oak Flooring Manufacturers Association (NOFMA),

There are two types of oak used in flooring, white oak and red oak. White oak flooring typically presents more variations in color than its consistently pinkish cousin, red oak, thus adding more depth to the decorator's palette. Less porous than red oak, white oak flooring produces a smoother, more open grain appearance. Longer rays are accented by occasional swirls and **burls,** giving the floor a rich look. When stains are used to complement a color scheme, the Select grade is often preferred for consistency of appearance in the finished floor. . . . White oak is also a very dense wood, making it an excellent choice for high traffic applications where its hardness provides greater resistance to heel dents and wear. Because it is plentiful, white oak strip flooring may cost from 5% to 20% less than the comparable grade in red oak.[1]

Weight is usually a good indicator of the relative strength of wood. Because wood is a natural material, it absorbs or eliminates moisture depending on the humidity to which it is exposed. Most shrinkage or swelling occurs in the width of the wood; the amount depends on the manner of the cut. **Quarter sawn** woods are the least troublesome.

Warping is the tendency of wood to twist or bend when drying. Warping may occur as a **bow, crook, twist,** or **cup** (Figure 4–2). The moisture problem can be reduced to a minimum by using kiln-dried lumber. In the kiln drying process, wood is stacked in an oven so heated air can circulate around each plank and thus render a uniform moisture content. Seven to 8 percent moisture content is acceptable in wood used for mak-

Warp

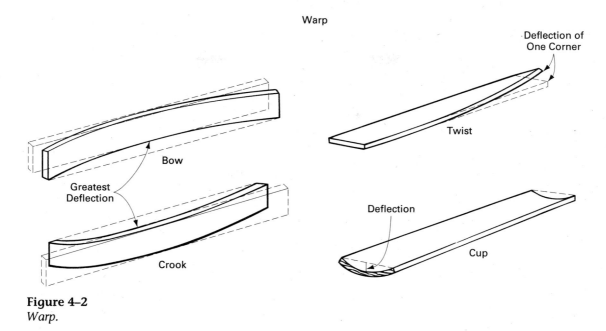

Figure 4–2
Warp.

ing floors and furniture, and 12 to 19 percent is acceptable for construction grades of wood.

According to the Hardwood Information Center,

Solid hardwood's natural response to extremely dry air is to lose moisture and contract a bit. Conversely, under high humidity conditions, the wood may absorb excess moisture from the air and expand. A humidifier in the winter and an air conditioner in the summer will stabilize the relative humidity at 25 to 35 percent. . . . Before a floor is installed, the hardwood should adjust to the new environment. It should be stored in the same room where it will be installed to reach a balance with the surroundings.[2]

Wood is composed of many cells that run vertically, thus giving wood its straight **grain.** At frequent intervals, **medullary rays** thread their way between and at right angles to the vertical cells. These rays are most noticeable in plain oak and beech.

We have all seen pictures or drawings of the circular rings of trees. Some of the giant sequoias of California and the ancient oaks of Great Britain have been dated by rings showing hundreds of years of growth. These rings show the seasonal growth and comprise springwood (formed early in the growing season) and summer wood or late wood. In some trees, such as ash or oak, the different times of growth are obvious, whereas in others, such as birch and maple, the seasonal growth is more blended. When there is an obvious difference in growth times, there is also a difference in weight and hardness. The faster-growing

trees, usually those in more moderate climates, are softer than the same trees grown in northern areas, where the growing season is shorter. Next to the bark is the sapwood, which contains the food cells and is usually lighter in color. Heartwood contains the currently inactive cells and is slightly darker because of chemical substances that are part of the cell walls.

Figure is the pattern of the wood fibers, and the wood grain is determined by the arrangement of the cells and fibers. Some grains are straight and others are patterned; this characteristic is enhanced by the method of cutting the boards.

There are two principal methods of cutting lumber. One is called plain sawn for hardwoods and flat grained for softwoods. The second is quarter sawn for hardwoods or edge grained for softwoods. When referring to maple as a flooring material, the words *edge grained* are used, although maple is a hardwood. Oak is quarter sawn, but fir cut in the same manner is called vertical grain. Interior designers will probably be dealing mainly with hardwoods, so the terms *plain sawn* and *quarter sawn* are used henceforth, with the exceptions mentioned previously. Each method has its own advantages: Plain sawn is the cheapest, easiest, and most economical use of wood, whereas quarter sawing gives less distortion of wood from shrinkage or warping.

Each method of cutting gives a different appearance to wood. Plain sawing gives a cathedral or pointed-arch effect, whereas quarter sawing gives more of a straight-line appearance. Sawmills cut logs into boards, producing 80 percent plain to 20 percent quartered lumber. Quartered oak flooring, therefore, is extremely hard to find and is expensive. Most production is mixed cuts (Figure 4–3).

Veneer is a very thin sheet of wood varying in thickness from 1/8 inch to 1/100 inch. Wood more than 1/4 inch thick is no longer considered veneer. The manner in which the veneer is cut also gives different patterns. The three methods are rotary sliced, flat sliced, and quarter sliced. (These are discussed in more detail in Chapter 5.) **Laminated or engineered wood** is used for some floors and is a sandwich with an uneven number of sheets of veneer, layered at right angles to prevent warping, with the better veneers on the face. Water-resistant glue should be used for bonding the layers, and the sandwich is placed in a hot press, in which pressure of 150 to 300 pounds per square inch (**psi**) is applied. Heat around 250° permanently sets the adhesive and bonds the layers into a single strong panel. Laminated prefinished floors are less affected by humidity and are therefore considered more stable. Only laminated wood floors may be installed below grade, but the manufacturer's installation procedures must be followed exactly. Laminated products expand little, so they may be fitted close to a vertical surface. It is predicted that laminated wood flooring sales will more than double in the next five years, because strong environmental trends are leading consumers to these products.

Grades of oak are determined by appearance alone. Flooring generally free of defects is known as clear, although it may contain burls, streaks, and pinworm holes. Select is almost clear, but this grade contains more of the natural characteristics, including knots and other marks. The common grades have more marking than either of the other two grades and are often specified because of these natural features and the character they bring to the flooring.

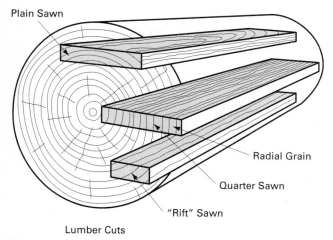

Plain Sawn

Radial Grain

Quarter Sawn

"Rift" Sawn

Lumber Cuts

Figure 4–3
Methods of sawing.

Types of Wood Flooring

The three different types of wood flooring are strip, random plank, and parquet.

Strip

Usually 2 1/4 inches wide, strip flooring is tongue and grooved on both sides and ends. This type of flooring is most commonly made of oak, although other woods may be used, such as teak and maple. Strip flooring may be laid parallel to the wall or diagonally. Gymnasium floors are always constructed of maple but require a special type of installation that provides a slight "give" to the floor.

The American Collection Longstrip, from Harris-Tarkett, has a top layer of hardwood, 1/7 inch thick with the four other layers making up a 9/16 inch thick by 7 1/2 inches wide by 95 1/2 inches long plank. Fourteen colors and six species are available, with a no-wax UltraBrite™ acrylic polyurethane finish that cleans easily with dust mop or vacuum. This product carries a 10-year finish warranty and can be sanded and refinished up to three times.

For residential installations, Mannington Wood Floors has a Lifetime Structural Guarantee, as long as the purchaser owns the house in which the floor was installed, on the following: separation of bonded parts, unsightly cupping of planks, buckling because of expansion, and warping or twisting. In addition, if the purchaser does not like the appearance of any plank before installation, the company will replace it free of charge. There is a full five-year warranty against subfloor moisture problems.

Another variation of plank, strip, and parquet flooring is acrylic impregnated flooring. Liquid acrylic is evenly forced into the pore structure of select hardwoods and then is permanently hardened. The finish, therefore, is as deep as the wood itself, is highly resistant to abrasion and impact, never requires refinishing, and is easy to repair and maintain. Dyes and fire retardants may be added to the acrylic, if required. The stain penetrates throughout the wood so worn areas need only be retouched with a topcoat. The floor never needs sanding, staining, or refinishing. With all these impregnated woods, it must be remembered that the color cannot be changed because it has penetrated the whole depth of the wood. This can be an asset or a liability, depending on the purchaser's requirements.

Regular strip flooring is sold by the board foot, and 5 percent waste allowance is added to the total ordered.

Plank

Plank flooring is 3 to 8 inches wide, and most installations comprise three different sizes. The widths selected should correspond to the dimensions of the room to keep the flooring in proper scale: narrower ones for small rooms and wider ones for larger rooms. Random plank comes with a **square** or **beveled** edge and may be factory finished or finished after installation.

Plank floors also have a tongue-and-groove side. The **prefinished** tongue and groove disguises any shrinkage, because the V-joint becomes a fraction wider; whereas with a square edge, the crack caused by shrinkage is more obvious. (This is why it is important that all wood be stored in the climatic conditions that will prevail at the installation site. Proper storage conditions will allow the wood to absorb or dissipate moisture and reach a stable moisture content.) A white finish will also emphasize any shrinkage.

In the past, some plank floors were installed using wooden pegs or plugs. A hole (or several holes for a wide plank) was drilled about 1 1/2 to 2 inches from the end of the plank. A **dowel** was pounded into the floor joist and glued into place. Any excess dowel was cut and sanded flush with the floor. Often, these plugs were constructed of a contrasting wood and became a decorative feature of plank flooring. Today it is recommended that, because of its width, plank flooring be screwed to the floor; then the screws should be countersunk and short dowels of walnut, other contrasting woods, or even brass are glued in to cover the screw for decorative purposes only. Unfortunately, some prefinished floors may have plugs made of plastic, which seems incongruous in a wood floor. Another decorative joining procedure used in the past was the butterfly or key, in which a dovetail-shaped piece of wood was used at the end joint of two boards. Plank flooring can also be of different species, which creates an interesting color combination (Color Plate 5).

The Timeless Series II from PermaGrain® is a 3/8 inch thick, laminated acrylic impregnated plank flooring. By mixing species and colors in combination with the three standard sizes—2 3/4″ × random length, 2 3/4″ × 46″ plank, or 2 3/4″ × 16 1/2″ slats—designers have almost limitless options to create patterns, borders, and accents.

Pattern-Plus® from Hartco® also mixes sizes for many pattern combinations. Pattern-Plus is sliced cut for fine grain beauty and has a HartWood® impregnated finish for unsurpassed durability. It is prefinished and backed by Hartco's 25-year wear warranty.

For those desiring the authentic look of an old floor, Aged Woods® has recycled antique planks with vary-ing amounts of character (i.e., knots and knot holes, nail holes, flat and vertical grain pattern, cracks and occasional insect marks, and **patina,** a dark, rich coloring). Aged Woods floors are available in oak, chestnut, pine, hemlock, and poplar in various finishes.

Plank flooring is sold by the square foot, and a 5 percent waste allowance is generally added to the total square footage.

Parquet

Parquet comprises individual pieces of wood, generally oak, from 3/8 to 3/4 inch thick, joined together to form a variety of patterns. These small pieces are held together by various methods: a **metal spline,** gluing to a mesh of paper, or gluing to a form of cheesecloth. Sizes vary from 9 to 19 inches square (Figure 4–4 and Color Plate 6).

Figure 4–4
This Citation patterned parquet floor is 3/4 inch thick by 36 inches and is made from select grade walnut with burl and figured diamonds and oak pickets. This pattern was given an ASID International Product Award. (Photo courtesy of Kentucky Wood Floors.)

There are many parquet patterns, as shown in Figure 4–5, and most manufacturers make a similar variety of patterns, but the names may vary. One company will name a pattern Jeffersonian, another Monticello or Mt. Vernon, but they are variations of the same pattern. This particular design is made with a central block surrounded by **pickets** on all four sides. The center may be made of solid wood, a laminated block, five or six strips all in the same direction, or a standard unit of four **sets.**

Designers need a word of warning about using some parquet patterns. Some parquets have direction (for example, the herringbone pattern). Depending on whether the pieces are laid parallel to the wall or at an angle, a client may see L's, zigzags, or arrows. The important thing is the client's expectations.

To reduce expansion problems caused by moisture, the oak flooring industry has developed several types of parquets. The laminated or engineered block is a product that displays far less expansion and contraction with moisture changes and, therefore, can be successfully installed below grade in basements and in humid climates. It can even fit tight to vertical obstructions. Blocks can be glued directly to the concrete with several types of adhesive, which the industry is making VOC compliant. One concern in the past has been the ability of a laminated block to be sanded and refinished. Because the face layer is oak, with proper maintenance the initial service life can be 20 to 30 years. Any of the laminated products on the market today can be sanded and refinished (at least twice) using proper techniques and equipment, so the expected life of a laminated block floor is 60 to 90 years.

The PermaGrain Series has acrylic impregnated parquet tiles in 12″ × 12″ parquet, or 12″ × 12″ or 6″ x 12″ one-directional 5/16″ tile, which may be combined with pickets and bands for even greater design freedom. This product exceeds all current ADA requirements and is UL listed for slip resistance.

Special custom-designed borders are available for use in a Victorian setting or for a contemporary custom look. These borders are made of contrasting woods and vary in width from 4 to 20 inches. Thin strips of semiprecious stones or metals, such as brass or aluminum, may also be incorporated in the design. Custom Borders from Kentucky Wood Floors are preassembled modules that can be glued down flush with 5/16 inch thick flooring or on top of underlay-

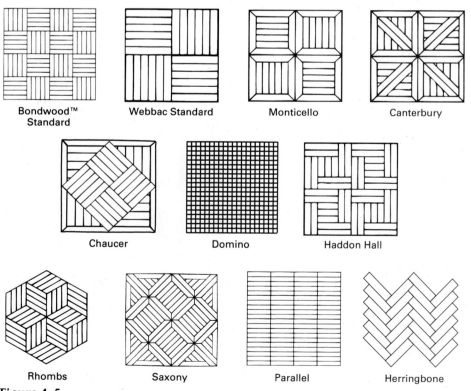

Figure 4–5
Parquet patterns from Harris-Tarkett. (Reproduced by permission of Harris-Tarkett.)

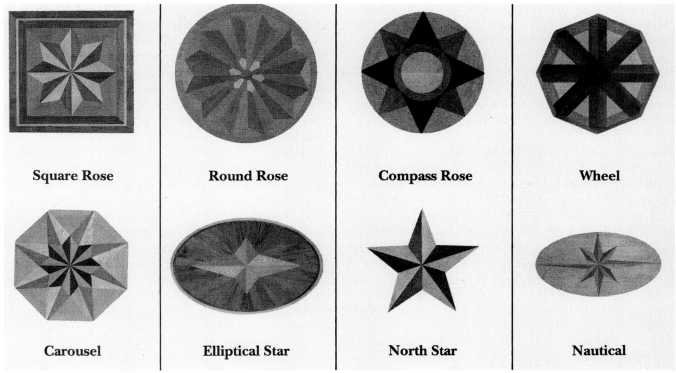

| Square Rose | Round Rose | Compass Rose | Wheel |

| Carousel | Elliptical Star | North Star | Nautical |

Figure 4–6
*Custom Accents are available in the designs shown or in a custom design,
such as a family crest or a corporate logo. The combination of species
(from Ash to Zebrawood), when used with Kentucky Wood Floors, will
match the adjacent hardwood flooring in grain and color. (Photo courtesy
of Kentucky Wood Floors.)*

ment with 3/4 inch thick flooring. Corner blocks are also available. Matching architectural millwork is available, such as quarter round, baseboard, nosing, and **reducer strips.** Custom Accents are medallion-style designs to accent any wood floor (Figure 4–6).

Parquet flooring comes packed in cartons with a specific number of square feet. When ordering parquet flooring, only whole cartons are shipped, so the allowance for cutting may be taken care of with the balance of the carton.

All the parquet woods mentioned in this subsection are quarter sawn or plain sawn, but some species are cut across the growth rings (end grained). End-grain patterns are formed by small cross-cut pieces attached into blocks or strips with the end grain exposed. The thickness may vary from 1 inch to 4 inches, depending on the manufacturer. One and a half inches of end-grain block have insulating qualities equal to 23 inches of concrete. Some end-grain block floors are still in place after more than 40 years of heavy industrial use. These blocks absorb noise and vibration and have been installed in museums and libraries.

Grade Levels

Figure 4–7 illustrates the differences among on, above, and below grade. Above grade is not a problem for installation of wood floors, because no moisture is pre-

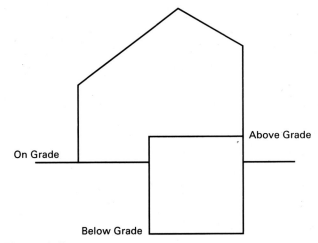

Figure 4–7
Grade levels.

sent. As mentioned earlier, moisture is the major cause of problems with wood. On grade means that the concrete floor is in contact with the ground. The floor usually has a drainage gravel as a base, covered by a polyethylene film to prevent moisture from migrating to the surface. The concrete is then poured on top of this polyethylene sheet. Below grade means a basement floor, in which the presence of moisture is an even greater problem. All freshly poured concrete should be allowed to **cure** for 30 to 60 days.

NOFMA provides the following information on testing for excessive moisture: Make tests in several areas of each room on both old and new slabs. When tests show too much moisture in the slab, do not install hardwood floors. For a moist slab, wait until it dries naturally, or accelerate drying with heat and ventilation; then test again. (If moisture is still present, consult a specialist in this field to avoid flooring problems.) There are four tests for moisture: rubber mat, polyethylene film, calcium chloride, and phenothalein.

1. *The rubber mat test.* Lay a smooth, noncorrugated rubber mat on the slab, place a weight on top to prevent moisture from escaping, and allow the mat to remain for 24 hours. If the covered area shows water marks when the mat is removed, too much moisture is present. This test is worthless if the slab surface is other than light in color originally.

2. *The polyethylene film test.* Tape a 1-foot square of 6 mil clear polyethylene film to the slab, sealing all edges with plastic moisture-resistant tape. If, after 24 hours, there is no "clouding" or drops of moisture on the underside of the film, the slab can be considered dry enough to install wood floors.

3. *The calcium chloride test.* Place a quarter teaspoonful of dry (anhydrous) calcium chloride crystals inside a 3-inch-diameter putty ring on the slab. Cover with a glass so the crystals are totally sealed off from the air. If the crystals dissolve within 12 hours, the slab is too wet.

4. *The phenothalein test.* Put several drops of a 3 percent phenothalein solution in grain alcohol at various spots on the slab. If a red color develops in a few minutes, too much moisture is present.

Particleboard underlayment is a product used widely as a substrate for floors in residential construction. Flooring manufacturers always specify the type of underlayment to be used with their products.

Substrates must be clean (free of dust, grease, or oil stains), dry, and level. As stressed in Chapter 3 and repeated throughout this book, SURFACE PREPARATION IS EXTREMELY IMPORTANT. The completed floor is only as good as the subfloor. Any high spots should be ground down and low spots filled using the correct leveling compound. One floor installer related a story about a client who complained of a loose wood floor installed over a slab. When the loose wood was removed, not only did the wood come up, but attached to it was the material used as a filler for the low spots. The person who leveled the floor had used the wrong leveling compound.

Two types of patching compounds are available for use under flooring: gypsum and portland cement. Whichever type is used, antimicrobial agents must be added to prevent mold and mildew growth.

Solid strip products are nailed down, and parquet products are glued down with such products as Hydroment® Ultra-Set Hardwood Adhesive. This adhesive is a one-part trowel applied, light gray, elastomeric, water-proof setting adhesive. Once cured, it is not affected by water. Laminated planks are the only product that can be either nailed or glued.

The National Oak Flooring Manufacturers Association suggests that several factors may contribute to an unsatisfactory installation. First, the wood floor should be scheduled at the end of construction. Because most other work is completed, the floors will not be abused. The building should be dry, with any moisture introduced during construction gone. Second, a subfloor of 5/8 inch or thicker plywood or 1" × 6" edge boards is preferred. A thicker, well-fastened subfloor provides better installation. Third, the wood flooring should be well nailed; there should be no skimping on the number of nails per strip, plank, and so forth. The illustrations in Figure 4–8 are taken from NOFMA's *Hardwood Flooring Manual* and show correct installation procedures.

Walls are never used as a starting point for installation because they are never truly square. Wood parquet must always be installed in a pyramid or stairstep sequence, rather than in rows, to avoid a misaligned pattern (Figure 4–9). Parquet may also be laid parallel to, or at a 45° angle to, the wall.

Reducer strips may be used at the doorway if there is a difference in level between two areas, and they are available to match the wood floor. Most wood floor **mastics** take about 24 hours to dry, so no one must walk on the floor or place furniture in the room during that period. Laminated planks must be rolled with a 150-pound roller before the adhesive sets. An unfinished wood floor is sanded with the grain using progressively finer grits until the floor is smooth and has an almost shiny appearance. After vacuuming to eliminate any dust particles, finishing

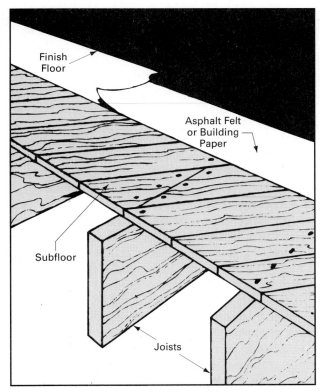

(a) Wood joist construction using square-edge board subfloor.

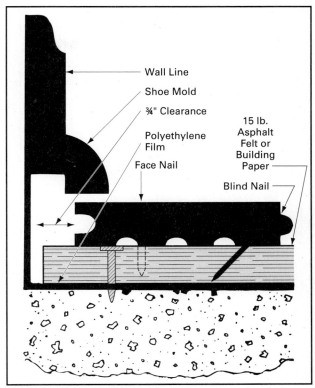

(b) Plywood-on-slab method of installing strip oak flooring.

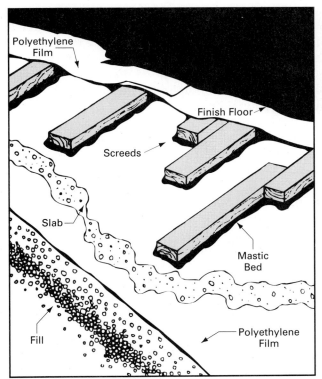

(c) Screeds method of installing strip oak flooring on slab.

(d) Use of power nailer for installing strip flooring.

Figure 4–8
Installation methods for wood floors. (Figures courtesy of National Oak Flooring Manufacturers Association.)

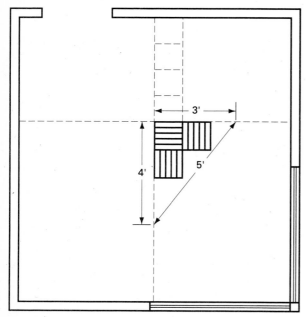

Figure 4–9
Method of laying parquet floor and other tile.

materials specifically manufactured for use on wood floors are applied. For open-grained wood such as oak, a filler with or without stain may be used after sanding to provide a more highly reflective surface. Often, there is a preference for natural-color hardwood floors, but stain may be used to bring out the grain or produce a darker tone. When a very light finish is wanted, the wood may be bleached or pickled. If a white floor is needed, a laminated wood floor is better because such floors are less likely to expand and contract (problems that show up as dark lines).

There are two main types of finish applied to wood floors: polyurethane and Swedish finish. Polyurethane finish will normally yellow with time, whereas the Swedish finish will not. Basic Coatings' Street Shoe® Commercial Wood Floor Finish system is a water-based finish that contains a special UV blocker designed to reduce the sun's damaging effects. This finish is used for both commercial and residential use. Glitsa®, a brand-name Swedish finish, is now VOC compliant.

Maintenance. Eight steps on a wood floor surface are needed to remove sand or dirt from the bottom of shoes. Therefore, walk-off mats at all exterior doors should be used. General housekeeping prolongs the life of a wood floor. The main problem with maintenance of any floor is *grit*, which can be removed by dust mop, broom, or vacuum. Another

problem is indentations caused by heels, especially women's high heels. A 125-pound woman with high heels exerts as much pressure as an elephant, and, therefore, indentations should be expected. If the floor is the type that may be waxed (very few are), a thin coat of wax should be allowed to dry and harden. Then an electric bristle brush buffer is used. Because old wax holds dirt and grease and a build-up of "scuffs," it should be removed periodically by means of a solvent type of wax remover specifically designed for wood floors. Food spills may be wiped up with a damp cloth.

Certain chemicals in wood oxidize in strong light, causing the wood to change color; therefore, rugs or area rugs should be moved periodically.

Wood and water do not mix. No matter what claims the manufacturer makes for the wood finish, water must never be poured onto the floor intentionally. A damp mop is fine for nonwaxed polyurethane and other surface finishes in good condition. Wax-coated finishes should *never* be cleaned with water, not even with a damp mop. (The *Wood Floor Care Guide* is available from the Oak Flooring Institute, an affiliate of NOFMA.)

Many manufacturers sell a line of maintenance products specially prepared for their own products. Custom finishes, such as polyurethane and Swedish finish, should not be waxed. Manufacturers of acrylic wood provide special cleaning materials for their products.

If cracks appear in the wood floor, they are probably caused by lack of humidity and can be reduced by installing a humidifier.

LAMINATE

In Europe, **laminate floors** have been used for many years. Wilsonart International manufactured the first laminate flooring in the United States. This type of floor is not to be confused with a laminated wood floor (also called engineered wood).

The following information is an overview of laminate flooring supplied by Wilsonart International:

Laminate Flooring generally comprises three layers:
Decorative surface: for design and abrasion resistance
Core board: for stability and impact resistance
Balancing backer: to prevent warpage and seal board.

The Decorative Surface can be made of:

Melamine paper: also called film or low pressure laminate; consists of a single layer of resin-treated decorative paper; or

High Pressure decorative laminate: HPDL; consists of a layer of resin-treated decorative paper bonded under heat and pressure to several layers of treated core paper.

The Core Board is usually some form of fiberboard; generally high density or medium density fiberboard (HDF or MDF).

The Balancing Backer, like the decorative surface, can be melamine or high pressure laminate, but is generally of the same composition as the top layer.

Wilsonart® Flooring is engineered to provide the best characteristics of each product: Decorative Layer: High pressure decorative laminate with a high abrasion-resistant surface. Provides increased wear, stain, fade resistance as well as impact resistance. Core Board: Medium density fiberboard, 55 lb. Provides optimum impact resistance and strength when combined with HPDL. Balancing Backer: nondecorative high pressure laminate.[3]

Other laminate floors may vary in core and surface. Wilsonart Planks are 7 3/4 inches wide by 46 inches long, and each carton contains eight planks or enough flooring to cover approximately 20 square feet. The tiles are 15 1/2 inches square and are designed so interesting patterns can be achieved when combined with the planks. One tile equals the width of two planks, and three tiles equal the length of a plank. (See the laminate floor in Figure 9–9 and Color Plate 7.)

There are 20 or more laminate floor products on the market. Because these products carry a 16-year warranty, it is probably best to stay with a nationally known brand, some of which are given in Appendix A.

Installation. According to Wilsonart International,

Laminate flooring is installed using the "floating floor" system: Planks or tiles are glued together using a tongue-and-groove system, and are installed over a padding which increases sound absorption and provides some flexibility to the floor. Laminate flooring is not nailed or glued to the subfloor; a small gap is left at walls allowing for expansion and contraction without damage to the floor. It can be installed over most existing floors, making it ideal for retrofit situations.

Reduced prep time prior to installation (e.g., tear out is often unnecessary) and the simple installation process provide both time and cost savings. Wilsonart Flooring features an exclusive, patented tongue-and-groove system that makes installation simple and ensures proper bonding and seal.[4]

MARBLE

Marble is a **metamorphic** rock derived from limestone. Pressure and/or heat created the metamorphic change that turned limestone debris into marble. Today all rocks that can take a polish come under the heading of marble. Dolomitic limestone ("hard" limestone), although technically limestone, is known commercially as marble. Travertine and onyx are related stones; travertine is more important for flooring purposes because it is easier to work. Onyx is brittle and is mostly relegated to decorative uses. Serpentine is of a different chemical makeup, but because it can be polished, it is classified as marble. All of the aforementioned stones are calcareous.

The colored veins of marble are as varied and numerous as the areas from which marble is quarried. One famous type, Carrara marble, is pure white. Michelangelo used this marble for many of his sculptures. Other Carrara marble may have black, gray, or brownish veining. The name *verd antique* is applied to marbles of prevailing green color, which consist chiefly of serpentine, a hydrous magnesium silicate. Verd antiques are highly decorative stones; at times the green is interspersed with streaks or veins of red and white. The pinks, reds, yellows, and browns are caused by the presence of iron oxides, whereas the blacks, grays, and blue-grays result from bituminous deposits. Silicate, chlorite, and mica provide the green colors.

Marble is the most ancient of all finished materials currently in use today. Some authorities believe that the onyx marble of Algeria was employed by the Egyptians as early as 475 B.C. Biblical references show that marble was used in King Solomon's Temple at Jerusalem, and in the palace of Sushun more than one thousand years before Christ. Parian marble from the Aegean Sea was found in the ruins of ancient Troy.

Pentelic marble was used in the Parthenon in Athens and is still available today. Phidias used this marble for the frieze of the Parthenon, and portions of this frieze known as the **Elgin Marbles** are intact today and are on display at the British Museum. Makrana marble, a white marble, was used in the Taj Mahal in India. Inside the Taj Mahal, sunlight filters through marble screens as delicate as lace and the white marble walls are richly decorated with floral designs in onyx, jasper, carnelian, and other semiprecious stones.

Knoxville, Tennessee, was known at the turn of the 20th century as the marble capital of the United States. Marble is found in many eastern states, from Vermont to Georgia, and in some western states. The Georgia Marble Company ranks as the world's largest producer of marble products (Figure 4–10). Dolomitic marble is quarried in Tennessee and Idaho. The famous Yule Quarry in Marble, Colorado (from which came the columns of the Lincoln Memorial and the massive block forming the Tomb of the Unknown Soldier) has just been reopened. The white from this quarry may be the purest marble in the world.

Marble floors were used in the Baroque and Rococo periods in Europe. During the French empire, black and white marble squares were used, and they remain a popular pattern for marble floors today. In the formal halls of Georgian homes, the marble floors were appropriate for mahogany tables and chairs. In his Barcelona Pavilion, Mies Van der Rohe used great slabs of marble as freestanding partitions. Today, marble is used for furniture, floors, and interior and exterior walls (see Figure 4–10).

Figure 4–10
Marble from Georgia Marble Company was used for the Registration and Office Area of the Key Largo Bay Beach Resort, Key Largo, Florida. The floor is Etowah Fleuri and Verde Oriental. The countertop is Etowah Fleuri. (Photographer Paul G. Beswick; photo courtesy of Georgia Marble Company.)

Marble does not come in sheets (slabs) and must be quarried. There are three principal quarrying methods utilized today. The first is by drilling holes and thus outlining the block. Then wedges are driven into the holes and the blocks are split from the surrounding rock. The second method uses wire saws. An exceedingly long steel cable with diamond teeth is passed over the stone with downward pressure, cutting the block of stone free from the deposit. The third method employs a large chainsaw-type machine to saw the stone free from the deposit. Marble chips are used in the production of **terrazzo, agglomerated** marble tiles, and cast polymer products.

Marble is a relatively heavy and expensive material for use on floors because of the necessity of using the conventional thick-bed installation method. Fiberglass and epoxy resins employed as a backing hold delicate stones together during fabrication, shipment, and installation. This mass-produced method allows expensive decorative stone to be furnished more economically than with conventional methods (i.e., permanent stone liners, also known as backer slabs).

Agglomerated marble tiles consist of 90 to 95 percent marble chips, combined with 5 to 10 percent resins and formed into blocks in a vacuum chamber. They are available as floor tile or marble wall veneers. Agglomerated marble may be classified as cast marble, but the term *cast* is also used to describe a polyester product containing ground marble.

The following properties must be considered for marble floors:

Density. Averages 0.1 pound per cubic inch. This figure may be used to calculate the weight of the marble.

Water absorption. Measured by total immersion of a 2-inch cube for 48 hours and varies from 0.1 to 0.2 percent, which is less than that for other natural stones. The maximum absorption, as established by ASTM C503, is 0.20 percent.

Abrasion resistance. Measured by a scuffing method that removes surface particles similar to the action of foot traffic. Abrasion resistance for commercial flooring should be at least a hardness value of 10, as measured by ASTM C241. The Marble Institute of America (MIA) recommends a hardness value of 12. This value is not necessary for single-family homes.

Marble is also classified A through C, according to the fabrication methods considered necessary and acceptable in each instance, as based on standard trade practice.

A polished finish reflects light and emphasizes the color and marking of the material. The polished finish may be used in residential installations, but not for commercial installations. The biggest problem with a polished floor is that the shine is removed in the traffic area but the edges retain the shine, emphasizing the difference in the two areas. A honed surface is satin smooth with little light reflection. A honed finish is preferred for floors, stair treads, thresholds, and other locations where heavy traffic will wear off the polished finish.

When using marble or any other natural stone, the weight of these materials must be calculated to ensure that the subfloor is strong enough to support the extra weight. This is where 3/8-inch marble materials come into use (especially in remodeling, the floor was probably not constructed to bear heavy stones). Subfloors must meet a maximum deflection of 1/180 of span. The stiffer the subfloor, the longer lasting the finished floor. Subfloors that have measurable deflection will fail.

One of the materials used to help provide rigidity to a stable subfloor is a cementitious backer unit (CBU), which is "a backing and underlayment designed for use with ceramic tile in wet or dry areas. Available in various lengths, this material can be applied over studs and subflooring. Ceramic tile can be bonded to it with dry-set, latex-portland cement or modified epoxy **mortars.** Complete interior installation and material specifications are contained in **ANSI** (American National Standards Institute) A108.11 and ANSI A118.9 or ASTM C1325."[5]

A crack-suppression membrane is another method of preventing cracks in hard flooring materials. It allows the stone setting bed to span cracks and narrow expansion joints without the fear of the stone floor following the crack. There are, of course, limits to which crack suppression membrane can work.

The following information is provided by Intarsia™. In Latin, *Intarsia* means "the process of inlaying fine materials to create lasting beauty and elegance." The art form of inlaid stonework blossomed during the Florentine Renaissance under the Grand Duke of Tuscany and expanded across Europe as a decorative treatment for flooring and furniture through the 19th century. Prized by royalty and the noble class, intarsia production fell dormant during the latter 19th century as class structures changed and the artisan tradition became more difficult to pass on. The emergence of waterjet cutting technology and computer-aided design has eliminated that dormancy.

Waterjet cutting technology has developed in the past few years to the point that hardened materials such as metals and stone can be cut. This is done using an abrasive grit (garnet sand) mixed with a fine stream of water at 60,000 psi. The waterjet directed by a CAD/CAM computer expert can cut marble and granite with tremendous precision (0.005), repeatability, and creative flexibility. Designs are almost limitless. Intarsia Inc. stocks 20 granites, 30 marbles, 8 semiprecious stones, 3 metals, 5 onyx, and 5 travertines for a total of 71 natural materials. Intarsia Inc. also has 96 proprietary patterns, which include medallions, borders, and accent tiles (Figure 4–11 and Color Plate 8).

Installation. Several associations are responsible for codes and standards based on the consensus of their membership. The natural stones, such as marble, travertine, and slate, use the specifications and test methods contained in the ASTM manual, Section 4, Construction; Volume 04.08, Soil and Rock; Building Stones. The ceramic tile industry uses ANSI A108 for installation specifications. A copy of these specifications and test methods may be obtained from the respective organizations (see Appendix B).

Because marble is the first hard surface material covered in this book, installation methods are dis-

Figure 4–11
A medallion from Intarsia Inc. is shown in a private residence in Palm Beach, Florida. Designer Cathy Ma, Design Group M., Inc., Minneapolis, Minnesota. The field of the medallion is Crema Marfil Marble. The detail is Empress Green Marble, Rojo Alicante Marble, and China Black Marble & Brass. (Photo courtesy of Intarsia Inc.)

cussed in detail. The same methods are used for all natural stones, ceramic tile, quarry tile, and other types of hard surface materials.

Setting materials account for only 10 percent of installation costs but 90 percent of problems, so proper specification and professional installation are crucial and will eliminate most problems. Skinning, a film that forms on the surface of the setting materials and causes improper bonding, is a common cause of installation failure for all setting materials. To cure this problem, the application tool should be used again to break up the skin.

According to the Tile Council of America,

Portland cement mortar is a mixture of portland cement and sand, roughly in proportions of 1:5 on floors and of portland cement, sand and lime in proportions of 1:5:1/2 to 1:7:1 for walls. Portland cement mortar is suitable for most surfaces and ordinary types of installation. A mortar bed, up to 2″ in thickness, facilitates accurate slopes or planes in the finished tile work on floors and walls.

The mortar bed can be modified with the inclusion of a latex polymer per the manufacturer's directions as part or all of the liquid portion of the mixture to enhance certain performance properties.

There are two equivalent methods recognized for installing ceramic tiles with a portland cement mortar bed on walls, ceilings and floors. They are: (1) the method covered by ANSI A108.1A, which requires that the tile be set on a mortar bed that is still workable, and (2) the method covered by ANSI A108.1B, which requires the tile to be set on a cured mortar bed with dry-set or latex-portland cement mortar. Absorptive ceramic tiles must be soaked before setting on a mortar bed that is still workable when using a neat portland cement bond coat.

Portland cement mortars can be reinforced with metal lath or mesh, can be backed with membranes and can be applied on a metal lath over open studding on walls, or on rough floors. They are structurally strong, are not affected by prolonged contact with water, and can be used to **plumb** and square surfaces installed by others. . . . Complete installation and material specifications are contained in ANSI A108.1A, A108.1B, and A108.1C. [6]

Thick-set or thick-bed *must* be used for setting materials of uneven thickness, such as flagstone and slate. It may also be used for hard-surfaced materials of uniform thickness. Tiles are placed on the mortar and are tapped into place until the surface is level. The mortar used on floors is a mixture of portland cement and sand, roughly in proportions of 1:6. According to TCA,

Dry-set mortar is suitable for **thin-set** installations of ceramic tile over a variety of surfaces. It is used in one layer, as thin as 3/32″, and after tiles are beat in, has excellent water and impact resistance, is water-cleanable, nonflammable, good for exterior work, and does not require soaking of the tile.

Dry-set mortar is available as a factory-sanded mortar to which only water need be added.

Cured dry-set mortar is not affected by prolonged contact with water but does not form a water barrier. It is not a setting bed and is not intended to be used in truing or leveling the work of others.

Suitable backings, when properly prepared, include plumb and true masonry, concrete, gypsum board, cementitious backer units, cured portland cement beds, brick, ceramic tile and dimension stone.

Complete specifications and material specifications are contained in ANSI A108.5 and ANSI A118.1. For conductive dry set mortar see ANSI A108.7 and ANSI 118.2. [7]

Another thin-set method is to use an adhesive that is spread with a trowel. The trowel is used not only for spreading, by using the flat edge for continuous coverage, but is also a metering device for determining the proper amount of adhesive. Oil-based adhesives should be avoided when installing marble, because they stain the marble. Again it must be repeated that thin-bed should be used only where the substrate is solid and level.

Almost all marble and granite tile produced today are manufactured for use with a joint and are furnished with a slight **chamfer** (bevel) at the junction of the face and edge.

Maintenance. The following information is condensed from the booklet *Care & Cleaning for Natural Stone Surfaces,* available from the Marble Institute of America, Inc. (see Appendix B). This Institute serves the Dimension Stone Industry. This information covers all natural stones, including marble, granite, limestone, onyx, and slate.

Blot the spill with a paper towel immediately. Do not wipe the area, it will spread the spill. Flush the area with plain water and mild soap and rinse several times. Dry the area with a soft cloth. Repeat as necessary. Identifying the type of stain on the stone surface is the key to removing it. Sometimes the location and color of the stain in proximity to possible culprits will make identification easier (i.e., plants, food service area, cosmetics). Surface stains can often be removed by cleaning with an appropriate cleaning product or household chemical. Deep-seated or stubborn stains may require using a poultice or calling in a professional.[8]

TRAVERTINE

Travertine is a porous limestone formed from the precipitation of mineral springs, has holes in it because of escaping gas, and is a calcareous stone. When it is used as a floor, travertine is filled with a cement fill. Epoxy-filled travertine is available only on special order and is much more expensive than cement-filled travertine. Epoxy is subject to color change and strength loss (failure) when subjected to sunlight (ultraviolet rays).

Maintenance. The maintenance of travertine is the same as for marble.

GRANITE

Granite is technically an igneous rock having crystals or grains of visible size. These grains are classified as fine, medium, or coarse. Granite is a type of siliceous stone.

Granite colors are white, gray, buff, beige, pink, red, blue, green, and black; however, within these colors, the variegations run from light to dark. The color gray, for example, may be light, medium, or dark, or vary between dark and purplish gray or dark and greenish gray. It is important to see an actual sample of the type of granite to be used. The National Building Granite Quarries Association (NBGQA) recommends submitting duplicate 12″ × 12″ samples to show the full range of color, texture, and finish. The designer retains one set, and the other is returned to the granite supplier for reference.

In addition to color, finish is important. The NBGQA has established the following definitions:

Polished: Mirror gloss, with sharp reflections.

Honed: Dull sheen, without reflections. (Preferred finish for floors, stair treads, thresholds, and other locations where heavy traffic will wear off the polished finish.)

Flamed: A rough textured surface. The flame finish is applied by mechanically controlled means to ensure uniformity. Surface coarseness varies, depending on grain structure of the granite. This finish is frequently used for granite floor tiles.

As with other stones, polished granite should not be used for floors because the mirror gloss and color will eventually be dulled by the abrasion of feet. If there is the possibility of water being present, flamed or thermal textures are used to create a nonslip surface.

Durastone offers 3/16 inch thick granite in a 48″ × 96″ size and in 11 colors for use on floors and walls.

The method of veneered construction used to make thinner and lighter-weight marble squares is also used with granite, and for the same reasons. When a feeling of permanence and stability is needed, granite is a good choice; therefore, granite is often used in banking institutions.

Installation. Honed granite is installed using the same methods as for marble. When more textured finishes are specified and when the granite has not been cut to a definite size, a mortar joint is used.

Maintenance. Granite floors, particularly those with rougher surfaces, require ordinary maintenance by means of a brush or vacuum cleaner. The more highly finished granite surfaces should be maintained in the same manner as marble.

GROUT

Grout is the material used to fill the joints between tiles. The type of grout employed, if any, depends on which variety of tile is being used (Table 4–1). Therefore, not only is the type of grout important, but also the spacing of the tile. Proper joint placement is crucial so both sides of the room have equal size pieces. The use of crack isolation membranes in thin-bed installations is necessary to prevent cracks in the substrate from cracking marble or ceramic tiles installed over them.

TABLE 4-1
Grout Guide

These guidelines cannot address every installation. The type and size of tile, service level, climatic conditions, tile spacing and individual manufacturer's recommendations are all factors that should be considered when selecting the proper grout.

Printed through the courtesy of the Materials & Methods Standards Association (rev. 1996) W = wall use F = floor use	GROUTS CONTAINING PORTLAND CEMENT					OTHERS			
	Commercial (Sanded) A118.6 H-2.1	Jobsite Mix (Sanded) A118.6	Dry-Set (Unsanded) A118.6 H-2.3	Commercial or Dry-Set with Latex (Polymer) A/118.6 H-2.4	Mod. Epoxy Emulsion A118.8	100% Solid Epoxy A118.3	Furan A118.5	Silicone or Urethane	Mastic Grout
	(4)	(4)	(4)	(4, 9)	(4)	(1, 3, 4, 6)	(1, 3, 4, 6)	(2, 4)	(3, 4)
TILE TYPE									
Glazed Wall Tile (7)	W		W	W		W		W	W
Glazed Floor Tile (7)	W, F	W, F	W, F	W, F	W, F	W, F			W, F
Ceramic Mosaics	W, F	W, F	W, F	W, F	W, F	W, F		W	W, F
Quarry, Paver, and Packing House Tile (8)	W, F	W, F		W, F	W, F	W, F	W, F		
Large Unit Porcelain or Vitreous Tile (8)	W, F	W, F	W, F	W, F	W, F	W, F	F	W	W, F
Dimension Stone (7, 8) (Including Agglomerates)	W, F	W, F	W, F	W, F	W, F				
USE									
Dry/Limited Water Exposure	W, F	W, F	W, F	W, F	W, F	W, F	W, F	W, F	W, F
Wet Areas (10)	W, F	W, F	W, F	W, F	W, F	W, F	W, F	W, F	
Exteriors (8, 9, 10)	W, F	W, F	W, F	W, F	W, F	W, F (4)	W, F (4)	W, F	
PERFORMANCE	Note: There are 5 performance ratings, from Best (A) to Minimal (E)								
Suggested Joint Widths (5)	1/8 to 5/8"	1/8 to 5/8"	1/16 to 1/8"	1/16 to 5/8"	1/16 to 5/8"	1/16 to 5/8"	3/8 to 5/8"	1/16 to 1/4"	1/16 to 1/4"
Stain Resistance	D	E	D	C	C	A	A	A	B
Crack Resistance	D	E	D	C	C	B	C	A	C
Color Availability	B	D	B	B	B	B	Black only	B	B

Notes:
(1) Mainly used for chemical resistant properties.
(2) Special tools needed for proper application. Silicone, urethane and modified polyvinylchloride used in pregrouted ceramic tile sheets. Silicone grout should not be used on kitchen countertops or other food preparation surfaces unless it meets the requirements of FDA Regulation 21, CFE 177.2600.
(3) Special cleaning procedures and materials recommended.
(4) Follow manufacturer's directions.
(5) Joint widths are only guidelines. Individual grout manufacturers products may vary. Consult manufacturer's instructions.
(6) Epoxies are recommended for prolonged temperatures up to 140°F; high temperature resistant epoxies and furans up to 350°F.
(7) Some types of glazed ceramic tiles, polished marble, marble agglomerates and granite can be permanently scratched or damaged when grouted with sanded grout or add sand to grout when grouting polished marble, marbled agglomerates and ceramic wall tiles with soft glazes. Check the tile or marble manufacturer's literature and test grout on a separate sample area prior to grouting.
(8) Some types of ceramic tiles and dimension stone may be permanently stained when grouted with pigmented grout of a contrasting color. WHITE GROUT IS BEST SUITED FOR GROUTING WHITE OR LIGHT COLORED MARBLE OR GRANITE.
(9) Latex modification may be required in areas subject to freezing temperatures. Consult grout manufacturer for recommended products and methods.
(10) Colored cementitious grouts may darken when wet.

Source: 1994 Handbook for Ceramic Tile Installation. Copyright © Tile Council of America, Inc. Reprinted with permission.

The Tile Council of America states that

Grouting materials for ceramic tile are available in many forms to meet the requirements of the different kinds of tile and types of exposure. Portland cement is the base of most grouts and is modified to provide specific qualities such as whiteness, mildew resistance, uniformity, hardness, flexibility, and water retentivity. Noncement based grouts such as epoxies, furans, and silicone rubber offer properties not possible with cement grouts. However, special skills on the part of the tile setter are required. *These materials can be appreciably greater in cost than cement-based grouts.* Complete installation and material specifications are contained in ANSI A108.10 and ANSI A118.6.[9]

Commercial portland cement grout for floors is usually gray (but colors are available) and is designed for use with ceramic **mosaics,** quarry, and paver tile. Damp curing is required, which is the process of keeping the grout moist and covered for several days and results in a much stronger grout. For areas that must be opened for traffic as quickly as possible, there are quick-set grout additives (see Table 4–1).

Grouts with sand are not used with highly reflective tiles, because the roughness of the grout is not compatible with the high gloss. For glazed tiles, unsanded grout or mastic grout is used. Special grouts are available that are chemical resistant; some are fungus and mildew resistant; and others of a latex composition are used when movement is anticipated. Intersept is incorporated into Portersept's grout sealer, which protects the grout against mold, mildew, and bacteria.

FLAGSTONE

Flagstones were used on the floors in Tudor England (1485–1603). Flagstone is defined as thin slabs of stone used for paving walks, driveways, patios, and so forth. It is generally fine-grained **sandstone, bluestone, quartzite,** or slate, but thin slabs of other stones may be used. One-inch-thick bluestone flagging in a random multiple pattern compares favorably in price to premium vinyl tiles. Flagstones are siliceous and durable because they are composed mainly of silica or quartzlike particles.

Flagstone may be irregularly shaped, the way it was when quarried, varying in size from 1 to 4 square feet, or the edges may be sawed to give a more formal appearance. Thickness may vary from 1/2 inch to 4 inches; therefore, the flagstone *must* be set in a thick mortar base to produce a level surface.

The extra thickness of the flagstone must be considered when positioning floor joists. One client had flagstones drawn and specified on her blueprints. The carpenter misread the plans, however, and assumed that it was to be a flagstone patterned floor and not the real thing. The client arrived at the house one day to discover that the entryway did not have the lowered floor necessary to fit the extra thickness of the stone. The contractor had to cut all the floor joists for the hall area, lower them 4 inches, and then put in additional bracing and supports in the basement—a costly error.

Another point to remember with flagstones is that the surface is usually uneven because it comes from naturally cleaved rock; therefore, flagstones are not suitable for use under tables and chairs. In addition, an entrance hall of flagstones is very durable, but the stone needs to be protected from grease, which can be absorbed into the stones.

The grout used in setting flagstones is a sand–portland cement type and fills all areas where flagstones adjoin.

Maintenance

Flagstones are relatively easy to clean with mild acidic cleaning solutions. There are sealing compounds on the market that make flagstones **impervious** to any staining and wear. These compounds are available in gloss and matte finishes and protect the treated surface against the deteriorating effects of weathering, salts, acids, alkalis, oil, and grease. The gloss finish does seem to give an unnatural shiny appearance to the stone, but where the impervious quality rather than the aesthetic quality is important, these sealers may be used. Vacuuming will remove dust and siliceous material from the surface, and a damp mop will remove any other soil from the sealed surface.

SLATE

Slate was also used as a flooring material in Tudor England (1585–1603). In 17th-century France, slate was combined with bands of wood. Slate is a very fine-grained metamorphic rock cleaved from sedimentary rock shale. One characteristic of slate is that this cleavage allows the rock to be split easily into thin slabs. The most common colors for slate range from gray to black, but green, brown, and red are also available. In areas of heavy traffic, honed black slate tends to show the natural scuffing of shoes, and the scratches give the black slate a slightly grayish appearance. All stones will eventually show this scuffing, and, therefore, highly polished stones should be avoided as a flooring material.

Different finishes are available in slate, as in other stones. The Structural Slate Company describes the following finishes:

Natural cleft: The natural split or cleaved face. This finish is moderately rough, with some textural variations. Thickness will have a plus or minus tolerance of 1/8 inch.

Sand rubbed: This finish has a slight grain or stipple in an even plane. No natural cleft texture remains. Finish is equivalent to **60-grit** and is obtained by wet sand on a rubbing bed.

Honed: This finish is equivalent to approximately **120-grit** in smoothness. It is semipolished, without excessive sheen.

The standard thickness of sawed flooring slate is 1/2 inch. Also available are 3/4 inch and 1 inch thicknesses, which are suitable for both interior and exterior use.

American Olean has two patterns and two color ranges of slate. Pattern 1 has sizes that range from 6″ × 6″ to 12″ × 12″, and Pattern 5 ranges from 6″ × 9″ to 15″ × 18″. The two color selections are mottled purple with predominantly green mottling and darker purple with slight green mottling. The black coloration ranges from gray black to blue black. The patterns each cover 15 square feet. The thicker slate is available in Pattern 5 rectangles, and squares in sizes from 6 to 24 inches square in multiples of 3 inches, whereas the sizes for 1/4-inch slate are 6 to 12 inches square, also in multiples of 3 inches (Figure 4–12).

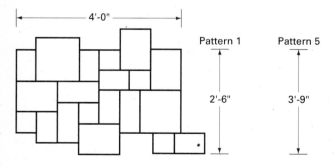

- Sizes include a 3/8" (1.0 cm) joint.
  Example: 6" × 6" (15.2 cm × 15.2 cm) is 5-5/8" × 5-5/8"
- 1/4" (0.6 cm) gauged thickness; other thicknesses available
  special order
- May be specified in single colors or a combination of colors

Figure 4–12
The two sizes of slate in Pattern 1 and Pattern 2 are shown in this illustration from American Olean. (Courtesy of American Olean.)

One-half-inch slate weighs 7 1/2 pounds per square foot, 3/4-inch slate weighs 11 1/4 pounds, and 1-inch slate weighs 15 pounds. The absorption rate of slate is 0.23 percent. One-quarter-inch slate is used for interior foyers in homes and commercial buildings using the thin-set method. This thickness is an excellent remodeling item over wood or slab and gives a rug-level effect when it adjoins carpet. One-quarter-inch slate weighs only 3 3/4 pounds per square foot.

Installation

As can be seen from the preceding types, slate is available for both thin-set and thick-set applications. When thin-set mastic or adhesive is used, a 1/4″ × 1/4″ notched trowel held at a 45° angle is suggested.

Several points need to be remembered with both types of installations. If grout is used with slate (the spacing varies from 1/4 inch to 1/2 inch), it is important that any excess be cleaned off immediately, because grout that has dried on the slate surface will probably never come off. If grout is not used, the slate tiles are butted against each other. Joint lines are staggered so no lines are more than 2 to 3 feet long in a straight line.

Thick-bed installation is similar to that for flagstones. All joints should be 1/2-inch-wide flush joints and should be **pointed** with 1:2 cement mix the same day the floor is laid to make joints and setting bed **monolithic.**

Maintenance

A slate floor is easily maintained with mild soap and water. Although waxing is not harmful, it detracts from the natural beauty of the stone, turns the floor a darker shade, and may yellow the grout.

CERAMIC TILE

Because ceramic tile was one of the most durable materials used by ancient civilizations, archaeologists have discovered that thin slabs of fired clay, decorated and glazed, originated in Egypt about 4700 B.C. Tile was, and is often, used in Spanish architecture to such a degree that a Spanish expression for poverty is "to have a house without tiles." The Spanish also use decorative ceramic tiles on the **risers** of stairs. The Romans used fired clay pipes to carry water and sewage and used terra cotta to construct and decorate their public and private buildings.

In England, many abbeys had mosaic tile floors, and the European cathedrals of the 12th century also had tile floors. In ancient times, tiles were used to make pictures on the walls, and these patterns were spread over many tiles. A good example is the bulls and dragons in the Ishtar Gate from Babylon, which is now in the Pergamon Museum in Berlin. Later, each tile was decorated with intricate patterns, or four tiles were used to form a complete pattern. Eighteenth- and 19th-century tiles used a combination of these two design types.

Tiles were named after the city where they originated: Faience, with its striking opaque glazes, from Faenza in Italy; Majolica, with bright decorations, from Majorca, Spain; and Delft tiles, from the town of Delft in Holland. Delft tiles, with their blue and white designs, are known worldwide.

Tiles are made by two methods: dust press and extruded. Floor and wall tiles for interior use are produced by the dust-process method. The clay mixture is forced into steel dies under heavy pressure and is fired at very high temperatures to form a **bisque,** a tile ready to be glazed. These tiles are then sprayed with a surface glaze and fired at a lower temperature than before. This second firing fuses the glaze to the tile. The dust-process method produces distinct shapes and sizes.

The second production method is an extruded or ram process in which the clay is mixed to form a thick mud and is then forced through a die. This process forms a slightly rougher-looking and larger tile, which is glazed in the same manner as the dust-process tiles. The temperature and proportions of the ingredients dictate the tile's use: walls, floors, interior or exterior, and residential or commercial.

Water absorption tests can also be used as a good indicator to predict the stain resistance of unglazed tile. The lower the water absorption, the greater the stain resistance.

Porcelain tiles are inherently impervious and are used frequently in heavy-use commercial and retail areas (Table 4–2). According to one tile manufacturer, its porcelain tiles

> are fired at a temperature that exceeds 2200° F, at which point they have a viscous liquid phase in which crystallization occurs. During the cooling stage, the materials fuse together and solidify again to gain strength and hardness. These tiles

TABLE 4–2
Porosity Variances

TYPE	WATER ABSORPTION RATE
Impervious	0.5% or less
Vitreous	More than 0.5% but less than 3%
Semivitreous	More than 3% but less than 7%
Nonvitreous	More than 7%

can be used in light colors that give an airy and spacious feeling to the installation. The color of the ceramic tile results from the addition of body stains, which consist of inert crystalline metals in oxides or salts. The breaking strength of porcelain tile is approximately three times stronger than that of a glazed tile. Additionally, the low absorption of porcelain tile yields a tile that is frostproof, unlike a glazed product, which when exposed to freezing and thawing may have the glazing separate from the body of the tile.[10]

Because of the low absorption rate of porcelain tiles, bond-promoting additives are added to the mortars and grouts.

Many types of finishes and patterns are available in ceramic tiles, ranging from a very shiny, highly reflective glaze to a dull matte finish and even an unglazed impervious tile. Tiles may be solid color or hand painted with designs.

The surface texture of ceramic tile relates to its reflectance qualities. For example, a perfectly smooth tile will have a much higher reflectance rate than a rough surface tile, although both tiles have identical glazes. Ceramic tiles are available in many different shapes and sizes. Instead of the traditional 4 1/4" × 4 1/4" tile, 8", 12", and even 18" square tiles are used widely.

Highly glazed tiles are not recommended for floor use for two reasons: First, the surface can become extremely slippery when wet; second, some wearing and scratching can occur over time, depending on type of use. Of course, if moisture and wear are not a problem, then glazed tiles may be used.

A coefficient of friction test provides a comparative measure for the slipperiness of a floor. The static coefficient of friction is a term used in physics to describe how much force is required to cause an object (shoe sole material) to start moving across a flooring material. By measuring the coefficient of friction, a quantitative number can be used to express the degree of slip resistance. A 50-pound weight is placed on a Neolite shoe heel that was previously placed flat on the tile surface. The heel and weight assembly is pulled across the tile with a spring or electronic scale. The maximum amount of force (pounds) needed to start the assembly in motion is then recorded. The measurement is divided by the weight (50 pounds) and is referred to as the coefficient of friction value. Although there is no current ANSI requirement, a coefficient of friction of 0.5 and above is the recognized industry standard for a slip-resistant flooring surface. The ADA recommends a coefficient of friction of 0.6 or greater.

The ASTM procedure states that the measurement made by this apparatus is believed to be one important factor relative to slip resistance. Other factors can affect slip resistance, such as the degree of wear on the shoe and flooring material; the presence of foreign matter, such as water, oils, and dirt; the length of the human stride at the time of the slip; the type of floor finish; and the physical and mental condition of the person. Therefore, this test method should be used to develop a property of the flooring surface under laboratory conditions and should not be used to deter-

mine slip resistance under field conditions unless those conditions are fully described. The coefficient of friction can, however, vary with each production run.

Most ceramic tile companies produce a raised dome surface tile that can be detected underfoot and by cane contact (which meets the guidelines set by the ADA). Its yellow color serves as a caution for platform and curb edges.

Figure 4–13
Cross-Quilt™ and Crossborder™, two custom-cutting programs from Crossville Tile Co., capture all the charm of heirloom quilts. Using the latest in custom-cutting technology, Crossville interprets vintage patchwork in any color and any texture of durable, stain- and fade-proof porcelain tile. (Photo courtesy of Crossville Ceramics.)

Cross-Colors® Mosaics, with the new Cross Sheen™ finish, are 3-inch mosaics that reduce grout problems commonly associated with smaller mosaics. Custom Color® is the name given to Crossville's custom colored tiles; for runs of sufficient size, the color and surface texture can be specified. These custom colors are made with porcelain tiles so, as described before, the color goes all the way through the body of the tile and is not merely on the surface. Other custom services from Crossville are Crosstyle™ and Geostyle™: Any tile can be precision cut in any straight-edged geometric shape (at least 2″ × 2″), which provides a factory-finished edge. Diagonal cuts and a multiple of trim types, including **bullnose**-edged beveling, are available in most surface textures (Figure 4–13).

Frenchquarter™, from Daltile™, has four different sizes: two squares, 12 and 6 inches, and two rectangular tiles, 12″ × 18″ and 6″ × 12″. By using a combination of these sizes, as shown in Figure 4–14, a large area of tile can be broken into a pleasing random design. This pattern has the appearance of antique slate with the performance of ceramic tile.

Another interesting aid for designers is the Designer CD from Daltile. By setting design preferences such as color, pattern, style, and budget, a search is made and the product samples are displayed to scale as photorealistic, true-color images with all pertinent information included.

The Laura Ashley™ ceramic tile collection by American Olean makes coordination possible with Laura Ashley fabrics and wallpapers.

When ceramic or quarry tiles are used on a floor, the floor is usually finished with a **base** or combination trim tile having a bullnose at the top and a **cove** at the bottom in the same material as the floor tiles. If ceramic tiles are to be continued onto the wall surface, a cove base is used (Figure 4–15).

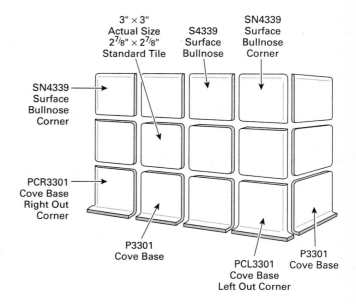

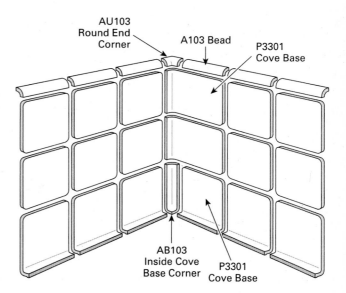

Figure 4–14
By using Frenchquarter from Daltile in a combination of sizes, a large area of tile can be broken up into a pleasing random design. (Photo courtesy of Daltile.)

Figure 4–15
Crossville line drawings. (Reproduced with permission from Crossville Ceramics.)

CERAMIC MOSAIC TILE

According to Compton's Interactive Encyclopedia,

> The earliest Greek patterned mosaics are made with small, naturally rounded pebbles set into fine cement. Early examples from the 8th century BC have been found at Fordion in Phrygia (Asia Minor). The technique may have been invented in Greece, where unpatterned pebble floors have been found to date from the Bronze Age. . . . In the Americas the Pueblo Indians of the Southwestern United States use turquoise to make mosaic plaques. Mexican mosaic made before Christopher Columbus includes examples of mosaic masks. There are references in surviving documents to architectural decoration in mosaic. Mosaic also reached a high level of excellence in ancient Peru. . . . By the 15th century mosaic was executed exclusively by craftsmen without the participation of the artist who supplied the design.[11]

Today, mosaic tile is used for intricate designs for floors, walls, and ceilings, copying the ancient art.

Ceramic mosaic tile is usually formed by the dust-press method and is 1/4 to 3/8 inch thick, with a facial area of less than 6 square inches. Pigments and, if required, abrasives, are added to the porcelain or clay mixture, and therefore the color is dispersed throughout the tile. Ceramic mosaic tiles are fired in kilns with temperatures reaching 2150°F. Ceramic mosaic tile is impervious, stain proof, dentproof, and frost proof. Because of a mosaic tile's small size, the individual tiles are mounted on a sheet to simplify setting. Back-mounted material may be perforated paper or a fiber-mesh. Face-mounted tiles have paper with a water-soluble adhesive applied to the face of the tile, and this paper is removed before grouting.

A paver tile has the same composition and physical properties as a mosaic tile, but it is thicker and has a facial area of more than 6 square inches.

Installation

The *Handbook for Ceramic Tile Installation* is published by the Tile Council of America, Inc., each year. Table 4–3 is from that publication. The designer can choose the correct tile installation for every type of floor use and specify a *Handbook* method number, grout, and setting method. The *Handbook* is also a guide in developing job specifications. As can be seen from Table 4–3, ceramic tile for floor use may be installed by both thick- and thin-set methods.

When ordering any tile, 2 percent extra of each color and size should be added for the owner's use. This will allow immediate replacement of damaged tiles, and the color will match exactly.

OTHER TYPES OF TILE

Conductive tile is made from a special body composition by adding carbon black or by methods resulting in specific properties of electrical conductivity while retaining other normal physical properties of a tile. Conductive tiles are used in hospital operating rooms, certain laboratories, or wherever the presence of oxygen and sparks from static electricity could cause an explosion. Conductive tiles should be installed using a conductive dry-set mortar with an epoxy grout.

Pregrouted tiles usually come in sheets of up to 2.14 square feet that have already been grouted with an elastomeric material such as silicone, urethane, or polyvinyl chloride (**PVC**) rubber, each of which is engineered for its intended use. The perimeter of these factory-pregrouted sheets may include all or part of the grout between sheets, or no grout. Field-applied perimeter grouting should be of the same elastomeric materials used in the factory-pregrouted sheets or as recommended by the manufacturer. Pregrouted tiles save on labor costs because the only grouting necessary is between the sheets, rather than between individual tiles.

Slip-resistant tiles contain abrasive particles that are part of the tile. Other methods of slip resistance may be achieved by grooves or patterns on the face of the tile.

Some tiles are self-spacing because they are molded with **lugs.** Other means of spacing are achieved by using plastic spacers to ensure alignment of tiles and an even grout area.

QUARRY TILE

A quarry tile is a strong, hard-body tile made from carefully graded shale and fine clays, with the color throughout the body. Depending on the geographic area where the clays are mined, the colors will vary from warm brown-red to warm beige. The face of a quarry tile may be solid colored, variegated with light and dark within the same tile, or flashed, in which the edges of the tile are a darker color than the center. A quarry tile is extruded in a 1/2-inch-thick ribbon and then cut to size. The qualities of the clays and temperatures at which they are fired (up to 2000°F) provide a variety of finished products. Quarry

TABLE 4-3
Floor Tiling Installation Guide

Performance-Level Requirement Guide and Selection Table
Based on results from ASTM Test Method C-627 "Standard Method for Evaluating Ceramic Floor Tile Installation Systems."

SERVICE REQUIREMENTS Find required performance level and choose installation method that meets or exceeds it.	FLOOR TYPE—Numbers Refer to Handbook Method Numbers			
	CONCRETE	PAGE	WOOD	PAGE
EXTRA HEAVY: Extra heavy and high impact use in food plants, dairies, breweries and kitchens. Requires quarry tile or packing house tile. (Passes ASTM C627 cycles 1 thru 14.)	F101, F102 F111, F112, F113 F114, F115 F121[b] F131, F132, F133 F134	12 13 14 15 16 17		
HEAVY: Shopping malls, stores, commercial kitchens, work areas, laboratories, auto showrooms and service areas, shipping/receiving and exterior decks. Heavy tile except where noted. (Passes ASTM C627 cycles 1 thru 12.)	F103[b] F111 (ceramic mosaic) F112 (ceramic mosaic) F113 (ceramic mosaic) F121[b] (ceramic mosaic) F125 RF918[c]	12 13 13 13 15 15 34	RF913, RF915[c] F143[a]	34 18
MODERATE: Normal commercial and light institutional use in public space of restaurants and hospitals. Ceramic mosaic or heavier tile. (Passes ASTM C627 cycles 1 thru 10.)	F112 (cured bed) F115 F122[d] (quarry tile) RF914, RF916[c]	13 14 15 34		
LIGHT: Light commercial use in office space, reception areas, kitchens, bathrooms. Ceramic mosaic or heavier tile. (Passes ASTM C627 cycles 1 thru 6.)	F122[d] RF912, RF917[c]	15 34	F121[b] F141 F143[a], F144 RF911	15 17 18 34
RESIDENTIAL: Kitchens, bathrooms, foyers. Ceramic mosaic or heavier tile. (Passes ASTM C627 cycles 1 thru 3.)	F116 (ceramic mosaic or TR711[e] glazed floor tile)	14 30	F142	17

Notes:
　　Consideration must also be given to (1) wear properties of surface of tile selected, (2) fire resistance properties of installation and backing, (3) slip-resistance.
　　Tile used in installation tests listed in Selection Table were unglazed ceramic mosaic and 1/2" thick quarry tile unless otherwise noted. Unglazed Standard Grade tile will give satisfactory wear, or abrasion resistance in installations listed. Glazed tile or soft body decorative unglazed tile should have the manufacturer's approval for intended use. Color, pattern, surface texture and glaze hardness must be considered in determining tile acceptability on a particular floor.
　　Selection Table Notes:
　　Tests to determine Performance Levels utilized representative products meeting recognized industry standards:
　　　　a. ANSI A118.3 epoxy mortar and grout.
　　　　b. Rating extrapolated from other test data.
　　　　c. Data in Selection Table based on tests conducted by Tile Council of America, except data for F144 and RF900 Methods, which are based on test results from an independent laboratory through Ceramic Tile Institute.
　　　　d. ANSI A118.1 latex portland cement mortar and grout.
　　　　e. Tile bonded to existing resilient flooring with epoxy adhesive.

Source: 1994 Handbook for Ceramic Tile Installation. Copyright © Tile Council of America, Inc. Reprinted with permission.

tiles are generally considered stain resistant but not stain proof.

The rugged, unglazed surface of quarry tiles develops an attractive patina with wear. An abrasive grit surface is available for installations in which slip resistance is important. Most quarry tiles are manufactured unglazed to retain the natural quality of the tile, but some quarry tile is available glazed.

Installation. Quarry tiles may be installed by either thick- or thin-set methods. The grout is either a sanded portland cement mix or an epoxy grout with a silica filler. It is the responsibility of the tile installer to remove all excess grout as part of the contract.

Maintenance. Ceramic or quarry tiles may be cleaned with a damp mop if the soil is light, or with water and a detergent if the soil is heavier. Tile and grout are two different materials, with grout being the more porous. Any soil that is likely to stain the grout should be removed as soon as possible.

MEXICAN OR SALTILLO TILE

In Mexican or saltillo tile, clay, taken directly from the ground, is shaped by hand into forms. Saltillo tile differs from ceramic and quarry tile in that the proportion of ingredients in the clay is not measured. The clay form is allowed to dry in the sun until it is firm enough to be transported to the kiln. Because Mexican tile is a product of families working together, it is common to find a child's handprint or a dog or cat paw imprinted in the surface of the tile. Leaf prints may also be noticed, in which a leaf drifted down when the tile was drying. These slight imperfections are part of the charm of using saltillo tile. Mexican tile is often named for the town in which it is made (thus the name *Saltillo,* the capital of Coahuila, Mexico). Today, Mexican factories are producing more consistent quality tiles.

Because of the uneven thickness of Mexican tile, it should be installed using the thick-set method. If it is being used in a greenhouse or similar area, where drainage is possible, Mexican tile may be laid in a bed of sand, which will adapt to any unevenness of the tile. All cracks or joints are then filled with sand.

Saltillo tile is extremely porous—the most porous of all tile—because of its natural qualities. If the tile is not sealed in the factory (and most are not), a "grout release" *must* be sponged, sprayed, or rolled on. Another method of preventing the grout from staining

the tile is to use a sealer before grouting. It is recommended that one of the many new sealer/finish products, which allow the combination of linseed oil and wax into one process application, be used. Additional coats can be applied to provide a matte or a gloss finish. The more coats applied, the higher the gloss will appear. The benefits are cost, labor, and an environmentally friendly finish. Plaza® from Johnson Wax is such a product.

Maintenance. A Mexican tile floor should be kept free of dust and dirt by sweeping or vacuuming and, when the floor shows signs of wear, applying another coat of wax or sealer/finish and buff. Traffic areas may need to be touched up frequently with wax or sealer.

GLASS BLOCK

The glass block for floors may be DELPHI® Paver Units, 6 inches square of solid glass, 1 inch thick, with a prismatic pattern and raised nonskid surface, and available in a sandblasted finish. VISTABRIK® units are 8 inches square and either 3 inches or 1 1/2 inches thick. The latter units provide excellent light transmission and good visibility, with high-impact strength. These blocks may also be used as covers for light fixtures recessed in floors. Glass block is also used where special lighting effects are required.

Maintenance. Simple cleaning with clean water and a sponge or mop should suffice. Any oily deposits should be removed by using soap and water and then rinsing with clean water.

CONCRETE

Concrete is a mixture of two parts: **aggregates** and paste. The paste, comprising portland cement and water, binds the aggregates (sand and gravel or crushed stone) into a rocklike mass as the paste hardens because of the chemical reaction of the cement and water. According to the Portland Cement Association,

aggregates are generally divided into two groups: fine and coarse. . . . Since aggregates make up about 60 percent to 75 percent of the concrete, their selection is important. Aggregates should consist of particles with adequate strength and resistance to exposure conditions. They should not contain materials that will cause deterioration of the concrete. . . . In properly made concrete, each particle of aggregate is completely coated with paste (portland cement and water), and all the space between aggregate particles is completely filled with paste.[12]

A good rule of thumb is as follows: the denser, the better.

The following was condensed from information supplied by R. Godfrey Consulting, Forensic Floor Covering Specialists: Irrespective of what may be claimed or in print, *all* concrete will allow the passage of water vapor. Concrete will always absorb and evaporate moisture until it is restricted. The source may be one or more of the following: subterranean moisture, lateral moisture absorbed through the edges of the slab, internal moisture from a leaking pipe, and topical moisture caused by excessive application of adhesive/wet installation. Moisture indicators include color (darker is generally wetter), smell, effervescence (alkali and salts from concrete), and touch (this is the worst way). Moisture will discolor most flooring materials.

The following should be used as a guide for the basic evaluation of vapor emissions and associated problems:

1. *All* concrete is permeable.
2. One volume unit of water in a liquid form is capable of producing as much as 1700 volume units of water in a vapor form.
3. Vapor emissions *can only be measured,* not calculated.
4. Water, whether it is in a liquid or vapor form, will *always* seek the path of least resistance.
5. Irrigation or landscaping surrounding irrigation and/or landscaping can contribute to vapor emission conditions.

A concrete floor is low in cost as compared with other materials and is very durable. Maintenance for interiors is difficult, however, unless the surface has been treated with a floor sealer specially manufactured to produce a dust-free floor. Color may be added when the concrete is mixed, or it may be dusted on the surface during the finishing operation. A concrete floor looks less like an unfinished floor or subfloor if it is stamped and/or colored into squares.

In addition, cracking is more likely to occur in the stamped grooves and be less visible. Several pattern products are available to mark the surface of the **plastic** concrete so it imitates the shapes and patterns of brick or natural stone.

Dark-colored concrete floors are used in passive solar homes because the large mass absorbs the rays of the sun during the day and radiates the heat back at night.

Concrete floors may be painted with an epoxy, polyurethane, or acrylic paint. Generally, epoxy paints are the best for adhesion.

Maintenance. Because cured concrete can sometimes absorb harmful chemicals, prewetting must be done before using any cleaning solution. Synthetic detergent should be used because soap will react with the lime and cause a scum.

TERRAZZO

Terrazzo was developed by the Venetians in the 16th century and is still used. Terrazzo as we know it today, however, was not produced until after the development of portland cement in the 18th century. Terrazzo is a composite material, poured in place or precast, that consists of marble chips and is **seeded** or unseeded with a binder that is cementitious, noncementitious (epoxy, polyester, or resin), or a combination of both. Terrazzo may be one color (e.g., white or cream) or may be a mixture of colors. The appearance will also change with the color and type of **matrix** used.

The National Terrazzo and Mosaic Association (NTMA) explains that the chips are mixed with the matrix in a 2:1 ratio aggregate to mix before pouring. After the terrazzo topping is poured in place (in a monolithic installation), additional chips are sprinkled or seeded and troweled into the terrazzo topping to achieve the proper consistency.

Terrazzo that is poured into forms should be cured for at least three days and then ground on a water-coated surface. First a coarse grit is used and then successively finer grits.

The NTMA gives the following sizes for aggregates:

Standard—1/4- to 3/8-inch chips

Venetian—1/4- to 1 1/8-inch chips

Palladian—3/8-inch-thick **spalls** up to 5 inches in breadth.

According to the NTMA,

Three types of binders are used to anchor marble chips or other aggregate in a terrazzo floor. One is a portland cement product: the second is a poly-acrylic modified portland cement that includes an acrylic additive. The third is an epoxy or polyester system, often referred to as a resinous **thin-set** system. Although each system has the role of anchoring the aggregate into the topping, the treatment of each does vary.

In portland cement systems, the terrazzo surface has a minimum 70% density marble chip surface exposure. The marble chips have a low porosity of absorption; thus, the portion of this floor system that needs protection is the portland cement binder that has 30% or less surface exposure. The NTMA requires a penetrating type sealer applied to the surface immediately following the final polishing. This helps inhibit the penetration of spilled materials upon initial contact with the terrazzo floor.[13]

This penetrating liquid does not produce a high-gloss sheen. Once the building is occupied, the floor must be stripped and resealed, and, if needed, finish coats may be applied to produce a higher sheen.

With resinous-type terrazzo systems (epoxy and polyester), the matrix is nonporous; therefore, no penetrating-type sealer is used.

Divider strips of brass, zinc, or plastic are attached to the subfloor and are used for several purposes: as expansion joints to take care of any minor movement; as dividers when different colors are poured in adjacent areas; and as enhancements of a design motif, logo, or trademark.

Because of the labor involved in a monolithic installation, terrazzo tiles consisting of portland cement with an aggregate of marble chips may be used. Wausau Tile is the only domestic manufacturer of cementitious terrazzo tile. The tile is available as 11 15/16 inches square by 3/4 inch thick, in both square and chamfered edges. With the tile set method, **chamfered** edge tiles are set with 1/16" to 3/16" joints, then grouted. With the new tight-joint method, square edge tiles are set with a 1/16" minus joint, then grouted flush and ground and polished on the job for a monolithic look. The size of the chips may be large or small, or a mixture of sizes. The finish may be polished or slip resistant (Figure 4–16).

Figure 4–16
Tiles of two different colors make up the floor of this reception area. The column bases in the background are also from Wausau Tile. (Photo courtesy of Wausau Tile.)

Installation. When cementitious terrazzo tiles are used, they may be installed using the thin-set method or other cement mortar methods. The installation of poured-in-place (monolithic) terrazzo was described previously.

Maintenance. Because there are three types of binders used to anchor marble chips or other aggregate in the terrazzo floor, it is necessary to know which type has been used in order to decide the correct maintenance procedure. The National Terrazzo and Mosaic Association specifically warns that soaps and scrubbing powders containing water-soluble inorganic salts or crystallizing salts should never be used in the maintenance of terrazzo. Alkaline solutions will sink into the pores and, as they dry, will expand and break the cells of the marble chips and matrix, causing **spalling.** (This is similar to the spalling problem that occurs with cement floors.) The NTMA has produced an excellent booklet, "The Care of Terrazzo."

After the initial cleaning, the terrazzo floor should be allowed to dry and then sealed with a water-based sealer in the acrylic family especially designed for terrazzo use. The Underwriters Laboratories classification of this sealer should include slip resistance with a coefficient of friction rating of minimum 0.5.

The NTMA recommends the following maintenance plan for terrazzo floors:

1. Sweep daily with yarn-wick brush treated with sweeping compound.
2. Weekly damp mop lightly soiled floors with a neutral cleaner.
3. Scrub heavily soiled floors with a mechanical buffing machine and neutral cleaner. Mop up residue with clean water before it dries. Allow to dry and buff with a dry brush.
4. Semiannually strip all old sealer and any finish coats. Reseal clean floors.

Stain removal for terrazzo is the same as for marble.

EXPOSED AGGREGATE

When an exposed aggregate floor is specified, the type of aggregate used is extremely important because it is visible on the finished floor. River stone gives a smooth rounded texture. Today, the river stone effect may be achieved by tumbling stones in a drum to remove sharp edges.

Installation. While the concrete is still plastic, the selected aggregate is pressed or rolled into the surface. Removal of the cement paste by means of water from a hose when the concrete is partially hardened will expose the aggregate and display the decorative surface. For interior use, most of the aggregate should be approximately the same size and color, but other values within that hue may also be used, with a scattering of white and black stones.

One drawback to the use of exposed aggregate is that, like any other hard-surfaced material, exposed aggregate is not sound absorbent and is hard on the feet during prolonged standing.

A clear polyurethane finish specially formulated for masonry surfaces can be applied. This finish brings out the natural color of the stone, similar to the way a wet stone has more color than a dry one. Coated exposed aggregate seldom seems to become soiled. A vacuum brush used for wood floors will pick up any loose dirt from between the stones.

BRICK

Prehistoric people made brick from dried mud, but they soon discovered that when mixed with straw, the shaped brick could withstand the elements. Kiln-burned brick made by the Babylonians 6000 years ago still exists. Sun-dried brick, or **adobe,** dates from around 5000 B.C. and is still used in some areas of the Southwestern United States, but with some modern-day materials added. Fired bricks and kilns first appeared between 2500 and 2000 B.C. in Mesopotamia and India, but the art was lost around 1700 B.C. and fired brick was not used again until 300 B.C.

The earliest recorded use of brick is in the Bible: The Egyptians made the Israelites work "in mortar and in brick" (Exodus 1:14). There was a limitless supply of clay from the bed of the Nile River. Sun-baked brick was used in the Tower of Babel and in the wall surrounding the city of Babylon.

The Chinese used brick in the 3rd century B.C. for building part of the Great Wall. The Romans used sun-dried bricks until about A.D. 14, when they started using bricks burnt in kilns. The Romans took this knowledge of brick making to Europe and Britain, but after they left in A.D. 410, the art died out and was not restored until the 11th and 13th centuries.

The first brick buildings in the United States were built in Jamestown, Virginia, by British settlers, and on Manhattan Island by the Dutch. Bricks used in Virginia were probably made locally because there are records of brick being exported in 1621. Of course, the Aztecs of Mexico and Central America also used adobe bricks for building purposes.

Until about the mid-1850s, brick was molded by hand, but from then on it was made using mechanical means. Bricks are made by mixing clays and shales with water and are formed, while plastic, into rectangular shapes with either solid or hollow cores.

During the process of heating the bricks, the clay loses its water content and becomes rigid, but it is not chemically changed. During the higher temperatures used in burning, the brick undergoes a molecular change: The clays and shales fuse, closing all pores, and the brick becomes vitrified or impervious.

The color of brick depends on three factors: chemical composition of the clay, method of firing control, and temperature of the kiln. A red color comes from the oxidation of iron to form iron oxide. Lighter colors (the salmon colors) are the result of underburning. The higher the temperature and the longer the heat is applied, the harder the brick will be. Harder bricks have lower absorption potential and higher compressive strength than softer ones. Generally, the denser the brick and the lower the absorption, the easier it is to clean and maintain. Flooring brick, used in such places as factories, where floors receive heavy use, is hard and dense.

Installation.   For areas in which spilled liquids are likely, such as in a kitchen or bathroom, a mortared installation is appropriate. When installing over a wood frame floor, a thin brick paver may be selected to reduce the additional dead weight of the floor assembly. Brick pavers weigh approximately 10 pounds per square foot (psf) per inch of thickness.

Installation methods are shown in Figure 4–17. Pavers are laid in a conventional manner in a 1/2-inch wet mortar bed with mortar joints. When the joints are thumbprint hard, they are **tooled,** compacting the mortar into a tight, water-resistant joint. Where moisture is not a problem, a mortarless method may be used.

Maintenance.   Brick may be vacuumed, swept, damp mopped, or spray buffed.

Linoleum

Linoleum was first patented in 1860 in Great Britain and was the only resilient flooring material available for many years. Modern technology has now produced vinyl sheet flooring, and linoleum has not been manufactured in the United States since 1974. Many people, however, persist in calling sheet vinyls "linoleum." Although the components of the two products are different, the results do appear similar.

Forbo imports linoleum, Marmoleum®, from Europe (Scotland and Holland). For the environmentally conscious user, linoleum is composed of natural materials obtained from sustainable farm crops cultivated in a controlled manner. The manufacture of linoleum requires less energy than the manufacture of most popular floor coverings. Beneficial bactericidal properties halt the spreading of many microorganisms, and the natural static resistance provides a safe environment for data processing facilities. There are no harmful VOC emissions, and natural antistatic properties repel dust and dirt. Because linoleum is made from natural materials, it is biodegradable. Forbo recycles 100 percent of its postproduction waste.

Installation.   One hundred percent solvent-free adhesive is used to install linoleum because solvents will dissolve or soften material.

Maintenance.   Forbo Industries recommends the following maintenance procedures: For initial cleanup and daily maintenance, remove all surface soil, debris, sand, and grit by sweeping or dust mopping. Damp mop with a neutral pH detergent, such as Butcher Sundance, TASKI R-50, Johnson Stride, or an equivalent. For a matte-satin shine, apply one or two thin coats of floor finish such as TASKI Ombra or equivalent, or for a high gloss shine apply two or three thin coats of floor finish such as Butcher Mainstay, TASKI Brilliant, Johnson Vectra, or an equivalent. These finishes are applied with a clean-finish mop or finish applicator, with 30 minutes dry time between each coat. For further maintenance instructions, see *Linoleum Maintenance* from Forbo Industries.

Asphalt Tile

Dark-colored asphalt flooring was developed in the United States in the 1920s. Like linoleum, however, asphalt tile is a flooring material that has been gradually phased out because of advanced technology. Asphalt tile was very inexpensive, but it was not resistant to stains and could be softened by mineral oils or animal fats. The individual tiles were brittle and had

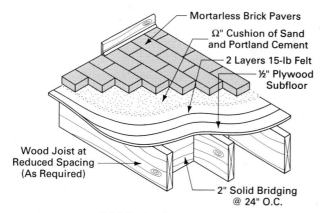

Mortarless Brick Pavers

Ω" Cushion of Sand and Portland Cement

2 Layers 15-lb Felt

½" Plywood Subfloor

Wood Joist at Reduced Spacing (As Required)

2" Solid Bridging @ 24" O.C.

Brick Paving Over Wood Joists

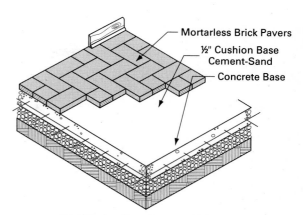

Mortarless Brick Pavers

½" Cushion Base Cement-Sand

Concrete Base

Brick Paving Over Concrete Slab

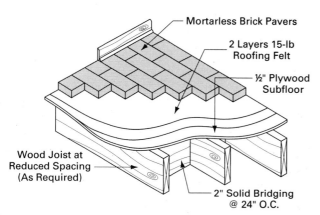

Mortarless Brick Pavers

2 Layers 15-lb Roofing Felt

½" Plywood Subfloor

Wood Joist at Reduced Spacing (As Required)

2" Solid Bridging @ 24" O.C.

Brick Paving Over Wood Joists

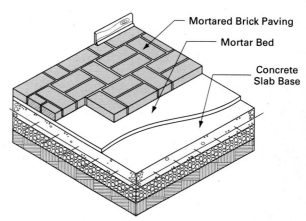

Mortared Brick Paving

Mortar Bed

Concrete Slab Base

Brick Paving Over Concrete Slab

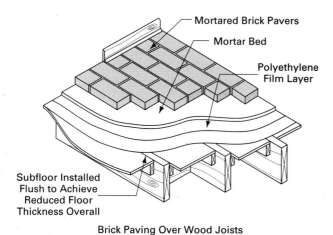

Mortared Brick Pavers

Mortar Bed

Polyethylene Film Layer

Subfloor Installed Flush to Achieve Reduced Floor Thickness Overall

Brick Paving Over Wood Joists

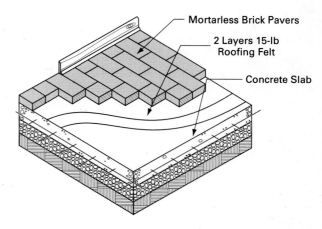

Mortarless Brick Pavers

2 Layers 15-lb Roofing Felt

Concrete Slab

Brick Paving Over Concrete Slab

Figure 4–17
Methods of installing brick. (Note: O.C. means "on center.")

poor recovery from indentation. Asphalt tile may still be found in some older homes.

Vinyl Composition

Vinyl composition tile (VCT) is a commonly used floor tile for less expensive installations. VCT is composed of binder (organic), fillers (inorganic), and pigments. The organic binder portion contains vinyl resins, plasticizer, additives, and, in the case of Mannington, 5 percent or greater recycled vinyl content (Figure 4–18). Color and pattern are commonly distributed evenly throughout the thickness of the tile. The mixture is formed into thin sheets under heat and pressure and is then cut into 12″ × 12″ tiles with a **gauge** of 3/32 inch or 1/8 inch. Inspirations™ and Essentials™ are vinyl composition tiles from Mannington Commercial (see Chapter 1).

Figure 4–18
Mannington Commercial vinyl composition tile is shown in a hallway of the Kingston Hospital/Family Maternity Center, Kingston, New York. (Photo courtesy of Mannington Commercial.)

Patterns in VCT may include a simulated brick paver, ceramic tile, and wood parquet. Accent strips are typically solid colors. (See Color Plate 9.)

Vinyl composition tiles were once made with asbestos. In recent years, however, asbestos has been proven to have adverse health effects, so VCTs are no longer made with asbestos fibers. The Occupational Safety and Health Administration has provided rigid rules for safely removing old vinyl asbestos floors.

The thickness, or gauge, as it is sometimes called, of VCTs is 3/32 inch or 1/8 inch. For commercial and better residential installations, the 1/8-inch gauge should be used.

The advantages of vinyl composition tile are that it (1) is inexpensive, (2) is easy to install and maintain, (3) may be installed on any grade, (4) resists acids and alkalis, and (5) withstands strong cleaning compounds. The disadvantages are that it (1) has low impact resistance, (2) has poor noise absorption, and (3) is semiporous as compared with solid vinyls and solid rubber.

Installation. Vinyl composition, vinyl, and some other tiles are all installed using the thin-set method. The most important step in this installation procedure is to be sure the subfloor is smooth and level. With thinner tile, any discrepancies in the subfloor will be visible on the surface of the tile. In a residential installation of thinner tile, a newly installed floor developed a wavy and bumpy appearance after only several weeks, because the wood subfloor had not been sanded.

Materials and the installation site should be at a minimum temperature of 65°F for 48 hours before, during, and after installation. The subfloor is troweled with the manufacturer's suggested adhesive and, as with the installation of parquet floors, the walls should not be used as a starting point.

Maintenance. Mannington Commercial suggests the following maintenance procedures for a newly installed floor, which are applicable to all VCT tile: Do not wash or scrub the floor for at least four to five days after installation to allow the floor tiles to bond to the underlayment/subfloor. Keep heavy furniture and equipment off the floor for at least 48 hours to allow the adhesive to set. Sweep or vacuum thoroughly, and remove any residual adhesive with a clean white cloth dampened with mineral spirits. Apply a minimum of two coats of a high-quality crosslinked acrylic floor polish to protect the floor temporarily until regular maintenance procedures can begin.

Floors should be maintained by using a good-quality nonalkaline floor cleaner and a floor machine. Thoroughly rinse the floor (but avoid flooding the floor) and allow the floor to dry completely. Apply three to five coats of the same polish mentioned previously. Wait at least 30 minutes between applications to allow for complete drying.

For regular maintenance, clean the floor frequently with a treated (nonoily) dust mop or clean, soft push broom. Damp mop the floor, as required, using a dilute, neutral-detergent solution. Light scrubbing with an automatic floor machine may be required in heavily soiled areas. Rinse the floor with clean water and allow to dry completely. After damp mopping or light scrubbing, spray buffing or high-speed burnishing may be performed to restore gloss. There are many liquid waxes on the market that may be used for commercial use. For commercial installations, Hillyard Chemical Company, for example, makes cleaners and waxes that may or may not require buffing. This company specializes in floor treatments and supplies finishing and maintenance information for every type of flooring discussed in this book. Many janitorial supply companies also provide suitable maintenance cleaners and wax for commercial installations.

Many of the same maintenance procedures may apply for commercial installations of other types of vinyl floors. See the manufacturer's specifications.

SOLID VINYL

Solid vinyl tile is really not all vinyl. It has a lower percentage of fillers and a higher percentage of PVC than vinyl composition tiles. It usually consists of a fiberglass-reinforced backing on which the pattern is printed. The final coat may be either clear vinyl or vinyl with urethane. The latter is tougher and wears longer.

Maintenance. Maintenance is the same as for vinyl composition tile.

PURE VINYL TILE

Pure vinyl tiles are homogeneous or, in other words, pure vinyl with few, if any, fillers, with the color throughout the tile. Vinyl tiles have a higher resistance to abrasive wear than VCT. They are available in faux-stone finishes, marble, travertine, brick, and slate. Pure vinyl tiles are also used as feature strips or for borders. Borders should be of approximately the same width at all walls.

A conductive tile is required in environments where static electricity poses a danger to sensitive electronic devices, and in areas where flammable gases or explosives may be present. If high voltages are used in the working environment, then a static dissipative vinyl tile should be used.

Vinyl wall base effectively trims off a floor installation and helps hide minor wall and floor irregularities. Its distinctive profile consists of a reclining curvature at the top and a descending thintoe line that conforms snugly with the wall and floor. Some vinyl cove bases can be hand formed to make the corners, whereas others come with both inside and outside corners preformed. The cove wall base comes either in 20-foot rolls or 48-inch strips in 2 1/4 inch or 4 inch heights.

Installation. Pure vinyl tiles are installed with a specified adhesive and are laid in a pyramid shape, as seen in Figure 4–9.

Maintenance. A new vinyl tile floor should not be washed, only damp mopped for a week to allow the adhesive to set. Spots of adhesive can be removed with a clean white cloth dampened with paste wax or lighter fluid. Periodically sweeping with a soft broom or vacuum will prevent the build-up of dust and dirt. Spills should be cleaned immediately. Damp mopping with a mild detergent is sufficient for slightly soiled floors, or scrubbing with a brush or machine for heavy soil. Soap-based cleaners should not be used because they can leave a dulling film. The floor should be rinsed with clean water after cleaning. The floor should never be flooded, and excess dirty water should be removed with a mop or wet vacuum. No-wax floors can be damaged by intense heat, lighted cigarettes, and rubber or foam-backed mats or rugs. If stubborn stains persist, they should be rubbed with alcohol or lighter fluid.

RUBBER

Rubber flooring is now made of 100 percent synthetic rubber. Although available with a smooth surface, multilevel rubber flooring (raised discs or pastilles, solid or duo-colored squares, or even rhythmic curves) has become increasingly popular where excessive dirt or excessive moisture is likely to be tracked inside. Raised portions have beveled edges, causing the dirt to drop down below the wear surface, which reduces abrasion on the wear surface. The same thing happens with water; most of it flows below the wear surface. Although the original purpose of this type of rubber tile was to reduce wear from moisture or dirt, rubber floors are now used to meet the minimum requirements of the Americans with Disabilities Act (ADA). Rubber flooring is considered an ideal product for public areas because it offers excellent traction, even when wet.

Rubber tiles are available in 9-, 12-, 20-, and 39-inch squares, with a thickness of 3/32, 1/8, or 3/16 inch. The tiles are usually marble or travertine patterned and are laid at right angles to each other. They may be laid below grade and are extremely sound absorbent. Stair treads are being made of rubber to comply with the California building code, which calls for a clearly contrasting color on the stair tread in public buildings.

Johnsonite® produces Tactile Warning Surface to address accessibility requirements where detectable warnings on walking surfaces are specified. Manufactured in strips, it is designed to extend across the full width of the hazardous area for a continuous depth of 3 feet. This product has an undulated surface to alert individuals to potentially dangerous areas, such as the top of open stairwells, in front of doors leading to loading platforms, and on theatrical stages and other areas where there are drop offs (Figure 4–19). Tactile Warning Surface meets all relevant ANSI requirements. Several other manufacturers have similar warning surfaces for the visually impaired.

Johnsonite also has a new-generation rubber flooring system, ComfortTech™, featuring an exclusive fused cushion core that provides enhanced walking comfort, sound absorption, and thermal insulation

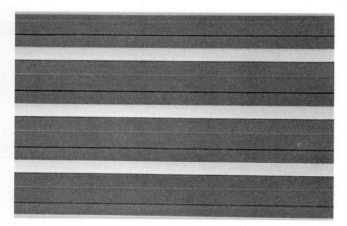

Figure 4–19
Johnsonite's Tactile Warning Surface was developed to address accessibility requirements where detectable warnings on walking surfaces are specified to meet ANSI A117.1-1986, section 4.27. (Photo courtesy of Johnsonite.)

with a slip-resistant surface that meets ADA recommendations. ComfortTech® is available in a raised profile checker pattern and a multicolor Optix™ design.

The explosion at the World Trade Center in New York accelerated Johnsonite's process of developing a supplemental evacuation solution. Johnsonite's Safe-T-First™ System integrates color with Permalight® self-illuminating technology in vinyl or rubber flooring products and accessories for low-location escape routing while enhancing present building safety systems. Johnsonite has received many awards for this extensive product offering (Figure 4–20). The Safe-T-First System has won many design awards.

Maintenance. Proper maintenance on a regular basis is essential to the appearance and wear life of rubber tiles. The tile should be swept and mopped daily with nonsudsing ammonia and hot water. Because buffing may dull the surface of newly installed tile, it should not be buffed for the first 90 days after installation.

New rubber flooring should be thoroughly machine stripped and scrubbed with a black stripping pad and stripper. The floor should be thoroughly cleaned with a good grade of mild detergent cleaner. The stripper or detergent solution should be vacuumed, mopped, or squeezed from the floor and the floor rinsed with a solution of 10 percent Clorox® in warm water. When the floor is dry, an ultra-high-speed buffer can be used. New floors will require more frequent buffing until a high sheen is acquired. For further maintenance, floors should be dry dusted or mopped (but mops treated with mineral oil or other petroleum products should not be used). Periodically, the cleaning procedure should be repeated and rebuffing done as needed.

SHEET VINYL

Sheet vinyl manufacturers have greatly improved not only the quality but also the designs of their products. Precise information regarding construction is a trade secret, but the following information is generic to the industry.

Sheet vinyl comes in widths of 6 feet, 6 feet 6 inches, 9 feet, and 12 feet and is manufactured by two methods—inlaid or rotogravure. Most inlaid sheet vinyls are made of thousands of tiny vinyl granules built up layer by layer, and then fused with heat and pressure. The result is a resilient, hefty flooring with a noticeable depth of color and a crafted look. Some

Figure 4–20
Johnsonite Permalight Safe-T-First is visible in light and sudden darkness, as can be seen in these two photographs. (Photos courtesy of Johnsonite.)

sheet vinyls have extra layers of foam cushioning to provide comfort underfoot and muffle footsteps and other noises. Color chips are distributed throughout the depth of the wear surface. A fibrous backing will produce a light, flexible flooring that virtually eliminates tearing and creasing and the telegraphing of irregularities from the old flooring to the new.

Rotovinyls, also called rotogravure vinyls, are made by a rotogravure process that combines photography and printing. Almost anything that can be photographed can be reproduced on a rotovinyl floor. The printed layer is protected by a topping (called the wear layer) of vinyl resin (PVC) either alone or in combination with urethane. Vinyl resin composition often produces a gloss surface, whereas urethane creates a high-sheen result. A mechanical buffer with a lamb's wool pad will bring back the satin gloss of the vinyl resin composition wear layers. Urethane wearlayer flooring should not be

buffed. All rotovinyls are made with an inner core of foamed or expanded vinyl, which means they are cushioned to some extent. At the lower end of the price scale, cushioning may be thin. Most sheet vinyls are flexible enough to be coved up the **toe space** to form their own base (check manufacturers' specifications).

The wearlayer is the final, protective topcoat on sheet vinyl or vinyl tile flooring products. Usually consisting of clear vinyl or urethane, wearlayers enable the flooring to resist scuffs, stains, and other evidence of wear. The thicker the wearlayer, the better the protection against the effects of foot traffic, dirt, and overall daily use. Generally, for residential rotogravure products, those with the thickest wearlayers often have long-term warranties. There is a definite distinction, however, between residential and commercial flooring. Product characteristics, maintenance, and warranties vary considerably.

For residential installations, high-gloss finishes are still available, but the trend seems to be patterns that copy natural materials, such as stone, wood, marble, and slate. The warranties, ranging from five to eleven years and more, cover manufacturing defects and wear.

Tarkett Inc. has twelve-foot-wide flooring, featuring a wearlayer with silicone, for seamless installation in most residential rooms. All manufacturers make a polish that will renew the shine. Some even recommend wax (again, follow the manufacturer's directions).

Mannington Commercial BioSpec™ homogeneous sheet vinyl was developed specifically for health care and clean room environments, where added protection against germs and moisture penetration is important. BioSpec features superior stain and chemical resistance and a rugged 80-mil wearlayer for durability and resistance against indentations and rolling load damage. Six of the patterns feature low-contrast colors, which makes it easier to see materials dropped on the floor and facilitates faster cleanup, especially in operating rooms. These six colors were developed with the input of health care designers and hospital staff, who requested warm, neutral colors to help reduce eye fatigue during long surgical procedures. BioSpec is also ideally suited for heavy traffic areas like classrooms and auditoriums, and it meets the ADA specification for static coefficient of friction.

Medintech® homogeneous, from Armstrong, is designed for health care spaces and those installations requiring superior stain resistance and durability. For wet areas, especially around freezers and refrigerator cases, Armstrong manufactures Step Master®, a slip-resistant floor covering.

Installation. Seaming methods vary from manufacturer to manufacturer, depending on the product and its application. Installation may be a perimeter-bond system stretched over the floor and secured only at the edges. The other—a full-adhered system—is set in a full bed of mastic. The correct trowel notch is important with resilient floors. The latter type should be rolled with a weighted roller to eliminate air pockets and form a good bond between the backing and the adhesive.

Installing new flooring over an existing floor is preferable to removal, particularly if it is known that the existing floor contains asbestos. As noted in Chapter 1 and previously in the vinyl asbestos section of this chapter, removal of old floor coverings or adhesives that might contain asbestos requires, in some states, a trained asbestos abatement contractor, whether or not the asbestos is friable.

The old floor must be fully adhered. A perimeter-bonded system must not be covered. When covering a textured or embossed surface, a manufacturer-recommended embossing leveler must be used. Asphalt tiles or asphalt adhesive must not be covered, because asphalt eats through vinyl.

Furniture should be equipped with the proper load-bearing devices; otherwise, indentations will mar the vinyl surface. Static load limitations vary for each product. Refer to each manufacturer's information (Figure 4–21).

Heavy refrigerators and kitchen or office equipment must not be dragged across the floor, because this will damage and tear the surface. These items should be "walked" across the floor on a piece of wood or on Masonite® runways. Runways must be used even if using an appliance dolly or if the heavy objects are equipped with wheels or rollers.

Discoloration has been a problem with some light-colored resilient floors. There are several ways the vinyl flooring may discolor. Bottom-up discoloration may result from any one of the following conditions:

Use of the wrong adhesives can cause discoloration. Follow the manufacturer's recommendations, and use the appropriate adhesives. These are specially formulated for that particular product.

Failure to remove existing adhesives or staining agents may discolor the vinyl surface.

Sometimes gypsum products, when combined with the slightest amount of moisture, can create an environment for fungus growth, causing discoloration. To eliminate this problem, use only portland cement–based patching compounds for *all* underfloor patching needs.

A synthetic polyurethane patch sometimes used for filling voids on the surface of wood panels will also cause discoloration in the shape of the patch. This problem can also be avoided by using an underlayment grade of plywood.

If there are dark pieces of wood or bark in wafer board and oriented strand board (OSB), they will cause staining.

The use of construction adhesives to cement underlayments of subfloors is a major cause of discoloration.

Rubber-backed mats may cause staining, and cocofiber mats may cause scratches.

Maintenance. Maintenance varies by product and manufacturer (no-wax does not mean no maintenance).

TYPE OF LOAD	KENTILE FLOORS INC. RECOMMENDS	KENTILE FLOORS INC. DOES NOT RECOMMEND	TYPE
HEAVY FURNITURE, more or less permanently located, should have composition furniture cups under the legs to prevent them from cutting the floor.	Right 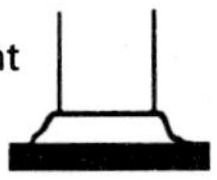 Wide Bearing Surfaces Save Floors	Wrong 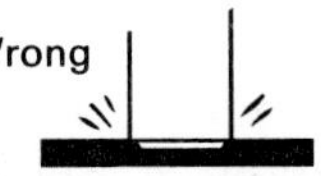 Small Bearing Surfaces Dent Floors	Composition Furniture Cups 
FREQUENTLY MOVED FURNITURE requires casters. Desk chairs are a good example. Casters should be 2" in diameter with soft rubber treads at least ¾" wide and with easy swiveling ball bearing action. For heavier items that must be moved frequently, consult the caster manufacturers as to the suitable size of equipment that should be used.	Right  Rubber Rollers Save Floors	Wrong 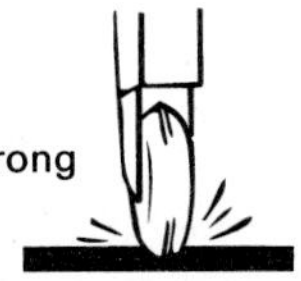 Hard Rollers Mark Floors	Rubber Wheel Casters 
LIGHT FURNITURE should be equipped with glides having a smooth, flat base with rounded edges and a flexible pin to maintain flat contact with the floor. They should be from 1¼" to 1½" dia., depending upon weight of load they must carry. For furniture with slanted legs apply glides parallel to the floor rather than slanted ends of legs.	Right 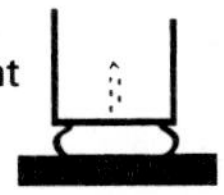 Use Flat Bearing Surfaces	Wrong 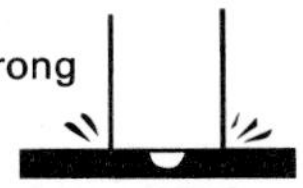 Remove Small Metal Domes	Flat Glides With Flexible Shank 

Figure 4–21
Static load for furniture. (Courtesy of Kentile Floors.)

CORK

Cork comes from the bark of the cork oak tree, which grows primarily in Spain and Portugal. Only the bark is harvested every nine years. The tree is never felled. The habitat remains undisturbed. First used in antiquity, cork today can be found in many products and applications, from a wine bottle stopper to the insulation panels of the NASA space shuttle. Frank Lloyd Wright, in 1937, used cork as a decorative durable flooring material in his renowned Falling Waters house in Pennsylvania, and he was one of the first Americans to do so.

Natural CORK™ has prefinished parquet tile suited for installation over smooth and level under-layment-grade plywood, above-grade and on-grade concrete. For below-grade installations (basements), the Natural Cork Company recommends prefinished Planks Plus™, which are ideal for remodeling because they may be installed over virtually any existing floor that is smooth and level. Humidity should be controlled (between 50 and 70 percent) because cork is a natural material and will react to extremes in humidity, shrinking in low humidity and peaking in high humidity, just like wood.

Unfinished tile and plank must be finished with a hardwood floor protective coating of either water-based or oil-based polyurethane or paste wax. Unfin-ished cork products may be stained a color before the protective coating is applied.

Installation. Because cork is a wood product, the floor tiles should be acclimatized to the installation site for 72 hours before installation. Because of cork's natural qualities, no two tiles are identical in pattern or color. Pieces may vary slightly in color, tone, and grain configuration. It is the installer's or client's responsibility to mix colors and patterns in an acceptable manner. The cork tiles should be "shuffled" to get the desired aesthetic mix. Only those sub-floor materials and adhesives specified by the manufacturer of the cork flooring should be used. Expansion and contraction, resulting from climatic conditions, will occur, so an approximate 1/8- to 1/4-inch space around the perimeter of the room must be allowed for. This space is covered by a base. Natural CORK Planks Plus do not require an underlayment, only a moisture barrier of 6-mil polyethylene film over the substrate.

Natural CORK provided the following information on installation on a concrete substrate: "Check concrete slab for moisture by chipping quarter size sections 1/8" deep in several places and applying two drops of 3% phenophalen in alcohol solution (readily available at drug stores) with a dropper in each section. If solution turns red, too much moisture is present for safe installation of Cork Parquet."[14] A calcium chloride test is also acceptable.

Maintenance. Walk-off mats should be used, provided they do not have a rubber back, which may cause permanent discoloration. Furniture guards should be used. Spills should be picked up immediately; wet spills or water should never be allowed to stand on the cork floor. With factory-prefinished cork parquet tiles and Planks Plus, a high-quality hardwood floor polyurethane cleaner should be used in accordance with the manufacturer's instructions. When the finish begins to show wear, the floor should be cleaned and one of Natural CORK's recommended topcoat finishes should be used.

FORMED-IN-PLACE OR POURED FLOORS

Formed-in-place floors come in cans and are applied at the site in a seamless installation. The basis of the "canned floors" may be urethane, epoxy, polyester, or vinyl, but they are all applied the same way. First, as with all other floor installations, the surface must be clean, dry, and level. Second, a base coat of any of the aforementioned materials is applied to the substrate according to manufacturer's directions. Third, colored plastic chips are sprinkled or sprayed on the base and several coats of the base material are applied for the wearlayer.

Formed-in-place or poured floors seem popular in veterinary offices, where a nonskid and easily cleaned surface is desirable. Such floors can also be bent up a base like sheet vinyl, which eliminates cracks between floor and base. Of course, this type of flooring may be used in any area where cleanliness is paramount.

Maintenance. Maintenance is the same as that for sheet vinyl.

BIBLIOGRAPHY

Berendsen, Anne, *Tiles: A General History.* New York: Viking Press, 1967.

Byrne, Michael, *Setting Tile.* Newton, CT: Taunton Press, 1996.

Oak Flooring Institute, *Hardwood Flooring Finishing/ Refinishing Manual.* Memphis, TN: Oak Flooring Institute, 1986.

Oak Flooring Institute, *Wood Floor Care Guide.* Memphis, TN: Oak Flooring Institute, 1986.

Plumridge, Andrew and Wlm. Meulenkamp, *Brickwork, Architecture and Design.* New York: Harry N. Abrams, 1993.

GLOSSARY

Adobe. Unburnt, sun-dried brick.

Agglomerate. Marble chips and spalls of various sizes, bonded together with a resin.

Aggregate. The solid material in concrete, mortar, or grout.

ANSI. American National Standards Institute.

Base. A board or moulding at the base of a wall that comes in contact with the floor; protects the wall from damage.

Beveled. In wood flooring, the top edge is cut at a 45° angle.

Bisque. Once-fired clay.

Bluestone. A hard sandstone of characteristic blue, gray, and buff colors, quarried in New York and Pennsylvania.

Bow. Longitudinal curvature of lumber.

Bullnose. A convex rounded edge on tile.

Burl. An abnormal growth or protuberance on a tree, resulting in a very patterned area.

Chamfer. Tile with a slight beveled edge.

Cove. A concave rounded edge on tile.

Crook. The warp of a board edge from the straight line drawn between the two ends.

Cup. Deviation of the face of a board from a plane.

Cure. Maintaining the humidity and temperature of freshly poured concrete for a period of time to keep water present so the concrete hydrates or hardens properly.

Dowel. Round wooden rod to join two pieces of wood.

Elgin Marbles. (Pronounced with a hard "g".) Lord Elgin, the British Ambassador to Turkey from 1799–1802, persuaded the Turkish government in Athens to allow him to remove the frieze of the Parthenon to the British Museum in London to prevent further damage.

Figure. The pattern of wood fibers.

Floorcloth. Painted canvas used in the early 1800s.

Gauge. Thickness of tile.

Grain. Arrangement of the fibers of the wood.

Grout. Material used to fill in the spaces between tiles.

Impervious. Less than 0.5 percent absorption rate.

Kiln. An oven for controlled drying of lumber or firing of tile.

Laminate floor. Same construction as a decorative laminate, only specially made for flooring.

Laminated or engineered wood. Bonding of two or more layers of material.

Lugs. Projections attached to the edges of ceramic tiles to provide equal spacing of the tiles.

Marquetry. Veneered inlaid material in wood flooring that has been fitted in various patterns and glued to a common background.

Mastic. An adhesive compound.

Matrix. The mortar part of the mix.

Medullary rays. Ribbons of tissue extending from the pitch to the bark of a tree, particularly noticeable in oak.

Metal spline. Thin metal wire holding strips of parquet together.

Metamorphic. Changes occurring in appearance and structure of rock caused by heat and/or pressure.

Monolithic. Grout and mortar base become one mass.

Mortar. A plastic mixture of cementitious materials, with water and fine aggregates.

Mosaic. A small size tile, ceramic or marble, usually 1 inch or 2 inches square, used to form patterns.

120-grit. A medium-fine grade of sandpaper.

Parquetry. Inlaid solid wood flooring, usually set in simple geometric patterns.

Patina. Soft sheen achieved by continuous use.

Pickets. Wood strips pointed at both ends, used in parquet floors in patterns such as Monticello.

Plastic. Still pliable and soft, not hardened.

Plumb. Exactly vertical.

Pointing. Act of filling joints with mortar.

PVC. Polyvinyl chloride. A water-insoluble thermoplastic resin used as a coating on sheet vinyl floors.

psi. Pounds per square inch.

Prefinished. Factory finished, referring to wood floors.

Quarter sawn. Wood sliced in quarters lengthwise that shows the grain of the wood to best advantage.

Quartzite. A compact granular rock, composed of quartzite crystals usually so firmly cemented as to make the mass homogeneous. Color range is wide.

Reducer strip. A tapered piece of wood used at the joining of two dissimilar materials to compensate for difference of thickness.

Riser. The vertical part of a stair.

Sandstone. Sedimentary rock composed of sand-sized grains naturally cemented from mineral materials.

Screeds. 2 × 4s between 18 and 48 inches in length, laid flat side down and randomly placed to support a subfloor.

Seeded. Sprinkling of marble chips on top of a base.

Semivitreous. Three percent but not more than 7 percent moisture absorption.

Sets. Groups of parquet set at right angles to each other, usually four in a set.

60-grit. A medium grade of sandpaper.

Spall. A fragment or chip, in this case of marble.

Spalling. Flaking of floor because of expansion of components.

Square. Edges cut at right angles to each other.

Stenciling. Method of decorating or printing a design by painting through a cut-out pattern.

Terrazzo. Marble chips of similar size combined with a binder that holds the marble chips together. This binder may be cementitious or noncementitious (epoxy resin).

Thin-set. The method of installing tile with a bonding material usually 3/32 to 1/8 inch in thickness. In certain geographical areas, the term *thin-set* may be used interchangeably for dry-set portland cement mortar.

Toe space. Area at base of furniture or cabinets that is inset to accommodate the toes.

Tongue and groove. A wood joint providing a positive alignment.

Tooled. A mortar joint that has been finished by a shaped tool while the mortar is plastic.

Twist. A spiral distortion of lumber.

Veneer. A very thin sheet of wood varying in thickness from 1/8 to 1/100 inch.

Vitreous. Moisture absorption of 0.5 percent to less than 3 percent.

NOTES

[1]The National Oak Flooring Manufacturers Association, *Oak Flooring Advocate.* Volume 4, Number 2 (boldface added).

[2]Hardwood Information Center, *Managing Natural Expansion and Contraction of Hardwood Floors.* www.hardwood.org/flooring

[3]Wilsonart International, *An Overview of Laminate Flooring.*

[4]Ibid.

[5]Tile Council of America, *1997 Handbook for Ceramic Tile Installation.* Clemson, SC, 1997, p. 7 (boldface added).

[6]Ibid., p. 5 (boldface added).

[7]Ibid. (boldface added).

[8]Marble Institute of America, *Care & Cleaning for Natural Stone Surfaces,* 1995, p. 6.

[9]TCA, *1997 Handbook for Ceramic Tile Installation,* p. 6 (italics in original).

[10]Letter from Crossville Tile, Crossville, Tennessee.

[11]*Compton's Interactive Encyclopedia™,* Version 2.01W ©1994 Compton's New Media Inc., a Tribune New Media Company.

[12]Portland Cement Association, *Design and Control of Concrete Mixtures,* 13th ed., p. 1.

[13]The National Terrazzo and Mosaic Association, "The Care of Terrazzo."

[14]Natural CORK Ltd. Co., *Installation Guidelines for Natural Cork Parquet Tiles Using Natural CORK's S-100 Adhesive,* revised 10/96.

5

Walls

In floors, the weight of flooring material is spread over a large area; however, when these same materials are used on walls, they create a heavy dead load. Thus walls, whether constructed or veneered with granite, stone, or brick, must have a foundation prepared to withstand this additional weight. **Compressive strength** is also important for wall installation materials.

There are two types of walls: load bearing and nonbearing. Interior designers need to know the difference between the two. Load-bearing walls are those that support an imposed load in addition to their own weight; a nonbearing wall is just for utilitarian or aesthetic purposes. The architect deals with both, but the interior designer probably deals more with nonbearing walls. A load-bearing wall should never be removed or altered without consulting an architect or engineer.

STONE

A stone wall is usually a veneer and may be constructed of any type of stone. **Rubble** is uncut stone or stone that has not been cut into a rectangular shape. **Ashlar** is stone that is precut to provide enough uniformity to allow some regularity in assembly. The rubble masonry is less formal, requires the use of more mortar, and is not as strong as the other types of bonds because of the irregularly shaped bonds. Uniform mortar joints are a mark of a skilled worker. **Fieldstone** or **cobble** has a more rounded feeling than does ashlar or rubble (Figure 5–1).

Maintenance. Stonework should be cleaned with a stiff brush and clean water. If stains are difficult to remove, soapy water may be used, followed by a clean-water rinse. Stonework should be cleaned by sponging during construction, which facilitates final cleaning. The acids used to clean brick should never be used on stone walls.

Regular maintenance consists of brushing or vacuuming to remove dust. It is important to remember that, generally, igneous types are impervious, but sedimentary and metamorphic stones are more susceptible to stains. Stone walls should not be installed where grease or any substance that may stain the stone is present.

GRANITE

Granite is used wherever a feeling of stability and permanence is desired, which is probably why one sees so much granite in banks and similar institutions. The properties of granite were mentioned in Chapter 4.

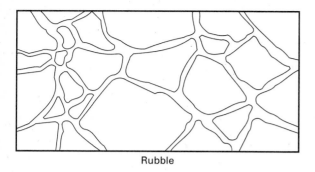
Rubble

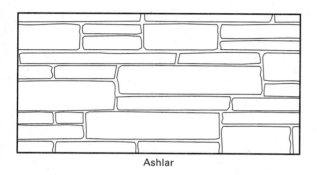
Ashlar

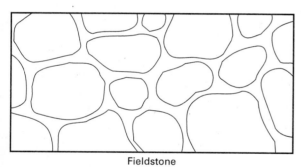
Fieldstone

Figure 5–1
Types of stonework.

Granite for walls may be polished or honed because abrasion is not a problem with walls.

Durastone produces 48" × 96" granite that is 1/16-inch thick, installs like wallpaper, and is strictly for wall use. This product has a rough stone finish.

Installation. Anchors, **cramps,** dowels, and other anchoring devices should be type 304 stainless steel or suitable **nonferrous** metal. A portland cement sand mortar is used and, where applicable, a sealant is used for pointing the joints.

Maintenance. If required, granite walls may be washed with a weak detergent solution and rinsed with clear water. The walls should be buffed with a lamb's wool pad to restore shine.

MARBLE

Marble has the same elegant and formal properties whether used for walls or for floors. According to the Marble Institute of America, interior marble wall facing may be installed by mechanical fastening devices utilizing nonstaining anchors, angles, dowels, pins, cramps, and plaster spots, or in a mortar setting bed to secure smaller units to interior vertical surfaces. The overall dimensions of the marble determine the setting method. Resilient cushions are used to maintain joint widths, which are then pointed with white cement or other approved material.

In addition to the traditional sizes, new thin marble veneers that are backed with lighter-weight materials have less weight per square foot and, depending on job conditions, may be set in either a conventional full mortar bed or by any of the several newer thin-bed systems.

Maintenance. Maintenance is the same as that for marble floors.

TRAVERTINE

When travertine is used in wall applications, it is not necessary to fill the voids. Unfilled travertine gives an interesting texture to the wall surface, but for a perfectly smooth installation, filling is required. Like flooring, wall applications of travertine may be filled with a clear, translucent epoxy or an opaque epoxy matching the color of the travertine. Filled travertine does tend to have less sheen on the opaque filled area than on the solid area. The surface of the travertine may be left in its rough state, providing texture, or it may be cut and sanded or ground smooth.

Installation. Installation methods of travertine are the same as for marble.

BRICK

Brick is used for both exterior and interior walls, and the surface of the brick may be smooth, rough, or grooved. Bricks with these surface textures create interesting wall designs with interesting shadows. Bricks are available in whites, yellows, grays, reds, and browns and may be ordered in special sizes or shapes. Firebrick is used for lining boilers and fireplaces and is made of special fire-resistant clays.

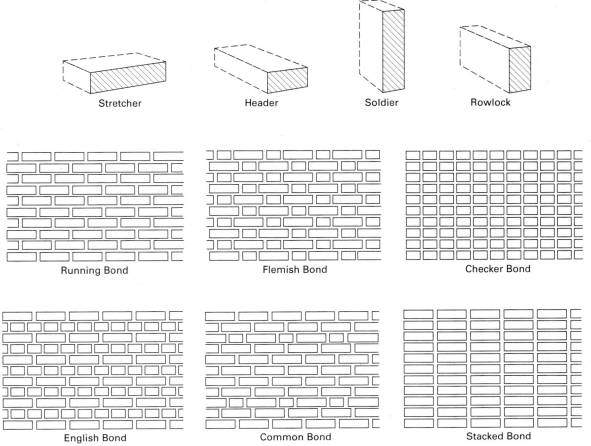

Figure 5–2
Stretchers, headers, and brick bonds.

The standard brick size is 3 3/4 inches wide by 8 inches long and 2 1/4 inches high. Bricks laid to expose the long side in a horizontal position are called **stretchers;** vertically they are called soldiers. When the ends of the bricks show horizontally, the bricks are called **headers,** but vertically they are called rowlocks (Figure 5–2). A bond is the arrangement of bricks in rows or courses. A common bond is defined as bricks placed end to end in a stretcher course with vertical joints of one course centered on the bricks in the next course. Every sixth or seventh course is made up of headers and stretchers. These headers provide structural bonding as well as pattern. A bond without headers is called a running bond. It is interesting to note that in some historical digs of buildings dating from the 1880s, it is possible to discover the nationality of the builders of brick walls (e.g., English and Flemish, as well as several other European nationalities) by the type of bond used (see Figure 5–2 for types of brick bonds).

Masonry walls may be hollow masonry, where both sides of the wall are visible, or they may be ve-

neered. When both sides are visible, the **header course** ties the two sides together. A veneered wall is attached to the backing by means of metal ties (Figure 5–3).

The joints in a wall installation are extremely important because they create shadows and special design effects. The joints of a brick wall are normally 3/8-inch thick. The mortar for these joints consists of a mixture of portland cement, hydrated lime, and sand. The mortar serves four functions:

1. It bonds the brick units together and seals the spaces between them.
2. It compensates for dimensional variations in the units.
3. It bonds to reinforcing steel and therefore causes the steel to act as an integral part of the wall.
4. It provides a decorative effect on the wall surface by creating shadow or color lines.

Mortar joint finishes fall into two classes: troweled and tooled joints. In the troweled joint, the excess

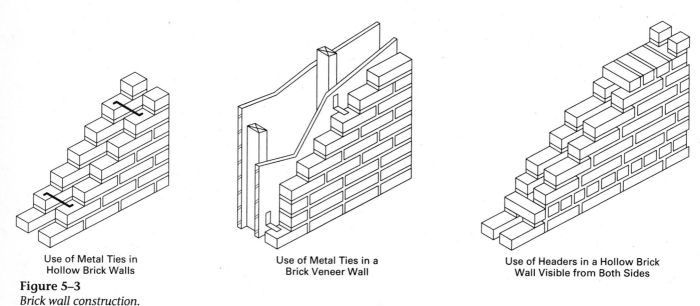

Use of Metal Ties in
Hollow Brick Walls

Use of Metal Ties in a
Brick Veneer Wall

Use of Headers in a Hollow Brick
Wall Visible from Both Sides

Figure 5–3
Brick wall construction.

mortar is simply cut off (**struck**) with a trowel and finished with the trowel. For the tooled joint, a special tool other than the trowel is used to compress and shape the mortar in the joint (Figure 5–4).

Installation. Brick and concrete blocks are both installed by masons. Bricks are placed in a bed of mortar and mortar is laid on the top surface of the previous course, or row, to cover all edges. The mortar joints may be any of the types shown in Figure 5–4.

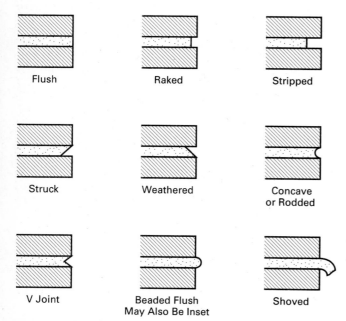

Flush

Raked

Stripped

Struck

Weathered

Concave
or Rodded

V Joint

Beaded Flush
May Also Be Inset

Shoved

Figure 5–4
Mortar joints for brick walls.

Maintenance. The major problem with finishing brick walls is the **mortar stain,** which occurs even if the mason is skilled and careful. To remove mortar stain, the walls are cleaned of surplus mortar and dirt; then scrubbed with a solution of trisodium phosphate, household detergent, and water; and then rinsed with water under pressure. If stains are not removed with this treatment, a solution of muriatic acid and water is used. The acid should be poured into the water, and not vice versa, to avoid a dangerous reaction. Just the bricks themselves should be scrubbed. The solution should not be allowed to dry but should be rinsed immediately with clean water. For cleaning light-colored bricks, a more diluted solution of muriatic acid and water should be used to prevent burning.

Regular maintenance for bricks includes brushing and vacuuming to remove dust that may have adhered to the rough surface. Masonry walls that may come in contact with grease, such as in kitchens, should be either impervious or sealed to prevent penetration of the grease.

CONCRETE

Currently, many architects of contemporary buildings, particularly in the commercial, industrial, and educational fields, are leaving poured concrete walls exposed on the interior. The forms used for these walls may be patterned or smooth, and this texture is reflected on the interior surface. The ties that hold the forms together may leave holes that, if properly placed, may provide a grid design.

From the interior designer's point of view, a poured concrete wall is a fait accompli. The surface may be left with the outline of the forms showing, patterned or plain (Figure 5–5), or it may be treated by the following methods to give a different surface appearance: bush hammering, acid etching, and sandblasting. Bush hammering is done with a power tool that provides an exposed aggregate face by removing the sand-cement matrix and exposing the aggregate. Sandblasting provides a textured surface. Bush hammering produces the heaviest texture, whereas the texture from sandblasting depends on the amount and coarseness of sand used. Acid etching just removes the surface.

If concrete is left in its natural poured state, the main problem facing the designer is using materials and accessories that will be compatible with cast concrete. Obviously, such materials need to imply weight and a substantial feeling, rather than delicacy or formality. The massive feeling of concrete can be overcome, however, by plastering over the concrete.

CONCRETE BLOCK

Concrete block is a hollow concrete masonry unit composed of portland cement and suitable aggre-

Figure 5–5
Countless texture and color combinations make concrete a cost-effective and popular material for many interior designers. Concrete walls throughout the Palm Springs Desert Museum, shown here, radiate with a fractured fin texture and a warm beige hue. The textures were created through the use of L. M. Scofield Company's LITHOTEX® Elastomeric Formliners. The color was created with the company's CHROMIX® Admixture, a coloring component that is integrally mixed into the concrete. (Photo courtesy of L. M. Scofield Company.)

gates. Walls of this type are found in homes, but they are more frequently used in commercial and educational interiors. There are several problems with concrete block: It has extremely poor insulating qualities if used on an exterior wall; if used on an outside wall and moisture is present, efflorescence will form; and it has a fairly rough surface that is difficult to paint, although coverage may be accomplished by using a specially formulated paint and a long-nap roller.

Installation. A mason erects a concrete block wall in a similar manner to a brick one except that, whereas a brick wall is viewed only from one side, a concrete block wall is often visible from both sides; therefore, the joints need to be finished on both sides of the block. Concrete block may be erected in either a running bond pattern or stacked (running bond is stronger).

Maintenance. Acid is not used to remove mortar smears or droppings, as with brick. Excess mortar should be allowed to dry and then chipped off. Rubbing the wall with a small piece of concrete block will remove practically all the mortar. For painting instructions, see Chapter 3.

GLASS BLOCK

In the 1920s and 1930s, glass block seemed to be used only in bathrooms and on the sides of front doors, but in the 1990s modern technology and the innovation of architects and designers have led to a revival and growth of its use in a variety of design environments. Glass block must only be used in non-load-bearing installations, but creative designers have nonetheless found many appealing uses for it.

Glass block, by definition, is composed of two halves of pressed glass fused together. The hollow in the center is partially **evacuated,** which provides a partial vacuum with good insulating qualities. The construction of the block is such that designs may be imprinted on both the inside and the outside of the glass surfaces. In all of their applications, glass blocks permit the control of light—natural or artificial, day or night—for function and drama. Thermal transmission, noise, dust, and drafts may also be controlled (Figure 5–6). For curved panel radius minimums refer to Table 5–1.

Pittsburgh Corning Corporation, the only American manufacturer of glass block, produces a variety of styles that may be used for both exterior and interior purposes. The range of privacy varies from the VUE® pattern, which is clear for the greatest combination of light transmission and visibility, to the ENDURA™ pattern, a thick faced block with narrow flutes that provide moderate light transmission with maximum privacy. There are specialty blocks for finishing a freestanding glass block wall in offices and residences. The newest block from Pittsburgh Corning is a sandblasted VUE pattern that provides a frosted look for complete privacy. Another new pattern is SPYRA™, which provides a ripple effect.

Standard glass block is 3 7/8 inches thick; the Thinline™ Series units are 3 1/8 inches thick. Glass block is available in 6-, 8-, and 12-inch squares, and some styles come in 4" × 8" and 6" × 8" rectangular blocks. Thinline block has the additional advantage of 20 percent less weight than standard glass block.

Specialty blocks such as VISTABRIK® units are solid glass and provide maximum protection from vandalism and forcible entry. "LX" inserts, of fibrous glass sheet, are sealed into the Pittsburgh Corning glass block unit to provide significant light and thermal control by tempering glare, brightness, light transmission, and solar heat gain. For a one-of-a-kind design, PC® Signature block can be custom manufactured with a corporate logo or design.

TABLE 5–1
Radius Minimums for Curved Panel Construction

BLOCK SIZE	OUTSIDE RADIUS IN INCHES	NUMBER BLOCKS IN 90° ARC	JOINT THICKNESS IN INCHES	
			Inside	*Outside*
6 × 6	52$\frac{1}{2}$	13	$\frac{1}{8}$	$\frac{5}{8}$
4 × 8	36	13	$\frac{1}{8}$	$\frac{5}{8}$
8 × 8	69	13	$\frac{1}{8}$	$\frac{5}{8}$
12 × 12	102$\frac{1}{2}$	13	$\frac{1}{8}$	$\frac{5}{8}$

Courtesy of Pittsburgh Corning Corporation.

Figure 5–6
The curved office wall of glass block provides both light and privacy for the conference room. (Photo courtesy of Pittsburgh Corning.)

Installation. The mortar-bearing surfaces of glass block have a coating that acts as a bond between the block and the mortar. Additionally, the coating acts as an expansion-contraction mechanism for each block. An optimum mortar mix is one part portland cement, one-half part lime, and four parts sand. Panel reinforcing strips are used in horizontal joints every 16 to 24 inches of height, depending on which thickness of block is used. Expansion strips are used adjacent to **jambs** and **heads.** Joints are struck while plastic and excess mortar are removed immediately. Mortar should be removed from the face of the block with a damp cloth before final set occurs.

For an all-glass look, blocks may be installed using Pittsburgh Corning's KWiK'N EZ® system, clear plastic spacer strips, silicone sealant, and a perimeter channel in place of mortar.

Maintenance. Ease of maintenance is one of the attractive features of glass block. Mortar or dirt on the face of glass block may be removed by the use of water, but not with abrasives (steel wool, wire brush, or acid).

PLASTER

The Egyptians and ancient Greeks used plaster walls that they painted with murals. The frescoes of early times were painted on wet plaster, which absorbed the pigment so it dried as an integral part of the plaster. The frescoes of Michelangelo's Sistine Chapel still retain their original brilliant color after 400 years. Historically plaster has been used for intricate mouldings and decorations. Today, plaster-covered walls are used only in commercial installations and expensive custom-built homes, because applications run as high as $2 per square foot, compared to about 50 cents per square foot for **drywall.** The plastering process is also extremely labor intensive, involving three coats of plaster over gypsum or metal lath.

Surface finishes called veneer plaster are on the market; they create the upscale look of solid plaster at a lower cost (about 25 percent more than gypsum board). Veneer plaster has high resistance to cracking, nail popping, impact, and abrasion failure. Veneer plaster is applied over a special veneer plaster base sometimes called blueboard (not to be confused with the water-resistant board used as a substrate for ceramic tile around the shower and bath area). This specially treated blueboard can become faded with light, which may affect the finish coats.

The one-coat Gold Bond® veneer plaster system from National Gypsum® can be applied directly to concrete block. National Gypsum's Uni-Kal® Tough Kote™ is specially designed for high abrasion resistance and has 10 times more surface abrasion resistance than standard plaster finishes. National Gypsum has a two-coat system with the same qualities as Tough Kote, but with even greater crack resistance.

Joints are reinforced with a fiberglass webbing; steel corners and **casing beads** protect corners. An alkali-resistant primer formulated for use over new plaster should be used if the surface is to be painted.

If a gypsum board wall is already installed, a plaster bonding agent must be applied before using the veneer plaster, which is then applied in two coats.

Lath is the foundation of a plaster wall. In the pyramids in Egypt, lath was made of intertwined reeds. The construction of the half-timbered homes of the English Tudor period is often referred to as daub and wattle (the daub being the plaster and the wattle the lath); the lath was a woven framework of saplings and reeds. When restoration work is done on houses built in the United States prior to the 1930s, the lath will probably be found to be thin wood strips nailed to the studs about 3/8 of an inch apart.

Modern lath is gypsum board, metal, or masonry block. The gypsum lath consists of a core of gypsum plaster between two layers of specially formulated, absorbent, 100 percent recycled paper. The gypsum lath is 3/8- or 1/2-inch thick, 16 inches wide by 48 inches long, and is applied horizontally with the joints staggered between courses. Other sizes are also available. Special types of gypsum lath may have holes drilled in them for extra adhesion or have a sheet of aluminum foil on one side for insulating purposes.

Metal lath is used not only for flat areas but also for curved surfaces and forms and is expanded metal that is nailed to the studs. The **scratch coat** is troweled on and some plaster is squeezed through the mesh to form the mechanical bond, whereas the bond with gypsum board is formed by means of **suction.** Beads or formed pieces of metal are placed at exterior corners and around casings to provide a hard edge that will not be damaged by traffic.

Plaster used to be troweled on the lath in three different coats. The first coat bonded to the lath; the second was the brown coat; and the third, the finish coat, was very smooth. The first two coats were left with a texture to provide tooth. A three-coat plaster job is still done sometimes, but two coats or even one may be used to complete the finished surface.

As mentioned in Chapter 3, because of its extreme porosity, plaster must be sealed before proceeding with other finishes.

GYPSUM BOARD

Gypsum board has the same construction as gypsum board lath. Sheets are normally 4 feet wide and 8 feet long, but they may be obtained in lengths up to 16 feet. The edges are usually tapered; some styles have the taper along the length. This allows for a tape and joint treatment to be applied, resulting in a finish that will be flat, smooth, and monolithic. The taper width is 2 inches. Some edges are square; the square edge was designed to be a base for a fabric covering or wallpaper, paneling, or tile. The square edge also can be used where an exposed joint is desired for a paneled effect. Tapered, round-edge gypsum board can be used for walls and ceilings in both new construction and remodeling. It is designed to reduce the beading and ridging problems commonly associated with standard-type gypsum board.

In some areas of the United States the term *drywall* is synonymous with *gypsum board*. The term *drywall* originated to differentiate between plaster or "wet wall" construction and any dry material, such as gypsum board, plywood, or other prefabricated materials, that does not require the use of plaster or mortar.

Another term mistakenly used as a synonym for *drywall* is Sheetrock®, a registered trademark of the U.S. Gypsum Company for its brand of gypsum board. The term *gypsum wallboard* should not be used either, because most gypsum board companies now produce a type of reinforced gypsum board specially for ceilings, which can withstand deflection. All gypsum board companies produce their product with 100 percent recycled paper on both the face and the back of the board.

Gypsum board is available with a foil back, which serves as a vapor retarder barrier on exterior walls. Another method of vapor retarder preparation is the use of a polyethylene sheet stapled to studs before erecting the gypsum board.

In new construction, 1/2-inch thickness is recommended for single-layer application; for laminated two-ply applications, two 3/8-inch thick sheets are used. Gold Bond Hi-Impact™ board has fibers in the gypsum core to provide added strength by helping to hold the core together during a fire. The fiber itself provides no resistance to heat transfer.

The horizontal method of application is best adapted to rooms in which full-length sheets can be used, because horizontal application minimizes the number of vertical joints. Today, screws are often used rather than nails, because screws can be installed by automatic screw guns and will not pull loose or "pop." Screws are placed a maximum of 12 inches on center (o.c.) on ceilings and 16 inches o.c. on walls where framing members are 16 inches o.c. Screws should be spaced a maximum of 12 inches o.c. on walls and ceilings where framing members are 24 inches o.c. In both cases, the screw heads should be slightly below the surface. A very good dry wall installation may also have an adhesive applied to the studs before installing the panels, in which case screws may be farther apart.

If, however, nails are used, the spacing is slightly different. Nails should be spaced a maximum of 7 inches o.c. on ceilings and 8 inches o.c. on walls along framing supports. The ceilings are done first and then the walls.

A thorough inspection of the studs should be made before application of the gypsum board to ensure that all warped studs are replaced. If this is not done, the final appearance of the plaster board will be rippled. Of course, this problem is not present when metal studs are used (e.g., in commercial construction).

After all the sheets have been installed, outside corners are protected by a metal corner or bead. The typical bead is right angled, but sometimes a curved bead is used. Trim strips are available for a **reveal** effect.

Joint cement, spackling compound, or, as it is called in the trade, "mud," is applied to all joints using a 5-inch-wide spackling knife. Tape is then placed to cover the joint and is pressed into the mud. (*All* seams or joints must be taped regardless of length; otherwise, cracks will soon appear. The outside beads have joint cement feathered to meet the edge.) Another layer of compound is applied, **feathering** the outer edges. After drying, the compound is sanded and a third coat is applied, with the feathering extending beyond the previous coats. All screw holes are filled with joint cement and sanded smooth. Care must be taken to sand only the area that has been coated with joint cement, because sanding the paper layer will result in a roughness that will be visible, particularly when a painted semigloss or gloss finish is applied. In fact, the Gypsum Association suggests that a thin skim coat of joint compound be applied over the entire surface to provide a uniform surface for paints. The drywall installer should be informed of the final finish so that attention can be paid to special finishing.

The surface of the gypsum board may be left smooth, ready for painting or a wallcovering, or it may have some type of texture applied. The latter is done for several reasons. Aesthetically, a texture may eliminate glare and is likely to hide any surface discrepancies caused by warping studs and/or finishing of joints. The lightest texture available is called an orange peel (the surface has the texture of the skin of an orange, just as the name suggests). Another finish is a skip-troweled surface: After the texture has been sprayed on, a metal trowel is used to flatten some areas. The heaviest texture is a heavily stippled or troweled appearance, similar to rough-finished plaster. A texture is preferred whenever there is a **raking light** on the wall surface; the texture helps hide surface discrepancies.

Gypsum board may also be installed on a curved wall by qualified drywall installers. Only **simple curves** may be used. **Compound curves** cannot be fabricated.

When water may be present, such as in bathrooms and kitchens, most building codes require the use of a water-resistant gypsum board. When ceramic tile is used, special water-resistant tile backers are used. If a pliant wallcovering is to be used, all plaster board must be sealed or sized, because the paper of the gypsum board and the backing of the wallcovering would become bonded and the wallcovering would be impossible to remove. Portersept with Surface Sealer® may be used in such cases.

Another type of gypsum board features fabric or vinyl wallcovering plastic in a variety of simulated finishes, including wood grains and other textures. This type of gypsum board can be applied directly by adhesive to the studs or as a finish layer over a preexisting wall. The edges may be square or beveled. Wood or metal trim must be applied at both floor and ceiling to create a finished edge. National Gypsum manufactures Durasan®, a vinyl-covered wall panel (also available in 30-yard rolls). Durasan yardage is for use on columns, curved surfaces, or where extensive cutouts would make Durasan panels difficult to use. Because field-applied vinyl is fabric backed, the Durasan panels and the complementary vinyl roll goods may vary slightly in color and texture.

Wallpaper and Wallcovering

The Chinese mounted painted rice paper on walls as early as 200 B.C. Although mention of painted papers has been historically documented as early as 1507 in France, the oldest fragment of European wallpaper, from the year 1509, was found in Christ's College, Cambridge, England. This paper has a rather large-scale pattern adapted from contemporary damask. Seventeenth-century paper, whether painted or block printed, did not have a continuous pattern repeat and was printed on sheets rather than on a roll, as is the modern practice. The repetitive matching of today's papers is credited to Jean Papillon of France in the late 17th century. In the 18th century, England and France produced hand-printed papers that were both expensive and heavily taxed.

Leather was one of the original materials to be used as a covering for walls. The earliest decorated and painted leathers were introduced to Europe in the 11th century by Arabs from Morocco and were popular in 17th-century Holland.

Flocked papers were used as early as 1620 in France. The design was printed with some kind of glue, which was then sprinkled heavily with finely chopped bits of silk and wool, creating a good imitation of damask or velvet. Flocked papers have been popular in recent decades but are less so now.

Scenic papers were used in the 18th century, many of them hand-painted Chinese papers. Wallpapers were imported to the United States during the second quarter of the 18th century. Domestic manufacturing did not start until 1800, and even then the quality was not equal to the fine imported papers.

After the Industrial Revolution, wallpaper became available to people of more moderate means, and the use of wallpaper became more widespread. In the late 19th and early 20th centuries, William Morris stimulated interest in wallpapers and their designs. In the first half of the 20th century, papers imitating textures and having the appearance of wood, marble, tiles, relief plasterwork, paneling, and moiré silk were in demand.

In the late 1930s and 1940s, wallpaper was in style, but in the 1960s, 1970s, and 1990s, painted walls were in fashion.

Today, designers are more discriminating with the use of wallpapers or, as they will be referred to from now on, wallcoverings. This change of name results from the fact that, although paper was the original material for wallcoverings, today these wallcoverings may be all paper, paper backed by cotton fabric, vinyl face with paper or cotton backing, or fabric with a paper backing. Foils or mylars have either paper or a nonwoven backing to ensure a smooth reflective surface.

The face of the paper wallcoverings is usually treated with a protective vinyl finish and provides a washable surface. *Washable* means that the surface can be wiped with a sponge and mild soap and water. Solid vinyl wallcoverings backed by woven cotton are more durable and are scrubbable, meaning that they can be cleaned with a soft brush and mild detergent.

Vinyl wallcovering is strippable, meaning that it peels off easily in one intact piece, without steaming or scraping. When a wallpaper is peelable, the face paper peels off, but the paper backing remains adhered to the wall. This backing can be removed or a new wallcovering can be applied over it.

Patterns

Today's wallcovering manufacturers produce pattern collections based on market research on consumer responses to specific patterns and demand for certain styles. Thus designers can use these collections to create the desired atmosphere in a client's installation.

Many of the Early American designs were inspired by valuable brocades and tapestries that adorned the homes of wealthy individuals. Several contemporary companies have made arrangements with museums to produce historical designs from the museum's collections. Bradbury & Bradbury Art Wallpapers have meticulously researched historical collections from the last quarter of the 19th century through Art Deco. Brunschwig & Fils has arrangements with The Historic New England collection of SPNEA (Society for the Preservation of New England Antiquities), the Musé des Arts Décoratifs in Paris, The Antiquarian and Landmarks Society of Connecticut, the Benaki Museum in Athens, Historic Charleston, the Winterthur Museum, and a number of other American museums. Scalamandre produces wallpaper for the Preservation Society at Newport, the Smithsonian Institute, and Historic Charleston, among others. Schumacher's licensers include Colonial Williamsburg, Historic Natchez, the National Trust for Historic Preservation, the Library of Congress, the Edith Wharton Restoration, and the Victorian Society. Thibaut Wallcoverings issues the Historic Homes of America collections based on samples from actual homes. Because Thibaut's papers are produced in large quantities, they are less expensive than the hand-screened prints mentioned previously, which are printed in smaller quantities (Figure 5–7).

Murals are large-scale, nonrepeat, hand-screened papers done on a series of panels and hung above a chair rail. They may be scenic, floral, architectural, or graphic in nature. **Chinoiserie** murals are the perfect background for English-style furniture. Murals are sold in sets varying from two to six or more panels per set. Each panel is normally 28 inches in width and is printed on strips 10 to 12 feet in length. The height of the designs varies greatly, but most fall somewhere between 4 and 8 feet. Some graphics go from ceiling to floor.

For a French ambience, wallcoverings with delicate scrolls or lacy patterns are suitable for a formal background, whereas **toile-de-Jouy** (see Figure 5-7) and checks are appropriate for the French Country look. Wallcoverings for a formal English feeling range from symmetrical damasks to copies of English chintzes and embroideries.

Geometrics include both subtle and bold stripes and checks, as well as polka dots and circles. The colors used will dictate where these geometrics can be used.

Trompe l'oeil patterns are three-dimensional designs on paper. Examples of realistic designs are a cupboard with an open door displaying some books, a view from a window, or a niche with a shell top containing a piece of sculpture. These trompe l'oeil patterns are sold in a set.

Pattern repeats are often mentioned in wallcovering books:

> The pattern repeat is the distance between one point and the next repeated same point. This distance may vary from no repeat or match (as in a texture) to repeats as large as 48 inches. Therefore, for an exceptionally large repeat, additional paper should be ordered.
>
> When a patterned wallcovering is hung, the left side of a strip will match or continue the design from the right side of the previous strip. If this match is directly across on a horizontal line, then it would be called a straight match. If the second strip has to be lowered to continue the design, it is a drop match. A drop match does not necessarily mean that more wallcovering must be ordered, but a drop match must be considered when cutting the strips.[1]

Types

Wallcovering textures include embossed papers, which hide any substrate unevenness, solid-color fabrics, and grasscloths. Embossed papers have a texture rolled into them during the manufacturing process. Care should be taken not to flatten the texture of embossed papers when hanging them.

Anaglypta® is an embossed product made from paper that has been imported from England since the turn of the century. Designed to be painted, this wallcovering provides the textured appearance of sculptured plaster, hammered copper, or even hand-tooled Moroccan leather. Anaglypta is a highly textured wallcovering that is applied to the wall like any other product. Once painted, the surface becomes hard and durable. The advantage of Anaglypta is that not only is it used on newly constructed walls in residential and commercial interiors, but it may also be applied after minimal surface preparation. In older dwellings and Victorian restoration projects, Anaglypta provides the added advantage of stabilizing walls while covering moderate cracks and blemishes. Friezes, with ornate embossed designs, are part of the heavier

Figure 5–7
The simple but elegant New Orleans Stripe in this front hall is from Thibaut's new Historic Homes of America V wallpaper and fabric collection. The original document for this design, and for its coordinating border, was of French manufacture. It came from the Gallier House, a beautiful townhouse in the heart of New Orleans's Vieux Carré. The house was built in the 1850s and designed for English-born architect James Gallier, Jr., his Creole wife, Agle, and their young family. The restored house is now open to the public as a house museum owned and operated by Tulane University. The bedroom pictured here is decorated with Rockwood Toile wallpaper and fabric, from Thibaut's new Historic Homes of America V collection. The design came from Rockwood, a fairy-tale Gothic house just north of Wilmington, Delaware. Rockwood, first occupied in 1855, is Delaware's finest example of Gothic architecture. Rockwood Toile was inspired by a fabric used in one of the bedrooms of the mansion. (Photos courtesy of Thibaut Wallcoverings.)

Lincrusta® line, the original extra-deep product. Low-relief and vinyl versions are also available.

Fabrics should be tightly woven, although burlap is frequently used as a texture. Walls are pasted with a nonstaining paste and the fabric, with the selvage removed, is brushed onto the paste. Custom Laminations, Inc. paperbacks fabrics for wallcoverings.

Grasscloth is made of loosely woven vegetable fibers backed with paper. These fibers may be knotted at the ends and are a decorative feature of the texture. Because the fibers are of vegetable origin, width and color will vary, thus providing a highly textured surface. In addition, because of the natural materials from which grasscloth is made, it is impossible to obtain a straight-across match, so seams will be obvious. Woven silk is frequently included in grasscloth collections; its finer texture gives a more refined atmosphere to a room.

Flocked papers, as mentioned previously, are one of the oldest papers on record. They are currently manufactured by modern methods but still resemble pile fabrics. One problem with flocked papers is that through abrasion or constant contact with the face of the paper, the flocking may be removed and a worn area will appear. A seam roller should never be used to press down seams because this also flattens the flocking.

Foils and mylars provide a mirrored effect with a pattern printed on the reflective surface; because of this high shine, the use of a lining paper is suggested to provide a smooth substrate. If the substrate is rough, the mirrored effect shows all the imperfections. Foils conduct electricity if allowed to come in contact with exposed wires. Some older foils had a tendency to show rust spots in moist environments. This is why most "metallic" wallcoverings are presently made of mylar. Foils are used to best effect in well-lit rooms because the light reflects off the foil surface and enhances the effect of the wallcovering.

Kraft papers are usually hand-printed patterns on good-quality kraft paper similar to the type used for wrapping packages. Unless specially treated, these kraft papers absorb grease and oil stains, so care should be taken in placement (i.e., it might not be a good idea to use them in kitchens).

For cork-faced paper, razor-thin slices of cork are applied by hand to tinted or lacquered ground papers. The base color shows through the natural texture of the cork and may blend or contrast with the cork itself. The sliced cork may also be cut into definite shapes for a repetitive pattern, or it may be printed with a design on top of the cork. Cork also comes in 12-inch square tiles varying in thickness from 1/8 to 5/8 of an inch. These solid cork tiles are of varying texture and provide good insulation from sound and temperature extremes.

Leather is cut into designs or blocks (much like blocks of Spanish tiles) because the limited size of the hide prohibits the use of large pieces. The color of the surface varies within one hide and from one hide to another; therefore, a shaded effect is expected.

Coordinated or companion fabrics are used to create an unbroken appearance where wallcovering and draperies adjoin. When using coordinated paper and fabric, the wallcovering should be hung first; then the draperies can be adjusted to line up with the pattern repeat of the wallcovering. The tendency is to call these companion fabrics "matching fabrics," but this is incorrect. It is extremely important to note that paper or vinyl will absorb dyes in a different manner than will a fabric, and many problems will be resolved by strict avoidance of the word *matching*.

Lining paper is an inexpensive blank paper recommended for use under foils and other fine-quality papers. It absorbs excess moisture and makes a smoother finished wall surface. A heavier canvas liner is available for "bad walls."

Printing of Wallcoverings

Roller printing is used for less expensive wallcoverings. The inks are transferred from a metal roller with raised design blocks to a large printing roller and then to the paper as it is fed through the press.

There are several means by which a wallcovering can be hand printed. First, it may be silk screened. A separate screen must be made up for each color used, and the screens must be meticulously positioned so that the patterns match at the edges. In silk screening, the wallcovering must be allowed to dry between application of different colors (Figure 5–8). Rotary screen printing machines are used for most orders today.

The following information is supplied by Bradbury & Bradbury and explains the process of custom silk screening. Printing tables are 90 feet long and each holds 6 rolls of wallpaper. Metal rails along the side of the table have adjustable knobs that are set to the particular repeat of the pattern to be printed. A complex pattern for an average size Victorian room can require more than 1,000 individual impressions. (See Figure 5–8a.)

Artwork is done by hand in the traditional manner by painting on acetate or cutting a stencil using a graphic arts film, as shown in Figure 5–8b. A separate stencil must be prepared for each color in the pattern, and all must align perfectly. Once a full repeat has been cut or painted by hand, computers aid in replicating the artwork.

Screen making is done by coating a silk screen with a photosensitive emulsion, essentially creating a large piece of film. The screen and artwork are sandwiched in a large vacuum frame and exposed to light. Areas exposed to the light become impervious; the other areas can be washed out. In the early days we used silk on a wooden frame; today monofilament polyester is used on a titanium frame (see Figure 5–8c).

Paint is forced through the stencil using a plastic-bladed squeegee. The printer must skip every other repeat to prevent the silk screen frame from falling in wet ink. Each screen lays down one color—if a pattern has eight colors it must be printed eight times with eight different screens (see Figure 5–8d). For completed patterns, see Color Plate 11.

Block printing produces a similar effect to silk screening, but instead of the paint being squeezed

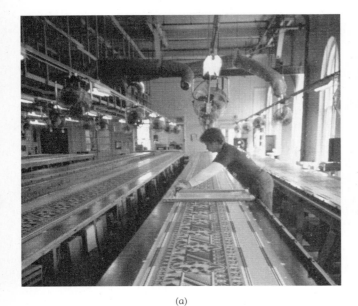

(a)

(b)

(c)

(d)

Figure 5–8
The process of silk screening. (a) Printing table. (b) Artwork done by hand. (c) An actual silk screen. (d) Paint being forced through the screen. (Photos courtesy of Bradbury & Bradbury Art Wallpapers.)

through the open pores of the silk screen, the paint or color is rolled on a block from which the negative, or unwanted, areas have been cut away. Block printing requires positive positioning (i.e., it has to be lined up properly). (The block printing method is similar to the process used to make potato blocks in grade schools.)

Because silk screening and block printing are hand processes, a machinelike quality is not possible or perhaps even desirable. The pattern does not always meet at the seams as positively as does the roller-printed pattern. Matching should be exact in the 3- to 5-foot area above the floor, where it is most noticeable.

Adhesives

There are several materials available to attach a wallcovering to a wall. The old standby is the wheat-base paste, which is used for many wallcoverings. However, certain wallcoverings, such as wet-look vinyls, handprints, naturals, and foils, require a special adhesive. The manufacturer will always specify which type of adhesive is to be used. If fabric or grasscloth is to be hung, a nonstaining cellulose paste should be used. Regular vinyls are hung using a vinyl adhesive that is not the same as the aforementioned special adhesive.

Prepasted papers come with a factory-applied dehydrated cellulose or wheat paste. To activate this paste, cut strips are soaked in water for a designated number of seconds and then applied in the same way as regular wallpaper. The prepasted papers are usually less expensive and are mainly for use by the homeowner in a do-it-yourself project.

Most machine-printed wallcoverings are **pre-trimmed** at the factory, but the majority of handprints and hand-made textures are untrimmed.

Packaging

A single roll of American wallcovering used to contain 36 square feet, but only the cloth-backed vinyls now contain this amount. All others are metric and use the European measurement equivalent to 28 square feet (8.4 square meters). To allow for waste and matching of patterns, it is advisable to calculate 30 usable square feet for the cloth-backed vinyls and 24 usable square feet for the metric system. This allowance is sufficient for a room with an average number of doors and windows, but for a room with window walls, more precise calculations should be made.

All wallcovering is priced by the single roll, but it is packaged in two- or three-roll bolts. A double-roll bolt is a continuous bolt containing the equivalent of two single rolls. The cost is twice the single-roll price. The same applies to a triple-roll bolt. By packaging wallcovering in bolts rather than in single rolls, the paperhanger has more continuous lineal yardage with which to work and, therefore, less waste. When ordering handprints from a retail store, there are a few things one must know: There is a cutting charge if the wallcovering order requires a cut bolt. Because the shading and even the positioning of the pattern on the roll may vary between dye lots or runs, SUFFICIENT BOLTS SHOULD ALWAYS BE ORDERED when the order is placed. The particular dye lot, which is stamped on the back of the roll, may not be available if it is necessary to order more in the future. Opened or partially used bolts are not returnable, and unopened bolts may be subject to a restocking charge.

Commercial Wallcoverings

Commercial wallcoverings are the exception to the single roll containing up to 28 square feet. Commercial wallcoverings are usually 52 to 55 inches wide and are packaged in 30-yard or more bolts. These wider coverings require a highly skilled professional paperhanger and a helper. The final appearance of the walls depends on the ability of the paperhanger.

Commercial wallcoverings are classified according to federal minimum performance standards. Until 1983, the specifications for commercial wallcoverings were based on the number of ounces per square yard. Previously, 100 percent cotton was used as a backing, but today a blend of polyester and cotton is used. Poly-

ester fibers are not as bulky as cotton fibers, but they have more **tensile strength.** Tensile strength is the single most important performance feature in commercial wallcovering. Abrasion resistance is important but mainly in key areas such as outside corners.

A second major change in federal standards is the inclusion of washability, scrubbability, and stain-resistance requirements. These qualities increase from Type I to the most durable, Type III. The three types are further classified into Class 1 (not mildew resistant) and Class 2 (mildew resistant). Advanced technology has produced a unique backing for Type II vinyl wallcoverings called apertured nonwoven. This backing combines the best qualities of regular woven and nonwoven backs and provides excellent print quality and pattern definition. It also allows for superior hangability and ease of application.

Mildew is a fungus that flourishes in a moist, dark environment. If mildew is present or suspected, the walls should be washed with a mixture of equal parts of household bleach and water. The correct paste or adhesive will help prevent mildew from forming under newly hung wallcovering. If proper precautions are not taken, any mildew that forms will permanently discolor the wallcovering.

ESSCAPE™ from Essex is a 54-inch wide, moisture-releasing wallcovering that contains Intersept to combat the mildew and bacteria that often plague hospitality and health care environments. Mildew forms when moisture becomes trapped in interior walls. Porous ESSCAPE discourages mildew formation and bacteria growth by allowing walls to evaporate moisture naturally.

Portersept® with Intersept Wallcovering Adhesive is a premixed wallcovering adhesive providing excellent initial tack, slip, and opentime for easier positioning. It can be used with light- to heavy-weight wallcovering. Types I, II, and III clean up with water. This nonflammable product contains Intersept to protect against microorganisms (see Chapter 1, page 5).

With plain textures, grasscloths, and suedes, it is advisable to reverse the direction of every other strip of wallcovering. This will provide a better finished appearance, particularly if one side of the covering happens to be shaded a little more than the other.

Commercial wallcoverings are no longer limited to using only texture for style diversity. JM Lynne manufactures a decorative overprint on its plain Renaissance texture. The print and the texture may be used in the same area for a touch of elegance (Figure 5–9).

As mentioned before, commercial wallcovering usually comes in 52- to 54-inch-wide bolts. However, MDC Wallcoverings produces a wallcovering, Quantex™, that is 108 inches wide and endless in length in

Figure 5–9
Illustration of JM Lynne's decorative overprint on Lynne's plain Renaissance texture. Design by Patty Madden. (Photo courtesy of JM Lynne.)

that the total width of all the walls is the length ordered. This woven textile has the best characteristics of olefins, such as durability and cleanability, but because of its extreme width it provides seamless installations and avoids panel shading. Quantex is made to be railroaded: In other words, instead of hanging vertically, Quantex is hung horizontally. The current Quantex collection is Teflon coated.

Koroseal® and Vicrtex® vinyl wallcoverings contain an Early Warning Effect formulation that, when heated to about 300°F, gives off a harmless, odorless, and colorless vapor that will set off the alarm on an ionization smoke detector located in the same room. These vinyls are also UL approved to Class A federal standards and contain antimicrobial and mildew-resistant elements. Koroseal Wallcoverings also produces Gossamer Steel® and Gossamer Basics™, Koroseal's polyolefin fabric lines. Vicrtex Sasso® received the ADEX award in 1996. This pattern is a menswear suiting design, and it looks like fabric on the walls. Vicrtex and Koroseal are UL labeled. The UL label is

recognized on products as a measure of safety and assurance for the customer.

Tassoglas™ is available in a variety of textures and patterns and is designed to be painted. Tassoglas offers tremendous design flexibility as an unfinished, paintable wallcovering for problem wall surfaces. It is made of all natural, environmentally friendly, woven glass textile yarns and comes in a bolt 54 1/2 yards long and 39 inches wide with pretrimmed edges. Tassoglas combines the versatility of paint with the strength and benefits of woven glass fiber yarns to provide a highly breatheable, mold- and mildew-resistant, durable, and long-lasting wallcovering. In areas of high humidity, it is recommended that a mildewcide/antimicrobial substance be added to the adhesive and paint unless the manufacturer already included such a substance. Beneath the surface, Tassoglas reinforces the substrate, easily bridges cracks, hides roughness or minor imperfections, and is ideal for use in both new construction and renovations. Novaglass™ hand-printed borders on woven fiberglass are also available.

A new concept in commercial wallcovering is the deeply embossed polyvinyl chloride (PVC) or expanded vinyl wallcoverings, which are not only attractive but offer acoustic values. They are packaged in full bolts, 29 inches wide by 55 yards in length.

All textile wallcoverings have good acoustic qualities and good energy-saving insulation qualities. Textiles may be backed by paper, and the fiber content may be 100 percent jute or a combination of synthetics and wool and jute and/or linen and cotton. These textiles usually have a flame spread rating of 25 or less.

Tretford Broadloom, a concentric ribbing in 38 colors from Eurotex, is mainly used in Europe for floors, but in the United States it is also used on walls. Face yarns are 80 percent wool/mohair and 20 percent nylon, with a primary backing of PVC and a secondary backing of jute. With a flame spread of 5, Tretford Broadloom is very suitable for contract work, absorbs sound, cushions impact, insulates to save energy, and is an excellent display surface that accepts Velcro® and push pins. Tretford can be installed on any dry, smooth surface, such as concrete, drywall, plaster, wood paneling, or particleboard. Installation on cinder or cement blocks or on surfaces covered with wallpaper or vinyl wallcovering is *not* recommended. Tretford is installed with an adhesive applied with a notched trowel, and maintenance involves brushing lightly in the direction of ribs and periodically vacuuming the surface.

Sisal is another wallcovering that has high sound absorption and is static free. Rolls are either 4 or 8 feet wide and 100 feet long. Sisal has an extremely prickly texture, as opposed to the other textiles, but this roughness can be an asset, as in the following case: A school found that when students lined up outside the cafeteria, the wall against which they were standing became dirty and defaced by graffiti. Installation of sisal prevented both problems and reduced the noise level.

One of the special surface treatments for wallcoverings is Tedlar®, which is a tough, transparent fluoride plastic sheet that is very flexible; chemically inert; and extremely resistant to stains, yellowing, corrosive chemicals, solvents, light, and oxygen. Most commercial wallcovering manufacturers produce wallcovering products that are, or may be, surfaced with Tedlar. Another stain-resistant product is PreFixx™, available on Essex 54 products, which protects invisibly with no loss of texture.

Some companies offer special-order printing of wallcoverings for minimum orders of 50 rolls or more. These prints may be designs already in a company's line or custom designs. Because such special orders involve hand painting, they are expensive; but they may solve a particular design problem.

In large public buildings, different colors of vinyl wallcovering are often used as a path-finding aid for patrons. The different colors can indicate certain floors or areas within floors.

Installation. Before hanging any wallcovering, the walls must be sized. Sizing is a liquid applied to the wall surface that serves several purposes: It seals the surface against alkali, also known as hot spots; it reduces absorption of the paste or adhesive to be used; and it provides tooth for the wallcovering. The sizing must be compatible with the paste or adhesive used.

Wallcoverings are installed in either of the following manners:

1. The wallcovering is table trimmed with a straight edge. This procedure involves cutting the selvage from both edges so that the panels can be butted. Table trimming reduces the amount of surface adhesive residues and facilitates cleanup.

2. Panels are overlapped on the wall, and seams are made by double cutting through both sheets. Care must be taken *not* to cut into the substrate surface. Various hooked knife-type cutting tools are available for this procedure. After the cut is made, the face strip may be removed and the adhesive cleaned off. Koroseal Wallcovering, manufacturer of Vicrtex wallcovering, offers the following extremely useful suggestions in its "Suggested Specification, Installation Instructions, Care and Maintenance" booklet: Remove excess paste from a

seam before making the next seam. Vertical joints should occur at least 6 inches from inside and outside corners. (Koroseal has also provided much of the information on which this section is based.)

Paste or adhesive is applied by means of a wide brush to the back of the wallcovering. Particular attention should be paid to the edges, because this is where any curling will occur. The wallcovering is folded or **booked,** without creasing. This allows the moisture in the adhesive to be absorbed by the fabric substrate or backing, thus allowing for any shrinkage before the wallcovering is applied to the wall surface. Booking also makes an 8- or 9-foot strip easier to handle and transport from the pasting table.

The first strip is always hung parallel to the **plumb line,** which has been marked previously. A seam roller is used on most wallcoverings, except as noted before. As mentioned previously, for some wallcoverings, the paste must be applied to the wall rather than to the backing. The manufacturer's instructions for installation methods should always be followed. Each roll must be inspected before the first strip is cut. If a damaged roll has been cut into, it cannot be returned.

Maintenance. All stains or damage should be corrected immediately. Paper-faced wallcoverings should be tested to ascertain if the inks are permanent before cleaning fluids are applied. Vinyls may be scrubbed with a soft brush and water if they have been designated scrubbable. Foils are washed with warm water and wiped with a soft cloth to avoid any scratching. Hard water tends to leave a film on the reflective surfaces of foil.

Grasscloths, suedes, fabrics, sisal, and carpeting may be vacuumed to remove dust. Again, the manufacturer's instructions for maintenance must be followed. Vinyl-covered walls should be washed at least once or twice a year. Grease and oils, in particular, should not be allowed to accumulate.

Koroseal recommends the following maintenance procedures:

1. For routine dirt and grime, use a mild detergent dissolved in warm water.

2. For severe dirt conditions use a concentrated solution of a mild detergent applied with a stiff brush. Remove the grimy suds by padding with a damp sponge. The wall should then be rinsed with clean water to remove detergent residue.

3. For surface stains such as lipstick, ball-point ink, heel marks, shoe polish, carbon smudges,

and the like: use anhydrous isopropyl alcohol as an efficient cleaner for removal of such stains from vinyl wallcovering. Ethyl alcohol or denatured alcohols are also efficient. Do not use strong alkaline or abrasive cleaners.[2]

TAMBOURS

Tambours are vertical slats of any material attached to a flexible backing, as in the front of a roll-top desk. The slats may be solid wood or hardboard. Other materials, such as wood veneer, high-pressure laminate, metal, metallic mylar, melamine, and melamine/mylar, are laminated to a tempered hardboard core with a flexible brown fabric backing approximately 3/16 of an inch thick overall. Slats are cut 1/2 to 1 inch o.c. with the angle of the groove varying between 30° and 90°. Depending on the face material and use, dimensions vary from 18 inches wide by 15 inches long for roll-top desks, to 48 inches wide by 120 inches long. Because of their flexibility, tambours are used for curved walls as well as for roll-up doors in kitchen appliance garages (Figure 5–10).

Flexible real glass mirror tambours may be clear, bronzed, or colored. The mirror is bonded to a cloth back in square, rectangular, or diagonal pattern cuts and gives a multifaceted or broken reflection. Mirrored sizes are smaller than wood tambour, depending on the type (12″ × 24″ to 23 1/2″ square).

Installation. The method of installation depends on the surface to which the tambour is to be attached. A special adhesive is usually required, but the manufacturers' instructions should always be followed.

WOOD

When selecting a wood or veneer, designers should ascertain whether it comes from a renewable source. It is possible for wood to be sustainable with proper management.

Wood is a good natural insulator because of the millions of tiny air cells within its cellular structure. For equal thickness, it is 4 times as efficient an insulator as cinder block, 6 times as efficient as brick, 15 times as efficient as stone, 400 times as efficient as steel, and 1770 times as efficient as aluminum. The production of the final wood product is also energy efficient: One ton of wood requires 1510 kilowatt-hours to manufacture, whereas one ton of rolled steel requires 12,000 kilowatt-hours and one ton of aluminum requires 67,200 kilowatt-hours.

Wood for walls comes in two different forms: solid wood strips and plywood. Solid wood may be used on the walls of residences, but it is not usually used for commercial applications, unless treated, because of the fire and building code restrictions. For residences, redwood, cedar, and knotty pine are the most commonly used woods, but walnut, pecan, and many others may also be used.

Figure 5–10
The variety of materials available in tambour form are shown in one photograph. (Photo courtesy of Flexible Materials.) A natural wood tambour is used on this undulating curved wall. (Photo courtesy of National Products Inc.)

There are several grades of redwood from which to choose. The finest grade of redwood is Clear All Heart, with the graded face of each piece free of knots. Clear All Heart gives a solid red color, whereas Clear redwood is also top quality but does contain some cream-colored sapwood and may also contain small knots. The cream-colored sapwood may be attractive to some, but to others its random appearance is bothersome; therefore, clients need to know the difference in appearance as well as cost between Clear All Heart and Clear. B Heart is an economical all-heartwood grade containing a limited number of tight knots and other characteristics not permitted in Clear or Clear All Heart. B Grade is similar to B Heart except that it permits sapwood as well as heartwood.

Redwood is available in vertical grain, which has straight vertical lines, and flat grain, which is cut at a tangent to the annual growth rings, exposing a face surface that appears highly figured or marbled. Smooth-faced redwood is referred to as surfaced; saw-textured lumber has a rough, textured appearance.

There are two types of cedar: aromatic cedar, which is used for mothproof closets, and regular cedar, which is used for both interior and exterior walls. Another soft wood frequently used for residential interiors is knotty pine, in which knots are part of the desired effect (unlike top-grade redwood).

Boards may be anywhere from 4 to 12 inches wide, with tongue and groove for an interlocking joint or **shiplap** for an overlapping joint. Tongue and groove may have beveled edges for a V-joint or may be rounded or even elaborately moulded for a more decorative effect. Shiplap boards come with their top edges beveled to form a V-joint or with straight edges to form a narrow slot at the seams.

Square-edged boards are used in contemporary settings and may be board and batten, board on board, reverse board and batten, or contemporary vertical. Board and batten consists of wide boards spaced about 1 inch apart; a narrow 1" × 2" strip of batten is nailed on top to cover the 1-inch gap. Board on board is similar to board and batten except that both pieces of wood are the same width. Reverse board and batten has a narrow strip under the joint or gap. In contemporary vertical installations, the battens are sometimes placed on edge between the wider boards.

For acoustical control, boards are often placed on edge and spaced about 2 to 3 inches apart on an acoustical substrate (Figure 5–11).

The National Oak Flooring Manufacturer's Association (NOFMA) suggests using oak flooring on walls and ceilings. It is now possible to obtain a Class A 0 to 25 flame spread rating (often required in commercial structures) by job-site application of an intumescent coating. Beveled oak strip flooring gives a three-dimensional effect when installed on a wall.

Several companies manufacture paneling that comes prepackaged in boxes containing approximately 64 square feet. The longest pieces are 8 feet and the shortest 2 feet, with beveled edges and tongue and grooved sides and ends. This type of paneling, although more expensive than regular strips, eliminates waste in a conventional 8-foot-high room.

Installation. Siding, planks, or strips may be installed horizontally, vertically, or diagonally. Each type of installation will give a completely different feeling to the room. Horizontal planking will appear to lengthen a room and draw the ceiling down, whereas vertical planking adds height to a room and is more formal. Diagonal installations appear a little more active and should be used with discretion or as a focal point of a room. Diagonal or herringbone patterns look best on walls with few doors or windows. Each application method requires its own type of substrate.

If installed horizontally or diagonally over bare studs or gypsum board, no further preparation of the surface is needed. The strips are attached to the wall in the tongue area, as with hardwood flooring, except

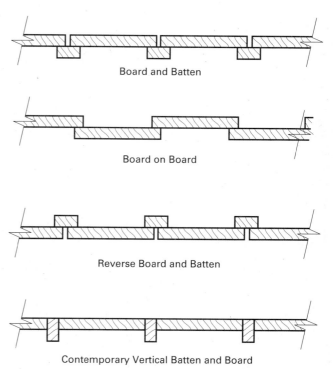

Board and Batten

Board on Board

Reverse Board and Batten

Contemporary Vertical Batten and Board

Figure 5–11
Board and battens.

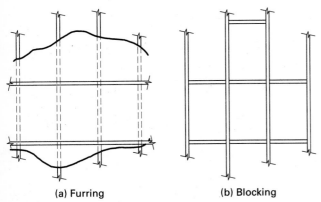

(a) Furring   (b) Blocking

Figure 5–12
Furring and blocking.

that with wall applications the nails penetrate each stud.

Vertical installations require the addition of nailing surfaces. The two types of nailing surfaces are blocking and furring. Blocking involves filling in horizontally between the studs with 2- to 4-inch pieces of wood in order to make a nailing surface. Blocking also acts as a fire stop. Furring features thin strips of wood nailed across the studs (Figure 5–12).

When wood is to be used on an outside wall, a vapor barrier such as a polyethylene film is required. In addition, wood should be stored for several days in the area in which it is to be installed so it may reach the correct moisture content. Some manufacturers suggest several applications of a water-repellent preservative to all sides, edges, and especially the porous ends (this is particularly important in high-humidity installations).

There are several suggested finishes for wood walls: wax, which adds soft luster to the wood; or a sealer and a matte varnish, for installations that will require cleaning. Paneling may also be stained, but it is important to remember that if solid wood is used, the natural beauty of the wood should be allowed to show through.

PLYWOOD PANELING

Plywood is produced from thin sheets of wood veneer, called plies, which are laminated together under heat and pressure with special adhesives. This process produces a bond between plies that is as strong as or stronger than the wood itself.

Plywood always has an odd number of layers that are assembled with their grains perpendicular to

each other. Plywood may also have a lumber core, Medium Density Fiberboard core, or particleboard core; however, lumber core plywood is virtually never used today in fine architectural woodworking (Figure 5–13).

The Architectural Woodwork Institute (AWI) is a not-for-profit organization that represents architectural woodwork manufacturers located in the United States and Canada. The discussion in this section would not be possible without the assistance and cooperation of AWI.

The side of the plywood panel with the best-quality veneer is designated as the face, and the back may be of the same or of lesser quality depending on its projected use.

AWI's *Architectural Woodwork Quality Standards* provide for three grades of plywood panel construction: economy, custom, and premium:

> *Economy Grade:* The grade defining the minimum expectation of quality, workmanship, materials, and installation within the scope of the 7th Edition Quality Standards Illustrated.
>
> *Custom Grade:* The grade specified for most high quality architectural woodwork. This grade provides a well-defined degree of control over the quality of materials, workmanship, and installation of a project. The vast majority of all work

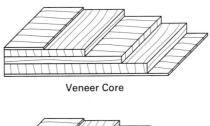

Veneer Core

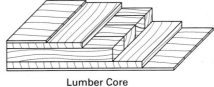

Lumber Core

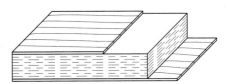

Particleboard Core

Figure 5–13
Types of plywood.

complies with 7th Edition Quality Standards Illustrated, Custom Grade.

Premium Grade. The grade specified when the highest degree of control over the quality of the execution of the design intent, and the highest quality of the materials, workmanship and installation under 7th Edition Quality Standards Illustrated, is required. Usually reserved for special projects, or feature areas within a project.

Prevailing Grade. When the AWI Quality Standards are referenced as part of the contract documents and no Grade is specified, AWI Custom Grade standards will prevail.[3]

Types of Veneer Cuts

According to the AWI,

The manner by which a log segment is cut with relation to the annual rings will determine the appearance of the veneer. When sliced, the individual pieces of veneer, referred to as **"leaves,"** are kept in the order in which they are sliced, thus permitting a natural grain progression when assembled as veneer faces. The group of leaves from one slicing is called a **flitch** and is usually identified by a flitch number and the number of gross square feet of veneer it contains. The faces of the leaves with relation to their position in the log are identified as the "tight face" (toward the outside of the log) and the "loose face" (toward the inside or heart of the log). During slicing the leaf is stressed on the "loose" face and compressed on the "tight" face. When this stress is combined with the natural variation in light refraction caused by the pores of the wood, the result is a difference in the human perception of color and tone between "tight" and "loose" faces.

Plain (or Flat Slicing) is the slicing method most often used to produce veneers for high quality architectural woodworking. Slicing is done parallel to a line through the center of the log. A combination of cathedral and straight grain patterns result, with a natural progression of pattern from leaf to leaf.[4]

Walnut is usually cut by this method. Figure 5–14 shows different methods of slicing.

The AWI also details the following slicing methods:

Quarter Slicing (or Quarter Cut) simulates the quarter sawing process of solid lumber, roughly parallel to a radius line through the log segment. In many species the individual leaves are narrow as a result. A series of stripes is produced, varying in density and thickness from species to species. **Flake** is a characteristic of this slicing method in red and white oak.

Rift Slicing (or Rift Cut Veneers) are produced most often in red and white oak, rarely in other species. Note that rift veneers and rift sawn solid lumber are produced so differently that a "match" between rift veneers and rift sawn solid lumber is highly unlikely. In both cases the cutting is done slightly off the radius lines minimizing the "flake" associated with Quarter slicing.

Comb Grain is limited in availability, and is a select product of the rift process distinguished by tight, straight grain along the entire length of the veneer. Slight angle in the grain is allowed. Comb grain is restricted to red and white oak veneers.

Rotary. The log is center mounted on a lathe and peeled along the general path of the growth rings like unwinding a roll of paper, providing a generally bold random appearance. Rotary cut veneers may vary in width and matching at veneer joints is extremely difficult. Almost all softwood veneers are cut this way. Except for a specific design effect, rotary veneers are the least useful in fine architectural woodwork.[5]

Other decorative veneer patterns may be obtained by using the crotch, burl, or stump of the tree. The crotch pattern is always reversed so that the pointed part, or V, is up. Burl comes from a damaged area of the tree, where the tree has healed itself and grown over the injury; it is a very swirly pattern. Olive burl is frequently used in contemporary furniture.

Matching Between Adjacent Veneer Leaves

It is possible to achieve certain visual effects by the manner in which the leaves are arranged. As noted, rotary cut veneers are difficult to match; therefore, most matching is done with sliced veneers. The matching of adjacent veneer leaves must be specified. Special arrangements of leaves such as "diamond" and "box" matching are avail-

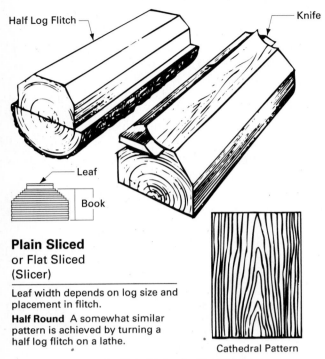

Plain Sliced
or Flat Sliced
(Slicer)

Leaf width depends on log size and placement in flitch.

Half Round A somewhat similar pattern is achieved by turning a half log flitch on a lathe.

Cathedral Pattern

(a) Plain Slicing (or Flat Slicing)

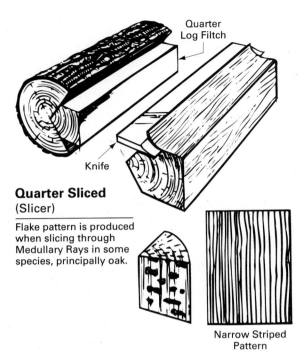

Quarter Sliced
(Slicer)

Flake pattern is produced when slicing through Medullary Rays in some species, principally oak.

Narrow Striped Pattern

(b) Quarter Slicing (or Quarter Cut)

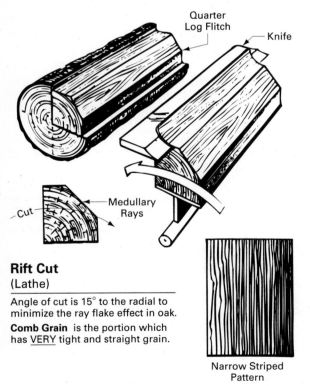

Rift Cut
(Lathe)

Angle of cut is 15° to the radial to minimize the ray flake effect in oak.

Comb Grain is the portion which has <u>VERY</u> tight and straight grain.

Narrow Striped Pattern

(c) Rift Slicing (or Rift Cut)

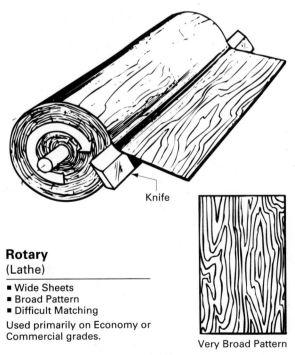

Rotary
(Lathe)

- Wide Sheets
- Broad Pattern
- Difficult Matching

Used primarily on Economy or Commercial grades.

Very Broad Pattern

(d) Rotary

Figure 5–14
Veneer cuts. (Reproduced by permission of the Architectural Woodwork Institute.)

able. Consult your AWI woodworker for choices. The more common types are:

Book matching is the most commonly used match in the industry. Every other piece of veneer is turned over so adjacent pieces (leaves) are opened like the pages of a book.

Visual effect: Veneer joints match, creating a symmetrical pattern. Yields maximum continuity of grain. When sequenced panels are specified, prominent characteristics will ascend or descend across the match as the leaves progress from panel to panel [Figure 5–15].

NOTE: May be used with plain-, quarter-, or rift-sliced veneers. Because the "tight" and "loose" faces alternate in adjacent leaves, they reflect light and accept stain differently, and this may yield a noticeable color variation in some species or flitches.

Slip matching is often used with quarter-sliced and rift-sliced veneers. Adjoining leaves are placed (slipped out) in sequence, without turning, resulting in all the same face sides being exposed [see Figure 5–15].

Visual effect: Grain figure repeats, but joints do not show grain match.

NOTE: The lack of grain match at the joints can be desirable. The relatively straight grain patterns of quartered and rift veneers generally produce pleasing results and a uniformity of color because all faces have the same light refraction.

In *random matching,* veneer leaves are placed next to each other in a random order and orientation, producing a "board-by-board" effect in many species.

Visual effect: Random matching provides a casual or rustic appearance, as though individual boards from a random pile were applied to the product. There is a conscious effort to mismatch grain at the joints [see Figure 5–15].

NOTE: Degrees of contrast and variation may change from panel to panel. This match is more difficult to obtain than book or slip match and must be clearly specified and detailed.

End matching is often used to extend the apparent length of available veneers for high wall panels and long conference tables. End matching occurs in two types: In architectural end match, leaves are individually book (or slip) matched, first end to end and then side to side, alternating end and side. The visual effect is the best for continuous grain patterns for length as well as width [see Figure 5–15].

For *panel end match,* leaves are book (or slip) matched on panel subassemblies, with sequenced subassemblies end matched, resulting in some modest cost savings on projects where applicable. The visual effect for most species is a pleasing, blended appearance and grain continuity.

Matching Within Individual Panel Faces

The individual leaves of veneer in a sliced flitch increase or decrease in width as the slicing progresses. Thus, if a number of panels are manufactured from a particular flitch, the number of veneer leaves per panel face will change as the flitch is utilized. The manner in which these leaves are "laid up" within the panel requires specification and is classified as follows (according to the AWI):

RUNNING MATCH—Each panel face is assembled from as many veneer leaves as necessary. This often results in a non-symmetrical appearance, with some veneer leaves of unequal width. Often, the most economical method at the expense of aesthetics is the standard for Custom Grade and must be specified for other grades. Running matches are seldom "sequence and numbered" for use as adjacent panels. Horizontal grain "match" or sequence cannot be expected.

BALANCE MATCH—Each panel face is assembled from veneer leaves of uniform width before edge trimming. Panels may contain an even or odd number of leaves, and distribution may change from panel to panel within a sequenced set. While this method is the standard for Premium Grade it must be specified for other grades, and it is the most common assembly method at moderate cost.

BALANCE AND CENTER MATCH—Each panel face is assembled of an even number of veneer leaves of uniform width before edge trimming. Thus, there is a veneer joint in the center of the panel, producing horizontal symmetry. A small amount of figure is lost in the process. [This method is] considered by some to be the most pleasing assembly at a modest increase of cost over Balance Match.[6]

Figure 5–16 shows different types of matching within panel faces.

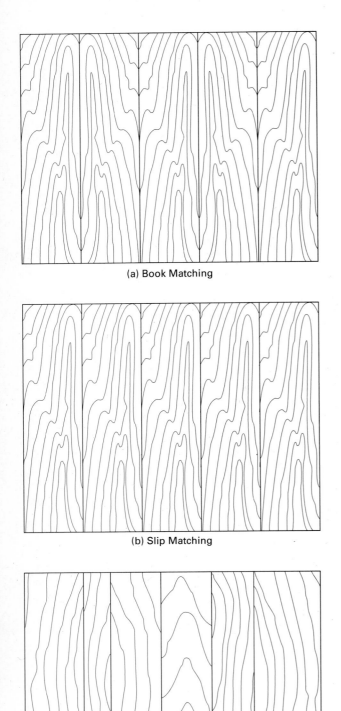

(a) Book Matching

(b) Slip Matching

(c) Random Matching

(d) End Matching

Figure 5–15
Matching of veneers. (Reproduced by permission of the Architectural Woodwork Institute.)

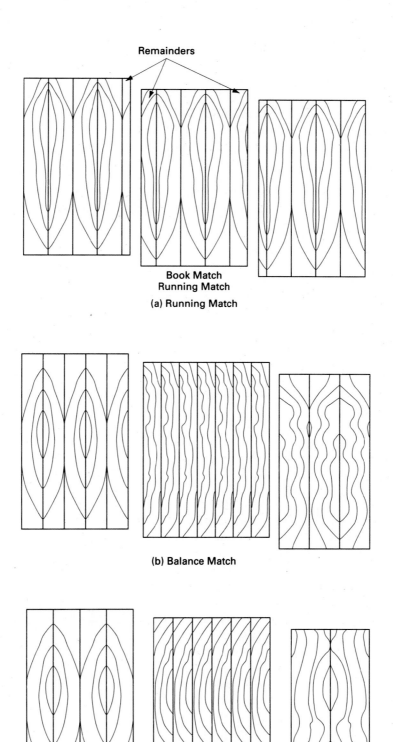

Figure 5–16
Matching within individual panel faces. (Reproduced by permission of the Architectural Woodwork Institute.)

Methods of Matching Panels

Veneered panels used in casework or paneling in the same area may be matched to each other. This important component of the project must be carefully detailed and specified. The natural growth patterns of the tree will cause the sequential panels to ascend, descend, or show a "grain progression" as the eye moves from panel to panel. The four common methods are:

1. *Premanufactured Sets—Full Width.* These are one step above "stock" plywood panels, usually made and warehoused in 4-foot × 8-foot or 4-foot × 10-foot sheets in sequenced sets. They may be produced from a single flitch or a part of a flitch, usually varying in number from 6 to 12 panels. If more than one set is required, matching between sets cannot be expected. Similarly doors or components often cannot be fabricated from the same flitch materials, resulting in noticeable mismatch. This is often the most economical type of special panel product.

2. *Premanufactured Sets—Selectively Reduced in Width.* These are panels just like Premanufactured sets—Full width, usually made and warehoused in 4-foot × 8-foot, and 4-foot × 10-foot sheets in sequenced sets. They are often selected for continuity, recut into modular widths, and numbered to achieve the appearance of greater symmetry. If more than one set is required, matching between the sets cannot be expected. Similarly, doors or components often cannot be fabricated from the same flitch materials, resulting in noticeable mismatch.

3. *Sequence Matched Uniform Size Set.* These sets are manufactured for a specific installation to a uniform panel width and height. If more than one flitch is required to produce the required number of panels, similar flitches will be used. This type of panel matching is best used when panel layout is uninterrupted and when the design permits the use of equal width panels. Some sequence will be lost if trimming is required to meet field conditions. Doors and components within the wall cannot usually be matched to the panels. Moderate in cost, sequenced uniform panels offer a good compromise between price and aesthetics.

4. *Blueprint-Matched Panel and Components.* This method of panel matching achieves maximum grain continuity, since all panels, doors, and other veneered components are made to the exact sizes required and in exact veneer sequence. If possible, flitches should be selected that will yield sufficient veneer to complete a prescribed area or room; if more than one flitch is needed, flitch transition should be accomplished at the least noticeable predetermined location. This method requires careful site coordination and relatively long lead times. Panels cannot be manufactured until site conditions can be accurately measured and detailed. This panel matching method is more expensive and expresses veneering in its most impressive manner.[7]

Figure 5–17 shows different methods of matching panels.

Rooms treated with paneling always produce a feeling of permanency. Architectural paneling is as different from ready-made paneling as a custom-made Rolls Royce is from an inexpensive production car. Ready-made paneling is discussed later in this chapter.

Fire-retardant Panel Flame Spread Classification

The various codes utilize "flame spread" classifications for wood and other materials. It is the responsibility of the specifier to determine which elements, if any, of the woodworking require special treatment to meet local codes. In most codes, the panel products used to fabricate casework and furniture are not regulated. For more detailed information, please refer to the AWI publication *Fire Code Summary.* Typical model code classifications are:

Class I or A	0–25
Class II or B	26–75
Class III or C	76–200

Flame Spread Factors

A. *Core*—The fire rating of the core material determines the rating of the assembled panel. Fire retardant veneered panels must have a fire retardant core. Particleboard core is available with a Class I (Class A) rating and can be used successfully with veneer or rated high pressure decorative laminate faces. MDF (Medium Density Fiberboard) is not currently available with a fire rating.

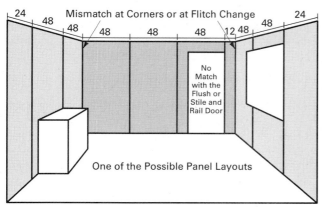

(a) Premanufactured Sets–Full Width

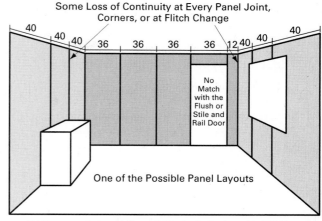

(b) Premanufactured Sets–Selectively Reduced in Width

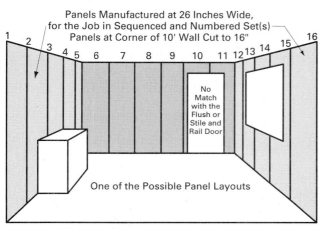

(c) Sequence Matched Uniform Size Set

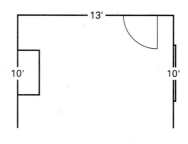

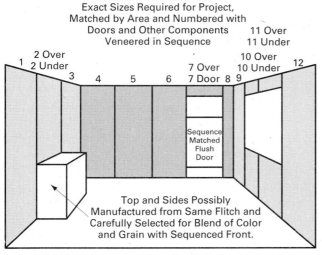

(d) Blueprint Matched Panels and Components

Figure 5–17
Matching of panels within an area. (Reproduced by permission of the Architectural Woodwork Institute.)

B. *Face*—Existing building codes, except where locally amended, provide that facing materials 1/28" or thinner are not considered in determining the flame spread rating of the panel. *NOTE: In localities where basic panel building codes have been amended, it is the responsibility of the specifier to determine whether the application of the facing material specified will meet the code.*

Face veneers are not required to be fire retardant treated, and such treatment will adversely affect the finishing process.[8]

There are several methods of installing panels for acoustical control. The panels may be floated or raised, or batten mouldings of wood, metal, or plastic may also be used.

Finishing. The Architectural Woodwork Institute has specific standards for factory finishing of woodwork, and its publication entitled *Architectural Woodwork Quality Standards* should be consulted.

PREFINISHED PLYWOOD

Prefinished plywood paneling varies from 1/4 to 1/2 inch thick. Standard panel size is 4 × 8 feet, but panels are also available in 7- and 10-foot heights. The face of the plywood is grooved in random widths to simulate wood strips. This feature also hides the joining, where each panel is butted up to the next, because outside edges are beveled at the same angle as the grooves.

The finish on prefinished plywood paneling is clear acrylic over a stained surface.

Some plywood paneling features a wood grain reproduction on the plywood or a paper overlay applied to **lauan mahogany** plywood and then protected with an oven-baked topcoat.

Installation. As with all wood products, paneling should be stored in the room it will be installed in for 24 hours prior to installation to condition for humidity and temperature. Paneling may be applied directly to the stud framing, but it is safer, from a fire hazard point of view, to install it over gypsum board. A 1/4-inch sound-deadening board used as a backing decreases sound transmission. Nails or adhesive may be used to install the panels. If nails are used, they may be color coated when exposed fasteners are acceptable, or countersunk and filled with colored putty (Figure 5–18).

Maintenance. Prefinished plywood panels require frequent dusting in order to prevent a build-up of soil, which dulls the finish. Each manufacturer supplies instructions for maintenance of its particular product, and these should be followed.

PARTICLEBOARD

Medium-density fiberboard (MDF) is used for walls, especially in retail stores or any other display areas. Marlite® manufactures Displawall®, slotted merchandise panels that have a base of MDF, a melamine topcoat, and factory-painted grooves to match, contrast, or harmonize with the surface selection. These grooves will accommodate a variety of hardware from which merchandise can be hung. Various-size modules and planks are also available.

Installation. Displawall panels may be applied directly to open studs or over drywall. Care must be taken to prevent moisture penetration through the walls.

HARDBOARD

Sheets or planks of hardboard are manufactured of compressed wood fibers by means of heat and pressure. Hardboard sheets or planks consist of a hardboard base that is textured during the pressing process, usually in a wood grain pattern. A dark base coat is then placed on top of the base; this layer gives the dark color to the V-joints. The light precision coat is applied next; it does not cover the V-joints. This precision coat is grained and coated with a melamine topcoat that is baked on and is resistant to most household chemicals and staining agents such as cosmetics and crayons. Tape should not be applied to the panel surface because it may damage the surface.

Hardboard paneling is also available in 4 × 8-foot sheets and may utilize harmonizing mouldings between panels or may be butted. Pigmented vertical grooves simulate joints of lumber planks, and edges are pigmented to match face grooves and to conceal butt joints. Hardboard panels are not to be used below grade, over masonry walls, in bathrooms, or in any area of high humidity.

When hardboard is covered with a photoreproduction of wood, it does not have the depth or richness of real wood and is probably best used for inexpensive installations, where price and durability are more important than the appearance of real wood. Because this paneling is not wood veneered but rather a

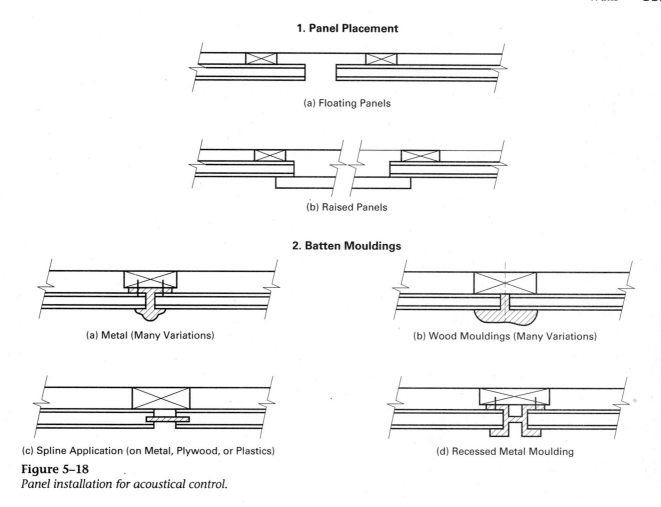

1. Panel Placement

(a) Floating Panels

(b) Raised Panels

2. Batten Mouldings

(a) Metal (Many Variations)

(b) Wood Mouldings (Many Variations)

(c) Spline Application (on Metal, Plywood, or Plastics)

(d) Recessed Metal Moulding

Figure 5–18
Panel installation for acoustical control.

reproduction, the same manufacturing methods may be used for solid colors or patterns. Fast food restaurants and many businesses requiring the feature of durability and easy cleaning use Marlite plank. The plank may be used vertically, horizontally, or diagonally, provided that furring strips have been installed over any sound, solid substrate.

Some hardboard is available in a stamped grille-type pattern or with holes (commonly known as Peg-Board®). The grille types are framed with wood and used for dividers. The perforated board is useful for hanging or storing items. Special hooks and supports are available for this purpose and are easily installed and removed for adjustment.

Installation. Thicknesses of hardboard vary from 1/8 and 3/16 of an inch to 1/4 of an inch. The 1/8-inch and 3/16-inch thicknesses must be installed over a solid backing, such as gypsum board. Panels are glued or nailed to the substrate.

Maintenance. To remove surface accumulation such as dust and grease, a lint-free soft cloth dampened with furniture polish containing no waxes or silicones may be used. More stubborn accumulations may require wiping with a soft cloth dampened in a solution of luke-warm water and a mild detergent. The hardboard must be wiped dry with a clean, dry cloth immediately following this procedure. (An inconspicuous area or scrap paneling should be used for experimental cleaning.)

DECORATIVE LAMINATE

Decorative laminates are made from layers of kraft paper that have been impregnated with phenolic resins, which give flexibility to the final product. The pattern layer is placed on top and is covered by a translucent overlay of melamine, a plastic that provides durability. When all these layers are bonded with heat (300°F) and pressure (1000 psi), the top translucent layer becomes transparent and forms the wearlayer. The pattern layer may be a solid color, a photo of wood, fabric, or an artist- or computer-drawn image. Decorative laminate is often mistakenly referred to as Formica®, but that is the brand name of a manufacturer of a decorative laminate.

The vertical surface of decorative laminate may be 0.050 inch (general purpose) or 0.030 inch (vertical surface). The 0.030-inch vertical surface type is not recommended on surfaces exceeding 24 inches in width. Decorative laminate for walls is often installed on the job site.

Balancing or backing laminates are used to give structural balance and **dimensional stability.** They are placed on the reverse side of the substrate to inhibit moisture absorption through the back surface.

Custom laminates are now available from Wilsonart®. They may be seamless inlay, in which a piece of Wilsonart patterned decorative paper is cut out like a stencil and then backed by another Wilsonart decorative paper, which, when bonded under heat and pressure, results in a two-color seamless inlay. The screen-print process is used when more than two colors are required. A multicolor, detailed image is screened onto a sheet of decorative paper, which is then made into a seamless, single-sheet laminate. A company logo could be placed on walls using this technique (Figure 5–19).

The Wilsonart Decorative Metal line consists of 26 decorative metals. New options include mirror-quality aluminum panels, with three solids in chrome, gold, and bronze, and seven etched patterns in chrome. In response to the increasing popularity of and demand for a matte finish, three cross-brushed patterns were added to the existing line of anodized aluminum metals, along with a new brushed stainless steel look.

There are other types of decorative laminate. Where antistatic properties are required, a standard-grade laminate is available. Several manufacturers of decorative laminate produce a laminate that does not have the usual dark edge associated with a square-edge installation (e.g., SOLICOR® and COLORCORE®). Many manufacturers of high-pressure decorative laminate **(HPDL)** produce a fire-resistant type that, when applied with approved adhesives to a fire-resistant core, results in wall paneling with Class 1 or A flame spread rating. Finally, Wilsonart has 12 different finish options available, with varying degrees of light reflectance, to suit any project.

Installation. When decorative laminates are to be used on a wall, 3/4-inch hardwood-faced plywood or particleboard should be used as a core. The use of an expansion-type joint (see Figure 5–19) is suggested. To permit free panel movement and to avoid visible fastenings, AWI recommends that panels be hung on the walls, utilizing metal panel clips or interlocking wood wall cleats.

Maintenance. Wilsonart recommends that decorative laminates be cleaned with warm water and mild soaps, such as those used for hands or dishes. If spots remain, an all-purpose cleaner or bathroom cleaner, such as Formula 409®, Glass Plus®, or Mr. Clean®, should be used.

For stubborn stains, a paste of baking soda and water should be applied to the stain with a soft bristle brush. The last resort is undiluted household bleach such as Clorox®, followed by a clean-water rinse. Use of abrasive cleansers or special cleansers should be avoided because they may contain abrasives, acids, or alkalines.

Metallic laminates other than solid polished brass may be cleaned as described previously. The surface of metallics, however, should always be wiped completely dry with a clean, soft cloth after washing. Stubborn smudges may be removed with a dry cloth and a thin, clean oil. For solid polished brass surfaces, only glass cleaners free of petroleum products should be used. The surface may be touched up with Fill 'n Glaze™ and a good grade of automobile wax. The manufacturer's instructions must be followed carefully during application.

PORCELAIN ENAMEL

Porcelain enamel is baked-on 28-gauge steel, laminated to 3/16 to 21/32 of an inch gypsum board or hardboard. It comes in many colors and finishes for use in high-abuse public areas, such as hospitals and food processing and preparation areas. It is also available with writing board surfaces that double as projection screens. Widths are from 2 to 4 feet, and lengths are from 6 to 12 feet. Weight varies from 1.60 to 2.7 pounds per square foot. Porcelain enamel is also used for toilet partitions in public rest rooms.

Maintenance. Maintenance is the same as that for ceramic tile (see p. 74).

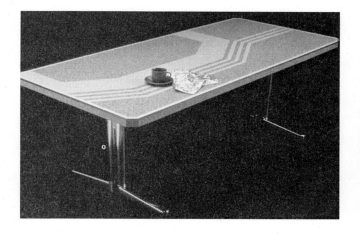

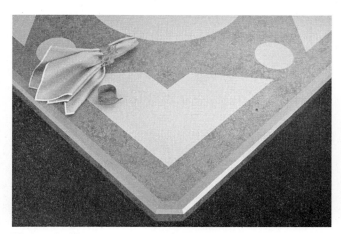

Figure 5–19
Using a special "seamless inlay" process, Wilsonart Custom Laminates allow the designer to specify a combination of two laminate patterns, or a pattern and a solid color, which are fused together into a single sheet of laminate and easily applied to counter tops, cabinetry, or other fixtures (shown here on table surfaces). Because laminate is made up of layers of paper, shapes that are cut out of the "top sheet" are seen as whatever color or pattern the "bottom sheet" happens to be specified in. The result is a custom-designed, unified sheet of laminate without the usual seams, where delamination or dirt collection may occur. (Photos courtesy of Wilsonart International.)

GLASS

Glass, one of our most useful products, is also one of the oldest (it was first used about 4000 B.C.). In ancient times, formed pieces of colored glass were considered as valuable as precious stones. In the past, glass was used mainly for windows, permitting light and sun to enter a home or building. Currently, as a result of modern construction methods, glass is used for interior walls or partitions. Of course, one disadvantage of glass is that it is breakable, but there are products specially made to reduce this problem.

There are three methods of manufacturing glass. The first is sheet or window glass, in which the molten glass is drawn out and both sides are subjected to open flame. This type of glass, which is not treated after manufacture, can show distortions and waviness. The second, plate glass, has both surfaces ground and polished, which renders its surfaces virtually plane and parallel. The third, float glass, is a more recently developed and less expensive process of manufacturing; molten glass is floated over molten metal and is used interchangeably with plate glass.

Insulating glass consists of two or three sheets of glass separated by either a dehydrated air space or an inert gas-filled space, together with a **desiccant.** Insulating glass limits heat transference and, in some areas of the country, may be required by the building codes in all new construction for energy conservation purposes. It also helps eliminate the problem of condensation caused by a wide difference in outside and inside temperatures.

There are various types of safety glass. The one with which we are most familiar is **tempered,** the kind used in entry doors or shower doors. In tempered glass, a heavy blow breaks the glass into small grains rather than sharp, jagged slivers. Another type of tempered glass, which has a wire mesh incorporated into its construction, can break under a blow but does not shatter.

Laminated glass can control sound, glare, heat, and light transmission. It offers security and safety through high resistance to breakage and penetration. In interior areas where glass is desired, laminated acoustical glass is effective in reducing sound transmission. Where exterior sounds (traffic, airplanes, etc.) are present and distracting, laminated acoustical glass may be used. Acoustical glass may be clear or colored.

Another form of glass used for energy conservation is a laminated glass with a vinyl interlayer that, depending on the color of the interlayer, may absorb or transmit light in varying degrees. The tinted glass may have a bronze, gray, green, blue, silver, or gold appearance, and these tints cut down on glare in a manner similar to sunglasses or the tinted glass in an automobile. Where 24-hour protection is required, such as in jewelry stores, banks, and detention areas, a security glass with a high-tensile polyvinyl butryal inner layer is effective. There are even bullet-resistant glasses on the market.

For those involved in historical restorations, Benheim Corporation offers Restoration Glass™. This glass is hand made using the original cylinder method, yet the glass easily meets today's tough building codes. It is available in two levels of distortion: full, for thicker and more distorting effects; and light, for thinner and less distorting effects.

Nippon Electric Glass America (N.E.G.) produces NeoClad, a product manufactured by the crystallization of specially formulated sheet glass. In the manufacturing process, the glass gains remarkable strength, a soft color, and a smooth, high-gloss surface. The edges can be shaped with various types of bevels on the front or back. NeoClad is for both interior and exterior use and is extremely resistant to environmental pollution and graffiti.

Viracon Inc. offers its own laminated glass:

Viracon Privacy Glass™ is a high-tech laminated glass that instantly switches from frosted to clear with a flip of a switch. It consists of a 3M™ film, composed of electrically-sensitive liquid crystals, which is laminated between two panes of tinted or clear glass. Each Privacy Glass window is wired to a standard 120V building electrical system. Viracon offers its Privacy Glass in clear, green, gray, or bronze and [the glass] is ideal for conference rooms, office and emergency hospital room partitions, control rooms, lobbies, executive office suites and glass displays. It may also be used for privacy in residences.[9]

Transwall features glass movable walls that are modular and may be combined with acoustical panels and/or a variety of other components.

MIRROR

The mirrors used 2000 years ago by the Egyptians, Romans, and Greeks were highly polished thin sheets of bronze. Today, many of these metal mirrors may be seen in museums. The method of backing glass with a metallic film was known to the Romans, but it was not until 1507 that the first glass mirrors were made in Italy. Plate glass was invented in France in 1691, enabling larger pieces of glass to be manufactured. The shapes of mirrors used in various periods of design should be studied by interior designers, but mirrors are no longer just accessories hung on the wall for utilitarian or decorative purposes. Walls are often completely covered with these highly reflective surfaces.

Quality mirrors are made of float glass and are silvered on the back to obtain a highly reflective quality. Also used in certain circumstances are two-way mirrors, which permit viewing from one side but not from the other (which appears to be an ordinary mirror). These two-way mirrors have many uses, such as in apartment doors, child observation areas, department stores, banks, and prison security areas.

Mirrors used on wall installations may be clear and brightly reflective or grayed or bronze hued. The latter are not as bright but do not noticeably distort color values. The surface may also be antiqued, which produces a smoky, shadowy effect. Mirrored walls always enlarge a room and may be used to correct a size deficiency or to duplicate a prized possession, such as a candelabra or chandelier. Mirrored walls may also display all sides of a piece of sculpture or double the light available in a room.

Mirrors are available for wall installations in many sizes, ranging from large sheets to small mosaic mirrors on sheets similar to mosaic tile. Sometimes a perfect reflection is not necessary and the mirrors may be in squares, **convex** or **concave,** acid etched, engraved, or beveled.

Mirror Terminology

The following terminology was provided by the North American Association of Mirror Manufacturers:

Acid etch: A process of producing a specific design or lettering on glass, prior to silvering but cutting into the glass with a combination of acids. This process may involve either a frosted surface treatment or a deep etch. This process can also be done on regular glass.

Antique Mirror: A decorative mirror in which the silver has been treated to create a smoky or shadowy effect. The antique look is often heightened by applying a veining on the silvered side in any one or more of a variety of colors and designs.

Backing Paint: The final protective coating applied on the back of the mirror, over copper, to protect the silver from deterioration.

Concave Mirror: Surface is slightly curved inward and tends to magnify reflected items or images.

Convex Mirror: Surface is slightly curved outward to increase the area that is reflected. Generally used for safety or security surveillance purposes.

Edge Work: Among numerous terms and expressions defining types of edge finishing, the five in most common usage are listed here.

Clean-Cut Edge: Natural edge produced when glass is cut. It should not be left exposed in installation.

Ground Edge: Grinding removes the raw cut of glass, leaving a smooth satin finish.

Seamed Edge: Sharp edges are removed by an abrasive belt.

Polished Edge: Polishing removes the raw cut of glass to give a smooth-surfaced edge. A polished edge is available in two basic contours.

Beveled Edge: A tapered polished edge, varying from 1/4 of an inch to a maximum of 1 1/4 inches thick, produced by machine in a rectan-gular or circular shape. Other shapes or ovals may be beveled by hand, but the result is inferior to machine bevel. Standard width of bevel is generally half an inch [Figure 5–20].

Electro-Copper-Plating: Process of copper-plating by electrolytic deposition of copper on the back of the silver film, to protect the silver and to assure good adherence of the backing paint.

Engraving: The cutting of a design on the back or face of a mirror, usually accomplished by hand on an engraving lathe.

Finger Pull: An elongated slot cut into the glass by a wheel, so that a mirrored door or panel, for instance, may be moved to one side.

First-Surface Mirror: A mirror produced by deposition of reflective metal on front surface of glass, usually under vacuum. Its principal use is as an automobile rear-view mirror or transparent mirror.

Framed Mirror: Mirror placed in a frame that is generally made of wood, metal, or composition material and equipped for hanging.

Hole: Piercing of a mirror, usually 1/2 inch in diameter and generally accomplished by a drill. Often employed in connection with installations involving rosettes.

Mitre Cutting: The cutting of straight lines by use of a wheel on the back or face of a mirror for design purposes. Available in both satin and polished finishes.

Rosette: Hardware used for affixing a mirror to a wall. A decorative rose-shaped button used in several places on the face of a mirror.

Sand Blasting: Engraving or cutting designs on glass by a stream of sand, usually projected by air.

Shadowbox Mirror: Mirror bordered or framed at an angle on some or all sides by other mirrors, creating multiple reflections of an image.

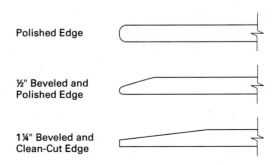

Polished Edge

½" Beveled and Polished Edge

1¼" Beveled and Clean-Cut Edge

Figure 5–20
Mirror bevels.

Stock-Sheet Mirrors: Mirrors of varying sizes over 10 square feet, and up to 7 square feet, from which all types of custom mirrors are cut. Normally packed 800 to 1,000 square feet to a case.

Transparent Mirror: A first surface mirror with a thin film of reflective coating. To ensure most efficient use, the light intensity on the viewer's side of the mirror must be significantly less than on the subject side. Under such a condition, the viewer can see through the mirror as through a transparent glass, while the subject looks into a mirror.

Installation. Both mastic and mechanical devices, such as clips or rosettes, should be used to install a mirror properly. Clips are usually of polished chrome and are placed around the outside edges. Rosettes are clear plastic fasteners and require a hole to be drilled several inches in from the edge so the mirror will accept the fastening screws and rosettes. Because of the fragile quality of mirrors, their use should be limited to areas where the likelihood of breakage is minimal.

CERAMIC TILE

Ceramic tile is frequently used on walls when an easily cleaned, waterproof, and durable surface is desired. One use of ceramic tile is as a **backsplash** in the kitchen or as a counter top. When ceramic tile is used for these purposes, the grout may be sealed by use of a commercial sealer or by using a lemon oil furniture polish. Ceramic tile is also used for the surrounds of showers and bathtubs and for bathroom walls in general. These three uses are probably the most common ones, but ceramic tile may also be used on the walls in foyers and hallways (plain, patterned, or displaying a logo) and as a heat-resistant material around fireplaces and stoves. Ceramic tile for countertops is discussed in Chapter 9.

If walls are completely covered with ceramic tile, there will be no need for trim pieces. In bathrooms or kitchens, however, or anyplace where tiling will not be continued from wall to wall or from ceiling to floor, trim pieces must be added. The type of tile trim used will vary with the method of installation. A thin-set installation will require a surface bullnose. With the thick-set method a separate piece of trim is used to finish off the edge and corners (Figure 5–21).

A bullnose for thick-set installations has an overhanging curved piece, whereas a bullnose for thin-set installations is the same thickness as the surrounding tiles but has a curved finished edge. For bath and shower installations, angle trims for the top and inside edges are used, and for walls meeting the floor, a cove is used (Figure 5–21).

The Tile Council of America offers the following installation advice:

> Use of wall-washer and cove type lighting, where the lights are located, either at the wall/ceiling interface, or mounted directly on the wall, are popular techniques of producing dramatic room lighting effects. When proper backing surfaces, installation materials and methods, and location of light fixtures are not carefully coordinated, these lighting techniques may produce shadows and undesirable effects with ceramic tiles. Similar shadows are created from side lighting interior walls and floors when light shines at that angle through windows and doors.[10]

Installation. Because of the force of gravity, mortar cement cannot be troweled directly onto the wall without sagging. To prevent this sagging, a metal lath, similar to the one used for a plaster wall, is attached to the solid backing and then troweled with mortar. The metal lath acts as a stabilizing force. The backing may be wood, plaster, masonry, or gypsum board. This procedure is equivalent to the thick-set method of floor installation. For wall use over gypsum board, plaster, or other smooth surfaces, an organic adhesive may be used. This adhesive should be water resistant for bath and shower areas (Table 5–2).

The *Handbook of Ceramic Tile Installation,* available from the Tile Council of America, is the nationally accepted guideline for tile installation, even for materials other than ceramic tile.

METAL

In the latter part of the 19th century, during the Victorian era, stamped tin panels were used on ceilings and dadoes. The dadoes even had a molded chair rail incorporated into them. (See Chapter 6 for more details on stamped metal.) While stamped metal is used primarily for ceilings, it can also be used on walls. Metal strips are sometimes used for ceilings and are often carried down onto the wall area (see Figure 6–3).

Perforated metal was developed for use in ventilation grilles and drainage grates. Today it has many interior uses. It can be used instead of a solid wall, providing a feeling of privacy yet with a slight see-through quality. A partition made from perforated metal gives a sense of separation without the thickness of a solid wall. Another use is metal for the doors of wood-framed kitchen cabinets.

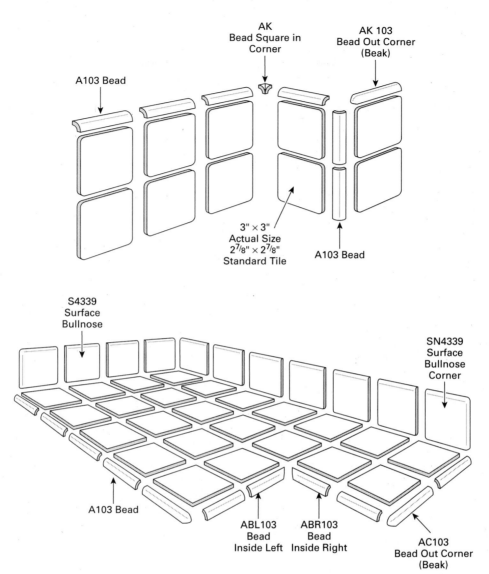

Figure 5–21
Wall trim from Crossville. (Reproduced courtesy of Crossville Ceramics.)

Perforated metal is made by stamping out holes of various sizes and shapes. The perforations can form almost any small geometrical pattern. A similar material is expanded metal, which, because of the manufacturing process, has an open mesh formed by slitting the metal sheet and is always diamond shaped.

ACOUSTICAL PANELS

Several manufacturers produce a mineral fiberboard or fiberglass panel that, when covered with fabric, absorbs sound and provides an attractive and individually designed environment. Because of the textured, porous surface of acoustical panels and the absorbent substrate, sound is absorbed rather than bounced back into the room. These panels may also be used as tack boards for lightweight pictures and graphics. In open-plan office areas, different colors of acoustical panels can be used to direct the flow of traffic through an open office and to differentiate between work areas. In addition to the acoustical qualities of these panels, there are two other beneficial features: (1) The panels are fire retardant, and (2) when installed on perimeter walls, there is a sound-insulating factor that varies with the thickness of the board used.

Acoustical panels may take the form of appliques in sizes of 2 × 4 feet or 2 × 6 feet, or they may cover the wall completely in panel sizes of 24 or 30 inches × 9 feet (Figure 5–22).

TABLE 5–2
Wall Tiling Installation Guide

Simplest methods are indicated; those for heavier services are acceptable. Some very large or heavy tile may require special setting methods. Consult ceramic tile manufacturer.						
SERVICE REQUIREMENTS	WALL TYPE (numbers refer to Handbook Method numbers)					
	Masonry or Concrete	*Page*	*Wood Studs*	*Page*	*Metal Studs*	*Page*
Commercial Construction—Dry or limited water exposure: dairies, breweries, kitchens.	W202 W221[a] W223	20 21 21	W223 W231 W243 W224	21 22 23 23	W223 W241 W242 W243, W244	21 22 22 23
Commercial Construction—Wet: gang showers, tubs, showers, laundries.	W202 W211 W221[a]	20 20 21	W231 W244 B411 B414	22 23 24 25	W241 W244 B411 B414, B415	22 23 24 25
Residential & Light Construction—Dry or limited water exposure: kitchens and toilet rooms, commercial dry area interiors and decoration.	W221[a] W223	21 21	W222[a] W223 W243 W244	21 21 23 23	W222[a] W242 W243 W244	21 22 23 23
Residential & Light Construction—Wet: tub enclosures and showers.	W202 W211 W223	20 20 21	W222[a] W223 W244 B412, B413 B415, B416	21 21 23 24 25	W222[a] W241 W244 B412, B413 B415, B416	21 22 23 24 25
Exterior	W201 W202	20 20	W231	22	W241	22

[a]Use these details where there may be dimensional instability, possible cracks developing in or foreign coating (paint, etc.) on structural wall which includes cleavage membrane (15 lb. felt or polyethylene) between wall surface and tile installation.

Source: 1997 Handbook for Ceramic Tile Installation. Copyright © Tile Council of America, Inc. Reprinted with permission.

Vinyl- or fabric-faced acoustical panels may be designed for various types of installations. For use on an existing wall, only one side needs to be covered. For open-plan landscapes, both surfaces are covered to absorb sound from both sides. Some panels are covered on the two side edges for butted installation, whereas another portable type is wrapped on all surfaces and edges. Sculptwall, with its rounded contour, provides an acoustical and aesthetic solution for sound absorbency. The surface area of the arc is 24 inches wide, and the arc covers 18 inches of wall surface. The internal construction is either 1- or 2-inch molded fiberglass core, which is adhered with the fabric or wallcovering of the client's choice.

Installation. Because there are numerous types of acoustical panels, no single installation method covers all panels. Depending on the type of panel, panels may be attached to the wall by means of an adhesive and/or may have moulding concealing the seams. Manufacturers' recommended installation methods should be followed.

Maintenance. Surface dirt is removed by vacuuming or light brushing. Spots can be treated with dry-cleaning fluid or with carpet shampoo.

Figure 5–22
NOVAWALL was used in this award-winning project to prevent acoustical hot spots. The walls form an ellipse in plan and cant inward as they ascend. The installation features a 1/4-inch-wide reveal grid concealing a 4-inch-thick acoustical fiberglass layer. Architect: Cesar Pelli & Associates. Fabric: Knoll Textiles Devon. (Photo courtesy of Novawall Systems Inc.)

Figure 5–23
QuarryCast, a moulded stone, was used for the Hexagonal columns, veneer panels, and signage with recessed lettering in the Nevada Supreme Courthouse, Carson City, Nevada. Eissman Pence Architects. (Photo courtesy of Formglas Interiors, Inc.)

Figure 5–24
At this telecommunications office, custom sliding panels about 40" × 108" cover the window wall lining the reception area/lobby of the sales center. Custom rosewood finish on poplar. (Project Manager: Laura Seccombel; design firm: Ehrlich-Rominger; photo courtesy of Design Shoji.)

CORK

Cork tiles or panels are available in a 12 × 36 inch size and in thicknesses of 1/2, 3/4, 1, and 1 1/2 inches. They may be used in residential, commercial, educational, and institutional buildings. Because of its porous nature, cork can breathe and, therefore, can be used on basement walls or on the inside surface of exterior support walls without the risk of moisture accumulation. Because of millions of dead-air spaces in the cork particles, cork also has good insulating properties.

Installation. Cork panels are applied by using a 1/8 × 1/8-inch notched trowel and the manufacturer-recommended adhesive.

Maintenance. Vacuuming periodically with the brush attachment is recommended. A light, dust-free sealing coat of silicone aerosol spray will give dust protection; a heavier spray protects against dust and gives the surface a glossier finish, providing more light reflection. A heavy spray tends to close the pores of the cork, however, thus decreasing its sound-deadening and insulating qualities. An alternative to the silicone spray is a 50-50 blend of clear shellac and alcohol.

OTHER MATERIALS

VITRICOR® is a high-molecular acrylic from Nevamar and is suitable for vertical surfaces that require a reflective gloss appearance with deep, rich, saturated color, much like that of hand-lacquered finishes.

QuarryCast®, from Formglas, is a mixture of natural aggregates and minerals and is colored throughout. The material is moulded in standard or custom shapes, is reinforced with glass fibers, and is therefore dimensionally stable and designated for interior wall applications. The material is nontoxic, lightweight, and easy to install (Figure 5–23).

Fixed Shoji panels can be used for walls (Figure 5–24).

BIBLIOGRAPHY

Ackerman, Phyllis, *Wallpaper, Its History, Design and Use*. New York: Frederick A. Stokes Company, 1923.

Architectural Woodwork Institute, *Architectural Woodwork Quality Standards Illustrated*, 7th ed., Version 1.0. Reston, VA: Architectural Woodwork Institute, 1997.

Byrne, Michael, *Setting Tile*. Newton, CT: Taunton Press, 1996.

Entwisle, E. A., *The Book of Wallpaper, A History and an Appreciation*. Trowbridge, England: Redwood Press Ltd., 1970.

Landsmann, Leanne, *Painting and Wallpapering*. New York: Grosset & Dunlap, 1975.

Pittsburgh Corning Corporation, *PC Glass Block® Products Specification Guidelines*. Pittsburgh, PA: Pittsburgh Corning, 1994.

Plumridge, Andrew and Wlm Meulenkamp, *Brickwork, Architecture and Design*. New York: Harry N. Abrams, 1993.

Schumacher, *A Guide to Wallcoverings*. New York: Author.

Time-Life Books, *Paint and Wallpaper*. New York: Time-Life Books, 1981.

Time-Life Books, *Walls and Ceilings*. Alexandria, VA: Time-Life Books, 1996.

Wilson, Ralph Plastics Co., *The ABC's of Easy Care for Wilsonart® Brand Decorative Laminate*. Temple, TX: Author, 1985.

GLOSSARY

Ashlar. Precut stone.

Backsplash. The vertical wall area between the kitchen counter and the upper cabinets.

Booked. Folding back of pasted wallcovering so that pasted sides are touching.

Book match. Every other leaf is turned over, so the right side of a leaf abuts a right side and a left side abuts a left side.

Casing. Exposed trim or moulding.

Casing bead. A carved protective reinforcement strip to protect the edge from damage.

Chinoiserie. (French) Refers to Chinese designs or manner.

Cobble. Similar in appearance to fieldstone.

Compound curve. Curving in two different directions at the same time.

Compressive strength. Amount of stress and pressure a material can withstand.

Concave. Hollow or inward-curving shape.

Convex. Arched or outward-curving shape.

Cramps. U-shaped metal fastenings.

Desiccant. Substance capable of removing moisture from the air.

Dimensional stability. Ability to retain shape regardless of temperature and humidity.

Drywall. Any interior covering that does not require the use of plaster or mortar.

Evacuated. Air is removed.

Feathering. Tapering off to almost nothing.

Fieldstone. Rounded stone.

Flake. A pattern produced when slicing through the medullary rays in some species, principally oak.

Flitch. Portion of a log from which veneer is cut.

Header. End of an exposed brick.

Header course. Headers used every sixth course.

Head. Horizontal cross member supported by the jambs.

HPDL. High-pressure decorative laminate.

Jamb. Vertical member at the sides of a door.

Laminated glass. Breaks without shattering. Glass remains in place.

Lauan mahogany. A wood from the Philippines that, although not a true mahogany, resembles mahogany in grain.

Leaves. Individual pieces of veneer.

Mortar stain. Stain caused by excess mortar on face of brick or stone.

Nonferrous. Containing no iron.

Plumb line. True vertical line.

Pretrimmed. Selvages or edges have been removed.

Raking light. Light shining obliquely down the length of a wall.

Reveal. A recessed space left between two adjoining panels for design purposes.

Rubble. Uncut stone.

Scratch coat. In three-coat plastering, the first coat.

Shiplap. An overlapping wood joint.

Simple curve. Curving in one direction only.

Stretcher. Long side of an exposed brick.

Struck. Mortar joint where excess mortar is removed by a trowel.

Suction. Absorption of water by the gypsum board from the wet plaster.

Tambours. Thin strips of wood or other materials attached to a flexible backing for use on curved surfaces. Similar in appearance to a roll-top desk.

Tempered glass. Glass having two to four times the strength of ordinary glass as the result of being heated and then suddenly cooled.

Tensile strength. Resistance of a material to tearing apart when under tension.

Toile-de-Jouy. Similar to the printed cottons made by Oberkampf in France during the 18th and 19th centuries.

Trompe l'oeil. French for "fooling the eye." Used on painted surfaces such as walls or furniture.

NOTES

[1]Schumacher, *A Guide to Wallcoverings.* New York: Author, n.d.

[2]Koroseal Wallcovering, "Suggested Specification, Installation Instructions, Care and Maintenance." New Jersey: Author, n.d.

[3]*Architectural Woodwork Quality Standards Illustrated,* 7th edition, Version 1.0. Reston, VA: Architectural Woodwork Institute, 1997, p. 6. All quotes from *Architectural Woodwork Quality Standards Illustrated* reproduced with permission.

[4]Ibid., p. 45 (boldface added).

[5]Ibid., pp. 45 and 46 (boldface added).

[6]Ibid., p. 48.

[7]Ibid., pp. 50–53.

[8]Ibid., p. 49.

[9]Viracon Privacy Glass brochure.

[10]Tile Council of America, Inc., *1997 Handbook for Ceramic Tile Installation.* Clemson, SC: Author, p. 8.

6

Ceilings

Early Greeks and Romans used lime stucco for ceilings, on which low, medium, and high **reliefs** were carried out. Italians in the 15th century worked with plaster, and in England Henry VIII's Hampton Court featured highly decorative plasterwork ceilings. In the Tudor and Jacobean periods, the plasterwork for ceilings had a geometric basis in medium and high relief. This style was followed by the classicism of Christopher Wren and Inigo Jones (an admirer of Palladio). In the late 18th century, the Adam brothers designed and used cast plaster ornaments for medallions with **arabesques, paterae,** and urns.

Stamped tin ceilings used in the 19th and 20th centuries disappeared from use in the 1930s but are now staging a comeback. In private residences, tin ceilings were occasionally used in halls and bathrooms. In commercial buildings, metal ceilings were used to comply with the early fire codes.

The ceiling should not be considered as merely the flat surface over our heads that is painted white. The ceiling is an integral part of a room; it affects space, light, heat, and sound, and the ceiling's design should reflect the overall ambience of the room. There are many ways to achieve this integration, such as beams for a country or Old World appearance, a stamped metal ceiling for a Victorian ambience, a wood ceiling for contemporary warmth, or an acoustical ceiling for today's noisier environments. Ceiling treatments are limited only by the designer's imagination.

PLASTER

There are times when the ceiling should be an unobtrusive surface in a room. If this is the case, plastering is the answer. The plaster surface may be smooth or highly textured or somewhere in between. A smooth surface will reflect more light than a heavily textured one of the same color.

The plaster for a ceiling is applied in the same manner as for walls, although scaffolding must be used in the application process so the surface will be within working reach. It will take longer to plaster a ceiling than it will to plaster wall area of similar size because of the overhead reach.

The ornately carved ceilings of the past are obtained today using one of three means:

1. Precast plaster, either in pieces or **tiles**
2. Molded polyurethane foam
3. Wood mouldings, mainly used as **crown mouldings.**

Urethane foam mouldings are discussed in detail in Chapter 7, in the section titled "Mouldings."

131

Gypsum Board

The main difficulty with installing gypsum board for ceilings is the weight of the board. Ceiling **panels** of 1/2-inch, however, are specially designed to resist sagging and are equal to 5/8-inch wallboard, installed perpendicular to framing. Gypsum board does require more labor and, again, scaffolding. It may be applied to a flat or curved surface. Spacing, whether using nails or screws, is required 6 to 8 inches apart. The seams and screw holes are filled in the same manner as for gypsum board walls. The surface may be perfectly smooth, lightly textured, or heavily textured. A smooth surface not only reflects the most light but also shows any unevenness of ceiling joists. Wallpaper may also be used on the ceiling, as shown in Color Plate 10.

Beams

Beams are probably the oldest of ceiling treatments, with the ceiling beams of the lower floor being the floor joists of the room above. Colonial New England houses had hand-hewn timbers that ran the length of the room; a larger **summer beam** ran across the width. The area between the beams was covered by the floor boards of the room above or, in the case of a sloped ceiling, the wood covering the outside of the roof timbers. Later these floorboards were covered with plaster and the timbers were left to darken naturally. The plaster in between the timbers had a rough or troweled surface. Today, instead of plaster, a plank ceiling is sometimes used in combination with beams.

Today, beamed ceilings are often used for a country setting with an Old World or contemporary feeling. The beams in early American homes were made of one piece of wood 12 inches or more square, but beams of this size are difficult to obtain today. Trus Joist MacMillan, however, produces Parallam® PSL, which is available in dimensions up to 11 inches by 19 inches and lengths up to 66 feet. These beams are made from 4-foot-long to 8-foot-long veneer strands that are dried and then bonded using adhesives via a patented, microwave pressing process.

There are several methods of imitating the solid, heavy look of hand-hewn beams. For example, a box beam may be built as part of the floor joists or as a surface addition. To make a box beam appear similar to a hand-hewn beam, the surface must be treated to avoid the perfectly smooth surface of modern lumber.

In contemporary homes, **laminated beams** are used. These consist of several pieces of lumber (depending on the width required) glued together (on the wide surface). Because of this type of construction, laminated beams are very strong. Laminated beams are commonly referred to as "lam" beams.

Wood

A natural outgrowth of a beamed ceiling is to use wood planks or strips to cover the ceiling joists. With the many types of wood available on the market today, wood ceilings are used in many homes, particularly contemporary ones.

Almost all types of strip flooring and solid wood for walls may be used on a ceiling. Because of the darkness of wood, it is most suitable for a cathedral or shed ceiling (the dark color appears to lower the ceiling).

Acoustical Ceilings

Residential

Because the ceiling is the largest unobstructed area in a room, sound is bounced off its surface without much absorption. Just as light is reflected from a smooth, high-gloss surface, so sound is reflected or bounced off the ceiling. Uncontrolled reverberations transform sound into noise, muffling music and disrupting effective communication. Textured ceiling tiles help reduce this reverberation and are often used today in both residential and commercial interiors.

Acoustical ceilings, however, do not prevent the transmission of sound from one floor to another. The only answer to sound transmission is mass—the actual resistance of the material to vibrations caused by sound waves.

Sound absorption qualities may be obtained by using different materials and methods. The most well known is the acoustical tile (a 12-inch square) or panel (larger than 1 square foot) composed of mineral fiber board. Other materials, such as fiberglass, metal, plastic-clad fiber, and fabric, may also be used. Sound absorption properties are produced by mechanical dies that perforate the mineral fiberboard after curing. Metal may also be perforated to improve its acoustical qualities if backed with an absorptive medium.

The noise reduction coefficient (**NRC**) is a measure of sound absorbed by a material. The NRC of different types of panels may be compared. The higher the number, the more sound reduction is indicated. For purposes of comparison, tests must be made at the same **Hertz** (Hz) range.

The sound transmission class (**STC**) is a single-number rating that is used to characterize the sound-insulating value of a partition (wall or ceiling). A partition prevents sound from being transmitted from one area to another; the STC rating denotes approximately how much the sound will be reduced when traveling through the partition. The higher the rating, the less sound will be transmitted through the wall or floor/ceiling.

The ceiling attenuation class **(CAC)** refers to the sound attenuation ability of ceiling systems. The CAC rates how much sound will be reduced when it is transmitted through the ceiling of one room into an adjacent room through a shared **plenum.** A higher rating indicates that the material will allow less sound transmission.

Another characteristic often included in acoustical mineral fiberboard charts is light reflectance **(LR),** which indicates the percentage of light reflected from a ceiling product's surface. The LR varies according to the amount of texture on the ceiling's surface and the value of the color. Some ceiling panels have a mineral fiber substrate with a needle-punched fabric surface.

Award-winning Cirrus Themes™ from Armstrong World Industries bring whimsy to ceiling design and create an ambience that encourages fun, comfort, and a sense of well-being. Cirrus Themes can be used in health and daycare facilities; designs include Primaries, Letters and Numbers, Trains, Critters, Animal paw prints, Stars, and Leaves.

Cirrus Borders™ help to break up a large ceiling expanse with a choice of classical, transitional, or contemporary panel detailing. Panel designs combine to create borders, continuous patterns, or island focal areas on the ceiling.

Installation. In private residences, any of three installation methods may be used: (1) If the tiles are to be used over an existing ceiling, they may be cemented to that ceiling provided the surface is solid and level. (2) Tiles have interlocking edges that provide a solid joining method as well as an almost seamless installation. If the existing ceiling is not solid or level, furring strips are nailed up so that the edges of the tile may be glued and stapled to a solid surface. (3) A suspended ceiling may be used, which consists of a metal spline suspended by wires from the ceiling or joists. The tiles are laid in the spline so that the edges of the panels are supported by the edge of the T-shaped spline. The splines may be left exposed or they may be covered by the tile. There are two advantages to using a suspended ceiling:

1. Damaged panels are easily replaced.
2. The height of the ceiling may be varied according to the size of the room or other requirements.

With an exposed spline, it is easy to replace a single panel; the damaged panel is merely lifted out. If the spline is covered, however, the damaged panel or panels are removed and, when replacing the last panel, the tongue is removed.

Maintenance. Celotex suggests that a soft gum eraser be used to remove small spots, dirt marks, and streaks from acoustical tiles. For larger areas or larger smudges, a chemically treated sponge rubber pad, or wallpaper cleaner is used. The sponge rubber pad or wallpaper cleaner must be in fresh condition. Nicks and scratches may be touched up with colored chalks. Dust is removed by brushing lightly with a soft brush or clean rag or by vacuuming with a soft brush attachment.

Acoustical tiles must not be soaked with water. They should be washed by light application of a sponge dampened with a mild liquid detergent solution: about 1/2 cup in 1 gallon of water. After the sponge is saturated, it should be squeezed nearly dry and then lightly rubbed on the surface to be cleaned using long, sweeping, gentle strokes. The strokes should be in the same direction as the texture if tile is ribbed or embossed.

Surface openings must not be clogged or bridged when acoustical tile is painted. A paint of high hiding power should be used because it is desirable to keep the number of coats to a minimum (paint greatly affects the NRC of the acoustical material). Some paint manufacturers provide specific formulations that have high hiding power and low combustibility and are not likely to bridge openings in the tile. The paint must be applied as thinly as necessary.

Commercial

Acoustical ceiling products have become a mainstay of commercial installations. Movable office partitions are prevalent today, so audio privacy is necessary. In this day of electronic word processors and data processing equipment, office din is somewhat less than in the days of noisy typewriters, but telephones and voices still cause distracting sounds. Productivity is increased in a quieter environment, but a noiseless environment is easily disrupted. USG Interiors' Cadre Executive, mainly a commercial product, can be adapted for use in a contemporary dining room (Figure 6–1).

The advantages of a residential suspended acoustical ceiling also apply to commercial installations, but the major reason for using a suspended ceiling in commercial work is easy access to wiring, telephone lines, plumbing, and heating ducts.

Installation. The traditional approach to lighting is to use **luminaires** recessed at specific intervals in the acoustical ceiling. The fixtures are often covered by

Figure 6–1
Cadre Executive panels are shown with a dome panel, from which the lighting fixture hangs, and corner and border panels in a pleasing combination. The dome and corner panels are 4′ × 4′ and the border panel is 2′ × 4′. (Photo courtesy of USG Interiors.)

lenses or louvers to diffuse the light. USG Interiors offers a variety of different luminous ceiling systems, including Rotunda®, Skylight™, Quadradome®, and Transparencies™ (Figure 6–2).

Today, not only lighting but also heating and cooling are often incorporated into acoustical ceiling installations. This is done in several ways. The heating and cooling duct may be spaced between the modules in one long, continuous line, or individual vents may be used. In one interesting innovation, the entire area

Figure 6–2
*Rotunda is a domed, luminous ceiling system available in any module
size or custom design (typical sizes are 8- to 24-inch radials). (Photo
courtesy of USG Interiors.)*

between the suspended ceiling and the joists is used
as a plenum area, with the conditioned air entering
the room through orifices in the individual tiles.

One word of warning: If you are replacing a ceiling that may contain asbestos, OSHA has some very

stringent regulations and safety precautions that must
be strictly adhered to.

For areas in which mold, mildew, or microorganisms may be present, an inorganic ceiling, such as
Eurostone from Chicago Metallic®, is recommended.

Eurostone won a 1997 Builder Show award for Technology Solutions.

METAL

Metal ceilings were originally introduced in the 1860s as a replacement for the ornamental plasterwork that decorated the walls and ceilings of the most fashionable rooms of the day. Once in place, it was discovered that metal ceilings offered two important benefits: (1) Unlike plaster, the metal could withstand rough use, and (2) it could be more easily maintained than plaster, which would flake, crack, and peel. Many of today's metal ceilings are actually steel, which can be prepainted or plated with copper, brass, or chrome.

Stamped metal ceilings now come in 1 foot squares, 1' × 2', 2' × 4', or 2' × 8', and are installed by attaching the units to furring strips with nails 12 inches apart. These stamped metal ceilings are suitable for Victorian restorations and may be ordered with cornice mouldings.

One contemporary metal ceiling is made of 3- to 7-inch-wide strips of painted or polished aluminum, which clip to special carriers. The polished metals also include bronze and brass finishes and can provide an almost mirrored effect. These ceilings may be used in renovations over existing sound ceilings or for new construction. The metal strips may be installed as separate strips, with the area between the strips left open to the plenum, or the open space may be covered with an acoustical pad. The metal strips may also be covered with a joining strip on the face to form a flush surface, or on the back for a board-on-batten effect. Metal strip ceilings may be installed as a flat, curved, or wavy surface (Figure 6–3).

For a special metal ceiling, the Gage Corporation International offers 24-inch square modules in a large collection of standard designs. Also available are custom designs, constructed of 50 percent recycled aluminum. One of Gage's custom designs is shown in Figure 6–4 and Color Plate 11.

OTHER CEILING MATERIALS

A vinyl-coated, embossed aluminum, bonded to a mineral fiber substrate, results in an easily maintained, corrosion-resistant, and durable ceiling product. Grease vapor concentrations may be wiped clean

Figure 6–3
Brooks Army Medical Center, San Antonio, Texas, features PLANAR®, an Interfinish™ brand product from Chicago Metallic. (Photo courtesy of Interfinish brand products of Chicago Metallic.)

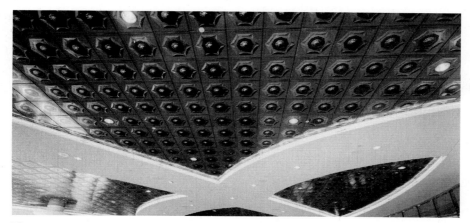

Figure 6–4
A porte cochere of a hotel and casino has a metal ceiling Design 413A, a colorful and durable surface. (Photo courtesy of Gage Ceilings.)

with a sponge or a mild detergent solution; thus these types of ceilings are suitable for commercial kitchens, laboratories, and hospitals.

Mirrors are not recommended for ceilings; instead, A-Look Mirror Quality Decorative Metals from Wilsonart® may be used. (A-Look Mirror Quality Decorative Metals are supplied by Mitsubishi KASEI America Inc.) A-Look ceilings are available in chrome, bronze, and gold colors; there are also seven etched designs.

Baffles are fabric-covered fiberglass panels hung from a ceiling by means of wire attached to eyelets installed in the top edge of the panel. Baffles are not only functional, but decorative too, with a sound rating of NRC 0.80. Baffles hung perpendicular to a ceiling are an established and highly effective way to create additional sound-absorbing surfaces, especially in interiors lacking sufficient surfaces for wall-mounted panels. Baffles can be used for signage or to denote areas or departments within a larger space.

Not all acoustical ceilings are flat. Many are **coffered** in 2- to 4-foot square modules. These panels may or may not include luminaires. An Interfinish brand product from Chicago Metallic, MAGNA T-CELL™ (Figure 6–5), creates visual interest while concealing service and mechanical systems (which, though hidden, are still accessible).

Compässo™ is a suspension ceiling trim from USG Interiors. The Compässo Design Kit includes a special template of the standard curves available to a 1/4- and 1/8-inch scale—it even includes a supply of graph paper. Designers can sketch their design using ideas such as the following:

Place dramatic accents with soffits a few inches below the ceiling.

Suspend a floating island far below the ceiling plane.

Build powerful peninsulas extending prominently from the wall. Separate or emphasize areas; create distinct spaces within spaces.

Bring special lighting or acoustical privacy closer.

USG then provides, at no charge, an AutoCAD® drawing for the designer's approval, complete with parts identification. The grid can also be used without the panels for an open-cell effect.

Figure 6–5
The Lake Charles Civic Center, Lake Charles, Louisiana, has a MAGNA T-CELL ceiling that creates visual interest while concealing service and mechanical systems. However, these systems are still accessible. (Photo courtesy of Interfinish brand products of Chicago Metallic.)

CERAMIC TILE

For a ceiling that is easy to wipe clean, or in very moist areas such as bathrooms and showers, ceramic tile may be installed.

BIBLIOGRAPHY

Rather, Guy Cadogan, *Ceilings and Their Decoration.* London, England: T. Werner Laurie, 1978.

Time-Life Books, *Walls and Ceilings.* Alexandria, VA: Time-Life Books, 1980.

GLOSSARY

Arabesques. Elaborate scroll designs either carved or in low relief.

CAC. Ceiling attenuation class. The CAC rates how much sound will be reduced when it is transmitted through the ceiling of one room into an adjacent room through a shared plenum.

Coffered. Recessed panels in the ceiling. May or may not be decorated.

Crown moulding. The uppermost moulding next to the ceiling.

Hertz. Unit of frequency measurement. One unit per second. Abbreviation: Hz.

Laminated beam. Several pieces of lumber glued to form a structural timber.

LR. Light reflectance. The amount of light reflected from a surface.

Luminaire. A complete lighting fixture with all components needed to be connected to the electric power supply.

NRC. Noise reduction coefficient. The average percentage of sound reduction at various Hertz levels.

Panel. A ceiling unit larger than one square foot.

Patera. A round or oval raised surface design.

Plenum. The space between a suspended ceiling and the floor above.

Relief. A design that is raised above the surrounding area.

Soffit. Underside of an overhang.

STC. Sound transmission class. A number denoting the sound-insulating value of a material.

Summer beam. A main supporting beam in old New England homes, in the middle of a room, resting on the fireplace at one end and a post at the other.

Tile. Ceiling tile (12 inches square).

7

Other Components

MOULDINGS

To an interior designer, trim and mouldings are what icing is to a cake: They cover, enhance, and decorate a plain surface. Basically, heavily carved or ornate trim is used in a traditional setting, whereas simpler trim is used where a contemporary ambience is desired.

The AWI lists four types of trim, all custom manufactured: **Standing trim** is fixed-length trim such as door and window **casings,** stops, **stools** or sills, and **aprons.** Such trim can usually be produced with single lengths of wood (depending on the species). **Running trim** is continuing lengths of trim (depending on species), such as **cornices, fascias, soffits, chair rails,** baseboards, and **shoe moulding. Rail** moulding is used on corridor walls of hospitals and nursing homes and for guard rails at glass openings. **Board paneling** is applied in the form of multiple boards (Figure 7–1).

Materials for trim and mouldings should be constructed from easily shaped stock. Both pine and oak are used when wood trim is desired, and both provide details that are easily discernible and smooth. Trim should always be **mitered** at the corners; that is, the joint should be cut at a 45° angle. Also available are Medium Density Fiberboard (MDF) mouldings for painted interior trims. Other trim materials include solid surface materials, such as Corian® and Gibraltar®, which are also used for counters. Depending on thickness, these materials are fairly easy to shape, and they are used most often in commercial and medical installations.

Bases are a type of moulding universally used to finish the area where the wall and floor meet. There are several reasons for using a base or skirting: It covers any discrepancy or expansion space between the wall and the floor; it forms a protection for the wall from cleaning equipment; and it may also be a decorative feature. The word *base* is used to describe all types of materials, including those mentioned earlier as well as vinyl or rubber.

Baseboard is the term used for wood bases only. When a plain baseboard is used, the wood should be sanded smoothly on the face and particularly on the top edge to facilitate cleaning. The exposed edge should be slightly beveled to prevent breaking or chipping. Traditional baseboards have a shaped top edge with a flat lower part. This design may be achieved with one piece of wood 3 1/2 to 7 inches wide or may consist of separate parts, with a base moulding on top of a square-edged piece of lumber. A **base shoe** may be added to either type. Traditional one-piece baseboards are available as stock mouldings from the better woodworking manufacturers (see, for example, Figure 7–1).

For residential use, windows come prefabricated with the **brickmould** or exterior trim attached. The interior casing (the exposed trim) may be flat or

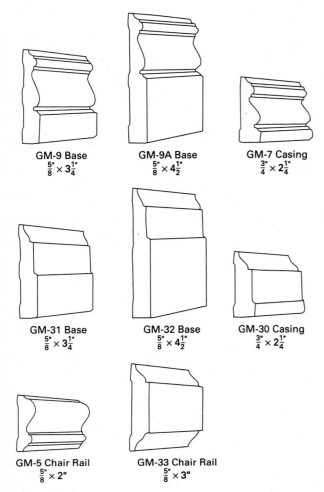

GM-9 Base
$\frac{5}{8}$" × 3$\frac{1}{4}$"

GM-9A Base
$\frac{5}{8}$" × 4$\frac{1}{2}$"

GM-7 Casing
$\frac{3}{4}$" × 2$\frac{1}{4}$"

GM-31 Base
$\frac{5}{8}$" × 3$\frac{1}{4}$"

GM-32 Base
$\frac{5}{8}$" × 4$\frac{1}{2}$"

GM-30 Casing
$\frac{3}{4}$" × 2$\frac{1}{4}$"

GM-5 Chair Rail
$\frac{5}{8}$" × 2"

GM-33 Chair Rail
$\frac{5}{8}$" × 3"

Figure 7–1
Wood bases, chair rails, and casings. (Courtesy of Granite Mill.)

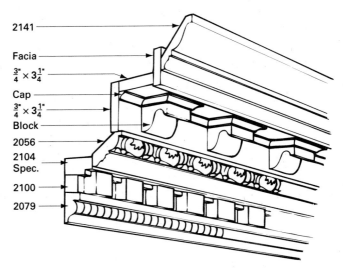

2141
Facia
$\frac{3}{4}$" × 3$\frac{1}{4}$"
Cap
$\frac{3}{4}$" × 3$\frac{1}{4}$"
Block
2056
2104
Spec.
2100
2079

Figure 7–2
Ten-piece wooden ceiling cornice. (Drawing courtesy of Driwood Period Moulding.)

moulded and is applied after the window and walls have been installed and the windows **caulked**, a crucial step in these days of energy conservation. The interior casing usually matches the baseboard design, although the size may vary (see Figure 7–1).

Doors, particularly for residential use, often come **prehung.** After installation of the door frame, the space between the jamb and the wall is covered by a casing. This casing matches the profile of the one used around the windows, with the width of the casing determined by the size, scale, and style of the room.

Crown and **bed mouldings** are used to soften the sharp line where ceiling and walls meet. Cove mouldings also serve the same purpose; the difference is that crown mouldings are intricately shaped and cove mouldings have a simple curved face. Cove mouldings may be painted the same color as the ceiling, thus giving a lowered appearance to the ceiling. Cornice

mouldings may be ornate and made up of as many as 10 separate pieces of wood (Figure 7–2).

Chair rails are used in traditional homes to protect the surface of walls from damage caused by the backs of chairs. These rails may be simple strips of wood with rounded edges, or they may have shaped top and bottom edges, depending on the style of the room (see Figure 7–1). The installed height of chair rails should be between 30 and 36 inches. When chair rails are to be painted, they should be made of a hard, close-grained wood. If they are to be left natural, they should be of the same material and should be finished in the same manner as the rest of the woodwork.

When plywood panels are used on walls, the edges are sometimes covered with a square-edge batten. In more traditional surroundings, a moulded batten is used.

Picture mouldings, as the name implies, were used to create a continuous projecting support around the walls of a room for picture hooks. Picture moulding has a curved top to receive the picture hook. Of course, when pictures are hung by this method, the wires used for hanging will be visible, but this

Figure 7–3
This room, as seen in House Beautiful *magazine, is a fine example of the use of stock mouldings to achieve a period appearance. Shown are a cove moulding in the coffered ceiling; fluted moulding for the cornice; Osborne Shell niche cap; cornice moulding for the broken pediment of the overmantel; cornice moulding for the mantel; and Linden frieze for the frame under the pediment. (Photo courtesy of Focal Point Architectural Products Inc.)*

method is still used in older homes, museums, and art galleries, where frequent rearranging is required. No damage is done to the walls, as it is with the modern method of hanging pictures. Picture moulding is placed just below or several inches below the ceiling. Wherever the placement, the ceiling color is usually continued down to the top of the moulding.

An infinite variety of patterns may be used for mouldings. They may be stock shapes and sizes or shaped to the designer's specifications by the use of custom-formed shaper blades. This latter method is the most expensive but does achieve a unique moulding.

Wood mouldings may be covered with metal in many finishes (including bright chrome, brass, copper, or simulated metal) for use as picture frame moulding, interior trim, and displays.

All the mouldings discussed thus far have been constructed of wood. When a heavily carved cornice molding is required, the material may be a **polymer.** Focal Point® makes a polymer molding by direct impression from the original wood, metal, or plaster article. This direct process gives the reproduction all the

personality, texture, and spirit of the original, but with several advantages: The mouldings are much less expensive than the hand-carved originals. They are lighter weight and therefore easier to handle; they may be nailed, drilled, or screwed; and they are receptive to sanding. Another feature is that, in many cases, the original moulding consisted of several pieces, but modern technology produces multiple mouldings in a one-piece strip, thus saving on installation costs. For contract installations where fire-rated materials must be used, Specicast™ meets ASTM E-84, Class A specifications.

Focal Point is authorized to reproduce architectural details for the Victorian Society of America, the Colonial Williamsburg Foundation, the National Trust for Historic Preservation (Figure 7–3), and the Historic Natchez Foundation. The contemporary market is not being ignored; Focal Point offers Santa Fe and Taos step mouldings in its contemporary line.

Polymer mouldings are factory primed in white; however, if a stained effect is desired, the mouldings may be primed beige and stained with Mohawk non-

Figure 7–4
On the left, the D'Evereux Rim from Focal Point. On the right, the Woodlawn Stair Brackets from Focal Point's National Trust for Historic Preservation Collection. (Photos courtesy of Focal Point Architectural Products Inc.)

penetrating stain. Careful brush strokes will simulate grain; when stain is skillfully applied, the effect is very convincing.

In Chapter 6, ceiling medallions were mentioned as a form of ceiling decoration. When these medallions were first used as **backplates** for chandeliers, they were made of plaster, but again the polymer reproductions are lightweight and easy to ship. The medallions are primed white at the factory, ready to paint. The use of medallions is not limited to chandeliers (Figure 7–4). They may also be used as a backplate for ceiling fans.

Other materials used in ornate ceiling cornices include gypsum with a polymer agent that is reinforced with glass fibers for added strength. A wood fiber combination may also be used.

Lightweight QuarryCast® or glass-reinforced gypsum and cement cast architectural products, including all types of mouldings mentioned previously, are used internationally. Round or tapered column covers, with capitals and bases, are also available (see Figure 5–23).

Other reproductions from the past include the dome and the niche cap. When first designed, they were made of plaster or wood, which was then hand carved. Domes and niche caps can provide a touch of authenticity in renovations; in fact, many of Focal Point's designs have been used in restorations of national historical landmarks. Niche caps have a shell design and form the top of a curved recess that usually displays sculpture, vases, flowers, or any other prized possession.

Stair brackets are another form of architectural detail and are placed on the finished **stringer** for a decorative effect (see Figure 7–4).

DOORS

An entry door makes a first impression, whether for a private residence or a business. Doors for residential use may be constructed of wood, metal, or fiberglass. In commercial applications, however, doors are not usually made of wood because of fire codes and the need for ease of maintenance.

Wood Doors

Flush doors are perfectly flat and smooth, with no decoration. There are several methods of constructing flush doors. A honeycomb hollow core is used for some interior residential flush doors. The core of the door is made of 2- to 3-inch-wide solid wood for the **rails** and 1 to 2 inches of solid wood for the **stiles**, with an additional 20-inch-long strip of wood, called a lock block, in the approximate hardware location. The area between the solid wood is filled with a honeycomb or ladder core. In less expensive doors, this core is covered by the finish veneer. More expensive doors have one or two layers of veneer before the finish veneer is applied. Thus, a flush door may be of three-, five-, or seven–ply construction.

Better-quality flush doors are constructed with a lumber core, also known as staved wood, and wood blocks are used in place of the honeycomb or ladder core of the hollow core door. The staved or lumber core may or may not have the blocks bonded together. With staved core doors, the inside rails and stiles are narrower than in other flush doors because this type of construction is more rigid. Species used for face veneers include hardwoods, such as oak, mahogany, cherry, and maple, and softwoods, such as pine and fir. If the door is to be painted, a "paint-grade" wood door made of softwood should be specified (Figure 7–5).

Another method of door construction utilizes a particleboard or flakeboard core with a crossband veneer to which the face veneer is attached. A particleboard door core is warp resistant and solid, has no knots or voids, and has good insulation properties and sound resistance (thereby limiting heat loss and transfer of sound waves).

Flush doors for commercial installations may have a high-pressure decorative laminate (HPDL) as the face veneer or, for low maintenance, a photogravure or vinyl covering similar to the paneling discussed in Chapter 5.

Commercial installations of doors do not always require a moulding; the doors are merely set into the wall. In other words, the wall meets the door jamb.

There are three methods of achieving a paneled look in doors. One uses a solid ornate **ogee sticking;** in other words, the stiles and rails are shaped so the moulding and stile or rails are all one piece of wood. The second method is the first but uses a simpler **ovolo** sticking. The third method uses a **dadoed** stile and rail, and the joining of panel and stile is covered by a separate applied moulding. If the panel is large, it will be made of plywood and a moulding will be used; if the panel is under 10 inches in width, it may be of solid wood (in Premium Grade, solid lumber is not permitted). Paneled doors reflect different periods, as do paneled walls. When period paneling is used, the doors should be of similar design.

There are an infinite number of designs for paneled doors. Panels may be horizontal or vertical, small or large, curved or straight, wood or glass (Figure 7–6).

Dutch doors for residential use consist of an upper and lower part. Special hardware joins the two

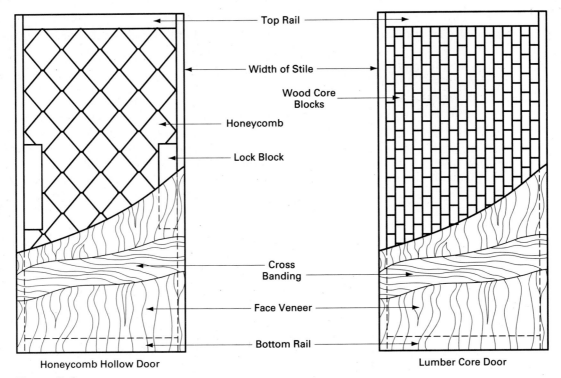

Figure 7–5
Door construction.

parts to form a regular door, or, with the hardware undone, the top part may be opened to ventilate or give light to a room, with the lower part remaining closed. Dutch doors are sometimes used commercially as a service opening. In this case, a shelf is attached to the top of the bottom half (Figure 7–7).

Louvers are used in doors to provide ventilation, such as in cleaning or storage closets, or to aid in air circulation. Louvers are made of horizontal slats contained within stile-and-rail frames. Louvers may be set into wood or metal doors, with the louver at the top and/or bottom, or the center may be all louvered.

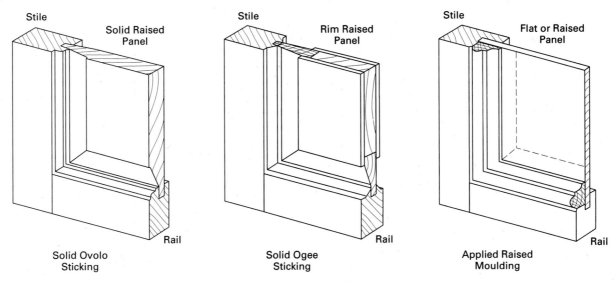

Figure 7–6
Paneled doors.

Color Plate 1
Designed by Gass Design, Pipersville, Pennsylvania, this Grand Prize–winning entry in the 1997 DuPont Antron® Design Award competition (it also was a first place winner in the Retail/Showroom category) is a concept-training center developed for Columbia Prescolite Moldcast, San Leandro, California. The carptet's strong graphics elements, combined with the ceiling-level product displays and flanking mirrors, provide a unifying design. Gass used a carpet of DuPont Antron Legacy nylon. (Photo courtesy of DuPont Flooring Systems.)

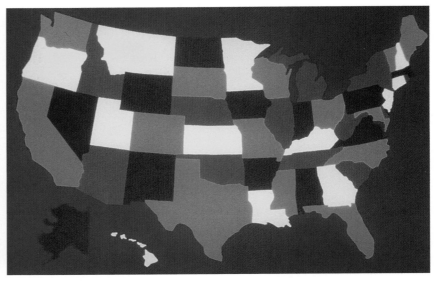

Color Plate 2
Imaginations™ designs provide a wide array of learning and visual aids incorporating bright, primary colors to make learning more creative and fun. On the left is the Learning Circle (actual size 10' x 10'). On the right is a colorful map of the United States (actual size 8' x 6'). (Photos courtesy of Collins & Aikman Floorcoverings Inc.)

Color Plate 3
These patterns and textures of "Piatto" from Lees are appropriate selections for commercial installations and large areas. (Photo courtesy of Lees, a Division of Burlington Industries.)

Color Plate 4

Stunningly designed with a prominent Bird of Paradise motif, Tropicale offers a unique look for contemporary designers. The bold, colorful pattern adds visual excitement while complementing a variety of settings, including hospitality and residential. A continuous filament nylon construction with Scotchgard® protection, Tropicale features four striking colorations. The carpet is manufactured by Philadelphia Commercial, a division of Shaw Industries, Inc. (Photo courtesy of Shaw Industries, Inc.)

Color Plate 5
*Contrasting planks of
quartered oak and American
walnut are used in a unique
manner to create this
interesting entrance way.
(Photo courtesy of Kentucky
Wood Floors.)*

Color Plate 6
*The flooring in this entertainment area is
a prefinished standard parquet floor in
natural red oak. (Photo courtesy of
Harris-Tarkett.)*

Color Plate 7

The floor of the reception area of a prestigious accounting firm is by Wilsonart International. The reception desk is covered with Wilsonart® SSV™ Solid Surfacing. (Photo ©Paul Bardagjy and courtesy of Wilsonart International.)

Color Plate 8

These two patterned medallions from Intarsia can be used as a focal point of either a floor or a table top. (Photos courtesy of Intarsia Inc.)

Color Plate 9

The Community Media Center in Grand Rapids, Michigan, represents one of the nation's first models for citizen access and training in radio, television, and information technology, including cable TV, broadcast radio, and the Internet. John McQueen, the designer of the floor, used a quilt motif, made up of diverse colors, fabrics, textures, and patterns all forming a unified whole, as a metaphor for the media center. Congoleum (VCT) was selected for the project because it offered generous color flexibility combined with durability and ease of installation. Four VCT lines—Selections®, Choices®, Alternatives®, and Special Effects™—were used to bring the quilt design from concept to reality. (Photo courtesy of Congoleum Corp.)

Color Plate 10

On the left is the Turkish Parlor of the Brune-Reutlinger House in San Francisco, California, taken from the Anglo-Japanese and Aesthetic movement room sets. On the right is a ceiling medallion adaption from the designs of P. B. Wight. (Photos courtesy of Bradbury and Bradbury Art Wallapers.)

Color Plate 11
A Celebrity Cruise ship uses Custom Design 403 from Gage Ceilings to create a festive mood in one of its casino areas. (Photo courtesy of Gage Corporation International.)

Color Plate 12
Jenn-Air's new Blue Creek line is shown in three colors: sapphire blue, jade, and Bordeau red. Shown are the double 27" wall ovens and the dishwasher. (Photos courtesy of Jenn-Air Company.)

Color Plate 13
Chatham's white beaded inset cabinets with mullion glass doors and simple trim help to create an open feeling that is at the same time intimate and reminiscent of turn-of-the-century bungalows. Note the glass shelves where ornaments and glassware are stored. The upper cabinets, however, have wood shelves that are almost hidden by the cross mullions of the glass doors. (Design: The Kitchen Works, Julie Vagts, ASID; photo courtesy of Wood-Mode.)

Color Plate 14
This colorful bathroom from American Standard features the compact fixtures Hamilton toilet, Seychelle pedestal lavatory, and an Ellisse built-in whirlpool. (Photo courtesy of American Standard.)

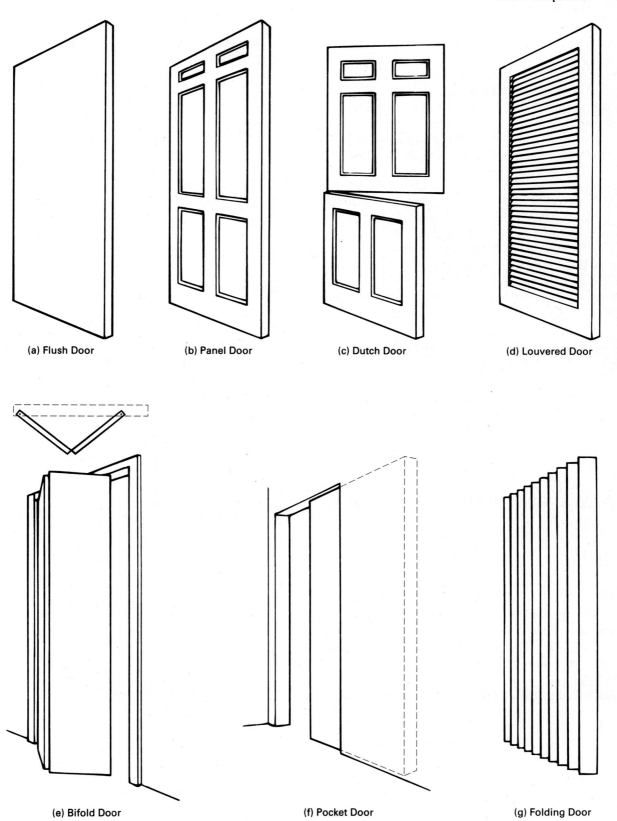

(a) Flush Door   (b) Panel Door   (c) Dutch Door   (d) Louvered Door

(e) Bifold Door   (f) Pocket Door   (g) Folding Door

Figure 7–7
Types of doors.

Some louvers are visionproof, some are adjustable, and others may be lightproof or weatherproof (see Figure 7–7).

One of the most common residential uses for a louvered door is a bifold door for a closet. For a narrow opening, a bifold door consists of two panels; larger openings require a double set of doors opening from the middle. The center panel of each pair is hung from the track, and the outer panels may or may not pivot at the jamb.

A pocket door, or recessed sliding door, requires a special frame and track that is incorporated into the inside of the wall. The finished door is hung from the track before the casing is attached. The bottom of the door is held in place by guides that permit the door to slide sideways while preventing back-and-forth movement (see Figure 7–7).

Folding or accordion doors are used where space needs to be divided temporarily. Folding doors operate and stack compactly within their openings. The panels may be wood-veneered lumber core or particleboard core with a wood-grained vinyl coating. Each panel is 3 5/8 inches or less in width, and folding doors are available in heights up to 16 feet 1 inch. Folding doors operate by means of a track at the top to which the panels are attached by wheels. The handle and locking mechanism is installed on the panel closest to the opening edge (see Figure 7–7).

For an Oriental ambience, fixed or sliding Shoji panels are available; these are wood-framed panels with synskin inserts, which have an Oriental rice paper look (see Figure 5–22). Pinecrest offers a wide variety of Shoji panels, standard or custom, both fixed and sliding.

Glass Doors

Sash doors are similar in construction and appearance to panel doors except that one or more panels are replaced with glass. French doors are often used in residences to open out onto a balcony or patio. They have wood frames and may consist of one sheet of plate glass or may have multiple **lights** in each door. French doors are most often installed in pairs and usually open out.

When French doors or other styles of doors are installed in pairs, one is used as the primary door. The second one is stationary, with a flush bolt or special lock holding it tight at top and bottom. To cover the joining crack between the pair of doors and to make the doors more weather tight, an **astragal** is attached to the interior edge of the stationary door. Both doors may be used to enlarge the opening.

Instead of using large sliding glass doors, the trend today seems to be to use patio doors, either singly or in pairs. These are similar in appearance to double French doors, except that they open into the house instead of out. If double doors are used, the astragal is on the exterior edge of the secondary door.

Glass doors for residential use may have a wood or metal frame and may pivot on hinges or have one sliding panel with the second panel stationary. Whenever full-length glass is used, by law it must be tempered or laminated.

Commercial glass doors must also be made of tempered or laminated glass and are subject to local building codes. The door may be all glass, framed with metal at the top and/or bottom, or framed on all four sides. Because of the nature of an all-glass door, the most visible design feature is the hardware.

Metal Doors

Most metal doors are made of steel, although some are available in aluminum. In the past, metal doors had a commercial or institutional connotation, but today many interior and exterior residential doors and many bifold doors are made of metal. Exterior metal doors were shunned in the past because wood exterior solid-core doors had better insulating qualities. The use of polystyrene and polyurethane as a core has provided residential metal exterior doors with similar insulating qualities that are not as susceptible to temperature changes and warping as are wood doors.

Surfaces may be factory coated with rust-resistant primer (to be painted on site) or vinyl or baked-on polyester finishes embossed with wood grain patterns. Some metal doors are given a wood-fiber coating that can be stained. Higher-end models are actually laminated with a real-wood veneer. Steel doors have a less convincing wood grain than fiberglass doors.

Fiberglass

Fiberglass or fiberglass-composite doors are an alternative to wood. Kaylien® invented the Fiberglass door. The manufacturing process has been perfected to such a degree that the doors bear an amazing resemblance to wood, even when viewed up close. These doors often have a long limited warranty—typically 30 years—and some even have a warranty for as long as the buyer owns the door. Fiberglass door styles are the same as for wood doors.

LustrMetl® from Kaylien are bonded, fire-rated, solid-core metal-faced doors. They are the product of a unique process of combining metal with resin, and they display the brilliance and strength of finely hand-worked bronze, brass, copper, or pewter. LustrMetl doors may be sealed or allowed to patina naturally. A Kaylien door is shown in Figure 7–8; this door has beveled glass with **came** (the black lead holding the glass together).

Specialty Doors

Special doors must be specified for installations in which X-ray machines will be used. These flush panel doors have two layers of plywood with lead between the layers; then a face veneer of wood, hardboard, or laminate is applied.

Fire doors have an incombustible material core with fire-retardant rails and stiles covered by a wood veneer or high-pressure decorative laminate. These

Figure 7–8
Royal American doors from Kaylien combine the art of metal/resin doors with that of beveled glass artisans, who use both lead and brass came to join the beveled glass panels into artistic motifs or scenes. The combination is compatible, even synergistic. (Photo courtesy of Kaylien.)

doors are rated according to the time they take to burn. Depending on materials and construction, this time will vary between 20 minutes and 1 1/2 hours. Local building codes should be consulted before specifying.

For exterior use, a wood door must be of solid construction. Hand-carved doors are available for exterior use, but manufacturer's specifications must be studied carefully because a door that appears to be hand carved may actually be moulded to imitate hand carving at less expense.

Specifications for Doors

Most doors are available prehung (that is, assembled complete with frames, trim, and sometimes hardware). The bored hole is ready for installation of the lock. This bored hole must have a **backset** that corresponds to the selected hardware. Most prehung doors come predrilled with a 2 3/8-inch hole; however, most designer-type hardware looks better with a 2 3/4-inch backset or even more. The 2 3/8-inch backset, with knob-type hardware, can sometimes result in scraped knuckles.

For prehung doors, door hand is determined by noting the hinge location when the door opens away from the viewer (i.e., if the hinge jamb is on his or her right, it is a right-hand door). In the case of a pair of doors, hand is determined from the active leaf in the same way. If prehung doors are specified, door handing should be included (Figure 7–9).

The following additional information should be provided when specifying doors:

Manufacturer.

Size—including width, height, and thickness.

Face description—species of wood, type of veneer (rotary or sliced). If not veneer, then laminate, photogravure, vinyl coating, or metal.

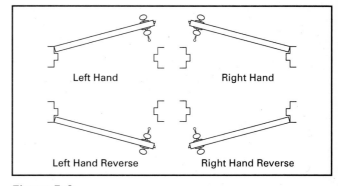

Figure 7–9
Door handing. (Reprinted with permission of Schlage Lock Company.)

Construction—crossbanding thickness, edge strips, top and bottom rails, stiles, and core construction.

Finishing—prefinished or unfinished.

Special detailing—includes specifying backset for hardware and any mouldings.

Special service (e.g., glazing, fire doors).

Warranty—differs for interior and exterior use.

Door Hardware

Some of the following material is adapted, by permission, from the Tech Talk bulletin, "Butts and Hinges," published by the **Door and Hardware Institute**'s (DHI) bulletin. This material is technical and has been simplified for ease of understanding.

Hinges

The two parts of a hinge consist of metal plates known as **leaves** joined by a **pin** that passes through the **knuckle** joints. **Countersunk** holes are predrilled in the leaves. **Template hardware** has the holes drilled accurately to conform to standard drawings, thus assuring a perfect fit. Template **butt hinges** have the holes drilled in a crescent shape (Figure 7–10).

Door hardware, in general, is not an issue unless it does not work properly. The door unit will not function properly if the proper hinging device is not specified.

There are hinges that will meet all types of applications. The standards developed by the Builders Hardware Manufacturers Association (BHMA) and promulgated through the American National Standards Institute (ANSI) are extremely helpful in making the correct selection of the proper hinge. These standards include ANSI/BHMA A156.1, A156.7, and A156.17.

The following eight points are intended to assist in proper hinge selection.

1. Determine the Type of Hinge. Before the type of hinge can be selected, there are several pieces of information that are needed, because certain types of hinges can be used only with certain types of construction. A door may be made of wood (WD) or hollow metal (HM), and the frame may be wood, hollow metal, or a channel iron frame (CIF).

The four classifications of hinges are as follows:

Full mortise. Both leaves are **mortised,** one leaf to the door and one leaf to the frame (WD or HM with WF or HMF).

Half mortise. One leaf is mortised to the door, and the other is surface applied to the frame (HM with CIF).

Full surface. Both leaves are applied to the surface, one to the door and the other to the frame (metal core door [MCD] or HM with CIF).

Half surface. One leaf is mortised to the frame, and the other is surface applied to the face of the door (WD with WF or MCD with HMF).

There is one easy way to remember the name of the hinge. The full mortise and the full surface are no problem. The half mortise and the half surface, however, can be difficult to keep straight. The name of the hinge refers to what is done to the door. A half mortise hinge is mortised to the door and surface applied to the frame. A half surface hinge is surface applied to the door and mortised to the frame.

Swaging is a feature of full mortise hinges. It is a slight offset to the hinge leaf at the barrel (or pin area). This offset permits the leaves to come closer together when the door is in the closed position. If the hinge were to be left in the natural state after the knuckle was rolled, the hinge would be referred to as **flatback.** A flatback hinge has a gap between the leaves of approximately 5/32 of an inch. This allows heat and air conditioning to escape and leaves an unsightly gap between the door and the frame.

The standard swaging on standard weight and heavyweight full mortise hinges provides 1/16 of an inch clearance between the leaves when the leaves are in the closed position.

The four types of hinges mentioned previously are named after the manner in which they are attached on the door. There are also several special-use hinges. One is the swing clear type, which is used primarily in hospitals and institutional buildings when the passage area must be the full width of the opening. One such use would be an 8-foot-wide corridor that requires a full opening for the passage of two beds or carts. With the use of swing clear hinges, this passage can be accomplished.

Swing clear hinges are designed to swing the door completely clear of the opening when the door is opened at a 95° angle. The standard way to accomplish this degree of opening is to build a pocket in the wall to accept the door. This allows the door to be concealed in the wall and not obstruct the flow of traffic.

Concealed hinges are used on doors when the design precludes the use of visible hinges. One side is mounted on the inside of the frame, and the second side is mortised into the door. These hinges are available in 90 to 100° openings or in a 176° opening.

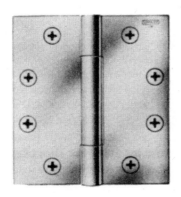

Full Mortise

Half Mortise

Half Mortise Swing Clear

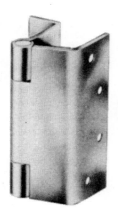

Full Mortise Swing Clear

Full Surface

Half Surface

Full Surface Swing Clear

Pivot Reinforced

Half Surface Swing Clear

Figure 7–10
Types of hinges.

Soss® Invisible Hinges from Universal Industrial Products are available for light-, medium-, and heavy-duty applications. They are also available for metal cabinet applications (Figure 7–11).

Concealed hinges for cabinets are different in construction from door concealed hinges. They are not visible from the outside of the cabinet but are surface mounted on the inside of the cabinet door (Figure 7–11).

Spring hinges may be single acting or double acting and are used when automatic closing is required. In some cases the spring hinge is used as a substitute for door closers. These are less costly than standard door closers, but they do not have the control or backcheck features that a door closer will offer. The tension is adjustable.

2. Select the Proper Weight and Bearing Structure. Two factors determine the weight and structure of the hinge: namely, weight of the door and frequency of use. Because of the large variety of door sizes and weights, hinges are divided into three groups:

Heavyweight—ball bearing

Standard weight—ball bearing

Standard weight—plain bearing

Bearings may be ball, oil impregnated, or antifriction. Ball bearing hinges are packed with grease to assure a quiet, long-life hinge. These types of bearings should always be specified for doors equipped with door closers.

3. Determine the Size of the Hinge. To determine the proper size of the hinge, the following information is necessary:

Door height

Door width

Door thickness

Door weight

Trim dimension required.

One hinge for every 30 inches of door height or fraction thereof is the general rule of thumb to determine the number of hinges per door leaf.

Doors up to 60 inches in height—two hinges

Doors over 60 inches but not over 90 inches in height—three hinges

Doors over 90 inches but not over 120 inches in height—four hinges.

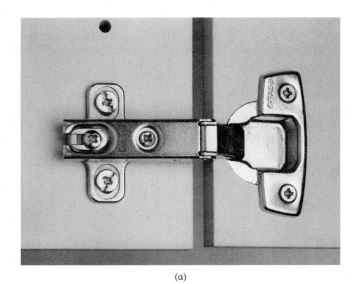

(a)

(b)

(c)

Figure 7–11
(a)The G 173 is an all-metal concealed hinge with a newly designed attractive hinge cup and is the first in a series of low-cost slide-on hinges from Grass. The hinge offers side and depth adjustment in the hinge arm. Height adjustment is achieved with the zinc die-cast baseplate with elongated holes. All adjustments are 2 mm. The hinge offers a 10.5 mm cup drilling depth. (Photo courtesy of Grass America Inc.) (b, c) Concealed door hinges. A phrase from a Soss Invisible Hinges brochure aptly describes how a Soss hinge appears when the door is open and when it is closed: Now you see it. . . . Now you don't. One is open—you see it; the other is closed—you don't see it. (Photo courtesy of Universal Industrial Products.)

4. Determine the Type of Material. There are three base materials from which hinges are manufactured: steel, stainless steel, and brass. Each base material has different qualities.

Steel has great strength but is a corrosive material. If the atmosphere in which steel is used is not stable (overly humid), the steel will begin to rust. The best application for steel is in a controlled environment, such as inside a building where the temperature and humidity are controlled.

Stainless steel also has great strength. It is rust resistant and has decorative value in that it can be polished to a satin or bright finish. Geographical factors may influence the decision to use stainless steel hinges. For example, such hinges may be a good choice for use on the seacoast or in industrial areas where acids or atmospheric conditions exist.

Brass is noncorrosive, rust resistant, and very decorative; however, it has less strength than steel or stainless steel material. Brass is often used where appearance is of great concern. Brass may be polished and plated in many various finishes.

Both steel and stainless steel hinges may be used on listed or labeled door openings (fire rated). Brass material may not be used on fire-rated or labeled openings because of its low melting point.

5. Determine the Type of Finish. All steel and brass material hinges can be plated to match the available finishes that are listed in ANSI/BHMA A156.18, Materials and Finishes. This standard will be extremely helpful during the specification process.

6. Determine Handing. In the architectural hardware industry, the position of the hinges on a door—in terms of right or left, as viewed from the outside of the building, room, or space to which the doorway leads—determines the hand.

The outside is the side from which security is necessary. In a series of connecting doors (as in a hotel suite), the outside will be the side of each successive door as one comes to it proceeding from the entrance. For two rooms of equal importance with a passage between, the outside is the passage side.

7. Determine Pin and Tip Style. The pins may be **loose, nonrising** loose, nonremovable loose, or **fast riveted.**

A loose pin hinge enables a door to be removed easily from the frame by merely pulling out the pin. A loose pin type of hinge is used for hanging less expensive residential doors. One problem with a loose pin is that the pin has a tendency to rise with use. If the pin of the loose pin hinge is visible, even a locked door can be removed from its frame by simply removing the pin. A nonrising loose pin has the same advantage of easy door removal as the loose pin, but without the rising problem.

The nonremovable pin has a small set screw in the body of the barrel. This set screw is tightened down against the pin. In most cases the pin has a groove in the position where the set screw makes contact, allowing the set screw to seat. The set screw is positioned so it cannot be reached unless the door is opened. If pin removal is necessary, the set screw is removed and the pin is tapped from the bottom in the usual manner.

Fast-riveted pins are pins that are **spun** on both ends, making the pin permanent.

Another security feature in hinges is the security safety stud, which places a stud in one leaf and a locking hole in the other leaf. When the door is closed, the stud is anchored into the opposite leaf. Even if the hinge pin is removed, the door is secure because the leaves are locked together.

One important point must be made: All of the aforementioned security features are intended as deterrents only. If someone wants to gain entry through a door badly enough, eventually that person will get through.

The tips of pins may be flat button or decorative. Flat button tips are normally furnished unless something else is specified. Decorative-type tips also are available from most manufacturers, such as Acorn, Ball, Steeple, and Urn. These types are used in highly decorative areas of offices and in more expensive residences. Steeple tips are used on New England hinges.

8. Determine Type of Electric Hinge. Over the past 15 years, hinge manufacturers have made some changes that have revolutionized the hardware industry. The introduction of electric hinges has made it possible to monitor the position of a door, transfer power, and incorporate both functions into the same hinge. It is now possible to electrify other hardware items, such as locks and exit devices.

Electric hinges can be modified to be exposed on the surface of the hinge or concealed in the hinge. When concealed, the modifications are not visible and normally go undetected by personnel using the openings.

Electrically modified hinges are for low-voltage power transfer only (50 volts or less). Normally, modifications are made to full mortise hinges. Monitoring can be supplied on a half surface hinge, however, when the need arises.

Most manufacturers require the use of a mortar box or jamb box to protect the wire terminations on the inside of the door frame. If this box is not used, the grout that may be poured into the frame will destroy the wiring and usually will void the warranty on the product.

Locks

The needs of the client and the expected usage of a lock will determine which lock will be selected. For residential uses, security is probably the foremost criterion, whereas for a commercial installation, heavy usage will necessitate not only a secure lock, but also one built to withstand constant use.

There are three weights or grades of locks: The most expensive is heavy duty, then comes standard duty, and light duty, or builders grade. The first two types are made of solid metal with a polished, brushed, or antique finish; the light-duty grade has a painted or plated finish that can be removed with wear.

The Door and Hardware Institute describes the types of locks as follows:

Bored type. These types of locks are installed in a door having two round holes at right angles to one another, one through the face of the door to hold the lock body and the other in the edge of the door to receive the latch mechanism. When the two are joined together in the door, they comprise a complete latching or locking mechanism.

Bored-type locks have the keyway (cylinder) and/or locking device, such as push or turn buttons, in the knobs. They are made in three weights: heavy, standard, and light duty.

The assembly must be tight on the door and without excessive play. Knobs should be held securely in place without screws, and a locked knob should not be removable. **Roses** should be threaded or secured firmly to the body mechanism. The trim has an important effect in this type of lock because working parts fit directly into the trim. The regular backset for a bored lock is 2 3/4 inches, but it may vary from 2 3/8 to 42 inches.

Preassembled type. The preassembled lock is installed in a rectangular notch cut into the door edge. This lock has all its parts assembled as a unit at the factory; when installed, little or no disassembly is required. Preassembled-type locks have the keyway (cylinder) in the knob. Locking devices may be in the knob or in the inner case. The regular backset is 2 3/4 inches. Preassembled-type locks are available only in a heavy-duty weight (Figure 7–12).

Mortise lock. A mortise lock is installed in a prepared recess (mortise) in a door. The working mechanism is contained in a rectangular-shaped case with appropriate holes into which the required components (cylinder, knob, and turn-piece spindles) are inserted to complete the working assembly. The regular backset is 2 3/4 inches. Mortise locks are available in heavy-duty and standard-duty weights (see Figure 7–12). **Armored** fronts are also available.

To provide a complete working unit, mortise locks, except for those with **deadlock** function only, must be installed with knobs, levers, and other items of trim.

Rim Lock. Rim locks were first used at the beginning of the 18th century and are attached to the inside of the door stile. They are used today in restoration work or in new homes of medieval English, Salt Box, or Cape Cod styles. Because rim locks are exposed to view, the case and other parts are finished brass.

The lock achieves its function by means of various types of bolts. The bolt is a bar of metal that projects out of the lock into a strike prepared to receive it. The Door and Hardware Institute describes types of bolts as follows:

Latch bolt. The function of a latch bolt is to hold the door in a closed position. A latch bolt is spring actuated and is used in all swinging door locks except those providing **deadbolt** function only. It has a beveled face and may be operated by a knob, handle or turn.

Auxiliary dead latch. An auxiliary dead latch is a security feature and should be required on all locks used for security purposes unless a deadbolt function is specified. This feature deadlocks the latch bolt automatically and makes it virtually impossible to depress the latch bolt when the door is closed.

Deadbolt. A deadbolt is a bolt having no spring action and is activated by a key or thumb turn. It must be manually operated. Deadbolts provide security. When hardened steel inserts are used, the security is greater. The minimum **throw** should be 1/2 inch, but today most throws are 1 inch.

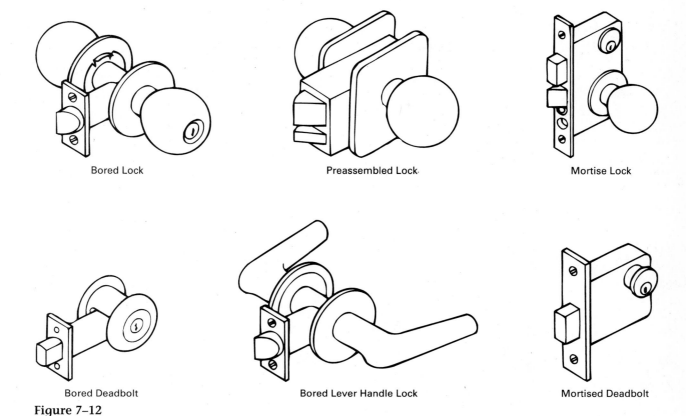

Bored Lock

Preassembled Lock

Mortise Lock

Bored Deadbolt

Bored Lever Handle Lock

Mortised Deadbolt

Figure 7–12
Types of locks.

Lock strike. A **lock strike** is a metal plate mortised into the door jamb to receive and to hold the projected latch bolt and, when specified, the deadbolt also, thus securing the door. It is sometimes called a keeper. The proper length lip should be specified so that the latch bolt will not hit the door jamb before the strike.

A wrought box should be installed in back of the strike in the jamb. This box will protect the bolt holes from the intrusion of plaster or other foreign material, which would prevent the bolt from projecting properly into the strike.[1]

Electric strike. This is an electro-mechanical device that replaces an ordinary strike and makes possible remote electric locking and unlocking. When a control mechanism actuates the electric strike, this allows the door to be opened without a key and relocked when closed. Used in secured apartment buildings.

The simplest type of door hardware is the passage set, in which both knobs are always free and there is no locking mechanism. An example would be the door between a living or dining room and a hallway. A **springlatch** holds this type of door closed.

Bathroom doors require a privacy lock, which locks from the inside in several ways. Some have a push button located on the interior rose, some have a turn or push button in the interior knob, and others have a turnpiece that activates a bolt. In an emergency, all privacy locks have some means of opening from the outside, either by using an emergency release key or a screwdriver.

When the type of use has been decided on, the style of the handle, rose, and finish is selected. There are many shapes of knobs (e.g., ball, round with a semiflat face, or round with a concave face, which may be decorated). Knobs may be made of metal, glass, porcelain, or wood (Figure 7–13). Grip handle entrance locks combine the convenience of button-in-the-knob locking with traditional grip handle elegance. Grip handles should be of cast brass or cast bronze. Interior Colonial doors may have a thumb latch installed on the stile surface (see Figure 7–13).

Lever handles are used in private residences but must be specified for all public and commercial doors, as per ADA. When blind persons have access to areas

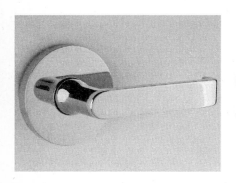

Figure 7–13
Hardware: Knobs, handles. Lever handle in brass 5105 Estate collection, textured knob #5067, black and gold knob #5080, and the Wilshire entry knob #6561, all from Baldwin Hardware Corp. (Photos courtesy of Baldwin Hardware Corp.) The E/B Series, Plymouth, ULTIMA™ Lifetime Finish (505), the Mediterranean Designer Series, Torino Lever and Capri, both with Bright Chrome Finish (625). (Photos courtesy of Schlage Lock Company.)

that might be dangerous, such as a doorway leading to stairs, the knob must be knurled or ridged to provide a tactile warning. Schlage® manufactures an access bow key with an easily identifiable 1 1/4-inch top.

Clear finishes take the color of the base metal in the product and may be either high or low luster. Applied finishes result from the addition (by plating) of a second metal, a synthetic enamel, or other material. The most popular of the plated finishes are the chromiums, both polished and satin.

Polished brass and bronze finishes are produced by buffing or polishing the metal to a high gloss before applying a synthetic coating. Satin brass and natural bronze finishes are obtained by dry buffing or scouring, and the resultant finish is then coated. Locks, which include all operating mechanisms, come with numerous finishes, including brass, bronze,

chrome, and stainless steel in bright polish, satin, antique, or oil rubbed. Baldwin Hardware Company, a Masco company, first produced brass hardware using physical vapor deposition (PVD), a process that uses low voltage ionization to create a stacked finish that is practically indestructible. This finish, when used on brass products from Baldwin, is called the Lifetime® finish. Currently, Weiser Lock® uses this PVD process and calls their finish Brilliance™ (used on other Masco company's products, i.e., Delta, Alsons, and others).

Roses are used to cover the bored hole in the door and may be round or square; roses may also be decorated. Some locks, particularly the mortise type, have **escutcheon** plates instead of roses. These are usually rectangular in shape. (See Figure 7–13 bottom left and bottom right.)

Security, function, and handing are all factors to be considered with regard to mortise locks.

Strictly speaking, the door itself is only right or left hand; the locks and the latches may be reverse bevel. It is necessary, however, to include the term *reverse* and to specify in accordance with the conventions shown on page 147. This will prevent any confusion regarding which side is the outside, especially important when different finishes are desired on opposite sides of the door.

Hardware, in general, may be

1. Universal. Used in any position (Example: surface bolt).
2. Reversible. Hand can be changed by revolving from left to right, or by turning upside down or by reversing some part of the mechanism. (Example: many types of locks and latches.)
3. Handed (not reversible). Used only on doors of the hand for which designed. (Example: most rabbeted front door locks and latches.)

    Although the hardware item specified may be reversible, or even universal, it is good practice to identify the hand completely, in accordance with the convention stated here.[2]

All Schlage locks are reversible. The correct hand, however, should be shown for all pin tumbler locks so they may be assembled to assure that keyholes are in the upright position. Hand information is also necessary to ensure proper finish of latchbolt and strike for locks that are to be installed on reverse bevel doors. The assembly diagram must be followed to determine the hand of the door. Some locks must be ordered as right or left handed.

Security has become an important feature of lockset selection. Most companies manufacture a lockset for which a key must be used on the outside. The lock features simultaneous retraction of both the latch and the deadbolt from the inside, by turning the knob or lever, providing panic-proof exiting (emergency). Such locks are recommended by police and fire departments to provide compliance with life safety and security codes. Schlage's H-Series Deadbolt/Springlatch combinations are available for the following backsets: 2 3/8, 2 3/4, and 5 inches. The ULTIMA Lifetime Finish is an environmentally clean, state-of-the-art vapor deposition coating process that outperforms and outlasts any lacquered finish on the market. It is available on the new Mediterranean Collection Designer Entrances and is guaranteed for a lifetime.

The patented MacLock 1500 replaces a deadbolt's single stress point with 28 inches of steel-to-steel surface contact between door and frame. A simple rotation of a key or thumb-turn extends the blade from the door into a strike plate mounted in the door frame. The deadlocked blade distributes stress across 28 inches of hardware, effectively eliminating door and frame tearout, which is common with kick-ins. From the outside, there's no hint that the MacLock is there; all that is visible is a keyed lock that looks like any other deadbolt installation (Figure 7–14).

A door should be controlled at the desired limit of its opening cycle to prevent damage to an adjacent wall or column, to equipment, to the door, or to its hardware. This control is achieved by stops and holders, which may be located on the floor or wall or overhead.

Floor stops are available in varied heights, sizes, shapes, and functions. They may have a mechanism, such as a hook or friction device, to hold the door open at the option of the user. The height of the door from the floor, shape of stops, and location of stops in relation to traffic are important considerations.

Wall stops or bumpers have the advantage of being located where they do not conflict with floor coverings or cleaning equipment. Thus they do not constitute a traffic hazard.

According to the Door and Hardware Institute, "there are two commonly used types of floor holders; the spring-loaded 'step-on' type and the lever or 'flip-down' type. Neither type acts as a stop."[3]

Door controls used in commercial installations may be overhead closers, either surface mounted or concealed, and floor-type closers. These devices are a combination of a spring and an oil-cushioned piston that dampens the closing action inside a cylinder. Surface-mounted closers are more accessible for maintenance, but concealed closers are more aesthetically pleasing. Overhead installations are preferred because dirt and scrub water may harm the operation of a floor-type closer. A three-second delay is required to provide safe passage for a disabled person (Figure 7–15).

In public buildings, all doors must open out for fire safety. A push plate is attached to the door, or a fire exit bar or panic bar is used. Slight pressure of the bar releases the rod and latch. For use by disabled individuals, this bar should be able to be operated with a maximum of 8 pounds of pressure.

An electronic eye is not a security measure but provides ease of access. When the beam is broken (i.e., someone steps in its path), the door opens. Locks that open without a key are frequently used for security purposes. Hotels use a specially coded plastic key card, similar to a credit card; the code is changed when the person checks out. Numbered combinations may also be used. The combination may be changed

Figure 7–14
The large photograph shows the MacLock 1500, with its 28-inch steel blade that fits into the 31 1/2-inch steel strike. The inset photograph shows the contrast with a regular deadbolt in case of a kick-in. (Photographer Winn Fugue; photos courtesy of MacLock.)

easily, thus eliminating the need to reissue keys. More sophisticated systems can scan and identify the unique pattern of blood cells inside a person's eye; recognize fingerprints or the distinctive profile of a hand; or even respond to a voice whose digitized sound was previously stored in the system.

Plastic key cards and combination codes are often used in restrooms of office buildings and other special areas where access is restricted to certain personnel.

To eliminate having to carry several keys for residential use, all the locksets for exterior doors may be keyed the same. This universal keying may be done

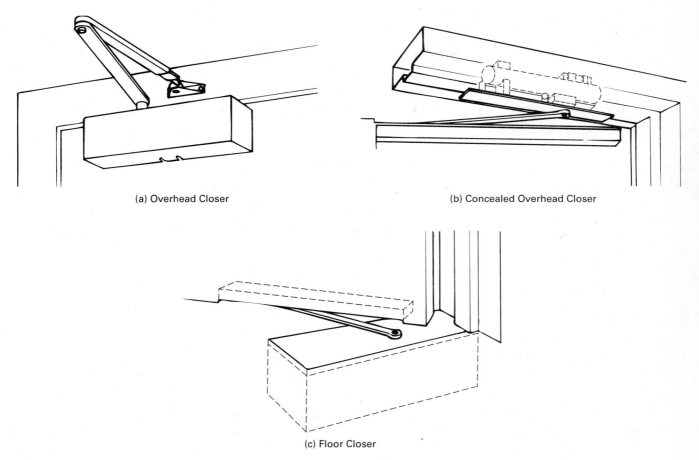

(a) Overhead Closer

(b) Concealed Overhead Closer

(c) Floor Closer

Figure 7–15
Door controls.

when the locks are ordered, or a locksmith can make the changes later (but at a greater expense).

When specifying locksets, the following information must be provided: manufacturer's name and style number, finish, style of knob and rose, backset, wood or metal door, thickness of door, and door handing.

Lockset installation should be performed by a professional locksmith or carpenter to ensure correct fit (i.e., no door rattles or other fitting problems).

HOSPITAL HARDWARE

Hardware for hospitals and health-related institutions includes items that might not be found in any other type of building. Because the hardware may be used by aged, infirm, sick, or disabled individuals, it must meet all the ADA requirements of safety, security, and protection and yet be operable with a minimum amount of effort.

Modifications of hinges may include hospital tips for added safety, special length and shape of leaves to swing doors clear of an opening, and hinges of special sizes and gauges to carry the weight of lead-lined doors.

Hospital pulls are designed to be mounted with the open end down, allowing the door to be operated by the wrist, arm, or forearm when the hands are occupied.[4]

BIBLIOGRAPHY

Buchard, H. Matt, Jr., AHC, "Butts and Hinges," *Tech Talk*. McLean, VA: Door and Hardware Institute, 1990.

National Particleboard Association, *Builder Bulletin, Particleboard Shelf Systems*. Gaithersburg, MD: National Particleboard Association, 1988.

Time-Life Books, *Doors and Windows, Home Repairs & Improvements*. Alexandria, VA: Time-Life Books, 1978.

GLOSSARY

Apron. Flat piece of trim placed directly under the window sill.

Armored. Two plates are used to cover the lock mechanism in order to prevent tampering.

Astragal. Vertical strip of wood with weather stripping.

Backplate. An applied decorative moulding used on ceilings above a chandelier or ceiling fan.

Backset. The horizontal distance from the center of the face-bored hole to the edge of the door.

Bed moulding. Cornice moulding.

Brickmould. Exterior wood moulding to cover the gap between a door or window and its frame.

Butt hinges. Two metal plates joined with a pin, one being fastened to the door jamb or frame and the other to the door.

Came. The slender grooved lead or brass rod used to hold together panes of glass, either stained or beveled.

Casing. The exposed trim moulding around a door or window.

Caulk. To fill a joint with resilient mastic. Also spelled calk.

Chair rail. Strip of wood or moulding that is placed on a wall at the same height as the back of a chair to protect the wall from damage.

Cornice. An ornamental moulding between the ceiling and the top of the wall.

Countersunk. Hole prepared with a bevel to enable the tapered head of a screw to be inserted flush with the surface.

Crown moulding. A moulding at the top of the cornice.

Dado. A groove cut in wood to receive and position another member.

Deadbolt or deadlock. Hardened steel bolt with a square head operated by a key or turn piece.

Door and Hardware Institute. (DHI) The organization that represents the industry.

Escutcheon. Plate that surrounds the keyhole and/or handle.

Fascia. The flat outside member of a cornice placed in a vertical position.

Fast-riveted pin. A pin that is permanently in place. Nonremovable.

Flatback. A hinge that has a gap between the leaves of approximately 5/32 of an inch.

Knuckle. Cylindrical area of hinge enclosing the pin.

Leaves. Flat plates of a pair of hinges.

Lights. Small panes of glass. Usually rectangular in shape.

Lock strike. A plate fastened to the door frame into which the bolts project.

Loose. Able to be removed.

Mitered. Two cuts at a 45° angle to form a right angle.

Mortised. Set into the surface.

Nonrising. Pins that do not ride up with use.

Ogee. A double curved shape resembling an S shape.

Ovolo. A convex moulding, usually a quarter of a circle.

Pins. The bolts of metal holding the leaves together.

Polymer. A high-molecular-weight compound from which mouldings are made.

Prehung. Frame and door are packaged as one unit.

Rails. Cross members of paneling (walls or doors).

Rose. The plate, usually round, that covers the bored hole on the face of the door.

Shoe moulding. A small moulding, such as a quarter round, nailed next to the floor on baseboards.

Soffit. The underside of an overhead surface, such as an arch, cornice, eave, beam, or stairway.

Springlatch. Latch with a spring rather than a locking action.

Spun. Moving the metal by means of a spinning action and applied pressure, which changes the shape of the metal.

Sticking. The shaping of moulding.

Stiles. Vertical members of paneling (walls or doors).

Stool. The flat piece on which a window shuts down, corresponding to the sill of a door.

Stringer. The inclined board that supports the end of the steps.

Swaging. A slight offset to the hinge at the barrel.

Template hardware. Hardware that exactly matches a master template drawing as to spacing of all holes and dimensions.

Throw. The distance a bolt penetrates when fully extended.

NOTES

[1]*Basic Architectural Hardware.* McLean, VA: Door and Hardware Institute, 1985, pp. 5, 8–10 (boldface added).

[2]Ibid., p. 25.

[3]Ibid., p. 23.

[4]Ibid., p. 23.

8

Cabinet Construction

To select or design well-made cabinet work, it is necessary to become familiar with furniture construction. By studying casework joints, specifiers will be able to compare and contrast similar items and make an informed decision on which piece of furniture, or which group of cabinets, offers the most value for the money.

When designing casework and specifying materials, several parts need definition. The AWI offers the following "Identification of Parts":

A. Exposed Parts—Surfaces visible when:
   1. drawer fronts and doors are closed;
   2. cabinets and shelving are open-type or behind clear glass doors;
   3. bottoms of cabinets are seen 42" (1067 mm) or more above finish floor;
   4. tops of cabinets are seen below 78" (1981 mm) above finish floor, or are visible from an upper floor or staircase after installation;
   5. portions of cabinets are visible after fixed appliances are installed;
   6. front edges of cabinet body members are visible or seen through gap greater than 1/8" with doors and drawers closed.

B. Semi-Exposed Parts—Surfaces visible when:
   1. drawers/doors are in the open position;
   2. bottoms of cabinets are between 30" (762 mm) and up to 42" (1067 mm) above finish floor;
   3. all front edges of shelving behind doors.

C. Concealed Surfaces—Surfaces are concealed when:
   1. surfaces are not visible after installation;
   2. bottoms of cabinets are less than 30" (762 mm) above finish floor;
   3. tops of cabinets are over 78" (1981 mm) above finish floor and are not visible from an upper level;
   4. stretchers, blocking and/or components are concealed by drawers.[1]

Note: A toe space is required for such items as kitchen cabinets and dressers, to provide a recessed space for toes under doors or drawers. This toe space is usually 3 inches high and 3 inches deep. For European kitchen cabinets, the toe space measures 5 7/8 inches high.

The three grades of wood mentioned in the wood paneling section of Chapter 5 (see pp. 108–109) apply to cabinetry (Figure 8–1).

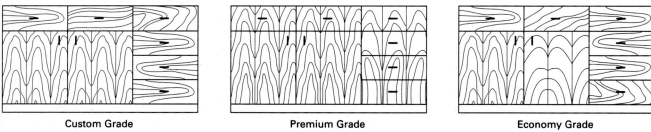

Figure 8–1
Illustration of grades in cabinetry. (Reprinted with permission from Architectural Woodwork Institute.)

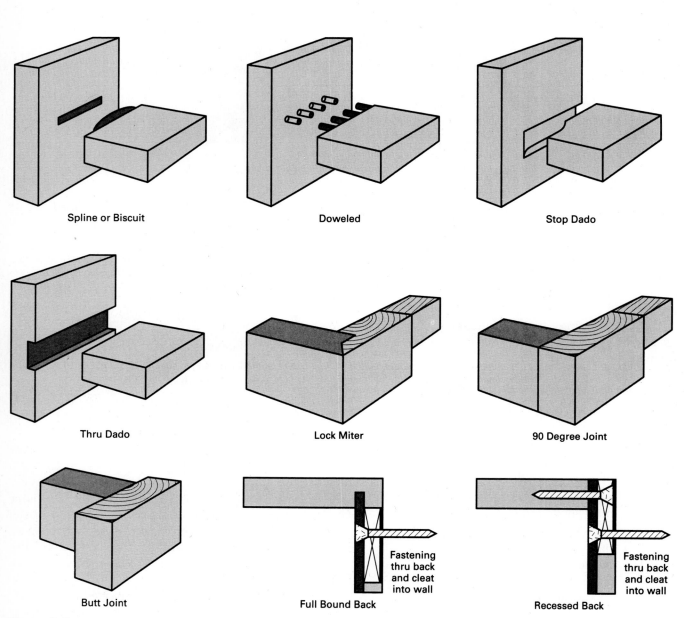

Figure 8–2
Joinery of face frames to cabinet body members. (Reprinted with permission from Architectural Woodwork Institute.)

JOINERY OF CASE BODY MEMBERS

According to the AWI,

> the type of joinery used for case construction varies according to the grade. For Tops, Exposed Ends and Bottoms the only acceptable joint for Custom grade is Spline or Biscuit, glued under pressure (approximately 3 per foot of joint). For Premium, a Stop Dado, glued and either nailed, stapled or screwed (fasteners will not be visible on exposed parts), doweled, glued under pressure (approximately 4 dowels per foot) or European assembly screws (37 mm from end, 128 mm on center, fasteners will not be visible on exposed parts). For Economy Thru Dado, glued under pressure or European assembly screws with trim caps.

> For exposed end corner details and face frame attachment. Custom grade requires butt joint, glued and finish nailed; for Premium, mitered joint: Lock miter or spline or biscuit, glued under pressure (no visible fasteners) or non-mitered joints, i.e., 90 degree applications: butt joint glued under pressure (no visible fasteners). For Economy grade butt joint, finish nailed is acceptable.[2]

Figure 8–2 shows examples of joinery.

EDGE TREATMENTS

Edge banding is required when materials other than solid wood are used. This edge treatment is used for case body members and shelves but varies according to the grade and finish of the work. When a transparent finish is used for premium grade cabinetry, the visible edge should be banded with the same species as the face and pressure glued. In custom grade cabinetry, the banding should be a compatible species and pressure glued. For economy grade, the compatible species may be nailed. When an opaque finish is used, premium grade requires close-grain material, pressure glued. Custom grade uses close-grain material glued and nailed. Economy grade edge is filled and sanded (Figure 8–3).

Figure 8–3
Edge treatments. (Reprinted with permission from Architectural Woodwork Institute.)

DRAWERS AND DOORS

Drawer or door fronts may be of one of the four following design categories, and construction will vary with the grade. Custom grade will use glue and finish nail, premium grade will be glued (no nails or other visible fasteners), and economy grade may be nailed.

1. Flush overlay construction
2. Reveal construction
3. Flush inset construction without face frame
4. Flush inset
5. Flush inset with face frame.[3]

The AWI defines the types of cabinet door and drawer construction as follows:

> *Flush Overlay Construction* offers a very clean, contemporary look because only the doors and drawer fronts are visible in elevation. When specified, grain matching between doors and drawer fronts can be achieved by having all pieces cut from the same panel. This style is increasingly popular and lends itself well to the use of plastic laminate for exposed surfaces. Conventional as well as concealed hinges are available for a variety of door thicknesses [Figure 8–4a].

> *Reveal Overlay Construction.* In this style, the separation between doors and drawer fronts is accented by the reveal. The style is equally suited to either wood or plastic laminate construction. The reveal may be at all horizontal and vertical joints, but can be varied by the designer. It should be noted that a reveal over 1/2" would require the addition of a face frame. The addition of a face frame will change the hinge requirements. With or without a face frame, this style allows the use of conventional or concealed hinges [see Figures 8–4b and c].

> *Flush Inset Construction without Face Frame.* With this style of construction, all door and drawer faces are flush with the face of the cabinet. This style is highly functional and allows the use of different thicknesses of door and drawer fronts.

> Conventional as well as concealed hinges are available for a variety of door thicknesses. The choice of case and door/drawer material influences the choice of hinges. Conventional butt hinges should be avoided when hinge screws would be attached to the end-grain of panel products.

> This is generally an expensive style due to the increased care necessary in the fitting and aligning of the doors and drawers. The design

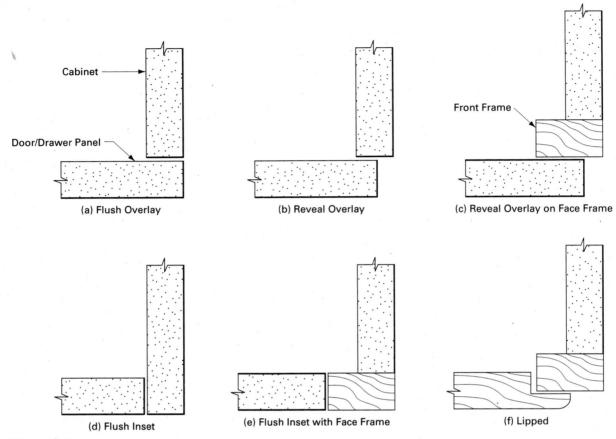

Figure 8–4
Plan view of door/drawer construction.

features of this casework style are the same as conventional flush with face frame except that the face frame has been eliminated. This style does not lend itself to the economical use of plastic laminate covering finishes [see Figure 8–4d].

Flush Inset Construction with Face Frame. With this style of construction, all door and drawer faces are flush with the face of the cabinet. This style is highly functional and allows the use of different thicknesses of door and drawer fronts.

This is generally the most expensive of the four styles described above, due to the increased care necessary in the fitting and aligning of the doors and drawers, in addition to the cost of providing the face frame. This style does not lend itself to the economical use of plastic laminate covering[4] [see Figure 8–4e].

There is another type of door and drawer front: the exposed face frame—lipped. The lipped design is the type used in traditional furniture. The door or drawer fronts are similar to reveal overlay construction except that the fronts have an overlapping edge

that partially covers the frame. This is an economical style because the fitting tolerances of the doors and drawers are less critical (see Figure 8–4f).

When an exposed face frame with a flush drawer front is designed, a **stop** must be incorporated to prevent too much inward travel. As mentioned previously, flush doors and drawers are the most expensive form of design because of the tolerances and hand fitting of such extras as drawer stops.

When doors or drawers are covered with a high-pressure laminate, a **balancing** laminate must be used on the reverse side of the substrate.

JOINTS

The types of joints for drawer construction also vary according to grade. The AWI lists the following grades and types of joints:

Premium Grade—Multiple Dovetail (all corners) or French Dovetail front/dadoed back, glued under pressure. Doweled, glued under pressure (min. 32 mm dowel spacing to 4″ [102 mm] high, 64 mm dowel spacing about 4″ [102 mm]). Lock Shoulder, glued and pin nailed and Square Shoulder, nailed or stapled.

Custom Grade, Lock Shoulder glued and pin nailed. Bottoms shall be set into sides and front (1/4″ [6 mm] deep groove with minimum 3/8″ [9 mm] standing shoulder).

Economy Grade, Square shoulder, nailed or stapled and Bottom installation technique mill option.[5]

A **dado** is a cross-grain machining feature with a square or rectangular section, and a **groove** is machined along the grain of the wood with a similar section. All drawer bottoms should have a minimum thickness of 1/4 inch and should be captured into dadoes on drawer sides, fronts, and backs. This construction creates a bottom panel that is permanently locked into position.

Wood may also be joined with a **butt joint,** in which two pieces of wood are at right angles to each other.

For a traditional type of paneling, **stile** and rail construction is used, which consists of a panel that may be flat, raised, or have a beveled edge. The vertical side strips are called stiles, and the horizontal strips at the top and bottom are called rails.

Rails, stiles, and **mullions** may themselves be shaped into an **ovolo** or **ogee** moulding; or, to give a more intricate design, a separate moulding may be added. For raised panels under 10 inches in width, solid lumber may be used in custom grade. For premium grade or wider panels, plywood is used with an attached edge of solid lumber, which is then beveled (Figure 8–5).

Panels are assembled by means of mortise and tenon, or dowel joints. At the joining of the panel and the stiles and rails, a small space is left to allow for the natural expansion and contraction of the panel. This type of construction may be called floating panel construction, and it is advisable where there are great variations in humidity. Panels that are glued have no allowance for this expansion and contraction and may split if movement is excessive.

Because the detail and design options in any type of paneling are virtually unlimited, the AWI suggests that the following minimum information be provided for proper estimation and specification:

Panel layout
Grain patterns and relationships
Stile and rail construction
Moulding details
Panel construction
Joinery techniques

DRAWER GUIDES

Drawer guides are an important feature of well-made casework. They may be constructed of wood or metal. If wood is selected, both male and female parts should be made of wood. Wood drawer guides are found mainly in wood furniture and are usually centered under the drawer, but they may also be attached to the side of the case, with the drawer sides being dadoed to accommodate the wood guide. The reverse procedure may also be used, with the guide attached to the drawer side and the frame dadoes receiving the guide. Paste wax should be applied to the wood guides to facilitate movement.

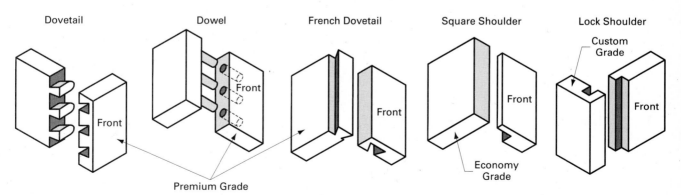

Figure 8–5
Drawer joinery. (Reprinted with permission from Architectural Woodwork Institute.)

The type of metal drawer slide selected depends on several factors: travel, width of drawer, action, and load factors. The AWI provides the following information:

> Travel is the maximum extension compared to the closed length. Typically, most slides are either 3/4 or full travel. Special extension lengths are available with modified travel. Generally, the longer the travel, the less load a slide can carry and vice versa.
>
> A "3/4 Travel" slide has extension of approximately 75% of its length.
> A "Full Travel" slide has extension approximately equal to its length.
> An "Over-Travel" slide has travel greater than its length.
>
> Drawer width affects the rigidity of the installation. In wide drawers, the slides will rack from side to side. Excessive racking can degrade performance and shorten life expectancy.
>
> The type of mechanism used to carry the load determines many of the quality aspects of a slide, such as performance, motion, noise, and the "fit and feel." Slides may use rollers, ball bearings, friction fits, or any combination in achieving movement. Generally, better action requires more rollers or ball bearings in supporting and distributing large loads.
>
> Knape & Vogt (KV) designates drawer slides in "Pounds Class" categories. KV uses **dynamic** loading to determine load ratings. **Static** and dynamic loads affect slide performance differently. Static load capacity is significantly higher than dynamic load capacity. A fixed static weight will gain momentum and other dynamic forces when set in motion. A load in motion induces more stress and fatigue.
>
> The "Pound Class" categories are used within the slide industry as general guidelines for drawer slide selection. These categories are general in nature, and *not* the same as actual load ratings. Specific load ratings vary by slide length and the application.[6]

Types of mounting include side mount, which requires adequate side clearance and drawer side height; bottom mount, which has limited selection, primarily for pullout shelf applications; and top mount, which also has limited selection, primarily for under-counter drawers.

Other features may include the following: "stay closed" slides have a built-in feature to prevent unintentional opening. Self-closing drawers will close without assistance from 4 to 6 inches of extension. A positive stop with trip latch removal means a trip latch must be activated to affect drawer removal. (This feature prevents drawers from accidentally being pulled completely out of position.) With lift-out removal, a drawer may be lifted from a cabinet when the drawer is fully extended.

CABINET HARDWARE

According to the AWI,

> European hinges with the screws set in synthetic inserts are fast becoming industry standard. These hinges have been found to be cost-effective alternatives to the more traditional hinges [shown in Figure 8–6]. There are conditions, however, in which the use of butt or wraparound hinges will continue to be the best solution. The owner and the design professional will be best served by involving an AWI member-manufacturer in the design and selection process early in the project.[7]

Figure 8-6, from *Architectural Woodwork Quality Standards,* explains the type of hinges to use with each application.

Grass offers a European-type hinge with a lifetime warranty. There are two different methods of installation: slide-on and snap-on. Grass's latest hinge is illustrated in Figure 7–11.

A piano hinge or continuous hinge is used on drop-leaf desks and on the doors of some fine furniture. Because piano hinges are installed the whole length of the edge, they support the weight of the door in an efficient manner.

Cabinet doors and drawers may be designed without pull hardware by using a finger pull either as part of the door or drawer construction, or by adding a piece of shaped wood, plastic, or metal to the front of the door. It is necessary to design these finger pulls in such a manner that the doors or drawers open easily.

Cabinet pull hardware consists of knobs (rounded or square) or handles, ranging from simple metal strips to ornately designed ones. The material from which this hardware is constructed may be wood, porcelain, plastic, or metal. It is necessary to select hardware that is compatible with the design of the cabinets or furniture. For traditional or period cabinets, authentic hardware should be chosen.

Some form of catch is needed to hold cabinet doors shut. There are five different types of catches:

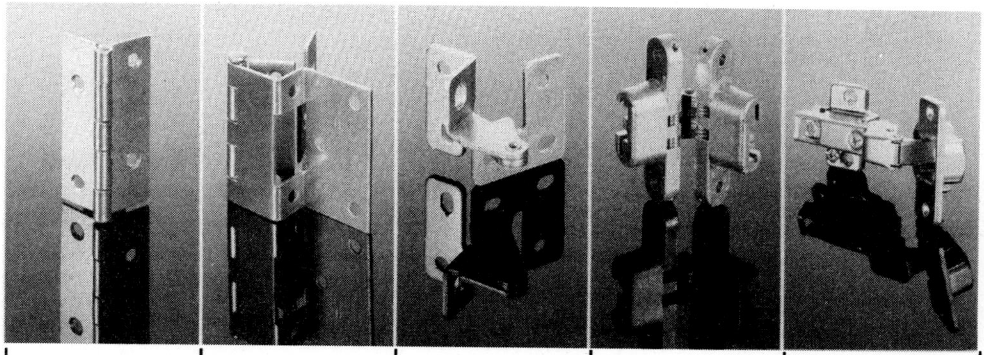

Applications	Conventional Flush Front with Face Frame	Conventional Flush Front Reveal Overlay Flush Overlay	Reveal Overlay Flush Overlay	Conventional Flush with Face Frame	Reveal Overlay Flush Overlay Conventional Flush without Face Frame
Strength	High	Very High	Moderate	Low	Moderate
Concealed when closed	No	No	Semi	Yes	Yes
Requires Mortising	Yes	Occasionally	Usually	Yes	Yes
Cost of Hinge	Low	Moderate	Low	High	High
Ease of Installation (cost)	Moderate	Easy	Moderate	Difficult	Very Easy
Can be easily adjusted after installation	No	No	No	No	Yes
Remarks	door requires hardwood edge			door requires hardwood edge	1. Specify degree of opening 2. No catch required

Figure 8–6
Architectural casework hardware. (Reprinted with permission from Architectural Woodwork Institute.)

friction, roller, magnetic, **bullet,** and touch catch. A friction catch, when engaged, is held in place by friction. A roller catch features a roller under tension that engages a recess in the **strike plate.** The magnet is the holding mechanism of a magnetic catch. In a bullet catch, a spring-actuated ball engages a depression in the plate. A touch catch releases automatically when the door is pushed. Many of these catches have elongated screw slots that enable the tension of the catch to be adjusted. Some hinges are spring loaded, eliminating the need for a catch (Figure 8–7).

SHELVES

For shelves, or when the case body is exposed, the following construction methods are used: Through dado is the conventional joint used for assembly of case

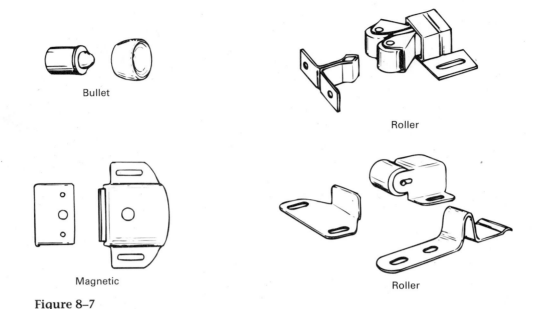

Bullet

Roller

Magnetic

Roller

Figure 8–7
Cabinet catches.

body members, and the dado is usually concealed by a case face frame. Blind dado has an applied edge "stopping" or concealing the dado groove and is used when the case body edge is exposed. Stop dado is applicable when veneer edging or solid lumber is exposed.

The span and thickness of shelves varies according to the purpose of the shelves. The AWI provides the following specifications for shelves: "For closet and utility shelving ends and back cleats to receive clothes rods or hooks shall be 3/4" × 3 1/2" minimum. Ends and back cleats which do not re-

TABLE 8–1
Maximum Shelf Spans in Inches for Uniform Loading

	END SUPPORTED Maximum Span						MULTIPLE SUPPORTS Maximum Span					
	INDUSTRIAL LOAD* PARTICLEBOARD (1-M-2)			MDF			INDUSTRIAL PARTICLEBOARD (1-M-2)			MDF		
Inches	$\frac{1}{2}$	$\frac{5}{8}$	$\frac{3}{4}$	$\frac{1}{2}$	$\frac{5}{8}$	$\frac{3}{4}$	$\frac{1}{2}$	$\frac{5}{8}$	$\frac{3}{4}$	$\frac{1}{2}$	$\frac{5}{8}$	$\frac{3}{4}$
50.0	15	19	23	15	19	23	21	26	31	20	25	30
45.0	16	20	24	16	19	23	22	27	32	21	26	32
40.0	17	21	25	16	20	24	22	28	34	22	27	33
35.0	17	22	26	17	21	25	23	29	35	23	28	34
30.0	18	23	27	18	22	27	25	31	37	24	30	36
25.0	19	24	29	19	23	28	26	33	39	25	32	38
20.0	21	26	31	20	25	30	28	35	42	27	34	40
17.5	22	27	32	21	26	31	29	36	43	28	35	42
15.0	23	28	34	22	27	33	31	38	45	30	37	44
12.5	24	30	35	23	29	34	32	40	48	31	39	46
10.0	26	32	38	25	31	37	34	43	50	33	41	49
7.5	28	34	40	27	33	39	37	46	54	36	45	53
5.0	31	38	44	30	37	43	41	51	60	40	49	58

*Load in pounds per square foot.
Courtesy of the National Particleboard Association.

ceive clothes rods or hooks shall be 3/4" × 1 1/2" minimum. Shelf thickness shall be a minimum of 3/4" if not specified, or shall be as specified by the design professional in relation to anticipated load."[8]

To increase a shelf's visible thickness, a dropped edge or applied moulding is used.

Particleboard and **Medium Density Fiberboard (MDF)** are often specified for shelves, and designers should be aware of fairly specific applications. Kitchen cabinets, for example, normally will be designed for a uniform load of 15 pounds per square foot (psf), closets 25 psf, and bookshelves 40 psf. (Table 8–1 lists maximum shelf spans in inches for uniform loading.) Table 8–1 has been abbreviated to include only information needed by designers. Underlayment and overhanging shelves have been omitted from the table. "The Builders Bulletin, Particleboard Shelf Systems," may be obtained from the NPA (now the Composite Panel Association).

Proper use of Table 8–1 is as follows:

1. *Design.* The critical factor in shelf design is the span between supports and the anticipated load on the shelf. Installation of extra support between the end supports will allow use of the Multiple Support values.

2. *Load factor.* Table 8–1 is based on pounds per square foot loading (psf). Known weight that is not in the form of uniform loading psf will have to be converted before the table may be used. To determine the uniform load in (psf), convert the inches of the shelf to square feet by dividing by 144 inches (one square foot); divide the expected load by the answer to get the uniform load. For example, a shelf is 9" × 36" or 324 square inches. To convert to square feet, divide by 144 inches to get 2.25 square feet. If you have a 50-pound load, divide it by the square footage (2.25) and your uniform load is 22.2 psf.

3. *Continuous support.* The most efficient use of load-bearing capacity involves using end supports with continuous support all along the rear edge of the shelf and fastened at 6-inch intervals. For shelves up to 12 inches wide, the span listed under the "End Supported" heading may be doubled when the same load is applied. For continuously supported shelves over 12 inches but less than 24 inches wide, first triple the load you are designing the shelf to hold. Then find the span listed under the "End Supported" heading for that treble loading. Next, double that span for the original load. (This analysis does not apply to shelves wider than 24 inches or longer than 6 feet.)

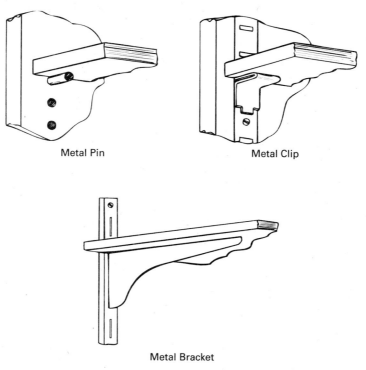

Metal Pin

Metal Clip

Metal Bracket

Figure 8–8
Shelf supports.

When shelves are to be installed permanently, some form of dado may be used for positioning. The type used depends on the frame construction. Another permanent installation uses a wood quarter round on which to rest the shelf (Figure 8–8.)

If, however, the shelves are to be adjustable, there are several methods of support. The type used in fine china cabinets is a metal shelf pin. A number of blind holes, usually in groups of three, are drilled 5/8 inch apart in two rows on each interior face of the sides. The metal shelf pins are then inserted at the desired shelf level.

Metal shelf standards have slots every inch, with two standards on each side running from top to bottom of the shelf unit. Four adjustable metal clips are inserted at the same level into these slots. The metal strips may be applied to the inside surface of the shelf unit, or they may be dadoed into the interior face.

When metal brackets are used, the shelf standards are attached to the back wall surface instead of to the sides (see Figure 8–8).

BIBLIOGRAPHY

Architectural Woodwork Institute, *Architectural Woodwork Quality Standards Illustrated*, 7th ed. Version 1.0. Reston, VA: Architectural Woodwork Institute, 1997.

GLOSSARY

Apron. A flat piece of wood attached vertically along the underside of the front edge of a horizontal surface; may be for support (as in bookshelves), or decorative.

Balancing sheet. In decorative laminate doors, the lighter-weight laminate on the interior face.

Bullet catch. A spring-actuated ball engaging a depression in the plate.

Butt joint. Two pieces of wood attached at right angles.

Concealed hinge. All hinge parts are concealed when the door is closed.

Dado. A cross-grained rectangular or square section.

Dowel joint. A joint, usually right angle, using dowels for positioning and strength.

Dynamic load. A moving load, as opposed to static.

Exposed hinge. All hinge parts are visible when the door is closed.

Flush. The door and frame are level and the frame is completely visible when the door or drawer is closed.

Friction catch. When engaged, the catch is held in place by friction.

Groove. A square or rectangular section cut with the grain.

Lipped door. A door with an overlapping edge. Partially covers the frame.

MDF. Medium Density Fiberboard.

Mullion. Vertical member between panels.

Ogee. A double curved shape resembling an S shape.

Overlay door. The door is on the outside of the frame and, when closed, the door hides the frame from view.

Ovolo. A convex moulding, usually a quarter of a circle.

Pivot hinge. Hinge leaves are mortised into the edge of the door panel and set in the frame at the jamb and top of the door. Some pivot hinges pivot on a single point.

Reveal. The small area of the frame that is visible when the door or drawer is closed.

Static load. A resting load without any motion. Static load capacity is significantly higher than dynamic load capacity.

Stile. Vertical pieces on paneling.

Stop. A metal, plastic, or wood block placed to position the flush drawer front to be level with the face frame.

Strike plate. Metal plate attached to the door frame, designed to hold the roller catch under tension.

NOTES

[1]Architectural Woodwork Institute, *Architectural Woodwork Quality Standards Illustrated*, 7th ed., Version 1.0. Reston, VA: AWI, p. 152.

[2]Ibid., pp. 126 and 127.

[3]Ibid., pp. 132, 134, 136, and 138.

[4]Ibid., p. 162.

[5]Ibid.

[6]Knape & Vogt, *Drawer Slides and Specialty Hardware*, 1994, pp. 4–5 (boldface added).

[7]AWI, p. 140.

[8]Ibid., p. 271.

9
Kitchens

The kitchen has undergone many changes over the years. In the Victorian era, the cast-iron cookstove was the main source of cooking and heating and, although it was an improvement over the open fire of Colonial days, much time and labor were required to keep it operating. The coal or wood had to be carried into the house, and the stove required blacking to maintain its shiny appearance. In winter, the heat radiating from the cookstove heated the kitchen and made it a gathering place for the family. In summer, however, to use the stovetop for cooking and the oven for baking, the fire had to be lit, which made the kitchen feel like a furnace. (Traditional wood- or coal-burning cookstoves are still available. Some models use gas or electricity but retain the look of a traditional cookstove.)

In the kitchens of the past, in addition to the cookstove, the only other pieces of furniture were tables, chairs, and a sink. All food preparation was done on the table or on the draining board next to the sink. There were no counters as we know them today and no upper storage cabinets. All food was stored in the pantry or in a cold cellar. Today, the kitchen has once again become a gathering place for the family. Much family life is centered around the kitchen, not only for food preparation but also for entertaining and socializing. In line with this, Joe Ruggiero, former Publishing Director of *Home* magazine, has said, "The kitchen will have more upholstery as well as new types of furniture, such as armoires, entertainment centers, and custom dish-racks, instead of traditional cabinetry. [There will be a] parade of gadgets such as wood-burning pizza ovens and built-in woks, . . . ice cream makers and sorbet freezers. Many kitchens will be outfitted with canning centers, special preparation areas and doors opening up to herb and vegetable gardens. The trend will be to more wood in the kitchen."

Regardless of the type of kitchen desired, there are some basic requirements for all kitchens. The appliances and work areas most used in a kitchen are the refrigerator for food storage, stove for cooking, and sink for washing. The **work triangle** connects these three areas, and the total size of the work triangle should not be over 22 feet and may be less than that in some smaller kitchens. The distance between the refrigerator and the sink should be 4 to 7 feet, with 4 to 6 feet between sink and stove and 4 to 9 feet between stove and refrigerator. In addition to an efficient work triangle, adequate lighting and adequate storage are important.

The type of kitchen desired depends on availability of space, life style, and ages and number of family members. Expense and space are the limiting factors in kitchen design. The best utilization of space will create a functional and enjoyable working area.

Kitchens are becoming larger and now account for almost 10 percent of the total square footage of a single-family home. They also feature more cabinetry and counter space, and barrier-free products are increasing in importance. GE Appliances publishes a booklet, *Basic Kitchen Planning for the Physically Impaired*, that provides necessary measurements.

Life style involves several factors. One is the manner of entertaining. Formal dinners require a separate formal dining room, whereas informal entertaining may take place just outside the work triangle, with guest and host or hostess communicating while meals are being prepared. If entertaining is done outside the home of a working host or hostess, then the kitchen may be minimal in size. Such things as how the grocery shopping is done also affect the type of cabinets. If grocery shopping is done twice a month, for example, the pantry space should be increased to allow for storage of foodstuffs.

A small kitchen will appear larger with an open plan (that is, without a wall dividing it from the adjacent room). It will also appear larger with a vaulted ceiling.

A young couple with small children might require a family room within sight of the kitchen. Teenagers like to be near food preparation areas for easy access to the refrigerator and snacks. All these factors need to be considered when planning a kitchen.

Some cooks prefer to work from a pantry and therefore do not need a lot of upper cabinets, whereas others prefer to have a bake center and work from both the upper and lower cabinets.

Ellen Cheever, Certified Kitchen Designer (CKD), ASID, gives the following work simplification techniques for planning a kitchen:

1. Build the cabinets to fit the cook.
2. Build the shelves to fit the supplies.
3. Build the kitchen to fit the family.

FLOOR PLANS

There are infinite variations on basic kitchen floor plans, and this is where customizing comes in (Figure 9–1). According to Linda Trent, "Islands, which may function as eat-in bars, room dividers, and/or work areas are probably the most sought-after design elements in today's kitchens, because they are attractive and make efficient use of space. Varying island shape can result in interesting angles and efficiencies."[1] One of the links between ergonomics and the new social role of the kitchen is the central island cooktop.

The simplest of all kitchen floor plans is the one-wall, otherwise known as **pullman, strip,** or **studio.** Here, all appliances and counter space are contained on one wall and, when required, folding doors or

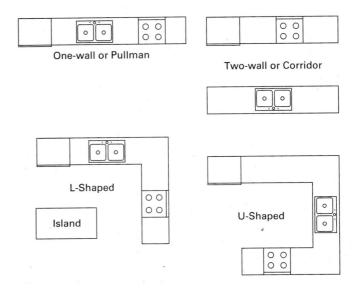

Figure 9–1
Kitchen floor plans.

screens are used to hide the kitchen completely from view. This is a minimal kitchen not designed for elaborate or family meals.

The **corridor** or two-wall plan utilizes two parallel walls and doubles the available space over the one-wall plan. The major problem with this design is through traffic. If possible, for safety's sake, one end should be closed off to avoid this traffic. The width of the corridor kitchen should be between 5 and 8 feet. A narrower width prevents two facing doors from being opened at the same time. For energy conservation, the refrigerator and stove should not face each other directly (see Figure 9–1).

In an L-shaped kitchen, work areas are arranged on two adjacent walls rather than on two opposite walls; the advantages of this are that there is no through traffic and that all counters are contiguous. The L-shaped kitchen may also include an island or a peninsula. This island may simply be an extra work surface, may contain the sink or stove, and may also include an informal eating area. If the island has a raised side facing an eating or seating area, the higher side will hide the clutter in the kitchen.

The U-shaped kitchen is probably the most efficient design. It has three walls of counter space, with no through traffic. Depending on the location of the window, there are at least two walls or more of upper cabinets. The work triangle is easy to arrange in this design, with the sink usually at the top of the U, refrigerator on one side, and range on the other. The refrigerator is always placed at the end of the U to avoid breaking up the counter area and to provide easy accessibility to the eating area. The stove, range, or cooktop is on the opposite side but more centered in the U. Islands also work in a U-shaped kitchen provided that the passageways are more than 4 feet wide.

When planning any kitchen, thought should be given to the activities of each area. The sink area serves a dual purpose. First, it is used for food preparation, such as washing and cleaning fruits and vegetables. Second, after the meal the sink is used for cleanup. In this age of the electric dishwasher, the sink area is generally used only for preliminary cleaning; but in the event of a large number of dishes, sufficient space should be provided next to the sink so a helper can dry the dishes.

Certain areas of the kitchen require a minimum amount of adjacent counter space. The sink needs 24 to 36 inches of counter space on the dishwasher side and 18 to 36 inches on the other side. For cooktops, 18 to 24 inches should be allowed on either side, and regardless of the type of design, there must be at least 16 inches of counter space on the handle side of the refrigerator, which should be at the end of one side of the counter near the entrance to the kitchen. The refrigerator should not be placed in such a manner that the counter is broken up into small areas.

The refrigerator should be plugged into its own individual 115-volt electrical outlet on a circuit separate from those used for heating and cooking appliances. The refrigerator should be placed in an area that will not receive direct sunlight or direct heat from the home heating system. It should not be placed next to sources of heat, such as the range or dishwasher.

The cooking area is considered to be the cooktop area. Many wall ovens are now located in separate areas from the cooktop.

KITCHEN APPLIANCES

Only those appliances that are necessary to a kitchen floor plan will be discussed—in other words, major appliances. Mixers and toasters are outside the scope of this book.

Major appliance manufacturers must comply with a law enacted by Congress in 1975 (PL 94-163). This law provides that energy costs for appliances must be calculated as so much per **kilowatt-hour** (kwh). This information must be supplied on a tag attached to the front of the appliance. Consumers can then calculate their yearly energy cost by finding out their local kilowatt-hour rate. It is important to bear in mind that the higher the local rate, the more important energy conservation features become. It is by using these figures that comparison shopping can be done.

The style of appliances selected may affect the style of cabinetry. Black appliances look better with white or light-colored wood cabinets, whereas free-standing Old-World style stoves may look better with French country cabinetry.

Colored as well as white appliances are available. Currently, the most popular color other than white is almond, which blends very well with wood cabinets. However, Jenn-Air has just introduced the Blue Creek™ line of appliances. The Water Color Collection features five colors: sapphire blue, champagne gold, copper, bordeaux red, and jade. The finish is tinted stainless steel. If a change in the decor of the kitchen is planned for the future, white is always a safe choice. All-black appliances are very popular in contemporary kitchens, with black glass fronts on microwaves and ovens. White appliances may have some chrome accents or be totally white but are more expensive than black appliances.

Another innovation from Jenn-Air is its Suncast Series cooktops. This series features specially engineered surface material in eight stone colors that dissipates heat and stays cool to the touch. The black granite, jade, gray granite, slate, sandstone, teton gray, plum, and lapis colors will not fade, because the colors are fused into the cooktops. The unique Crescent Cooktop's boomerang shape allows it to fit perfectly anywhere—even in a tight-fitting corner. Three Ultra Quick-Start™ radiant elements and one Ultra Quick-Twin Dual element give cooks the power options of five elements in the space of four. The former radiant elements heat to full power in a remarkable three to four seconds (Figure 9–2).

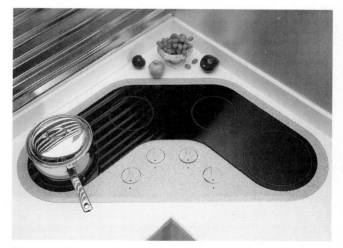

Figure 9–2
The Blue Creek by Jenn-Air Crescent Cooktop, with its boomerang shape, gives cooks an entirely new perspective on kitchen appliances. This sleek, ultra-stylish cooktop creatively utilizes shape and color, allowing kitchen designs to reflect personal style and imagination, with colors designed to coordinate with the most popular countertop colors. (Photo courtesy of Jenn-Air Co.)

Porcelain enamel is most frequently used on surface tops and oven doors because it resists heat, acid, stains, scratches, yellowing, and fading. Baked enamel or electrostatically applied polyester is less durable than porcelain enamel because it is less resistant to stains and scratches; however, it resists chipping better than porcelain enamel.

Stainless steel [Color Plate 12] is resistant to corrosion, dents, and stains and is easy to clean. It may turn dark, however, if it is overheated. Chrome-plated finishes are durable and will not dent easily. Excess heat may cause chrome to discolor over a period of time.[2]

Refrigerators

The most costly kitchen appliance to purchase and to operate is the refrigerator. In fact, the U.S. Department of Energy mandated that 1993 models operate 30 percent more efficiently than 1990 models, and this efficiency will probably increase. By July 1, 2001, all refrigerators must use 30 percent less energy than at present. These savings will be accomplished by improvements in the compressor, thicker insulation, more efficient fans, and increased surface area of the condenser and evaporator coils. Different methods of refrigeration are being studied, and the initial increased cost of such methods may be offset by better efficiency over a period of years.

For our purposes, the word *refrigerator* will be used instead of *refrigerator/freezer* because we assume that all refrigerators have some form of freezer section. The freezer section is commonly on top (which is the most energy efficient), but some refrigerators have the freezer section below the regular food storage area. Side-by-side refrigerators have separate vertical doors for the freezer and refrigerator sections; because the narrower doors have a shorter swing radius, they work well in a galley kitchen or across from appliances with doors. Other exterior features include panel adapter kits, which are used on the face of the refrigerator to match other appliances; the latest are stainless fronts for appliances. Doors that can be reversed are an important feature for those who move frequently.

Refrigerators are sold by their storage capacity (in other words, by cubic feet of space). It is interesting to note that whereas families and kitchens generally are getting smaller, the size of the refrigerator is staying around 16 to 17 cubic feet. This may be a result of working parents who have less time to food shop and need to stockpile food, or it may mean that people are entertaining frequently and need to keep food on hand for guests. Sizes of refrigerators vary from 13 cubic feet to 28 cubic feet. The most energy-efficient refrigerator is in the 15- to 20-cubic-foot range.

The average size for refrigerators is 66 1/2 inches high, 35 3/4 inches wide (that is, the refrigerator fits into a 36-inch space), and 30 1/2 inches deep. This depth measurement means that the door of the refrigerator extends beyond the counter by several inches. To design the refrigerator as an integral part of the cabinetry, many manufacturers have recessed the coils or placed them above the refrigerator, which makes the refrigerator flush with the edge of the counter; however, this type is usually considerably more expensive than usual models. The refrigerator door can be covered to match the cabinets, and it can have custom handles. Because this style has no bottom vent, the toe-kick panel can extend from the cabinet across the base of the refrigerator. For new construction, 37 inches of floor space should be allowed for a refrigerator, even if the planned unit is narrower, and accommodations for a water hook-up should be made even though the hook-up may not be used at the time.

The most common refrigerator features include meat keepers, vegetable storage bins, unwrapped food sections, adjustable shelves, and humidity-controlled vegetable storage areas. Other interior features might include egg storage, handy cheese and spread storage, and glass shelves that prevent spilled liquids from dripping onto other shelves (these solid glass shelves may prevent full air circulation). The shelves on the doors of both refrigerator and freezer may be fixed or adjustable. The latest feature is a door deep enough to hold gallon containers. Other features include frozen juice can dispensers, ice makers, and ice cream makers within the freezer compartment.

An ice-water dispenser with cubed and/or crushed ice that is accessible without opening the refrigerator door may conserve energy and justify the additional expense. All Profile refrigerators from GE feature water and ice activators with a LightTouch® dispenser (instead of the stirrup type usually used) that delivers crushed ice, cubes, and chilled water. This series also offers a 30-cubic-foot refrigerator, the largest manufactured.

Frigidaire was the winner of the 1997 Good Buy Award for its PureSource™ Ice and Water Filter. The PureSource Filter is a class I filter that reduces lead by 94 percent, chlorine by 99 percent, cysts by 99.5 percent, and particulates by 99 percent. The filter system is built into the refrigerator, and the old filter can be twisted off easily and a new one twisted on. The cost of using this filter is less than 10 cents per gallon.

One manufacturer offers a third door for access only to the ice cube compartment. Another offers a storage unit in the door that can be opened for access to snack items without opening the full-length refrigerator doors.

Some companies offer see-through storage bins in their refrigerators. Frigidaire has lighted storage drawers with clear fronts. Frigidaire also features separate components that can be stacked or placed side by side or in a cubical arrangement of four units. The components include wine coolers with optically coated, double-pane thermal glass doors to protect the wine from harsh lighting. There are separate units for white and red wines, as well as the conventional refrigerator and freezer components.

Most manufacturers are interested in energy conservation, and efficiency has greatly improved over the past 15 years. A self-defrosting refrigerator consumes more energy than a manual defrost, but it is much more convenient.

Frigidaire refrigerators feature an exclusive Frigi-Foam® insulation with reduced ozone-depleting chlorofluorocarbons (CFCs). It also offers a new design feature: the gently rounded edges on the sides of its UltraStyle™ refrigerator.

Sub-Zero refrigerators are designed to be built in and flush with the adjacent cabinetry. The company offers a complete range of models, from 27 to 48 inches in width and in a variety of configurations. Its core products, which have the compressors at the top of the units, are 84 inches high and 24 inches deep, the same depth as most cabinets. Sub-Zero's standard units are the only combination units that have two compressors, one for the refrigerator and the other for the freezer, which contributes to fresher food and better energy usage. On the Sub-Zero 700 Series units, one unique energy-saving feature is a door/drawer alarm that emits an audible beep after 15 seconds, reminding users that the door or drawer is ajar. Sub-Zero also manufactures two-drawer units, either refrigerators or freezers. These drawers are 34 1/2 inches high, 27 inches wide, and 24 inches deep and can be used in kitchen islands, low peninsulas, or next to a sink. All Sub-Zero's freezer units have an automatic ice maker (Figure 9–3).

White-Westinghouse manufactures 11- and 13-cubic-foot refrigerators that are small enough that all the contents can be reached from a wheelchair. These refrigerators meet accessibility requirements because the midpoint of the freezer section is less than 54 inches from the floor. This company also offers a side-by-side model that has adjustable shelves, which can be positioned low to reach from a seated position or high to prevent bending over. All White-Westinghouse refrigerators feature an energy saver switch that conserves energy in less humid weather, when cabinet moisture removal is not needed.

Figure 9–3
Two Sub-Zero freezer/refrigerator combinations are shown either side of a counter area. (Note that each unit has the handle side nearest the counter.) The center island includes two refrigerator drawers, used here for fresh fruits and vegetables. (Photo courtesy of Sub-Zero Freezer Company Inc.)

Nylon rollers are provided for moving or rolling the refrigerator from the wall. If the refrigerator is to be moved sideways, a **dolly** should be used to avoid damaging the floor covering.

Ranges

Old-fashioned stoves have been replaced by **freestanding, drop-in,** or **slide-in** range units. Slide-in models can be converted to freestanding by addition of optional side panels and a backguard. Some ranges contain the cooking units, **microwave,** and/or oven in one appliance, or the oven and cooktop may be in two separate units (often in two separate locations in the kitchen).

Many 30-inch ranges now come with a second oven above the cooktop surface. This may be another **conventional oven** or a microwave. An exhaust fan is incorporated beneath some of the microwave ovens.

Freestanding ranges vary from 20 to 40 inches wide, but most are 30 inches wide. Slide-in ranges usually measure 30 inches wide. A freestanding range has finished sides and is usually slightly deeper than the 24-inch kitchen counter. This type of range may be considered if a change of residence will take place in the near future.

Built-in ranges come in two types: slide-in units or drop-ins, both of which are designed for more permanent installation and are usually placed between two kitchen cabinets. Slide-ins fit into a space between cabinets, and drop-ins fit into cabinets connected below the oven. Drop-ins lack a storage drawer, but both types look alike. The cooking medium may be gas or electricity. Some ranges have the cooking surface flush with the counter, whereas on others the cooking surface is lowered an inch or so. The only difference is that if several large or wide pans are used at the same time, such as during canning or for large parties, the lowered surface is more restrictive. The flush surface permits the centering of the larger pans. The surface of ranges may be white or colored with porcelain-coated steel, stainless steel, tempered glass, or ceramic glass.

For those who desire state-of-the-art technology combined with authentic 19th-century styling, old-fashioned-type ranges are now available with gas or electricity. These decorative ranges conceal features such as self-cleaning convection ovens, digital clock timers, and exhaust vent systems. There are several companies that manufacture these types of products. Heartland Appliances makes traditional-style built ovens, refrigerators, and wood- or coal-burning cookstoves.

The U.S. Department of Energy estimates that the typical annual cost of operating an efficient gas range is about half the cost of operating an electric range. This only amounts to a dollar or two per month, however, so individual preference is more of a consideration.

Electric Ranges

There are several different types of element choices for electric ranges. The least expensive and most common is the coil element. The most expensive is the European solid disk of cast iron sealed to the cooktop, which some manufacturers refer to as a **hob.** With the solid-electric element, a red dot indicates that the element is thermally protected and will shut down if a pan boils dry. Some elements have a silver dot, a pan sensor that maintains a fairly constant preselected temperature, sometimes with a variance of 20°. Electric elements heat quickly and can maintain low heat levels.

Another type of element is the radiant **glass-ceramic cooktop,** or smoothtop. When first introduced in 1966, these cooktops were white; now they can be black or patterned grayish-white ceramic glass. The patterned surface shows smudges and fingerprints less than a shiny black surface. All these surfaces are heated primarily by conduction; however, some use halogen. Some smoothtops have quick-heating elements, and for safety's sake the indicator lights will stay on as long as the surface is hot. This type of cooktop has a limiter that cycles the burners on and off, restricting the temperature reached by the glass surface. Smoothtops should be cleaned with a special cream, which both cleans and shines the ceramic. These cooktops are usually 30 inches wide. Both radiant and induction methods require flat-bottomed pots of the same diameter. Jenn-Air offers a 48-inch designer line downdraft triple electric with three convertible bays that use an Energy Saver grill and a choice of cartridges.

Two new methods of heating are halogen and induction, both of which are used with glass-ceramic cooktops. The halogen units have vacuum-sealed quartz glass tubes filled with halogen gas that filter out the white light and use infrared as a heating source. The surface becomes a bright red when turned on. Halogen units provide instant on and instant off, and, as with the induction method, the surface unit itself does not get hot. The only heat the glass top may retain is absorbed from a hot pan.

Induction units are the most expensive type of elements. According to Jenn-Air,

> Induction is literally, the "cool" way to cook. In technical terms, induction uses electromagnetic force to heat cookware of ferromagnetic material (iron, nickel, cobalt, and various alloys). When controls are turned on, the coils produce a high-frequency alternating magnetic field which ultimately flows through the cookware. Molecules in the cookware move back and forth rapidly, causing the cookware to become hot and cook the food. Plus, the cooktop's glass-ceramic surface is unaffected by the magnetic field since it contains no ferromagnetic material. The heat of the pot will warm the glass but will remain much cooler to the touch than other smoothtop surfaces.[3]

When induction-type smoothtops sense overheating, they beep and shut off the power to that burner. Because of the method of heating, induction units turn off the power when a pot is removed. Induction models use electronic touchpads.

For greatest efficiency, all cooking utensils used on an electric range must be flat bottomed to allow full contact with the cooking unit, although induction units will work with slightly warped pans. Usually there are four cooking units, but some of the larger glass cooktops have five or even six units.

Some electric ranges have the controls and clock on a back panel. On separate cooktops, controls are in the front or at the side of the cooktop. On electric ranges, controls may be divided left and right, with the oven controls in between, giving a quick sense of which control works which elements. Controls on the latest cooktops are electronic touchpads.

Electric cooktops may be modular, such as the ones from Jenn-Air, with interchangeable coil, solid, halogen, or radiant elements. Accessories include a **griddle, grille** with exclusive Excalibur® nonstick grill grate finish for easy cleanup, wok, cooker-steamer, and rotiss-Kebab units. For safety, backlit controls or light bar indicators show at a glance if heating elements are on.

Cooktops now have concealed or visible hinges that make it easy to clean under the cooktop, where the overflow from drip bowls ends up. Porcelain drip bowls are much easier to clean than the shiny metal bowls and can be cleaned in the oven during the self-cleaning cycle.

Gas Ranges

Gas cooktops can be made of glass, porcelain-coated steel, or stainless steel. One advantage of using gas is that it is easier to moderate temperature changes. Conventional gas burners have grates that hold the pan above the flame. These grates should be heavy enough to support the pan and be easy to clean. Propane burns a little cooler than regular gas. Sealed gas burners are fused to the cooktop, and there are no drip pans; all spills remain on the glass surface.

Newer gas ranges have pilotless ignition systems that light the cooking unit automatically from either a spark ignition or a coil ignition. By eliminating the standard, always-burning pilot light, these ranges reduce the gas needed for cooking by 30 percent, keep the kitchen cooler, and prevent pilot outage caused by drafts or other conditions. Electricity must be run to the range to operate the pilotless ignition. In case of electricity failure, the burner may be lit by a match; however, as a safety precaution, the oven cannot be used by lighting a match. If electricity cannot be run to the pilotless range, models with pilot lights are still available.

With today's emphasis on fat-free cooking, the Gaggenau Vario Series Built-In Steamer makes quick work of vegetables or rice and doubles as a cooktop warmer for holding entrees until serving time. The compact steamer basin installs seamlessly into counter surfaces and comes equipped with interchangeable perforated or solid stainless-steel inserts that allow cooks to switch from steaming broccoli to stewing meats in stock or wine. Gaggenau's pressureless steam system monitors temperatures and steam output for consistent results. A temperature control ranges from 104° for warming to 203° for quick steaming, and a glass cover lets cooks keep an eye on the food's progress. For easy liquid disposal, the model VK 111-160 Built-In Steamer connects directly to the kitchen drainage system (Figure 9–4).

One of the trends of the 1990s has been the use of multiburner restaurant-type gas ranges with six or even eight burners in home kitchens. (Truly commercial ranges are not permitted in a private residence because of the excessive heat generated.) These ranges are freestanding and are very useful when catering for a large crowd. Most are stainless steel, but the Russell Range may be obtained in a solid brass edition. Most of the restaurant-type ranges have grates covering the entire cooktop, which means that pots and pans can be slid and not lifted aside from the burner.

Russell Range's Plus Steam™ is available in 30- and 36-inch models. The Plus Steam operates as a standard convection oven, but, with the touch of a button, steam circulates through the oven cavity. Seafood is steamed to perfection, breads are baked and proofed to a golden brown, and leftovers are restored to their original flavor and appearance.

Gas appliances produce exhaust gases that are better expelled by means of an exhaust fan.

Ovens

Electric ovens come in 24-, 27-, and 30-inch widths, but some 30-inch ovens require a 33-inch cabinet. Ovens come in two types: self-cleaning **(pyrolytic)**

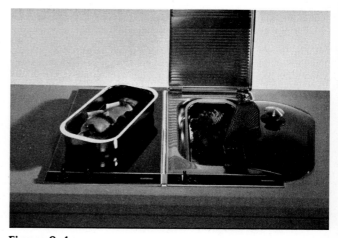

Figure 9–4
The Gaggenau Vario Series Built-in Steamer is a healthy way of cooking vegetables. (Photo courtesy of Gaggenau USA Corp.)

and continuous cleaning (**catalytic**). Self-cleaning ovens have a special cleaning setting that is activated by the timer for the required length of time. This cleaning cycle runs at an extremely high temperature and actually incinerates any oven spills, leaving an ash residue. One of the excellent byproducts of a self-cleaning oven is that, because of the high temperatures required to operate the cleaning cycle, the oven is more heavily insulated than is customary and so retains heat longer and uses less energy when baking. There are now some gas ovens that are self-cleaning.

Continuous-cleaning ovens feature a special porous ceramic finish that disperses and partially absorbs food spatters to keep the oven presentably clean. Running the oven at the highest temperature for a while will help clean up remaining spatters. Oven-cleaning products available at the grocery store may *not* be used on the continuous-cleaning surface.

Ovens cook by one of three methods: radiation, convection, or microwave. Radiant baking is the method used in most ovens. According to Jenn-Air,

> While a conventional oven uses radiant heat to warm the food, oven interior and air, **convection** uses a fan inside the oven cavity to circulate that warm air. The moving air strips away a layer of cooler air that surrounds the food, thus speeding up the baking or roasting process. . . . Jenn-Air's convection ovens have radiant heating elements at the oven's top and bottom, with the fan built into the back for maximum space usage. . . . Meats are juicier, since circulating air seals the outside surface and reduces the evaporation. . . . Because of the way in which the air circulates, cooks can bake three racks of cookies, pizza or other items instead of just one or two.[4]

Therefore, it is possible to cook a greater quantity of food in a small convection oven cavity than in a larger conventional one. On low heat settings, foods can also be dehydrated for long-term storage. The defrosting setting works on the same principle. Convection ovens are more expensive than other ovens, however.

Built-in ovens are required when using a separate cooktop. These may be single conventional oven units or double oven units with one a conventional type and the other a microwave. They are available in widths of 24, 27, and 30 inches. The 24- and 27-inch ovens fit into a standard 27-inch cabinet, but not all 30-inch models fit into a 30-inch cabinet. Some require a 30-inch opening, which only a 33-inch cabinet provides.

Electric ovens may have a solid door, a porcelain enamel door with a window, or a full black glass window door. The porcelain enamel is available in many colors. (A glass door is shown in Figure 9–8.) Controls may be knobs or electronic touchpads. Electric ovens require the door to be left ajar when the broiling mode is in use, or food will roast. Many new ovens turn off automatically after 12 hours (this is a safety feature).

Most ovens have a drop-down door, but for people who are physically challenged, Frigidaire offers a side-swing door, which is reversible so it can be set to open from either side. Sometimes double ovens are used, but they do not offer the advantage of waist-level shelves (which are better for disabled individuals). Timers for ovens vary in length from 99 minutes to 10 hours.

Warming drawers are becoming more prevalent in upscale kitchens. These thermostatically controlled drawers are designed to keep hot foods hot or crisp prior to serving, and they may also be used for proofing bread.

Microwave Ovens

Microwave cooking activates the molecules in food about 2 1/2 billion times per second. The friction between molecules produces the heat. Today, most microwave ovens are operated by means of touch controls that electronically monitor the amount of energy from full power to a warming setting or defrost cycle.

Microwave ovens may be programmed to cook whole meals on a delayed-time basis. Some feature recipes that are available at a touch on the control panel, whereas others use a meat probe to produce meat that is rare, medium, or well done.

A microwave's size refers to the cooking cavity. Most microwaves are designed to sit on a countertop. Small models can be mounted under upper cabinets. Some medium-sized models are specifically designed to be mounted over the range, under specially sized cabinets. Sizes vary from 0.5 cubic foot to 1.3 cubic feet. Microwave ovens are rated by watts, from 600 to 1000 watts. The greater the wattage, the more quickly the oven heats food.

Microwave ovens may be counter models, under-the-cabinet (UTC) models without a vent, or over-the-range (OTR) models with built-in recirculating exhaust fans. Spacemaker Plus™ from GE features high wattage and a bottom-feed microwave distribution system. Some new features are Auto Cook, Auto Popcorn, and Auto Reheat, which rely on a humidity sensor to determine precisely when the food has been cooked properly.

Most microwave ovens have a door that swings open, but the GE Monogram® microwave oven has a door that pulls down to open. This particular microwave oven may cook by convection either alone or in combination with the microwave. The combination method means that food can be browned while being cooked by microwave. The feature used most frequently on a microwave oven is the defrost cycle.

Unlike regular ovens, the microwave cooking time varies with the amount of food to be cooked; thus, four potatoes require about 70 percent less energy when microwaved, but 12 potatoes bake more efficiently in a conventional oven.

For safety's sake, some microwaves have child lockouts with keypad releases.

Ventilation Fans

There are many methods of venting cooking fumes from the kitchen. Ducted fans may be either updraft or downdraft. With updraft, the hood over the cooking surface collects the heat, odors, and fumes and exhausts them to the outside. This method takes up some space in the cabinet over the cooking surface. The Slim Telescoping Hidavent™ canopy, when not in use, takes up only 2 inches in height.

There are three types of downdraft on the market. The most well-known downdraft is from Jenn-Air, the original manufacturer of cooktops and grill ranges, with a built-in downdraft ventilation and a two-speed fan for flexibility. The higher speed is ideal for grilling and drying, whereas the lower speed provides ventilation for lighter cooking. Jenn-Air has a vent that goes from the back to the front of the cooking surface. It will also vent the fumes and heat that escape the oven during the self-cleaning cycle. Downdraft cooking is ideal for peninsula kitchen designs.

Some manufacturers use a raised vent at the back of the cooktop, which may not always completely exhaust fumes from the front burners, particularly if the pans are very high. A split downdraft consists of two vents on each side of the cooktop surface. Broan® offers Eclipse® for island and peninsula cooking, where updraft venting is impractical.

For outside walls, an exhaust fan that vents directly outdoors may be used.

Ductless or recirculating systems have a washable **charcoal filter** that filters out odors.

Dishwashers

Dishwashers are 24 inches wide and are usually installed adjacent to the sink so that the plumbing connections are made easily. Dishwashers discharge the dirty water through the sink containing the garbage disposal. For older-style kitchens with no under-counter space for a dishwasher, movable models are available that connect to the faucet in the sink and dis-

charge into the sink. GE makes an under-sink model for small kitchens.

The features most desired in dishwashers are quiet operation, energy and water conservation, and versatile loading. Available features in dishwashers include a heavy-duty cycle for cleaning heavily soiled pots and pans, a regular cycle for normal soil, rinse and hold for a small number of dishes requiring rinsing, and low-energy wash cycles.

If the utility company offers lower off-peak rates, a delay-start feature may be desirable. Some models will display an alert message, such as "blocked wash arm" or "PF," should a power failure occur.

Dishes may be dried by the heated cycle, or for energy efficiency a no-heat drying cycle may be programmed. Newer dishwashers require little or no rinsing of soiled dishes because a soft food disposer or filtration system is built in. Racks and even dividers are now adjustable, allowing for large-size dishes or wider items that do not fit over the fixed dividers. Some dishwashers have a separate rack on top for silverware, which makes the silverware easier to get at, easier to clean, and more scratch resistant. Water-saver dishwashers are now available that use only 6 gallons. Frigidaire, in its Precision Wash System™, uses microfilters that continuously filter 100 percent of the cleaning water. A unique glass trap captures any accidental glassware breakage or small utensils if they are accidentally dropped into the tub, eliminating the potential hazard of items jamming water lines and motors.

The American Council for an Energy-Efficient Economy, an independent research group, has proven that ASKO dishwashers are very quiet, because the stainless steel tank is wrapped in a blanket of asphalt and heavy felt padding, which absorbs 10 times more sound than the fiberglass used in ordinary brands. In addition, the circulation and drain pumps and motors are mounted with rubber dampeners and hoses to a special galvanized-steel base pan isolated from the tank, to reduce vibration and noise further. In model 1805, there are hidden touch controls that disappear when the door is closed. The controls are set with the door open; the dishwasher starts when the door is closed. The dishwasher stops automatically if the door is opened and resumes when the door is closed.

Trash Compactors

Trash compactors reduce trash volume by 80 percent in less than one minute. Most have some form of odor control and use a compacting ram with the force of approximately 3000 pounds. In today's society trash disposal has become an expensive service, and trash compactors do reduce the volume of trash considerably. They may make trash less biodegradable, however, because of its compacted volume. Trash compactors vary in width from 12 to 18 inches.

In some areas of the United States, as a result of recycling laws, trash compactors may becoming obsolete. Trash compactors can be used to crush recyclable aluminum cans and plastic bottles, however, making them less bulky. Where recycling is not required, trash compactors can still be used in the conventional manner.

Kitchen Sinks

Kitchen sinks are constructed of stainless steel, enameled cast iron, enameled steel, or manufactured materials (usually compression-molded modified acrylic). Each material has its pros and cons.

Stainless steel sinks give a contemporary look to a kitchen and are less likely to cause breakage if dishes are accidentally dropped into them. Finishes may be satin or gloss. Any water spots will leave a spot on the shiny surface, however. In addition, heat from the hot water dissipates more rapidly with a metal sink than with a porcelain enamel one. When selecting a stainless steel sink, the lower the number of the gauge is, the thicker the metal will be. Undercoating absorbs sound, protects against condensation, and helps maintain sink water temperature. Like all kitchen sinks, there is a great variety of sizes, depths, and number of bowls in stainless steel.

Porcelain enamel sinks show stains easily, and a scouring powder is usually required to remove such stains. The porcelain may become chipped when hit with a heavy object. Enameled cast iron sinks provide a colorful touch in the kitchen, however.

Enameled steel sinks are low cost and lightweight but also less durable than the other types. Sinks made of solid surfaces are easily cleaned, but colors are limited and require an experienced installer, which raises the cost.

Porcelain sinks are highly chip resistant but can break when a heavy object is dropped into them. Porcelain sinks are made from high-fired clay with an enamel finish, a combination that is used more in Europe than in the United States.

Composite or quartz acrylic is the latest material for kitchen sinks. This material produces a color-through sink impervious to stains and scratches. Composite sinks are a combination of natural materials and synthetics. Elkay makes three models of top-mounted Corian® sinks in three colors: glacier white, cameo white, and almond.

Some kitchen sinks, such as stainless steel sinks and those designed to be used with a metal rim, are flush with the counter. Any water spilled on the counter may be swept back into the sink. Self-rimming sinks are raised above the surface of the counter, and any water spilled must be mopped up.

Some self-rimming sinks have predrilled holes, which must be ordered to suit the type of faucet to be used. The old standard had three holes, or four holes if a spray or soap dispenser will be used. With the increasing use of single-lever faucets with self-contained pullout sprays, however, only one hole may be needed. Some models have knockout holes started in their undersides. An extra hole may be needed if a water purifier is desired. Under-mounted, flush-mounted, and integral or molded sinks have the faucets on the counter.

Single-compartment sink models should be installed only where there is minimum space. One-bowl models do not provide a second disposal area if the bowl is in use. Two-bowl models may be the same size and depth, or one bowl may be smaller and shallower. For corner installations there are L-shaped double models. A single-bowl sink, called a bar sink or hospitality sink, is often placed in a separate area of the kitchen, usually in an island. These sinks typically have a high arc bar faucet (Figure 9–5).

In triple sinks one of the bowls is usually shallower and smaller than the other two and may contain the garbage disposal unit. Some sinks with small bowls have a strainer for draining pastas or cleaning vegetables. Other sinks have a ribbed area for draining dishes. A variety of kitchen sinks are shown in Figure 9–5.

For those interested in composting waste, Kohler offers the Ecocycle sink, which has two 10-inch-deep basins and a chute system accessed by an opening in the wide saddle between the two basins. Accessories with the sink include the Ecocycle chute and bucket system, a cutting board, a colander, and the Duo-strainer® Dry, a new remote control cable drain. The Ecocycle comes in self-rimming and tile-in versions.

Corian, when used as a material for kitchen sinks, may or may not be an integral part of the counter. (Corian is discussed on page 184.)

The width of a kitchen sink varies between 25 and 43 inches. Some sinks with attached drain boards are almost 50 inches wide. New sinks have the drain at the rear, which means there is a flat area for food preparation and more accessible storage space under the sink.

Accessories for sinks may include a fitted cutting board, where waste material may be pushed off one corner into the sink. Wire or plastic colanders are another feature and are useful for holding food or vegetables that require rinsing.

The Assure™ kitchen sink from Kohler extends accessibility into the kitchen. It is made from cast iron

Figure 9–5
Life in the Country™, a new pattern from Kohler's Artist Edition portfolio of decorated fixtures, is the perfect complement to today's country casual kitchens. Vignettes of fishing, harvesting, and gardening scenes are paired with bands of country fowl, strawberries, plums, and grapes, all rendered in colors from a soft, natural palette. GIBRALTAR® solid surface material from Wilsonart provides the perfect frame for these under-counter artistic works. Kohler's Revival™ faucet in brushed chrome is shown here. (Photo courtesy of Kohler Co.) Also shown is undermount sink model ELU-3119-L with Regency Single Lever faucet LK-4371-F-CR. (Photo courtesy of Elkay Manufacturing Company.) The bar sink shown is model BILGR-2115-L with Polished Brass Hi-Arc faucet LK-2088-13-D. (Photo courtesy of Elkay Manufacturing Company.)

and features high and low basins that make kitchen sink tasks easy to perform from a seated or standing position. An optional polyethylene cutting board, polypropylene colander, and drain board with wire dish rack are all specifically designed for Assure. This design has a front apron that curves gently inward to bring the basins closer to a seated user and a wide front ledge that users can grasp to pull themselves toward the sink and rest their arms while working. A polystyrene shroud designed to fit over the drain and water pipes prevents a seated user's knees or legs from coming in contact with hot pipes. The Assure kitchen sink was designed with the following points in mind: users' specific limitations of reach, upper-body mobility, and gripping strength; the amount of room needed to turn or position a wheelchair, walker, or crutches; and accessibility to working surfaces and appliance controls from a seated position (Figure 9–6).

Maintenance. Kitchen sinks should be cleaned with only mild powders or paste cleaners. Steel wool or heavy-duty abrasive powders should not be used. A mirrored-finish stainless sink can be cleaned with a special automotive polishing compound to maintain its sheen.

Kitchen Faucets

Faucets do not come with the kitchen sink and can sometimes be as expensive as the sink itself. Faucets constructed of chrome-plated steel should be all chrome-plated steel, with no parts chrome-plated plastic, because plating over plastic will gradually peel off with use. Delta, a Masco company, also uses the brass finish Brilliance (as described in Chapter 7, page 154). Due to this finishing method, brass faucet sales for kitchens and bathrooms have dramatically increased in the past year. Several other companies have a similar process; however, the brass color does vary with each manufacturer.

A mixing type of valve, with which hot and cold may be blended with one handle, allows one-handed operation (see Figure 9–6). One problem is that the handle may be accidentally turned on when in the hot position, and a burn can result. This problem should be eliminated by legislation enacted on January 1, 1994, which requires all new and replacement faucet valves to have pressure balance and antiscald controls by January 1996. To prevent burns, the water heater should be set at 120°F. Most kitchen faucets have a hose attached for spraying the sink and washing vegetables.

Several manufacturers provide lifetime warranties on their valves. Price Pfister offers the Pforever

Figure 9–6
The new Assure wheelchair-accessible kitchen sink by Kohler becomes a complete work station with the addition of a polyethylene cutting board, colander, and drainboard. The Coralais™ faucet with integral pull-out sprayhead brings the spout to the seated user. (Photo courtesy of Kohler Co.)

Warranty™, which covers material and workmanship for the life of the product on all noncommercial products. Pfister's commercial products carry a 10-year warranty.

Moen® warrants to the original purchaser that its faucets will be leak and drip free during normal domestic use for as long as the purchaser owns them. If the faucet should ever develop a leak or drip during this time, Moen will provide, free of charge, the parts necessary to put the faucet back in good working condition.

A gooseneck faucet is higher than normal and may be used for the kitchen but is more frequently used in a bar sink (see Figure 9–5). Moen has designed its new kitchen faucet longer than the customary faucet length (Figure 9–7). Delta's Signature® line also has a 9-inch-high spout, with the escutcheon plate (the base) sloped toward the sink area for easy run off of water.

The Kohler Coordinates™ is a relationship between Kohler Co. and its multiple partners. This collaboration translates to well-coordinated, high-style products for the kitchen and bath. Kohler manufactures plumbing products for kitchen and bath; Canac® produces cabinetry for any area in the house, including kitchens and baths; Sub-Zero is a refrigeration specialist; Dacor manufactures kitchen appliances; Ann Sacks Tile and Stone manufactures and imports tile, marble, granite, and limestone; Dutch Boy Paint manufactures paints; DalTile produces ceramic tile; Wilsonart International manufactures products for counters, walls, tub and shower surrounds, and flooring; and Robern Co. specializes in the design and manufacture of mirrored bath cabinetry and lighting for the home.

Several hot water dispensers on the market provide very hot water (about 190°F) for use in making hot drinks and instant soups. Franke and In-Sink-Erator have recently introduced models that dispense both hot and cold water through one faucet. The extra hole in the sink may be used for these dispensers as well as for purified water.

Because of increasing awareness of water conservation, plumbing manufacturers are now making 2.5- to 2.7-gallons-per-minute-flow kitchen faucets.

KITCHEN CABINETS

Stock kitchen cabinets usually start at 15 inches wide and come in 3-inch increments up to 48 inches. The depth of lower cabinets is 24 inches, and the depth of

Figure 9–7
(a) The Chateau® kitchen faucet is Moen's new longer-length faucet. It is shown here with a hose spray in the deck plate and a lotion dispenser. (Photo courtesy of Moen Corp.) (b) Kohler adds the convenience of a handspray to its popular Essex kitchen faucet. The 9-inch gooseneck spout makes it easy to fill large containers and tall glasses; easy-to-operate wristblade handles are embossed with a fleur-de-lis *(a French royal lily) design. (c) Finial Traditional with high arc spout combined with a lever handle with traditional rolled accents, both from the Finial Traditional collection, reflect Early American influences. (Photos courtesy of Kohler Co.)*

upper cabinets is 12 inches. Filler strips are used between individual cabinets to make up any difference in measurements.

Kitchen cabinets are usually made of all wood or wood with decorative laminate doors. Solid wood is required for raised panel designs. For dimensional stability, a medium density or multi-density fiberboard (MDF) is used for the case and shelves, and the edges are banded with a wood veneer that matches the door and drawer fronts. The interior of the cabinets is often coated with a PVC plastic material that reflects light, making it easier to find items inside and easier to clean. Under-cabinet appliances are also popular and clear the counter of clutter.

One of the many products available from St. Charles of New York is the steel cabinet. Because of the strength of steel, steel cabinets are thinner and taller and feature an added shelf for more storage. They are resistant to temperature and humidity changes and will not twist, warp, swell, or absorb odors. Steel cabinets are also available in hypoallergenic material, which is important for those clients who need a chemical-free environment.

The kitchen is a very personal room, and the style of cabinets selected should reflect the client's life style. At one extreme are kitchens in which everything is hidden from sight (behind solid doors) and counters are empty. The other extreme is the kitchen with raised panel doors, shaped at the top, often with glass inserts, and shelves on which personal collections and/or kitchen utensils are displayed. Glass doors should be used with glass shelves for displaying decorative items, or the impact on the viewer is lost. (It is also important to consider what will be visible through the glass doors.) (See Color Plate 13.) Another style of kitchen uses open shelves for the storage of dishes and glasses; a pantry is used for food storage. Most kitchens fall somewhere between these extremes, but kitchens should be personalized for the client.

Wood cabinets may have flush overlay, reveal overlay, or, for more traditional styles, an exposed frame with a lipped door. The face surface of the door may be plane, have a flat or raised panel, or have mouldings applied for a traditional approach. Contemporary kitchens may have not only flush overlay doors, but flush overlay in combination with linear metal or wood decorative strips, which also function as drawer and door pulls. Perma-Edge® from Wilsonart has matching mouldings for doors and drawers.

The traditional front frame cabinet construction and the European-style frameless construction (sometimes referred to as 32-mm cabinets) are both popular. Thirty-two millimeters is the spacing of predrilled holes in the cabinet sides for shelf spacing. Shelves in all cabinets should be fully adjustable to accommodate the needs of the user. A well-stocked kitchen requires a minimum of 50 square feet of shelf space and a minimum of 11 square feet of drawer space. Pots and pans are more readily accessible if drawers, rather than base cabinet shelves, are used for storage.

When the frameless type of construction is used, it will have an opening 1 1/2 inches wider than that in conventionally constructed cabinets. A quality frameless cabinet is as strong as a face frame cabinet, with 1/2-inch-thick sides and 1/4-inch-thick back. There is very little cost difference between framed and frameless construction (Figure 9–8).

Many special features may be ordered for the custom-designed kitchen, which will add to the cost of the installation but may be ordered to fit the personal and budgetary needs of the client. Base sliding shelves make all items visible, which eliminates the need to get down on hands and knees to see what is at the bottom of a base unit. A bread box may be contained within a drawer with a lid to help maintain freshness. A cutting board, usually made of maple, that slides out from the upper part of a base unit is convenient and will help protect the surface of the counter from damage. A cutting board should not be placed directly over a drawer that might be needed in conjunction with the cutting board.

Lazy susans in corner units or doors with attached swing-out shelves utilize the storage area of a corner unit. Another use for the corner unit is the installation of a 20-gallon water heater, which provides instant hot water for the kitchen sink and the electric dishwasher and prevents waste of water. A second water heater can be installed close to the bathroom to

Figure 9–8
The softened contours of Tarsia II in cherry provide a pleasing counterpoint to Biscayne bevels, shown here in the solid surface material. Note the two different types of materials used for the cabinets, which provides a pleasant contrast. (Photo courtesy of Wood-Mode®.)

conserve energy and to avoid having to wait for the hot water to reach the bathroom.

Dividers in drawers aid in drawer organization, and vertical dividers in upper or base units utilize space by arranging larger and flat items in easily visible slots (thus avoiding nesting).

Bottle storage units have frames to contain bottles. Spice racks may be attached to the back of an upper door or built into a double-door unit. A special spice drawer insert allows for easy visibility of seasonings. Hot pads may be stored in a narrow drawer under a built-in cooktop. A tilt-down sink front may hold sponges, scouring pads, and the like. Wire or plastic-coated baskets for fruit and vegetable storage provide easily visible storage. A wastebasket attached to either a swing-out door or a tilt-down door or sliding out from under the sink provides a neat and out-of-sight trash container.

Appliance garages are built into the back of the counter and enclose mixers, blenders, and other small appliances. The garage may have tambour doors or may match the cabinets.

Portable recycling units have been on the market for some time. Some states and cities have comprehensive recycling laws, and both custom and stock cabinets offer multibasket recycling units (the four-unit model is most popular). Manufacturers recommend putting one single recycling unit near the sink for compostables, and then two away from the food preparation area, one for aluminum cans and the other for bottles. Local building codes should be checked to see whether some type of venting is necessary for the cabinet under the sink.

Several kitchen cabinet companies publish brochures that will assist in kitchen planning. These brochures include questionnaires that cover such issues as height of primary user, type of cooking to be performed, and what the client may or may not like about the current kitchen plan.

COUNTER MATERIALS

Counters may be of the following materials: decorative laminate, ceramic tile, wood, marble, travertine, solid surface materials, solid surfacing veneer (SSV), stainless steel, granite, or slate.

Decorative Laminate

In some areas of the United States, decorative laminate is the most commonly used counter material. The construction is exactly the same as for laminate used on walls. For countertop use, two thicknesses are available; a choice of one or the other depends on the type of counter construction. For square-edged counters, the general-purpose grade is used. If it is necessary to roll the laminate on a simple radius over the edges of the substrate, a **postforming** type is specified. The postforming method eliminates the seam or brown line at the edge of the counter. Another method of eliminating the brown line is to use one of the colorthrough laminates.

Installation. Postformed countertops must be constructed at the plant rather than at the job site, because heat and special forming fixtures are used to create the curved edge. The counter may be manufactured as a single unit, or each postformed side may be manufactured separately. By manufacturing each side separately, any discrepancy in the alignment of the walls can be adjusted at the corner joints.

For square-edged counters, the edge is applied first and then routed smooth with the substrate. The flat surface is then applied, and the overlapping edges are routed flush with the counter surface.

Another method is to apply the flat surface first and rout the apron to accommodate such edge treatments as Perma-Edge mouldings. These mouldings may be laminate with a beveled edge, all one color; laminate with a beveled edge, two different colors; half-round wood with 2-, 4-, or 6-inch radii to match; or wood with a laminate insert.

For counters, the adhesive is applied to both the countertop substrate and the back of the laminate. When the adhesive is dry, scrap plastic, thin wood, or metal strips are placed on the substrate to prevent contact before the laminate is properly positioned. These strips are gradually removed, and the bond is complete. The excess at the front is then trimmed with the router.

A decorative laminate surface is durable, but it is not a cutting surface and will chip if heavy objects are dropped onto it. For areas where chemical spills or other destructive or staining substances may be used, a chemical- and stain-resistant laminate may be specified. Specific uses are chemistry laboratory tops, photographic lab tops, medical and pathology labs, and clinics.

For high-use and heavy-wear areas such as fast-food countertops, supermarket check-out stands, and bank service areas, a 0.125-inch thickness of decorative laminate is available.

Maintenance. Decorative laminate may be cleaned with warm water and mild dish soaps. Use of abrasives or special cleansers should be avoided because they may contain abrasives, acids, or alkalines. Stubborn stains may be removed with organic solvents or two minutes of exposure to a hypochlorite bleach, such as Clorox®, followed by a clean water rinse. Manufacturers' specific instructions and recommendations for cleaning should be followed.

Ceramic Tile

Ceramic tile has become a popular material with which to cover kitchen counters. To facilitate cleaning, the **backsplash** may also be covered with tile. Ceramic tile is a durable surface; the most vulnerable part is the grout, which will absorb stains unless a stain-proof grout is specified. A grout sealer or lemon furniture oil will also seal the surface of the grout so stains will not penetrate.

Around the sink area, the ceramic tile counter may be carried down the front to the top of the doors below. This is reminiscent of old farmhouse kitchens and protects wood cabinets from water.

Because of the hard surface of the tile, fragile items that are dropped on the counter will break, and if heavy objects are dropped, the tile may be cracked or broken. Sufficient tile for replacements should be ordered.

Installation. When installing a ceramic tile counter, it is recommended that an exterior-grade plywood be used as the substrate. The remaining installation procedure is the same as for floors and walls.

Maintenance. Maintenance of ceramic tile counters is the same as that for ceramic tile floors.

Wood

Wood counters are usually made of a hard wood, such as birch or maple, and are constructed of glued strips of wood that are then sealed and coated with a varnish. Unsealed wood will permanently absorb stains. Wood counters should not be used as a cutting surface because the finish will become marred. Any water accumulating around the sink should be mopped up immediately; a wood surface can become damaged from prolonged contact with moisture. (See Color Plate 13.)

Wood counters may be installed in a curved shape by successively adding a strip of wood, gluing, and clamping it. When dry, another piece is added.

Marble

In the past, marble was used as a material for portions of the countertop. Today, in some expensive installations, marble is used for the entire counter area. Some people like to use a marble surface for rolling out pastry or making hand-dipped chocolates. As mentioned in the section on marble floors (p. 65), marble may absorb stains. This tendency may cause unsightly blemishes on marble countertops. Heavy items dropped on a marble surface will crack it.

Maintenance. Stain removal from marble countertops is the same as for marble floors.

Travertine

When travertine is used as a counter material, it must be filled. Maintenance of travertine countertops is the same as for marble floors.

Solid Surface Materials

Corian, a product invented by DuPont, is acrylic based and combines the smoothness of marble with the solid feel of granite and the workability of wood. Corian is available in sheets of 1/4, 1/2, and 3/4 inch thicknesses and in a wide variety of double- and single-bowl kitchen sinks and lavatory styles. Corian is nonporous and highly resistant to abuse; even cigarette burns, stains, and scratches can be removed with household cleanser or a Scotch-Brite® pad. Because Corian is acrylic, it can be formed to a very tight radius before the inside of the curve becomes too compressed and the outside too stretched. Other brands of solid surface materials are made of polyester, which resists tight radii. Dark colors may perform differently from light colors.

Solid surface materials may have thicker, built-up edges, made by using joint adhesive, and can be routed into a variety of decorative treatments, including bull-nose edges and "sandwich" inserts (Figure 9–9). Solid surface manufacturers may be able to supply custom colors for large projects.

Wilsonart SSV (Solid Surfacing Veneer) is 1/8 inch thick and was used on the reception desk in Color Plate 7. Gibraltar®, also from Wilsonart International, is 1/2 inch thick, and both materials match their laminates exactly, so a coordinated look can be obtained although different materials are being used.

Fountainhead is a solid surface material from Nevamar and can be routed to provide curves. Contrasting color can be used to fill in the routed designs. FH Coordinates from Nevamar is a collection of hardware designed to coordinate with Nevamar's solid surfacing material and laminates. Swanstone® is a fiberglass-based solid surface material manufactured by Swan.

The edges of solid surface materials may be shaped like wood, and seams may be made for longer lengths, provided there is support for the seam.

Maintenance. Most stains on solid surface materials wipe right off with a regular household detergent. Because of the solid composition of these materials, most stains stay on the surface and may be removed with any household abrasive cleanser or

| Set-back or Recessed | Double Chamfer | Roman Ogee | Bullnose | Double Roundover | Wood Inlay | Inlay of CORIAN |

Figure 9–9
Edge treatments for counters.

Scotch-Brite pad gently rubbed in a circular motion. Cigarette burns and cuts may be removed with very fine sandpaper, 120–140 grit, and then rubbed with a Scotch-Brite pad. If the surface was highly polished, repolishing may be required to blend the damaged area.

Stainless Steel

All commercial kitchens have stainless steel counters because these counters can withstand scouring, boiling water, and hot pans. Stainless steel counters can be installed in private residences, if desired, providing a high-tech look.

Maintenance. One of the problems with stainless steel is that the surface may show scratches, and with hard water the surface shows water spots. Water spots may be removed, however, by rubbing the damp surface with a towel, and scratches gradually blend into a patina. Apart from possible scratches and spots, stainless steel is extremely easy to maintain.

Granite and Slate

Both granite and slate may be used as counter materials, although construction of the cabinets must be strong enough to support the extra weight of stone. As noted in Chapter 4, granite and slate vary in porosity, and care should be taken to prevent stains from penetrating the surface.

Maintenance. Maintenance of granite and slate countertops is the same as that for granite walls and slate floors.

Other Materials

In composition, Nuvel® does not fit any of the previous classifications. It is a high-density thermoplastic polymer sold in sheet form and used in edge profiles and double-bowl kitchen sinks. It may be used for countertops, tabletops, kitchen and bath cabinets, shelving units, and for postforming and thermoforming. Nuvel is not manufactured with and does not contain or emit ozone depleting compounds. Nuvel is completely recyclable.

Installation. Nuvel surfacing material is not recommended for application directly to composite substrates such as hardboard, cardboard, and solid lumber because of their dimensional instability. The recommended substrates for Nuvel are industrial-grade particleboard, medium density fiberboard, hardwood-faced grade plywood, or metal. Although contact adhesives commonly used in high-pressure laminate fabrication are suitable for use with Nuvel, it is recommended that Nuvel Seaming Cartridge be used.

Maintenance. Although Nuvel will not be damaged by inadvertent and short-term exposure to extreme heat, it is advised that Nuvel not be exposed for prolonged periods to temperatures in excess of 175°F. Nuvel may be cleaned with spray detergent and a damp cloth. More difficult stains may be removed with a cleanser and damp cloth. A Scotch-Brite pad will aid in removing difficult stains.

FLOORS

Kitchen floors may be ceramic tile, quarry tile, wood, laminate (Figure 9–10), or any resilient flooring. The choice of flooring will depend on the client's needs

Figure 9–10
Wilsonart laminate floor in contrasting squares was used for this kitchen floor. The cabinetry is by Fieldstone and the tabletop is Wilsonart Gibraltar with a colored insert. (Photo courtesy of Wilsonart International.)

and personal wishes. Some people find a hard-surfaced floor to be tiring to the feet, whereas others are not bothered by the hard surface. Wood floors need to be finished with a durable finish that will withstand any moisture that may be spilled accidentally. Resilient flooring may be vinyl, cushioned or not, or the new rubber sheet flooring.

WALLS

Kitchen walls should be painted with an enamel that is easily cleansed of grease residue. The backsplash may be covered with the same decorative laminate as used on the counter, applied either with a cove or a square joint. Ceramic tile may be used in conjunction with a ceramic tile counter or with a decorative laminate one. Mirror may also be selected for kitchen walls; it provides reflected light and visually enlarges the appearance of the counter space. A completely scrubbable wallcovering is another alternative material for the backsplash.

CERTIFIED KITCHEN DESIGNERS

A certified kitchen designer **(CKD)** is a professional who has proven knowledge and technical understanding through a stringent examination process conducted by the Society of Certified Kitchen Designers, the licensing and certification agency of the American Institute of Kitchen Dealers. A CKD has technical knowledge of construction techniques and systems used in new construction and light exterior and interior remodeling, including plumbing, heating, and electrical.

A CKD will provide a functional and aesthetically pleasing arrangement of space depicted in floor plans and interpretive renderings and drawings. In addition to designing and planning kitchens, the CKD supervises installations of residential-style kitchens.

An interior designer would be well advised to work with a CKD.

BIBLIOGRAPHY

American Gas Association, *Buyer's Guide, Efficient Gas Ranges*, 1991.

Consumer Reports, "Cooktops, a Remodelers Dream?," July 1994.

Consumer Reports, "Wall Ovens, a Cooktops Complement," July 1994.

Jenn-Air Company, *Solid Element Cooktops*. Indianapolis, IN: Author, 1985.

Whiteley, Peter O., "Choosing a Kitchen Sink," *Sunset Magazine*, January 1993.

GLOSSARY

Backsplash. A protective area behind a counter.

Catalytic. A porous ceramic finish that accelerates the dispersion of food spatters.

Charcoal filter. A frame that contains charcoal particles, which filter the grease from the moving air.

CKD. Certified kitchen designer.

Convection oven. Heated air flows around the food.

Conventional oven. Food is cooked by radiation.

Corridor kitchen. Two parallel walls with no contiguous area.

Dolly. Two- or four-wheeled cart used for moving heavy appliances.

Drop-in range. Ranges designed to be built into base units.

Freestanding range. Ranges having finished sides.

Glass-ceramic cooktop. A smooth ceramic top used as a cooking surface in electric ranges.

Griddle. A unit with a flat cooking surface used for cooking pancakes.

Grille. A unit specially for broiling food.

Hob. Sealed solid element providing a larger contact area with the bottom of the pan and better control at low-heat settings.

Kilowatt-hour (kwh). A unit of energy equal to 1000 watt hours.

Microwave oven. Heat is generated by the activation of the molecules within the food by the microwaves.

Postforming. Heating a laminate to take the shape of a form.

Pullman kitchen. A one-wall kitchen plan.

Pyrolytic action. An oven that cleans by extremely high heat, incinerating any residue to an ash.

Rotisserie. An electrical accessory that rotates food on a spit or skewer.

Shish-kebab. A rotisserie accessory combining alternate small pieces of meat and/or vegetables on a skewer or spit.

Slide-in range. Similar in construction to a drop-in range, except that the top edges may overhang the side; therefore, this type must be slid in rather than dropped in.

Strip kitchen. One-wall kitchen plan.

Studio kitchen. One-wall kitchen plan.

Work triangle. An imaginary triangle drawn between the sink, refrigerator, and cooking area.

NOTES

[1]Linda Trent, "Combining Kitchen and Bath Elements," *Interiors & Sources,* April 1994.

[2]*Buyer's Guide to Energy-Efficient Gas Furnaces & Appliances.* Arlington, VA: American Gas Association.

[3]Jenn-Air, *Masterful Cooking—Convection.* Indianapolis, IN: Jenn-Air.

[4]Ibid. (boldface added).

10

Bathrooms

Ancient Greek cities featured large public baths where one could take a hot and cold bath and then get a rubdown with olive oil. Public bathing was also practiced by the Romans, who used aqueducts to bring water to the people of Rome. Roman bathing facilities consisted of dressing rooms, warm rooms, hot baths, cold baths, steam rooms, swimming pools, and recreation rooms (where the bather exercised). These bathing facilities were an early version of present-day spas. After the fall of the Roman Empire, during the Dark Ages, bathing became much less frequent. In the 1800s and early 1900s, the Saturday night bath was a ritual. A metal tub was brought into the heated kitchen, and hot water was poured in by hand. Almost 90 percent of the modernization of bathrooms has occured in the past 25 years.

American hotels originated the idea of bathing rooms, and the first one was built at the Tremont House in Boston in 1829. The idea proved very popular and spread to other hotels and private homes throughout the United States. As a nation, Americans take more baths and showers than any other people in the world. The realities of the 1990s, however, include both energy and water conservation. According to Linda Trent, "The graying of America combined with new awareness of the needs of the physically challenged have increased demand for both safety features and barrier-free or accessible products that are attractive and functional, particularly in hospitality, commercial and multi-housing construction and renovation."[1]

Because all bathrooms have the same three basic fixtures, it is the designer's challenge to create a bathroom that is not only unique but functional. A knowledge of the different materials used in these fixtures and the variety of shapes, sizes, and colors will help designers meet this challenge.

PLANNING A BATHROOM

Eljer offers the following suggestions for planning a better bathroom: The size of the family needs to be considered. The more people who will use a bathroom, the larger it should be. There should also be more storage, more electrical outlets, and perhaps more fixtures. If the bathroom is to be used by several people at the same time, compartmenting can often add to utility.

The family schedule should also be considered. Where several people depart for work or school at the same time, multiple or **compartmented** bathrooms should be considered. Two lavatories will allow a working couple to get ready for work at the same time.

The most economical arrangement of fixtures is against a single **wet wall.** Economy, however, is not the only factor to be considered. Plumbing codes, human comfort, and convenient use require certain minimum separation between and space around fixtures. The minimum size for a bathroom is approximately 5 feet by 7 feet, although, if absolutely necessary, a few inches may be shaved off these measurements. Deluxe bathrooms may be very large and incorporate a seating area or an exercise room and/or a **spa.**

In a corridor-type bathroom, there should be 30 inches of aisle space between the bathtub and the edge of the counter or the fixture opposite. The bathtub should only be placed under the window if there is privacy and the walls and window frames are tiled to retain watertight integrity. This window location is usually used in the master bathroom. There should be a minimum of 24 inches in front of a toilet to provide knee room. When walls are on either side of the toilet, they should be 36 inches apart. If the **lavatory** or bathtub is adjacent to the toilet, then 30 inches are sufficient. The lavatory requires elbow space. Five feet is the recommended minimum length of a countertop with two lavatories. The lavatories should be centered in the respective halves of the countertop. For a sitdown **vanity,** the counter should be 7 feet long, with 24 inches between the edges of the lavatories for greatest comfort. Six inches minimum should be allowed between the edge of a lavatory and any side wall.

The location of the bathroom door is extremely important. The door should be located so it will not hit a fixture, because such poor placement would eventually cause damage both to the door and the fixture. A sliding pocket door may have to be used to prevent this.

All bathroom fixtures, whether tubs, lavatories, toilets, or **bidets,** come in white and in standard colors, which are more expensive than white fixtures. High-fashion colors—even black—cost 40 percent or more than white fixtures. Care should be taken not to select fad colors that will become dated, because bathroom fixtures are both difficult and expensive to replace when remodeling. To obtain a perfect match, all fixtures should be ordered from the same manufacturer. Colors, even white, vary from one manufacturer to another.

FLOORS

Bathroom floors should be of a type that can be cleaned easily, particularly in the area of the bathtub, shower, and toilet. Ceramic tile may be used, but it should not be highly glazed because glazed tiles, when used on a floor, can be slippery when wet.

Other types of flooring material that can be used for the tub area include wood with a good finish or any of the resilient flooring materials.

Carpeting may be used in the master bath but is not suggested for a family bath because of the likelihood of excessive moisture, which can cause mold and mildew.

Wallcoverings are often used in bathrooms. Vinyls or vinyl-coated wallcoverings are recommended because they are easy to wipe dry and maintain. Bathroom walls should be treated before applying wallcovering to prevent mildew (see Chapter 2, p. 20).

WALLS

Most of the manufactured materials used for counters can be used to cover vertical surfaces, either on the wall or as a shower enclosure (e.g., Syndecrete®, discussed in Chapter 1).

Only semigloss paint or enamels that can withstand moisture should be used on bathroom walls.

If an acrylic shower and tub surround is not used, ceramic tile is installed because of its vitreous quality.

BATHTUBS

The typical tract home bathtub is 5 feet long, 30 inches wide, and, in less expensive styles, only 14 inches deep. Tubs that are 6 feet long are available, however, for those who like to soak. Tub height, measured from the floor, may vary (15, 16, or even 22 inches). Tub heights of 14 inches are convenient for bathing children. The depth figures represent the outside tub measurements, however, and, allowing for the **overflow** pipe, a 14-inch tub height does not permit the drawing of a very deep bath.

Many semicustom homes feature 5' × 42" or 6' × 42" oval tubs in master baths. There are so many sizes and shapes of tubs, however, that there is no longer an "average" size.

Most state laws require that all bathtubs installed today have a **slip-resistant** bottom. Many tubs also come with a handle on one or both sides, which is extremely useful for the elderly or infirm.

The straight end of the bathtub contains the drain and the plumbing, such as faucets or **fittings,** and the overflow pipe; therefore, the location of the bathtub must be decided before the order is placed. Bathtubs may be ordered with a left or right drain, all four sides enclosed, the front and two sides enclosed, or the front and one side enclosed. For a completely built-in look, a drop-in model may be specified.

The drop-in model is sometimes installed as a sunken tub. Although a sunken tub may present a luxurious appearance, it can be difficult to get in and out of such tubs. In addition, sunken tubs can be difficult to clean. Cleaning a sunken tub means lying flat on the floor to reach the interior. Sunken or recessed tubs can represent a safety hazard in that small children may crawl into the bathtub and hurt themselves or, at the worst, drown.

Bathtubs are manufactured of several materials. The old standby is the porcelain enameled cast-iron tub, which was originally a high-sided bathtub raised from the floor on ball-and-claw feet with the underside exposed. This style is still available today in a modernized version. The porcelain enamel gives better color than other materials and is approximately 1/16 of an inch thick, but this finish can be chipped if a heavy object is dropped on it. Therefore, bathtubs should be kept covered with a blanket or a special plastic liner until construction has been completed.

A cast-iron bathtub is the most durable bathtub available, but it is expensive and heavy; it may weigh as much as 500 pounds. Therefore, the floor should be strong enough to bear the combined weight of the tub, the tub full of water, and the bather.

Formed steel tubs with a porcelain enamel finish were developed to provide a lightweight (about 100 pounds) tub that would be less expensive than cast iron. Formed steel tubs are ideally suited for upper-story installations or for remodeling because they are easier to move into place than cast-iron tubs. A formed steel tub is noisier than a cast-iron tub, but a sound-deadening coating may be applied to the underside at extra cost. If the bathtub does not come with an insulated coating on the outside, a roll of fiberglass insulation can be wrapped around the tub. This insulation not only helps the tub retain heat longer, but it also helps reduce noise. Because of the properties of steel, formed steel bathtubs may flex; therefore, they do not have as thick a layer of porcelain enamel as do cast-iron tubs.

If a cast-iron or steel bathtub is badly stained or chipped, it can be "replaced" without tearing out the walls to get access to the old tub. The product that makes this possible is called Re-Bath®, a bathtub liner made of nonporous ABS (acrylonic butadiene styrene) acrylic, custom molded to fit into any bathtub without disturbing flooring, walls, or plumbing. Re-Bath wall systems, which are designed to go over existing tile walls, are also available. A new overflow and drain are provided with Re-Bath tub liners.

Heavy-duty polyester reinforced with fiberglass and surfaced with a **gel coat** can be used for bathtubs. In specifying this type of tub, it is important to select a name brand. There are currently many poor-quality units on the market produced by a process that does not require a large investment. Consequently, the tubs can crack easily and lose their surface rapidly. Good maintenance practices and avoidance of abrasive cleansers are mandatory for polyester-reinforced tubs. Some manufacturers recommend using a coat of marine wax or a good automotive wax to restore the shine to dulled surfaces of gel-coated tubs.

Another type of lightweight bathtub is acrylic reinforced with fiberglass. This type of bathtub does not have as high a gloss as gel-coated tubs, but maintenance is easier.

There are several advantages to acrylic-reinforced fiberglass bathtubs. First, they are much lighter weight than steel or cast iron, although they may not be as durable. Second, the tub **surround** can be cast as an integral part of the bathtub and can include such features as a built-in seat, soap ledges, and grab bars. The latter type of tub can be installed only in new construction, because the tub and surround are too large to be placed in a remodeled bathroom. For remodeling, there are molded tub units with wall surrounds in two, three, or four pieces that pass easily through doorways and join in the recessed bathtub area to form a one-piece unit.

Soaking tubs are also made from reinforced fiberglass. Instead of sitting or laying in the tub, one sits on a molded, built-in seat, and the tub is filled to the requisite depth. Some soaking tubs are recessed into the floor, and the bather steps over the edge and down into the tub; others are placed at floor level and require several steps to reach the top. Soaking tubs should not be installed in every bathroom in the house, because it is impossible to bathe small children in such tubs and the elderly or infirm will find it too dangerous to enter and leave a soaking tub. A regular bathtub should be installed in at least one bathroom in the house.

Whirlpool baths are generally bathroom fixtures; they must be drained after each use. Jacuzzi®, the inventor of the whirlpool bath, uses continuous cast acrylic, reinforced with fiberglass for added strength. Quiet jets are placed low in the bath for the best results in hydrotherapy. These whirlpool jets create a circular pattern of bubbles as the air/water mixture flows into the tub, providing deeply penetrating massage (see Figure 10–1 and Color Plate 14).

Most companies manufacture a corner bath, which can be either a plain bath or, more often, a whirlpool. The corner location gives a feeling of openness because the tub does not have walls surrounding it and is only used for bathing, not for showering.

For the active elderly or for any person who might have difficulty stepping over the edge of a bathtub,

(a)

(b)

Figure 10–1

(a) A simple but elegant Repertoire suite from American Standard shows the scalloped-edge pedestal Repertoire lavatory, Infinity EL toilet, and Heritage® whirlpool bath. (Photo courtesy of American Standard Inc.) (b) A contemporary bathroom, Symbio's curvilinear design blurs the line separating the shower and bath, resulting in a space-saving unit that is both practical and beautiful. The acrylic whirlpool bath offers five or seven Flexjet whirlpool jets, depending on the whirlpool size. Shown in white with Finial Fundamentals faucets in polished chrome. (Photo courtesy of Kohler Co.)

Kohler's Precedence™ whirlpool bath, with a swing-open door, is the answer (Figure 10–2). The Freewill™ line of barrier-free bathing products from Kohler is designed to meet the strict ANSI standards, with slip-resistant bottoms for safety and grab bars fabricated of rigid nylon to provide a firm grip even when wet. The Freewill line features a removable transfer seat so bathers can sit and swing legs over the edge of the tub instead of stepping into it. The fold-up seats make Freewill tubs ideal for installation in a residence where one family member may have limited mobility.

Spas are similar to whirlpool baths but need not be drained after each use. They are equipped with heat and filtration systems. Because the same water is recirculated, daily testing and maintenance of the proper water chemistry are required. Spas may be installed outside in warmer climates or in an area other than the bathroom. They have many of the same features as whirlpool baths but are larger (64 to 84 inches long, 66 to 84 inches wide, and 28 to 37 inches high). Spas come with factory-installed redwood skirts and rigid covers.

Tub surrounds and shower enclosures may also be reinforced fiberglass, as mentioned previously, or they may be decorative laminate, ceramic tile, solid ABS, or solid acrylic. Many of these surrounds and en-

Figure 10–2

The Precedence™ bath whirlpool from Kohler features a water-tight door that provides easy access to the bathtub and a seat that can be used for bathing or showering and can be folded up to become a backrest for a deep-soaking bath. The tub's dimensions, 60" × 38" × 25 1/2" deep, allow the tub to fit into the space allowed for a conventional bathtub. (Photo courtesy of Kohler Co.)

closures have integrated tubs with built-in whirlpool systems. The all-in-one type eliminates the need to caulk around the area where the tub and surround meet. Failure to install and caulk the tub surround properly is the major cause of leaks in the tub area. When designing a bathroom, the bathtub should be placed where an access panel can be installed to simplify future plumbing repairs. Access *must* be provided to any whirlpool equipment to facilitate future maintenance.

Ceramic tile is installed as described in Chapter 3. The substrate must be exterior-grade plywood or a special water-resistant grade of gypsum board. The backer board, mentioned in Chapter 4, also makes a suitable substrate. Particular attention must be paid to the application of the grout, because it is the grout that makes ceramic tile a waterproof material. When a cast-iron tub is used, its weight may cause a slight sagging of the floor. Any space caused by this settling should be caulked immediately.

SHOWERS

Showers may be installed for use in a bathtub, or they may be in a separate shower stall. There should always be at least one bathtub in a house, but stall showers may be used in the remaining bathrooms. When used with a bathtub, the tub spout contains a **diverter** that closes off the spout and diverts the water to the shower head. A bathroom with a shower instead of a tub is designated as a three-quarter bath.

The standard height of a shower head is 66 inches for men and 60 inches for women, which puts the spray below the hairline. These measurements mean that the plumbing for the shower head must break through the tub or shower surround. Therefore, it is recommended that the shower **feed-in** be 74 inches above the floor. When placed at this height, the shower head should be adjustable so it can be used to wash hair or to hit below the hairline.

A hand-held shower can easily be installed in any bathtub, provided the bathroom walls are covered with a waterproof material. This type of shower comes with a special diversion spout, and the water reaches the shower head by means of a flexible metal line. One type of shower head is hung on a hook at the required height. Another type is mounted on a 5-foot vertical rod and attached to the water outlet by means of a flexible hose. This full-range sliding spray holder or grab bar locks at any desired height. The spray holder is both adjustable and removable.

There are several advantages of hand-held showers. Such showers can be hung at a lower level for use by children and can be used to rinse the hair of young children without the complaint of "the soap is getting in my eyes." In addition, hand-held units may be used to clean and rinse the interior of the bathtub.

Shower heads more than five years old use between 3 and 8 gallons of water per minute. Replacing one of these with a model achieving a flow of 2.4 gallons per minute or less will save the average household almost 12,000 gallons of water annually. Water is a limited resource and should be conserved. Some cities have mandated 2.4-gallon shower heads. Water conservation does not mean a skimpy shower. Speakman Anystream® shower heads will automatically adjust water flow to compensate for available pressure. Their output ranges from bracing needle spray to gentle rain.

Stall showers are 34 × 32 inches wide; a slightly larger 36-inch square is recommended if space is available. These are minimum requirements; deluxe showers may be 48 inches square or even 60 × 36 inches wide. They usually include a seat.

Stall showers may be constructed entirely of ceramic tile; in other words, the sloping base and walls are all made of tile. When installing a ceramic tile shower area, particular attention should be paid to the waterproof base and to the installation procedures supplied by the manufacturer or the Tile Council of America. Other stall showers have a **preformed base,** with the surround touching the top of the 5- to 6-inch-deep base. This preformed base is less slippery than a base of tile but not quite as aesthetically pleasing. Shower walls may be constructed of any of the solid surface materials (see Chapter 9, p. 184).

For a massage effect, a 20-inch-wide cascade of water streams from the waterfall ledge atop the 10-jet BodySpa™ tower from Kohler. The electronic keypad independently controls each of the five pairs of jets (to direct the massage action where it is needed most), activates the waterfall (for a deep massage at the neck and shoulders), and controls massage intensity. A variable-flow pump allows for infinite control of the massage action and recirculates the water, as little as 35 gallons, at speeds of up to 80 gallons per minute. The 2-horsepower pump with integral heater recirculates the water and maintains water temperature (Figure 10–3).

The J-Allure™ from Jacuzzi Whirlpool Bath presents the ultimate bathing environment for two. An ideal union of luxury and convenience, the J-Allure treats bathers to dual multifunction shower heads, 12 invigorating body sprays, soothing steam as well as a full-size whirlpool bath complete with four PowerPro jets and two lumbar jets. An electronic control panel customizes the shower. The unit has built-in AM/FM

(a)

(b)

Figure 10–3
(a) The 10-jet BodySpa from Kohler, as shown here, is a 52" × 52" × 13"
deep neoangle footbath and glass enclosure. The unit is equipped with
Kohler's Taboret® bath valves and spout to fill the BodySpa basin, and a
Taboret Rite-Temp™ pressure-balancing shower valve and Master-
Shower™ three-way showerhead, for those who wish to use their BodySpa
enclosure for showering. (Photo courtesy of Kohler Co.) (b) J-Allure™ is
the ultimate combination whirlpool bath, shower system, and steam bath
built for two. There are tempered-glass doors, accessory compartments,
two full-length mirrors, as well as a steam bath. Designed for corner
installations, the J-Allure measures 52" long × 52" wide × 94" high.
(Photo courtesy of Jacuzzi Whirlpool Bath.)

stereo and CD system with four speakers, coupled with an optional television monitor with remote control. Both the BodySpa and J-Allure are the ultimate in sybaritic pleasure.

There are several ways to keep water within the shower area. One way is to hang a shower curtain from rings at the front of the shower. A shower curtain is a decorative feature, but unless care is taken to ensure placement of the shower curtain inside the base when using the shower, water may spill over onto the floor, causing a hazard. Glass shower doors are also used (the type depends on local building codes). All shower doors are made of tempered glass, but some codes require the addition of a wire mesh. These glass doors may pivot, hinge, slide, or fold. The major maintenance problem with glass doors involves removing soap and hard water residue from the glass surface and cleaning the water channel at the base of the door. A water softener greatly reduces or even eliminates this residue. Some shower units are designed with close-fitting doors that completely enclose the front of the unit and become steam systems with a **sauna** effect. An example of a multiple-use shower is the J-Dream™ family, which combines an adjustable shower head with hydromassage and a steam bath.

Master bath showers are often designed so no door or curtain is required. These shower stalls have walls placed so water is contained within the wet area.

Wheelchair-accessible stall showers are available and vary in size from 42 by 36 inches to 65 by 36 inches, all with an interior threshold height of only 1/2 inch. Units with integral seats have the seat placed toward the front of the enclosure for easier access.

TUB AND SHOWER FAUCETS

The old-fashioned type of faucet is ledge mounted: The fitting is mounted on the edge of the tub or tub enclosure, usually with an 8-inch to 18-inch **spread.**

Tub/shower combinations may be of two different types: deck mounted or wall mounted. Deck mounted are used only for tubs. Both types are available in single or dual control (hot and cold water are controlled together or separately). A shower-only unit has wall-mounted controls, which may be single or dual control. Single controls regulate the temperature of the water more easily. Two choices are available with a tub/shower combination: two sets (one for the tub and the other for the shower) or one set, with a diverter. The diverter in tub/shower combinations is most commonly a diverter-on-spout. After the water temperature is balanced, the diverter is pulled up to start the shower. To stop the flow of water to the shower head, the diverter is pushed down. The handle diverter design has three handles. By twisting the middle handle, the water is diverted to the shower head. The other two handles control the hot and cold water. This handle diverter had 8-inch **centers.**

Most shower heads are adjustable and change the flow of water to drenching, normal, or fine spray. Some shower heads have a pulsating flow that provides a massaging action. Conventional shower heads use from 6 to 8 gallons of water per minute. Plumbing codes are being amended to make 2.7 gallons of water per minute at 60 psi the maximum amount of water that can be used. Antiscald controls are required by law on all shower heads.

Fast-flowing Roman tub valves feature high-flow 3/4-inch valves. This type of valve enables whirlpool baths to be filled rapidly, provided a large-capacity water tank is used.

LAVATORIES

Lavatories come in many sizes, shapes, and materials according to personal and space requirements. Many types of materials are used, but most lavatories are made of vitreous china. All of the following materials may be used, however: glass, cast iron, sculpted marble, china or ceramic, enameled formed steel, polished brass, or solid surface materials.

Lavatories are usually round or oval, but they may also be rectangular, or even triangular for corner installations. Sizes range from 11×11 inches for powder rooms to 38×28 inches.

Pedestal lavatories are the latest style of lavatory to be used, but they are probably more suitable in a master bathroom because they do not provide the adjacent counter area usually needed in family bathrooms. They may be as streamlined or decorative as desired. To compensate for the lack of counter space, some pedestal lavatories are as large as 44×22 inches, with a wide ledge surrounding the bowl area. (Figures 10–4 and 10–1 show different styles.)

Built-in lavatories may be one of six types:

1. They may be self-rimming (a hole is cut into the counter smaller than the size of the lavatory and the bowl is placed so the edge is raised above the level of the counter). With a self-rimming sink, water cannot be swept back into the bowl and must be mopped up (Figure 10–5).

2. For a flush counter and bowl installation, the lavatory may be installed with a flush metal rim. This is a popular and inexpensive style but can cause a cleaning problem at the juncture of the rim with the countertop.

3. The integral bowl and counter, such as those made of solid surface materials, is another option. With this type, which may be placed virtually anywhere on the vanity top, the countertop and bowl are seamed for a one-piece look, with the faucets usually mounted on the counter.

4. An old-fashioned wall-hung installation is often used in powder rooms or for wheelchair users.

5. The lavatory can be installed under the counter. This type of installation is generally used with a tile, marble, or synthetic countertop. Various types of solid surface materials are available, and under-the-counter installations are becoming very popular. Under-the-counter installations require that the fittings be deck mounted.

6. The lavatory can be installed above the counter; this is a modern version of the pitcher and bowl set of the Victorian era (Figure 10–6).

(a)

(b)

(c)

Figure 10–4
(a) The squared, footed pedestal and stately basin styling for the largest Memoirs™ lavatory offer a bold profile. Measuring 30 by 22 by 35 inches, this lavatory is designed to accommodate single-hole faucets or, as shown here, 8-inch faucets. The faucet is Finial Traditional in polished brass. (Photo courtesy of Kohler Co.) (b) The same style lavatory in the Console Table model. (Photo courtesy of Kohler Co.) (c) The pedestal lavatory shown is 61 inches wide by 21 1/4 inches deep and 33 5/8 inches high. The wider areas on each side can be used as a counter. This pedestal lavatory is Siena Lavatory from Absolute by American Standard and is accented by two F Series-colored framed door cabinets by Robern. (Photo courtesy of Robern Inc.)

(a)

(b)

Figure 10–5
(a) Graceful stems of mauve and lavender blue Iris bloom on Sherle Wagner's hand-painted china over edge bowl. (Photo by Lynton Gardner.) (b) Floral Chinoiserie design combines delicate floral nosegays with the all-over egg and dart pattern rimmed in 24 karat gold. The over-edge bowl and coordinating basin fittings are in green. Other color options are blue or pink. (Photos courtesy of Sherle Wagner International.)

(a)

(b)

(c)

Figure 10–6

Glass lavatories. (a) The Lava Cienega Glass Sink on a fused Glass Countertop. (Photo courtesy of Alchemy.) (b) Vessels glass lavatories interject an eclectic, one-of-a-kind look that complements a range of Kohler fixtures and decors. A Vessels lavatory is shown here in aquamarine with Kohler's Falling Water faucet in polished chrome. The Vessels Spun lavatory may be mounted on the wall with a wrought iron bracket designed for Kohler's Vessels collection of lavatories. This series may also be used for an above-counter installation. (Photo courtesy of Kohler Co.) (c) MTS Sink module from Robern consists of a mirrored backsplash and glass top with integral bowl and comes with a Kohler Falling Water faucet. The cabinet and lights are purchased separately. (Photo © Tom Crane; photo courtesy of Robern Inc.)

Cherry Creek Enterprises laminates glass for its Vitraform sinks, which are available in clear and several colors, all in a polished or frosted finish. Custom engraved options are available.

Alchemy manufactures 18-inch-diameter glass sinks either in monochromes or fused glass. The company's Cienega Glass is a unique kind of glass made by fusing layers of glass together, trapping metals and other minerals inside the glass. The colors vary not only from piece to piece, but also within a piece depending on how the piece is lit and from what angle it is viewed. The color in the center will always be some shade of copper, ranging from the color of a new penny to a deep burgundy. The color along the edge of the glass and bordering the center area is usually darker in contrast to the center and has a greenish base color with either wisps of smoky gray or dots of blue and magenta, depending on the Cienega type. The Vitraform sink and the Alchemy sink stand on top of a flat surface and are not built in.

Vessels™ from Kohler is an above-counter handcrafted glass lavatory, with air bubbles formed during the casting process. The glass lavatories are available in clear glass, cobalt, and aquamarine (see Figure 10–6).

A specialty lavatory is a solid brass self-rimming bowl, which adds an elegant look to a bathroom. For a unique lavatory, a self-rimming painted ceramic washbasin may be used. These specialized sinks have wall- or counter-mounted faucets.

Lavatories come punched with one hole or three holes. The single hole is for European-style single-hole faucets. With single-control fittings and 4-inch center-set fittings, the third hole is for the **pop-up rod.** In wide-spread fittings, however, the third hole is used for hot and cold water.

Some lavatories are punched with one or two extra holes. These holes are used as a shampoo lavatory and have a retractable spray unit. The second extra hole is for a soap or shampoo dispenser. Shampoo lavatories are extremely useful for a family with children because the bowl is usually installed in a 32-inch-high vanity (in contrast to the 36-inch height of a kitchen sink). Some styles of shampoo lavatories feature spouts that swing away from the sink.

LAVATORY FAUCETS

There are many types of lavatory faucets. **Center-fit** faucet fittings have been used for the past few decades. With these units, the two handles and spout are in one piece, with a 4-inch spread. The single-control unit with a 4-inch spread has a central control

that regulates both temperature and rate of flow. This single-control unit may also work by means of a lever that, when pulled up, increases the flow of water and, when pushed down, decreases the flow. Temperature is controlled by moving the lever to the right for cold and to the left for warm or hot water. For arthritis sufferers, a lever faucet is easier to operate than a knob type.

Placement of the faucets depends on the design of the sink. Some sinks have predrilled holes for the faucets, and others require a deck-mounted style. Faucets must be ordered after the sink has been selected.

The popularity of center-fit faucets has been declining; spread-fit fittings now comprise 80 percent of the market, and their market share is growing. Center-fit faucets may be making a comeback, however, as consumers look to the past. With spread-fit faucets, the hot and cold handles and the spout are independent of each other. To make installation and choice of faucet sets easier, the fittings should be joined by means of flexible connectors. If flexible connectors are not used, faucet choices may be limited to the spread of the holes in the selected lavatory. When center-fit fittings are used, a plate covers the center hole. When a spread-fit fitting is used, the center hole accommodates the spout. Mini-wide faucets offer the appearance of spread-fit faucets and fit the common 4-inch center fit. Mini-wides are difficult to clean, however, because the faucets are very close together.

To conserve water, bathroom faucets are now set to a flow of 2 gallons per minute. Most manufacturers are using a ceramic disc cartridge inside the faucet; ceramic disc cartridges are considered the most durable, especially with problem water. The cartridge helps prevent dripping, which can waste gallons of water a year.

Several companies are now manufacturing faucets designed as barrier-free products with water conservation in mind. When the faucet's electronic sensor beam is broken by the hands, water flows at the preset temperature. Savings of up to 85 percent over normal water usage are typical. Additional energy savings are realized because hot water is conserved.

Faucets may be polished chrome, black chrome, polished brass, or even gold plated. A current trend is to use two different finishes on the same faucet, such as black chrome with polished chrome and/or polished brass, or wood and brass. Brushed nickel with brass is often used. Two finishes are often used on what is known as the ring handle (circular handle with no extended parts). Delta Faucet Company manufactures ring handles suitable for retrofit, so the bathroom can be given a new appearance. Usually chrome is the most durable finish, followed by colors and then brass. With the introduction of the PVD process, brass is now a viable choice. Delta, a Masco company, uses Brilliance on its brass bathroom fittings, with the pop-up drain (usually the first part of the faucet assembly to show wear) also being coated.

Translucent and metal handles have slight indentations to provide a nonslipping surface. The handles may also be of a lever type. The traditional shape for spouts is being replaced by a more delicately curved shape, which is popular in Europe. The Roman-style faucets previously used for bathtubs are now being used for lavatories.

Pull-out spouts, which have previously been a feature of kitchen faucets, are now used for bathroom lavatories. Delta manufactures a 4-inch center-set faucet with a pull-out spout that can extend to 21 inches and may be used for washing hair, bathing infants, filling containers, and even washing the family pet (in the utility room, of course).

Wrist-control handles, which meet the standards of the Americans with Disabilities Act, do not require turning or pulling but are activated by a push or pull with the wrist rather than the fingers.

Toilets

In Europe, a toilet is often called a water closet. The plumbing trade frequently uses that term, or *closet* when referring to what the layperson calls a toilet. In some areas of the United States, the toilet may also be called a commode. We will use the word *toilet* in the text because this is the more common word, but when talking to a plumber, *closet* is more correct.

Toilet bowls, and tanks, are constructed of vitreous china. Only vitreous china can withstand the acids to which a toilet is subjected. Most toilets are designed with water-saving devices that are important both economically and environmentally.

There are two basic shapes to a toilet: the regular or round bowl and the elongated bowl. Most toilets do not come with a toilet seat; therefore, it is important to know the shape of the toilet before ordering a seat. Some special shape expensive toilets come with a seat. More space (usually 2 inches) is required for installing an elongated bowl. Local building codes will provide space requirements.

Toilets may be wall hung, which leaves the floor unobstructed for easy cleaning, or floor mounted.

Wall-hung toilets have a wall outlet; in other words, they flush through a drain in the wall. To support the weight of a wall-hung toilet, 6-inch studs must be used and an L-shaped unit called a chair carrier must be installed.

Floor-mounted toilets flush through the floor or the wall. For concrete floor construction, wall outlets are suggested to eliminate the extra cost of slab piercing.

Another choice in the design of toilets is whether tank and bowl should be a **low-profile,** one-piece integral unit, or whether the tank and bowl should be in two pieces. For space saving in powder rooms or bathrooms, a corner toilet, an Eljer exclusive, is available. An old-fashioned ambience can be created by using an overhead wall-hung tank with a traditional pull chain. In areas where condensation on the toilet tank is a problem, an insulated tank may be ordered.

All toilets are required to have a visible water turn-off near the bowl on the back wall in case of a faulty valve in the tank.

Toilets for elderly and disabled individuals have an 18-inch-high seat, whereas regular toilet seats are 15 1/2 inches high. Higher toilets may also have a set of metal rails or armrests for extra support. The height of the seat on one-piece toilets may be less than 18 inches.

Toilets have different flushing actions. The washdown is the least expensive but is also the least efficient and the noisiest. The least inexpensive of the siphon-action toilets is the reverse trap, in which the rush of flushed water creates a siphon action in the trapway, assisted by a small water jet at the trapway outlet. More of the bowl is covered by water, so the bowl stays cleaner. The washdown and siphon action are gravity flush toilets. The siphon jet used on most newer toilets is much quieter and more efficient than those previously mentioned but usually more expensive. According to American Standard, "pressure assisted flushes is a tank within a tank. Incoming water compresses the air. When released, it creates a pushing action, complete in about 4 seconds. It is a little louder, but a second flush is never needed. Also, there is no condensation or 'sweating' on the outer tank."[2] (Figure 10-7)

The 1992 National Energy Policy Act limits water use for new toilets to 1.6 gallons per flush, compared with the typical 3.5-gallon flush. For a family of four, that means a savings of more than 11,000 gallons of water per year. A European import even has double-handed flushers to vary how much water is used in each flush.

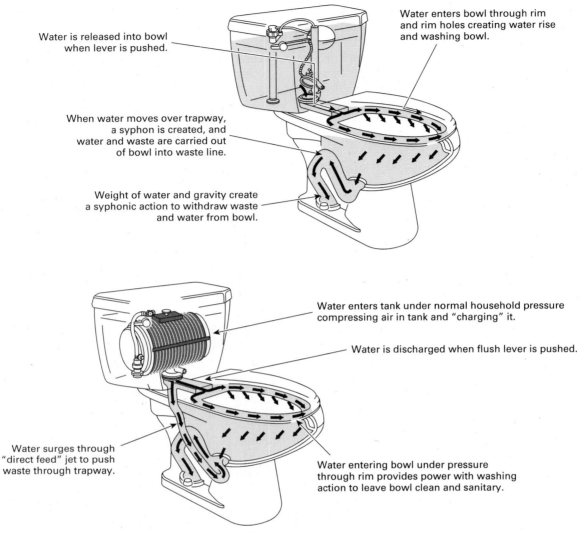

Water is released into bowl when lever is pushed.

Water enters bowl through rim and rim holes creating water rise and washing bowl.

When water moves over trapway, a syphon is created, and water and waste are carried out of bowl into waste line.

Weight of water and gravity create a syphonic action to withdraw waste and water from bowl.

Water enters tank under normal household pressure compressing air in tank and "charging" it.

Water is discharged when flush lever is pushed.

Water surges through "direct feed" jet to push waste through trapway.

Water entering bowl under pressure through rim provides power with washing action to leave bowl clean and sanitary.

Figure 10–7
Flushing action. (Courtesy of American Standard Inc., The Bathroom Book.*)*

BIDETS

Although bidets are common in Europe, they are only now becoming an accepted fixture in American bathrooms, and then only in more sophisticated types of installations. A bidet is generally installed as a companion and adjacent to the water closet or toilet and is used for cleansing the perineal area. Bidets do not have seats. The user sits astride the bowl, facing the controls that regulate water temperature and operate the pop-up drain and transfer valve. Water enters the bidet via the spray rinse in the bottom of the bowl. A bidet may also be used as a foot bath when the pop-up drain is closed.

When the fresh water supply is below or directly involved with piping, a **vacuum breaker** must be installed.

COUNTERTOPS

The term *vanity cabinet* is not technically used in the architectural profession. Ready-made bathroom cabinets containing the lavatory are so often called and sold by this name, however, that this term is used to refer to the prefinished cabinet with doors underneath the counter top. Vanity cabinets may be ordered with or without a finished counter top. The lavatory is purchased separately. Other types of vanities come with the countertop and bowl molded in one.

A ready-made vanity is between 29 and 30 inches in height. For a master bathroom in a custom-designed house, the counter can be raised to suit personal requirements; however, at least one vanity in the house must be at the lower height.

Most custom-designed bathrooms have specially designed cabinets containing the lavatory with a storage area beneath. A bathroom countertop may be made of the same materials as a kitchen counter, although marble is more frequently used in bathrooms than in kitchens.

Solid surfacing materials for countertops, vanities, lavatory bowls, showers, and bathtubs are becoming increasingly popular because they are versatile and attractive.

ACCESSORIES

There should be 22 inches of towel storage for each person. Towels should be within convenient reach of the bath, shower, and lavatory. Soap containers may be recessed into the wall, such as those used in the tub area. For the lavatory with a counter, a soap dish can be a colorful accessory. A toilet tissue dispenser should be conveniently placed next to the toilet. Many faucet manufacturers that make designer model faucets also make bath accessories to match.

Ground fault interrupter **(GFI)** electrical outlets should also be provided for the myriad of electrical gadgets used in the bathroom. All switches should be located so they cannot be reached from a tub or shower area. (This is usually stated in local building codes.)

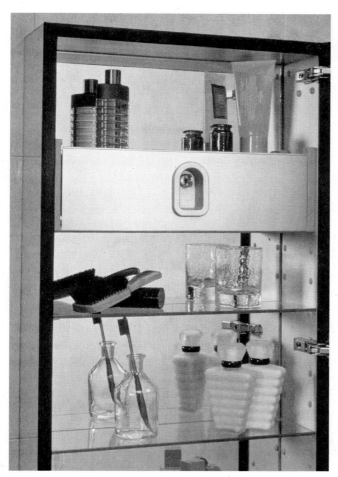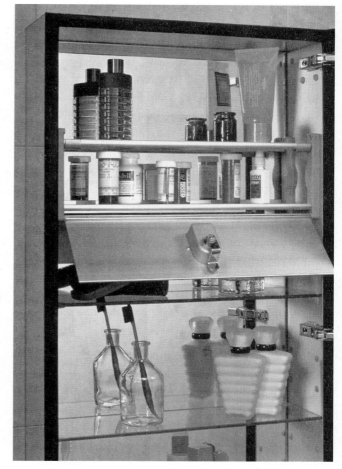

Figure 10–8
The Safety Lock box medicine cabinet from Robern is shown open and closed. The Safety Lock box offers a safe place to store prescription drugs, out of the reach of children. (Photo courtesy of Robern Inc.)

Mirrors may be on the door of a built-in medicine cabinet, or they may be installed to cover the entire wall over the counter area. When used in the latter manner, mirrors visibly enlarge the bathroom. The top of the mirror should be at least 72 inches above the floor.

Robern Inc. manufactures a wide selection of mirrored wall cabinets. All Robern's swing-door cabinets include a swing-out magnifying mirror. When opened, the mirror projects out over the sink for comfortable use. Glass shelves are 1/4 to 3/8 inch thick. Most of these cabinets have mirrored interiors and are available in 4-, 5-, and 8-inch depths; they come with an optional defogging door and concealed 110-volt outlets for recharging and using electrical appliances (see Figure 10–4).

Robern manufactures a Safety Lock box that slides into a wall cabinet, as shown in Figure 10–8, and stores prescription drugs safely out of reach.

Heated towel rails are sometimes installed in upscale bathrooms. These rails may be heated by constantly recirculating hot water, or the heating element may be activated by an electrical switch.

Ventilating fans are required in bathrooms that do not have windows that can be opened. Broan manufactures a wide range of ventilation products for residential and light commercial applications, from the Solitaire® Ultra Silent™ Series, which features the industry's lowest sound levels, to attic ventilators. Ventilating fans for bathrooms often incorporate a light and sometimes a heater.

Certified bathroom designers **(CBDs)** perform the same services for bathroom design as CKDs do for kitchen design.

PUBLIC RESTROOMS

The bathrooms previously discussed were designed to accommodate one or two people at a time. For public restrooms, however, conditions and location may mean that the bathroom will be used by many people at the same time. (This includes not only people who can walk, but those who use wheelchairs and those who walk with impaired mobility.) According to Bobrick Washroom Equipment Inc.,

Public washrooms are one of the most critical building amenities with regard to accessibility and function for people with disabilities. This applies to virtually every building type: commercial office buildings, government facilities, factories, schools, public stadia, theaters, and all forms of food service establishments and entertainment centers. With one in four persons becoming disabled sometime during their life, washrooms need to be responsive to a wide range of human needs and abilities: including people without disabilities and those using wheelchairs and walking aids, people with sight or hearing disabilities, impaired coordination, cardiac or pulmonary disorders, and even people affected by temporary illness, pregnancy, or advanced age. . . .

The ADA requires that all washrooms, whether newly constructed or remodeled, be usable by people with disabilities. . . . **All building plans, however, should be confirmed with local jurisdictions to ensure job compliance.**[3]

Bobrick publishes a brochure, *Barrier-Free Washroom Planning Guide*, which includes diagrams to aid in making public restrooms accessible for wheelchair-bound individuals.

Public restrooms receive much physical abuse, most of which is not premeditated but occurs through normal wear and tear. Unfortunately, vandalism is a major problem; therefore, fixtures and materials must be selected for durability. Bobrick manufactures a line of Maximum-Security Accessories™ that are mostly secured from the rear. Mirrors are bright polished stainless steel. A two-stall restroom in a small restaurant and a multistall restroom in a huge recreational facility must be designed differently with the potential for vandalism in mind.

Maintenance is another factor in the selection of materials and fixtures for public restrooms. Floors are usually made of ceramic tile or similar material and require a floor drain, not only for an emergency flooding situation, but also to simplify cleaning and disinfecting of the floor.

For hospitality establishments such as hotels, durable and functional commercial accessories are available.

Lavatories

To aid in cleaning the counter areas of public restrooms, vitreous china lavatories with flush metal rims are most frequently specified. Such lavatories allow quick cleaning of any excess water on the counter. White sinks are usually selected in restrooms for two reasons: They are cheaper, and their cleanliness is easily visible.

Lavatories come with three holes punched in the top, but soft or liquid soap dispensers may be installed in a four-hole sink. Or the soap dispenser may be attached to the wall above each lavatory or between two adjacent ones. For freestanding applications, wall-hung vitreous china lavatories may be specified.

A specially designed lavatory that meets ADA requirements must be installed to enable the seated person to reach faucet handles. Faucets, toilets, and washroom accessories for the physically disabled must meet ADA Accessibility Guidelines for Buildings and Facilities (ADAAG). The controls and operating mechanisms (push buttons, valves, knobs, and levers) must be operable with one hand, without tight grasping, pinching, or twisting of the wrist, and with a force that does not exceed 5 pounds.

Because some wheelchair occupants are paraplegic, it is important to turn down the temperature of hot water to 110°F and wrap waste pipe with some form of insulation. These measures will prevent inadvertent burns.

Faucets

Some companies specialize in manufacturing faucets designed for public restrooms. These faucets are available with **metering devices,** usually with push-buttons, which can be adjusted to flow for 5 to 15 seconds. This metering conserves energy and water and prevents accidental flooding. Other faucets, such as the Eagle Eye™, have an electronic eye; when the beam is broken, the faucet turns on and stays on as long as there is continuous motion (such as hand washing) in the sensor field. By reacting to motion and not to beam obstructions, Eagle Eye can help conserve water, minimize vandalism, and reduce maintenance time. The electronics of Eagle Eye adjust to the environment: Common obstructions, like soap and water, will not disrupt normal operation. If the sensor is covered completely, the faucet will shut off in 15 seconds. Eagle Eye meets ADA requirements (Figure 10–9).

(a)

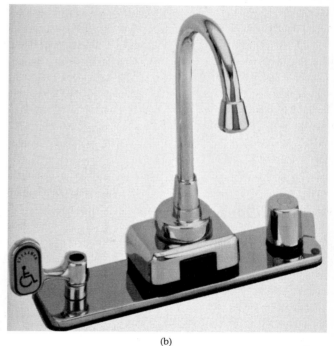

(b)

Figure 10–9
(a) Speakman Company's MICROFLO™ battery-operated metering faucets are easily retrofitted into older buildings. The self-contained units fit into preexisting sinks and do not require wiring. Factory programmed at 10 seconds, the new programmable feature can easily reset the water to flow from 5 to 120 seconds. While conserving water, reducing maintenance, and providing accurate, dependable, push-button operation, MICROFLO meets ADA requirements. (b) Speakman SENSORFLO® Plus Electronic Sensor Faucet incorporates a manual override that permits the system to be conveniently used for continuous running and filling applications. Especially useful in hospital, institutional, and laboratory facilities, this expanded flexibility does not compromise the important features of sensor operation. (Photos courtesy of Speakman Company.)

Faucets manufactured for commercial use can be fitted with antivandal devices, which require special tools to dismantle.

Toilets

Wall-hung toilets are often used in public restrooms to facilitate cleaning. The toilet seats do not have lids and must have an open front. To aid in quicker maintenance and to avoid vandalism, toilets in public restrooms do not usually use a conventional tank but instead have a **flush valve.** This valve requires greater **water pressure** than residential toilets but uses less water and is easier to maintain. This type of valve is not used in private residences because it is too noisy. It may be operated by hand or sometimes by a foot pedal.

Another method of flushing is electronic. After the toilet has been used and there is no longer pressure on the seat, it will flush automatically.

There is a great need for more stalls in ladies' rooms than in the men's restrooms. Some architects are beginning to realize this need after seeing long lines outside the ladies' rooms at sporting events and other public affairs.

Several different types of **urinals** may be used in the men's room. All are constructed of vitreous china and all have integral flushing rims. One type is a stall urinal mounted on the floor. Others may be wall hung. A wall-hung unit with an elongated front is designed for use by the physically disabled and meets Americans with Disabilities Act requirements.

Stall Partitions

There are many different styles of stall dividers and many different materials from which to select. The **pilasters** may be floor anchored, ceiling hung, overhead braced, or floor and ceiling anchored. The ceiling type minimizes maintenance but requires structural steel support in the ceiling. Stalls are 32 to 36 inches wide with sides 56 to 60 inches high. Doors are 22 to 29 inches wide for in-swinging doors and 32 to 36 inches wide for out-swinging doors. The difference in the width measurement is made up by stiles, which vary between 3 to 24 inches depending on requirements. Doors of regular stalls open into the stall, whereas some wheelchair-accessible stalls have out-swinging doors.

Bobrick, in its *Barrier-Free Washroom Planning Guide,* offers complete instructions regarding size and location of stalls, toilets, lavatories, and all accessories (Figure 10–10).

The material used for partitions may be galvanized steel primed and finished with two coats of baked enamel, stainless steel, seamless high-pressure decorative laminate, or even marble. All of these finishes come in a variety of colors and may be coordinated with the colors used for washroom accessories, vanity centers, shelves, and countertops.

When the design of restrooms dictates, entrance screens for privacy should be used. It is important to consider the direction the door opens and placement of mirrors to ensure privacy.

Urinal screens are used in men's restrooms. These screens may be wall hung, floor anchored, ceiling hung, or supported by a narrow stile going from floor to ceiling, in a similar manner to the stall partitions. Urinal screens are placed between each urinal or between the urinal area and other parts of the restroom (Figure 10–11).

Accessories

Washroom accessories must not project more than 4 inches into a clear access aisle if their leading edge is between 27 and 80 inches above the finish floor; if their leading edge is at or below 27 inches, then they may project any amount as long as the required minimum width of an adjacent clear access aisle is maintained. This standard is specifically designed to ensure detection by visually impaired people. It is recommended that all floor-standing and surface-mounted units projecting more than 4 inches be located in corners, alcoves, or between other structural elements so as not to be a hazard to visually impaired people or interfere with access aisles or wheelchair turning areas. Fully recessed accessories are the preferred choice throughout universally designed washrooms.

As was mentioned previously, soap dispensers may be installed on the lavatory rim itself. This type is preferable because any droppings from the dispenser are washed away in the bowl; the dry powder type usually leaves a mess on the counter area. To meet standards, soap dispensers installed over lavatories must be mounted so their push buttons are no higher than 54 inches above the finish floor. Paper towel dispensers should be within easy reach of the lavatory, along with towel disposal containers. Sometimes both these accessories come in one wall-hung or wall-recessed unit. Another method of hand drying is the heated air blower. At the push of a button, heated air is blown out and the hands are rubbed briskly until dry. This type of hand dryer eliminates the mess of paper towel disposal, but if the dryer breaks down, there is no way to dry the hands. Newer hand dryers operate electronically, similar to automatic faucets; in other words, they start when the hands are positioned under the blower and turn off when the hands are removed.

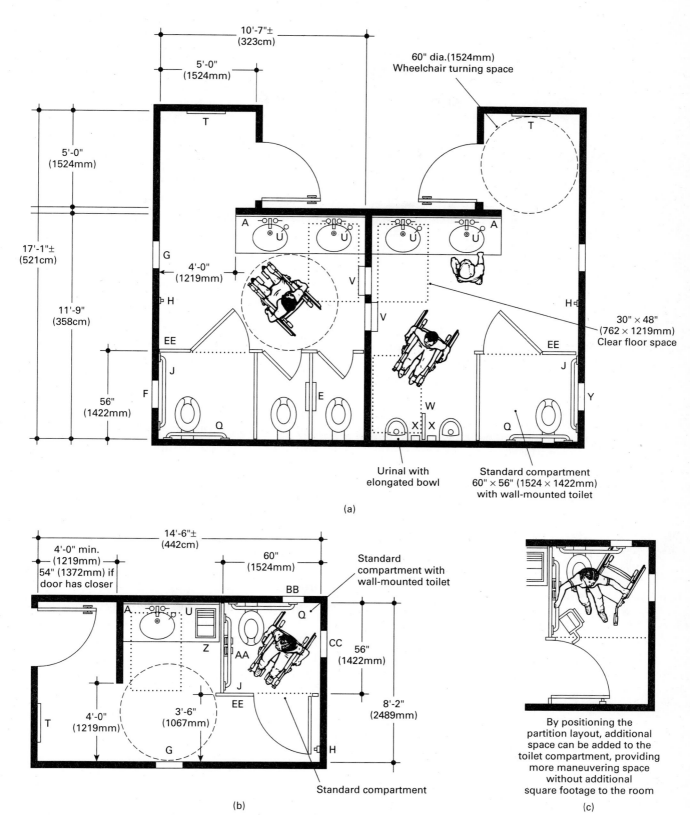

(a)

(b)

(c)

By positioning the
partition layout, additional
space can be added to the
toilet compartment, providing
more maneuvering space
without additional
square footage to the room

Figure 10–10

Small barrier-free public washrooms. (a) Small public washroom with single compartment. (b) Standard compartment meeting minimum ADAAG requirement. (c) Standard alcove compartment provides greater accessibility. By positioning the partition layout, space can be added to the toilet compartment, providing more maneuvering space without adding square footage to the room. (Courtesy Bobrick Washroom Equipment Inc.)

Figure 10–11
Marblstal®, made of Georgia Marble®, is perfect for toilet compartments and urinal screens, as shown in this photograph. Marblstal is prefabricated and ready to install, with rugged chrome-plated hardware included. (Photo courtesy of the Georgia Marble Co.)

Each toilet compartment requires a toilet tissue dispenser; an optional accessory is a toilet seat cover dispenser. A feminine product disposal is necessary in each stall in a ladies' room. A napkin and tampon vending machine should be placed outside, near the toilet stalls. A hook for hanging pocketbooks and jackets is optional in toilet stalls. The preferred location for a hook is on the handle side of the door so no personal items are left behind. Another optional accessory in ladies' toilet stalls is a flip-down shelf that holds packages off the floor area.

In stalls for use by disabled individuals, stainless steel grab bars are required by law to be mounted on the wall nearest the toilet. They are 1 1/2 inches in diameter and 1 1/2 inches from the wall and 33 inches from the floor. Local building codes vary, so it is important to consult the codes for exact measurements.

There are two methods of transfer for wheelchair-bound people, depending on their abilities. Those who are able to stand with support can pull themselves upright by means of the grab bars. Others have to use the side transfer method, in which the arm of the wheelchair is removed and the individuals lean across the toilet and pull themselves onto the seat. The side transfer method requires a larger stall, because the chair must be placed alongside the toilet; front transfer requires only the depth of the chair plus standing room in front of the toilet.

BIBLIOGRAPHY

Bobrick, *Barrier-Free Washroom Planning Guide*. Los Angeles, CA: Bobrick, 1996.

Mazzurco, Philip, *Bath Design*. New York: Whitney Library of Design, an imprint of Watson-Guptil Publications, 1986.

GLOSSARY

Bidet. A sanitary fixture for cleansing the genito-urinary area of the body.

CBD. Certified bathroom designer.

Center fit. Two handles and one spout mounted on a single plate.

Centers. Another way of saying "on centers"; in other words, the measurement is from the center of one hole to the center of the second hole.

Compartmented. Bathroom divided into separate areas according to function and fixtures.

Diverter. Changes flow of water from one area to another.

Feed-in. Where the rough plumbing is attached to the fittings.

Fittings. Another word for the faucet assembly; a term used by the plumbing industry.

Flush valve. Designed to supply a fixed quantity of water for flushing purposes.

Gel coat. A thin, outer layer of resin, sometimes containing pigment, applied to a reinforced plastic moulding to improve its appearance.

GFI. Ground fault interrupter. A special electrical outlet for areas where water is present.

Lavatory. The plumbing industry's name for a bathroom sink.

Low profile. A one-piece toilet with almost silent flushing action. There are almost no dry surfaces on the bowl interior.

Metering device. A preset measured amount of water is released when the metering device is activated.

Overflow. A pipe in bathtubs and lavatories used to prevent flooding. The pipe is located just below the rim or top edge of these fixtures.

Pedestal. A lavatory on a base attached to the floor rather than set into a counter surface. The base hides all the waste pipes that are usually visible.

Pilaster. Vertical support member, varying in width.

Pop-up rod. The rod that controls the raising and lowering of the drain in the bottom of the lavatory.

Preformed base. Shower pan or base of terrazzo or acrylic.

Sauna. A steam bath of Finnish origin.

Slip resistant. Special material on the bottom of the tub to prevent falls.

Spa. Whirlpool-type bath for more than one person, with a heating and filtration system. Frequently installed outside in warmer climates.

Spread. Distance between holes of a bathtub or lavatory faucet.

Surround. The walls encircling a bathtub or shower area.

Urinals. Wall-hung vitreous plumbing fixtures used in men's rooms, with flushing devices for cleaning purposes.

Vacuum breaker. A device that prevents water from being siphoned into the potable water system.

Vanity. Laypersons' term for a prefabricated lavatory and base cabinet.

Water pressure. Measured as so many pounds per square inch. Usually 30 to 50 psi.

Wet wall. The wall in which the water and waste pipes are located.

Wrist control. Long lever handles operated by pressure of the wrist rather than the fingers.

NOTES

[1] Linda Trent, "Combining Kitchen and Bath Elements," *Interiors & Sources*, April 1994.

[2] American Standard Inc., *The Bathroom Book*, 1997.

[3] Bobrick Washroom Equipment Inc., *Barrier-Free Washroom Planning Guide*, p. 2

The Newest Products on the Market

TRENDS

One new trend is the use of textured carpet and patterned carpet for residential use. Many of the patterns are tweed colors woven into geometric patterns.

New technology has brought an increase in flexible trim. Previously, curved pieces were small and had to be joined together. Now, however, the flexible trim is available in long strips (up to 12 feet).

Security has become a major concern of hardware manufacturers, with many new innovations from all manufacturers.

The newest designs for kitchens locate the sink in an island facing the entertainment center. Also, many new kitchens feature a second single sink for preparing vegetables. Herb gardens are often included in today's kitchens. The demand for quieter dishwashers has also been addressed by manufacturers, with many kitchen designers raising the dishwasher to avoid the bending required with conventionally located dishwashers.

CHAPTER 1, ENVIRONMENTAL CONCERNS

Avonite® has a new recycled solid surface material called Kaleidoscope. This product uses waste from Avonite's plain colored solid surface materials; therefore, the recycled product has a speckled appearance. Finishes include gloss, satin, or matte.

CHAPTER 3, CARPET

As mentioned in Chapter 3, the raw material for the carpet fibers comes from chemical companies. Each of the carpet fiber–producing companies has introduced a new form of carpet protection for residential carpet. These are listed alphabetically.

All Anso® nylon brands use Anso IV® with soil and stain resistance and now feature 7-year Limited Stain Resistance and 7-year Limited Soil Resistance warranties.

BASF Fiber Products Group has introduced *Color*STAY®, a premium solution-dyed nylon filament product. *Color*STAY offers excellent resistance to fading from exposure to sunlight and ozone. *Color*STAY can be cleaned with harsh detergents without losing color. Carpets made with *Color*STAY yarn come with a 10-year stain removal guarantee, 10-year light fastness guarantee, and a lifetime antishock guarantee.

New Stainmaster™ carpets from DuPont now have DuPont Advanced Teflon® Repel System for a cleaner carpet. This company has also extended its stain and soil warranties to 7 years.

Solutia™, the manufacturer of Wear-Dated® carpets, has now added another feature (at about $3 a square yard) called Pet-Agree™ to any Wear-Dated line. This new process keeps liquids from seeping through the carpet into the padding and onto the floor, thereby causing odors. This new Wear-Dated Pet-Agree comes with an impervious polyethylene backing that traps liquids where they can be found and cleaned thoroughly. If the liquid reaches the padding, it is impossible to get to the root of the stain and the stain will keep reappearing.

CHAPTER 4, FLOORS

The National Oak Flooring Manufacturers Association now represents not only manufacturers of oak and prefinished oak flooring, but also flooring using such species as beech, birch, hard maple, hickory/pecan, and ash. The NOFMA has official flooring grading rules that must be adhered to in order to conform to membership in NOFMA.

Applied Radiant Energy Corporation, which manufactures Gammapar, has added a 3-ply floor using the same species of wood in all three plies.

Wilsonart International now manufactures a parquet laminate floor that must be ordered in both A and B packages in order to show the difference in color. Parquet from one or the other box will not be attractive.

Tarkett® now manufactures a sheet vinyl product featuring a wearlayer with silicone. This new Naturelle™ line has a satin finish; previously the silicone wearlayer had a high gloss finish.

Azrock® has introduced a new line of flooring especially for areas that may become wet.

Johnsonite, the manufacturer of Permalight Safe-T-System shown in Figure 4.19 also manufactures all types of signage with this fluorescent finish for walls.

CHAPTER 5, WALLS

James Hardie™ Interior Products now produces Hardibacker 500™, a 1/2-inch ceramic tile backerboard for walls. This new thickness allows for smoother drywall transitions, as the other walls in the bathroom are usually constructed of 1/2-inch gypsum board.

Today's *Home Owner Magazine* gave Pittsburgh Corning a Best New Products of 1998 award for its

Lightwise™ Window. The Lightwise Window installs like traditional windows (in one piece). The sizes are based on 8″ × 8″ nominal glass block, and come in 8-inch multiples. The smallest size is 16″ × 16″; the largest is 80″ × 16″. There are three styles of glass block from which to choose: Decora® pattern, which provides maximum light transmission with subtle visual distortion; Delphi® pattern, with maximum light transmission combined with maximum privacy; and the Mistique™ pattern, providing moderate light transmission with maximum privacy. These Lightwise windows also provide more security than a regular window, which can be easily broken. Available frame colors are white and sandstone.

Seabrook Wallcoverings has introduced the Carey Lind Neo Classic Vol II. This new line contains wide and narrow borders used over a background paper. Coordinated fabric is also available.

CHAPTER 7, OTHER COMPONENTS

Will-Trim® MDF Moulding is a wood substitute that is an ideal and economical alternative to solid wood or overlay moulding. Willamette's manufacturing process produces straight, uniform, defect-free moulding with a premium primed surface that is unattainable with solid wood. The primed surface is applied on the face and both sides in a six-step process. The primer is an excellent surface for latex and oil-based paints. Will-Trim MDF Moulding is available in a full line of traditional and contemporary profiles, including casings, bases, chair rails, crowns, jambs, and stools. These mouldings are available in lengths up to 16 feet, reducing the need to splice baseboards.

Heritage Architectural Moulding is a composition moulding with a primer coating over wood with a two-dimensional section of polymer added over the primer.

Flex Trim Mouldings are available in a paint or stain grade. The paint grade has a smooth surface, and the stain grade is available in a variety of wood textures that do not require a primer because of their lack of porosity.

Focal Point is now producing The Frank Lloyd Wright Collection® of architectural details, replicated from properties designed by America's preeminent 20th-century architect. The Collection spans Wright's career, and reflects Prairie designs from the Oak Park Home and Studio outside of Chicago to the contemporary look of the Harold Price Home in Arizona.

New-Tech® Doors has a selection of more than 40 standard designs in 6′8″, 7′, and 8′ (the normal heights), but 12- and even 14-foot doors can be produced on special order, with the appropriate number of hinges. These doors do not come prehung or with a finish. Wood doors are left natural and the paint grade is white.

The patented MacLock 1500 as seen in Figure 7–14 is now available with a remote control.

G-U Hardware, Inc., manufactures the US CRE-MONA, 3-point locking system, featuring double reinforced shoot bolts, top and bottom for maximum security and protection against warping of door panels. Also featured is a 90° locking mechanism. The locking points are engaged by lifting the lever handle and released by pushing the handle down.

Weiser Lock has introduced the new Powerbolt 3000™ home access system. This single remote control, small enough to carry in a pocket or a purse, operates home door locks, garage doors, and interior lights. Like all bright brass door hardware from Weiser Lock, Powerbolt comes in the patented Brilliance Lifetime Anti-Tarnish Finish. Powerbolt™ keyless entry system has an electronic touchpad control that eliminates the need to carry keys. Children do not have to worry about lost or hidden keys, and jogging enthusiasts do not need to carry them.

CHAPTER 9, KITCHENS

Amana has just introduced the revolutionary new Wave Oven. The Wave Oven cooks food by using infrared waves rather than heat. Foods not only brown on all sides, but retain their natural juices. A system of halogen lamps is strategically placed in both the oven ceiling and floor. The Amana Wave Oven requires no preheating, thereby saving time. It cooks food more quickly than a conventional oven or outdoor grill, cutting cooking time by up to 75 percent. It monitors the temperature inside the oven, automatically adjusting power and total cook time for a perfect finish every time. A single touch will commit up to 10 preset menus to memory. The Wave Oven comes with preprogrammed heat and time settings for 39 commonly used foods. For example, one button is for pizza. Among the questions that appear in the lit panel are, Is it frozen? Does it have a French bread crust? Has it been partially cooked? Is it a fresh pizza? Each response requires a different cooking time.

Viking has a built-in gas wok, 24 inches wide and 24 inches deep. The components include a 20-inch stainless steel wok with a top, a two-piece cast iron removable surface burner grate, and a center trivet to use with large pots.

Moen has Pure Touch™, a faucet that filters water on demand. The electronic filter life indicator provides visual and audible feedback (it beeps when it reaches 5 percent efficiency). There are three grades of filter: the MicroTech™ 1000 filter reduces chlorine taste and odor; the MicroTech 3000 filter cartridge also reduces lead; and the Micro Tech 5000 filter cartridge has all the benefits of MicroTech 3000 plus it reduces cysts (crypto sporidium and giardia). Beneficial fluoride is not removed. Each cartridge filters approximately 200 gallons (3 months average use). The MicroTech filter cartridge was designed by Culligan®, America's leader in water quality. The faucet can also supply an unfiltered stream or spray for everyday kitchen use.

The Best® series of range hoods from Broan is designed and handcrafted in Italy. There are 16 contemporary designs available.

Kohler® Colors is a water-based, high-gloss caulking compound developed to closely match and accent Kohler kitchen and bathroom fixture colors.

The In-Sink-Erator® Septic Disposer™, designed for any size septic system, injects a measured amount of Bio-Charge™ Enzyme Treatment each time it is operated to break down food and other household waste. The Bio-Charge easily replaceable cartridge is highly concentrated to last up to 4 months. It also helps prevent odors and backups.

Grohe® manufactures a line of solid stainless steel kitchen faucets, the Ladylux™ and Ladylux Café™ pull-out spray faucets. The Ladylux Plus faucet has a 10 3/8" spout. This line features a singularly styled handle that makes one-finger (or wet finger) control of both water temperature and volume effortless, a critical consideration for those with physical limitations.

CHAPTER 10, BATHROOMS

Broan has a new exhaust fan, Solitaire® Ultra Silent™ Series, with the industry's lowest sound levels, as low as 0.3 sones (a unit of loudness), which is silent to the ear and measurable only by machines. These fans incorporate a 7-watt nightlight for safety and security. Because the Solitaire Ultra Silent fans and fan/lights are so quiet, a lighted switch indicates when the fan is on.

Delta Faucet has introduced four new shower heads in its plumbing line, with Delta's Push-Clean™ and Touch-Clean® features, which make the showerhead easy to maintain: (1) The Push-Clean showerhead requires pushing in on the flat head surface to remove buildup of mineral deposits. (2) The Touch-Clean showerhead is cleaned by wiping the face of the showerhead to loosen and flush away deposits. (3) Dual-spray Touch-Clean also features a shell-top divot adjustment that provides a massage spray. (4) Ultimate Touch-Clean provides the additional feature of a soft aerated spray. These showerheads allow full flow at a very low water pressure, as little as 5 psi. There are seven finishes available, including the Brilliance, with a lifetime antitarnish finish.

Kohler has introduced San Raphael Power-Lite™, a new one-piece low-profile toilet with a seat height of 16 inches from the floor. The San Raphael Power-Lite employs a 0.2 horsepower electric pump to propel water through the toilet. The resulting jet of water forcefully removes waste through the 2 1/4-inch trapway, while the 11″ × 14″ water surface helps keep the bowl clean. The dual flushing system allows the user to save water by choosing between a 1.1- or a 1.6-gallon flush. Both flushes are activated by Kohler's easy-to-operate Twin-Touch™ side-mounted push button.

The Briolette™ bath from Kohler offers a myriad of installation options. Featuring a diamond-shaped, angular design, Briolette lends itself perfectly to the increasingly popular corner installation, fitting easily into a 60″ × 60″ corner. Designers can also make a dramatic statement by installing Briolette in a peninsula or island, or by recessing it into a bay window. With a center drain location, this bathtub will accommodate two bathers. Briolette is available in both a tub-only version as well as a whirlpool style.

Appendix A: Measurements, Manufacturers, and Associations

METRIC CONVERSION TABLE

This simple metric conversion chart contains equivalents only for the linear measurements taken from the textbook.

Some other quantities such as gallons, pounds, square yards, and temperatures may be converted from the following figures:

To convert square yards to square meters multiply square yards by .80

To convert gallons to liters, multiply gallons by 3.8

To convert pounds to kilograms, multiply pounds by 0.45

To convert Fahrenheit to Celsius, subtract 32 from the Fahrenheit amount and multiply by 5/9

Some materials, such as stones, are not manufactured, of course; these materials may be found only through Yellow Pages listings. For information on other manufacturers not listed in the Yellow Pages, write to the addresses listed in Appendix B.

Remember that the companies listed here are just a few of those manufacturing that particular product. The listed products are nationally distributed items, but there are many local products that may be similar in quality.

Associations and Institutes represent their members in sales promotions and informational services only. They do not sell products, but many can provide a list of suppliers in your area.

IN.	CM	IN.	CM	IN.	CM	FT	M
1/000	0.003	4	10.16	36	91.44	1	3.05
1/16	0.16	4 1/4	10.80	37	93.98	2	6.10
3/32	0.24	5	12.70	39	99.06	3	9.14
1/8	0.32	6	15.24	40	101.60	4	12.19
5/32	0.40	7	17.78	42	106.68	5	15.24
3/16	0.48	8	20.32	44	111.76	6	18.29
1/4	0.64	9	22.86	46 1/2	118.11	7	21.34
5/16	0.79	10	25.40	48	121.92	8	24.38
3/8	0.95	11	27.94	52	132.08	9	27.43
7/16	1.11	12	30.48	54	137.16	10	30.48
1/2	1.27	14	35.56	55	139.70	12	2.7
5/8	1.59	15	38.10	59	149.86	15	4.5
3/4	1.91	18	45.72	60	152.40	22	6.6
7/8	2.22	19 1/2	49.53	64	162.56	25	7.5
1	2.54	20	50.80	66 1/2	168.91	28	8.4
1 1/16	2.70	22	55.88	72	182.88	37	11.1
1 1/4	3.18	23	58.42	78	198.12	64	19.2
1 1/2	3.81	24	60.96	82	208.28	66	19.8
2	5.08	27	68.58	84	213.36	100	30.0
2 1/4	5.72	29	73.66	90	228.60		
2 3/8	6.03	30	76.20	91	231.14		
2 3/4	6.99	30 1/2	77.47	96	243.84		
3	7.62	32	81.28				
3 1/8	7.94	33	83.82				
3 5/8	9.21	34	86.36				
3 7/8	9.84	35 3/4	90.81				

CHAPTER 1

Composite Panel Association
Envirosense Consortium
Green Seal
Gridset from Rockland React Rite
Syndecrete from Syndesis
TOPsiders

Recycled Carpet
Collins & Aikman Floorcoverings Inc.

CHAPTER 2

*Paints**
Benjamin Moore & Co.
The Glidden Company
Porter Paints, Courtaulds Coatings Inc.
Sherwin-Williams
Wm. Zinsser & Co. Inc.

Applied Finishes
Duroplex from Triarch Industries
OMNIPLEX from Seagrave Coatings Corp.

Multicolor Wall Coatings
Aquafleck from California Products Corp.
Polomyx from Surface Protection Industries International
Zolatone, Surface Protection Industries International

Flame-retardant Paints
Flame Control Coatings Inc.

*Stains**

*Danish Oil**

CHAPTER 3

The Carpet and Rug Institute (CRI) is the trade association representing the dynamic carpet and rug industry. The Carpet Cushion Council represents the carpet cushion industry.

Wool
Helios

*Denotes that the local distributor may be found in the Yellow Pages under the particular product, brand name, or manufacturer's name.

Carpet Modules
Interface Flooring Systems Inc.
Lees Modular Carpets

Commercial Carpet Manufacturers*
Bentley Mills
Collins & Aikman
J & J Commercial
Shaw Carpet Corp.
Stark Carpet

Sisal, Coir, and Natural Fibers
Alison T. Seymour
Merida Meridian

Natural Carpet Cushion
Dixie Manufacturing Corp.

Synthetic Rubber Cushion
Sponge Cushion Inc. (SCI)

Recycled Carpet Cushion
Dura Undercushions
Hartex from Leggett & Platt

Installation Systems
TacFast

Dirt Control Foot Mats and Grating
J.L. Industries
Nuway Matting Systems, Inc.

CHAPTER 4

Associations and Institutes

The American National Standards Institute (ANSI) sets codes and standards based on membership consensus.

The American Society for Testing and Materials (ASTM) sets standards for all types of products.

The Hardwood, Plywood & Veneer Association (HPVA), with ANSI, sets standards for hardwood and decorative plywood.

The International Cast Polymer Association, formerly the Cultured Marble Institute, promotes the use of cast polymers that may be used on floors, walls, counters, sinks, and bathrooms.

The Marble Institute of America represents the marble industry. It has a publication, *Care and Cleaning for Natural Stone Surfaces*, that is available from the address listed in Appendix B.

The National Oak Flooring Manufacturers Association (NOFMA) sets the standards by which wood flooring should be installed.

The National Terrazzo and Mosaic Association, Inc. represents the terrazzo industry.

The National Wood Flooring Association represents the wood floor industry.

The Resilient Floor Covering Institute (RFCI) is a trade association representing six resilient flooring manufacturers, including Armstrong World Industries; Burke Industries; Congoleum Corporation; Domco Inc.; Mannington Mills, Inc.; and Tarkett Inc. To obtain a free copy of RFCI's brochure, "Recommended Work Practices for the Removal of Resilient Floor Coverings," write to the Resilient Floor Covering Institute at the address listed in Appendix B.

The Tile Council of America, Inc. publishes *CERAMIC TILE: The Installation Handbook* annually. These specifications cover all types of tile installations and are a guide for the tile industry.

Strip—Factory Finished
Bruce Hardwood Floors
Harris-Tarkett
Hartco Flooring Co.
Kentucky Wood Floors Inc.
Memphis Hardwood Flooring Co.
Robbins Hardwood Flooring

Strip—Unfinished
Bruce Hardwood Floors
Kentucky Wood Floors Inc.
Memphis Hardwood Flooring Co.
Robbins Hardwood Flooring

Plank—Factory Finished
Bruce Hardwood Floors
Hartco Flooring Co.
Kentucky Wood Floors Inc.
Memphis Hardwood Flooring Co.
Robbins Hardwood Flooring

Plank—Unfinished
Aged Woods
Bruce Hardwood Floors
Kentucky Wood Floors Inc.
Memphis Hardwood Flooring Co.
Robbins Hardwood Flooring

Parquet—Factory Finished
Bruce Hardwood Floors
Harris-Tarkett
Hartco Flooring Co.
Kentucky Wood Floors Inc.
Memphis Hardwood Flooring Co.
Robbins Hardwood Flooring

Parquet—Unfinished
Kentucky Wood Floors Inc.
Memphis Hardwood Flooring Co.
Robbins Hardwood Flooring

Acrylic—Impregnated
WearMaster, Bruce Hardwood Floors
Gammapar, Applied Radiant Energy Co.
Hartco Flooring Co.
PermaGrain

Foam-backed Parquet
Bruce Hardwood Floors
Hartco Flooring Co.

End Grain
Kentucky Wood Floors Inc.

Recycled Woods
Aged Woods

Inlaid Borders and Accents
Kentucky Wood Floors Inc.

Laminated Wood Floors—Factory Finished
Kentucky Wood Floors Inc.
Robbins Hardwood Flooring

Custom Flooring
Kentucky Wood Floors Inc.

Wood Adhesives
Hydroment from Bostik

Wood Finishes
Glitsa American
Street Shoe from Basic Coatings, Inc.

Laminate Flooring
Brace Floors
Formica Corp.
Pergo
Wilsonart International

Marble
Georgia Marble Co.
Intarsia Inc.

Marble Veneers
Terrazzo & Marble Supply Co.
Georgia Marble Co.

Backer Boards
Hardibacker® from James Hardie Building Products
UTIL-A-CRETE distributed by American Olean

Grout Sealer
Portersept, Porter Paints

Agglomerate
Terrazzo & Marble Supply Co.

*Granite**
Durastone
Terrazzo & Marble Supply Co.

*Flagstone**

*Slate**
Buckingham-Virginia Slate Corp.
Structural Slate Co.

*Ceramic Tile**
American Olean Tile
Ann Sacks Tile & Stone
Crossville Ceramics
Dal-Tile Corp.
Summitville Tiles Inc.

*Ceramic Mosaic Tile**
Dal-Tile Corp.
Summitville Tiles Inc.

*Pregrouted Ceramic Tile**

*Quarry Tile**

*Mexican Tile**
Vasquez Enterprises

Glass Block
Pittsburgh Corning Corp.

*Monolithic Terrazzo**

Terrazzo
General Polymers Corp.
Intarsia Inc.
Wausau Tile Inc.

*Brick**

*Floor Maintenance**
Hillyard, Inc.

Linoleum
Linosom from Azrock Products
Marmoleum, Forbo Industries Inc.

Vinyl Composition
Azrock
Mannington Commercial Flooring
VPI Inc.

Vinyl Tile
Azrock from Amtico
Roppe Corp.
VPI Inc.

Conductive Vinyl Tile
VPI Inc.

Vinyl and Rubber Bases
Azrock Industries
Burke Industries
Johnsonite Inc.

Rubber Tile and/or Sheet
Burke Industries
Johnsonite Inc.
Roppe Corp.

Sheet Vinyl
Armstrong Corp.
Azrock
Congoleum
Tarkett Inc.
Mannington Commercial, Inc.

Cork
Natural CORK Ltd. Co.

CHAPTER 5

Associations and Institutes

The Architectural Woodwork Institute (AWI) is a nonprofit organization devoted to the elevation of industry standards, to continuing research into new and better materials and methods, and to the publication of technical data helpful to architects and specification writers in the design and use of architectural woodwork. Write for the price list covering all the books mentioned in this book as well as many others.

The North American Association of Mirror Manufacturers promotes the many uses of mirror and produces a compilation of outstanding mirror ideas by leading interior designers.

Granite* Veneer
Durastone Corp.
Stone Panels Inc.

Marble*
Georgia Marble Co.

Travertine*

Brick*

Concrete Forms
L.M. Scofield

Concrete Block*

Glass Block
Pittsburgh Corning Corp.

Plaster*

Gypsum Board
Gold Bond Building Products, National Gypsum
SHEETROCK, US Gypsum Co.

Embossed Gypsum Board
Pittcon Industries Inc.

Vinyl-Surfaced Gypsum Wall Panels
Durasan, National Gypsum

Veneer Plaster
National Gypsum Co.
United States Gypsum (USG) Co.

Wallcoverings
Anaglypta from Crown Corp.
Bradbury & Bradbury Art Wallpapers
Brunschwig & Fils
Schumacher
Thibaut Wallcoverings

Paperbacking Fabrics
Custom Laminations, Inc.

Commercial Wallcoverings
Innovations in Wallcoverings Inc.
ESSCAPE from Essex
Koroseal, Sasso and Vicrtex from RJF International Corp.
J. M. Lynne Co., Inc.
MDC Wallcoverings
Seabrook Wallcoverings
Tasso Wallcoverings
Tretford from Eurotex

Adhesives
Portersept, Porter Paints

Tambours
National Products
Flexible Materials

Protective Finishes
Tedlar, DuPont

Redwood*
California Redwood Association

Solid Wood Strips*

Plywood Paneling*
Consult a member of the Architectural Woodwork
    Institute.

Prefinished Plywood*

Particleboard
Marlite

Hardboard*
Masonite
Peg-Board from Masonite

Decorative Laminate
Formica Corp.
Nevamar Corp.
Wilsonart International

Glass
NeoClad
Nippon Electric Glass America
Restoration Glass from Bendheim Co.
Transwall Corp.
Viracon, Inc.

Mirror*

Metal*

Acoustic Panels
Novawall Systems Inc.

Other Materials
Pinecrest
QuarryCast from Formglas Interiors
VITRICOR from Nevamar

CHAPTER 6

Plaster Ceiling Tiles
Above View from Tiles Inc.

Wood*
Any of the wood flooring manufacturers

Manufactured Beams
Trus Joist MacMillan
Willamette Industries, Inc.

Acoustic Ceilings—Residential
Armstrong
USG Interiors, Inc.

Acoustic Ceilings—Commercial
Armstrong
AutoCAD from Autodesk
Eurostone, Chicago Metallic
USG Interiors, Inc.

Mirrored Effect
The Gage Corporation, Int.
USG Interiors, Inc.
Wilsonart International

Stamped Metal Ceilings
AA Abbingdon Affiliates, Inc.
Chelsea Decorative Metal Co.
W.F. Norman Corp.
Pinecrest Inc.
Shanker Industries Inc.

Strip Metal Ceilings
Chicago Metallic Corp.

CHAPTER 7

The Door and Hardware Institute promotes the door
and hardware industries.

Mouldings
Driwood Moulding Co.
Focal Point
Formglas Interiors Inc.
Old World Moulding
Willamette Industries, Inc.

Doors
Kaylien
Kentucky Millwork
Marlite
Pinecrest Inc.

Shoji
Cherry Tree Design
Design Shoji
Pinecrest Inc.

Hinges
Grass America
Hager Hinge Co.

Hardware*
Baldwin Hardware Corp.
Forms + Surfaces
Gainsborough Hardware
MacLock
Paul Decorative Products
Sargent
Schlage Lock Co.
Stanley Hardware
Yale Security

Glass Door Hardware
HEWI Inc.
J.L. Industries

Closers*
LCN Closers

CHAPTER 8

Drawer Guides
Accuride
Knape & Vogt Manufacturing Co.

CHAPTER 9

Kitchen Appliances
Amana Refrigeration Inc.
Asko
DACOR
Frigidaire
Gaggenau USA Corp.
General Electric
Jenn-Air
KitchenAid
Sub-Zero Freezer Co.
Thermador
Whirlpool

Commercial Refrigerators
Traulsen & Co., Inc.
U-Line

Warming Drawers
Frigidaire

Restaurant-type Ranges
Russell Range Inc.
Viking Range Corp.

Wood/Coal Cookstoves
Heartland Appliances, Inc.

Under-counter Refrigerators and Coolers
Marvel Industries
U-Line Corp.

Ventilation Fans
Broan Mfg. Co.
Thermador

Kitchen Sinks
Elkay Manufacturing Co.
Kohler Company
Moen Inc.

Kitchen Faucets
Delta Faucet Co.
Elkay Manufacturing Co.
Kroin Inc.
Moen Inc.

Kitchen Cabinets
Canac Kitchens
St. Charles of New York
Wood-Mode Cabinetry

Kitchen Counter Materials
Formica Corp.
Nuvel
Surell, Formica Corp.
Wilsonart Laminate
Wilsonart Solid Surface Veneer

Solid Surface Materials
Avonite, Avonite, Inc.
Corian, DuPont
Fountainhead, Nevamar
GIBRALTAR, Wilsonart International
Swanstone, Swan Corp.

CHAPTER 10

Plumbing Fixture Manufacturers
American Standard Inc.
Eljer Plumbingware
Jacuzzi Whirlpool Bath
Kohler Company

Bath Repairing
Re-Bath Inc.

Specialty Lavatories
Alchemy
Robern Inc.
Sherle Wagner

Faucets
Chicago Faucet Company
Delta
Kroin Inc.
Moen Inc.
Speakman Company

Accessories
Broan Mfg. Co.
HEWI Inc.

Commercial Bathroom Fixtures
Chicago Faucet Company
Eljer Plumbingware

Stall Partitions
Accurate Partitions Corp.
Georgia Marble Co.
Marlite

Bathroom Accessories—Commercial
Bobrick Washroom Equipment Inc.
Broan Mfg. Co.
HEWI Inc.

Appendix B:
Resources

AA Abbingdon Affiliates Inc.
2149 Utica Avenue
Brooklyn, NY 11234

Accuride
12311 Shoemaker Avenue
Santa Fe Springs, CA 90670
www.accuride.com

Aged Woods
2331 East Market Street
York, PA 17402
www.agedwoods.com

Alchemy
3143 South Cienega Boulevard
Los Angeles, CA 90016
www.alchemy-glass.com/sinkshots.html

Amana Refrigeration Inc.
Amana, IA 52204
www.amana.com

American National Standards Institute
1430 Broadway
New York, NY 10018
www.ansi.org

American Olean Tile
P.O. Box 271
Lansdale, PA 19446-0271
www.aotile.com

American Society for Testing and Materials
1916 Rose Street
Philadelphia, PA 19103
www.astm.org

American Society of Interior Designers
608 Massachusetts Avenue NE
Washington, DC 20002–6006
www.asid.org

American Standard Inc.
P.O. Box 6820
Piscataway, NJ 08855–6820
www.americanstandard.com

Amtico International Inc.
6480 Roswell Road
Atlanta, GA 30328
www.amtico.com

Ann Sacks Tile & Stone
8120 N.E. 33rd Drive
Portland, OR 97211
www.annsackstile.com

Applied Radiant Energy Co.
P.O. Box 289
Forest, VA 24521
www.gammapar.com

Architectural Woodwork Institute
1952 Isaac Newton Square
Reston, VA 20190
www.awinet.org

Armstrong World Industries Inc.
P.O. Box 3001
Lancaster, PA 17604
www.armstrong.com

Asko
P.O. Box 851805
Richardson, TX 75085-1805
www.askousa.com

Autodesk Inc.
111 McInnis Street
San Rafael, CA 96903
www.autodesk.com

Avonite Inc.
1945 Highway 304
Belen, NM 87002
www.avonite.com

Azrock Industries Inc.
P.O. Box 34030
San Antonio, TX 78265
www.domco.com

Baldwin Hardware Corp.
P.O. Box 15048
Reading, PA 19612

Basic Coatings
2124 Valley Drive
Des Moines, IA 50321
www.basiccoatings.com

S. A. Bendheim Co., Inc.
61 Willett Street
Passaic, NJ 07055

Bentley Mills
14641 E. Don Julian Road
City of Industry, CA 91746
www.ifsia.com

Bobrick Washroom Equipment Inc.
11611 Hart Street
North Hollywood, CA 91605
www.bobrick.com

Bostik
211 Boston Street
Middleton, MA 01949
www.bostik.com

Bradbury & Bradbury Art Wallpapers
P.O. Box 155
Benica, CA 94510
Cost of brochure $12
www.bradbury.com

Broan Mfg. Co. Inc.
Hartford, WI 53027
www.broan.com

Bruce Hardwood Floors
16803 Dallas Parkway
Dallas, TX 75248
www.sweets

Brunschwig & Fils
979 Third Avenue
New York, NY 10022-1234

Buckingham-Virginia Slate Corporation
P.O. Box 8
Arvonia, VA 23004–0008
www.bvslate.com

Burke Industries Inc.
2250 South Tenth Street
San Jose, CA 95112

California Products Corp.
P.O. Box 569
Cambridge, MA 02139–0569

California Redwood Association
405 Enfrente Drive, Suite 200
Novato, CA 94949
www.calredwood.org

Canac Kitchens
360 John Street
Thornhill, ON Canada
www.canac.com

Carpet & Rug Institute
P.O. Box 2048
Dalton, GA 30720
www.carpet-rug.com

Carpet Cushion Council
P.O. Box 546
Riverside, CT 06878

Chelsea Decorative Metal Co.
9603 Moonlight
Houston, TX 77096
www.telluscom.com/chelsea

Cherry Tree Design
34154 E. Frontage Road
Bozeman, MT 59715

Chicago Metallic
4849 S. Austin Avenue
Chicago, IL 60638
www.chicago-metallic.com

Collins & Aikman Floorcoverings, Inc.
P.O. Box 1447
Dalton, GA 30720
www.powerbond.com

Composite Panel Association
18928 Premiere Court
Gaithersburg, MD 20879
www.pbmdf.com

Congoleum Corporation
P.O. Box 3127
Mercerville, NJ 08619-3127
www.congoleum.com

Crossville Ceramics
P.O. Box 1168
Crossville, TN 38557
www.crossville-ceramics.com

Crown Corp., NA
3012 Huron Street, #101
Denver, CO 80202

Custom Laminations, Inc.
P.O. Box 2066
Paterson, NJ 07509-2066
www.customlaminations.com

DACOR
950 South Raymond Avenue
Pasadena, CA 91109–7202
www.dacorappl.com

Dal-Tile Corp.
P.O. Box 17130
Dallas, TX 75217
www.daltile.com

Delta Faucet Co.
P.O. Box 40980
Indianapolis, IN 46280
www.deltafaucet.com

Design Shoji
3000 King Ranch Road
Ukiah, CA 95482

Dixie Manufacturing Corp.
109 Colley Avenue
Norfolk, VA 23510

Door and Hardware Institute
14170 Newbrook Drive
Chantilly, VA 22021–2223
www.dhi.org

Driwood Moulding Company
P.O. Box 1729
Florence, SC 29503

DuPont Answers Program
www.dupont.com/antron

DuPont Corian
P.O. Box 80012
Wilmington, DE 10880-0012
www.corian.com

Durastone Corp.
P.O. Box 992
Florence, AL 35631

Dura Undercushions Ltd.
8525 Delmeade Road
Montreal, Quebec H4T 1M1

Eljer Plumbingware
901 10th Street
Plano, TX 75086

Elkay Manufacturing Co.
2222 Camden Court
Oak Brook, IL 60521
www.elkay.com

Envirosense Consortium
100 Chastain Center Blvd., Suite 165
Kennesaw, GA 30144
www.envirosense.org

Essex Wallcoverings
Three University Plaza
Hackensack, NJ 07601

Eurotex
165 West Ontario Street
Philadelphia, PA 19140

Flame Control Coatings Inc.
1120 Hyde Park Blvd.
Niagara Falls, NY 14305
www.flamecontrol.com

Flexible Materials Inc.
11209 Electron Drive
Louisville, KY 40299
www.flexwood.com

Flex Trim Inc.
P.O. Box 4227
Rancho Cucamonga, CA 91730
www.flextrim.com

Focal Point Architectural Products Inc.
P.O. Box 93327
Atlanta, GA 30377-0327
www.focalpointap.com

Forbo Industries Inc.
P.O. Box 667
Hazelton, PA 18201
www.marmoleum.com

Formglas Interiors, Inc.
20 Toro Road
North York, Ontario
Canada, M3J 2A7
www.formglas.com

Formica Corp.
10155 Reading Road
Cincinnati, OH 45241
www.formica.com

Forms + Surfaces
6395 Cindy Lane
Carpenteria, CA 03013
www.forms.surfaces.com

Frigidaire
635 West Charles Street
Greenville, MI 48838
www.frigidaire.com

The Gage Corporation, Int.
803 S. Black River Street
Sparta, WI 54656

Gaggenau USA Corp.
425 University Avenue
Norwood, MA 02062
www.gaggenau.com

Gainsborough Hardware
Design House Inc.
W. 180 N. 11691 River Lane
Germantown, WI 53022

GE Monogram
GE Appliances
Louisville, KY 40225
www.ge.com

General Polymers Corp.
145 Caldwell Drive
Cincinnati, OH 45216
www.gencorp.com

Georgia Marble Co.
P.O. Box 238
Tate, GA 30177
www.georgiamarble.com

The Glidden Company
925 Euclid Avenue
Cleveland, OH 44115
www.ici.com/paints

Glitsa American Inc.
327 South Kenyon
Seattle, WA 98108
www.glitsa.com

Grass America Inc.
P.O. Box 1019
Kennersville, NC 27284
www.grassusa.com

Green Seal
1400 16th Street, N.W., Suite 300
Washington, DC 20036-2215
www.greenseal.org

Grohe America Inc.
241 Covington Drive
Bloomington, IL 60108

G-U Hardware Inc.
11761 Rock Landing Drive, Suite M6
Newport News, VA 23606
www.g-u.com

Hager Hinge Co.
139 Victor Street
St. Louis, MO 63104
www.hagerhinge.com

James Hardie Building Products, Inc.
Elm Avenue
Fontana, CA 92337
www.jameshardie.com

Hardwood Plywood & Veneer Association
P.O. Box 2789
Reston, VA 22090-0789
www.hpva.com

Harris-Tarkett
P.O. Box 300
Johnson City, TN 37601
www.harristarkett.com

Hartco Flooring Co.
P.O. Drawer A
Oneida, TN 37841
www.hartcoflooring.com

Heartland Appliances, Inc.
5 Hoffman Street
Kitchener, Ontario N2M3M5

Helios
www.helioscarpet.com

HEWI Inc.
2851 Old Tree Drive
Lancaster, PA 17603
www.hewi.com

Hillyard, Inc.
P.O. Box 909
St. Joseph, MO 64502–0909
www.hillyard.com

J.L. Industries
4450 West 78th Street Circle
Minneapolis, MN 55435
www.jlindustries.com

Innovations in Wallcoverings, Inc.
22 West 21st Street
New York, NY 10010
www.innovationsusa.com

Intarsia Inc.
1851 Cypress Lake Drive, Suite B
Orlando, FL 32837

Interface Flooring Systems, Inc.
P.O. Box 1503
Lagrange, GA 30241
www.ifsia.com

International Interior Design Association
341 Merchandise Mart
Chicago, IL 60654
www.iidia.com

Jacuzzi WhirlPool Bath
P.O. Drawer J
Walnut Creek, CA 94596
www.jacuzzi.com

J & J Industries Inc.
P.O. Box 1287
Dalton, GA 30722-1287
www.jj-invision.com

Jenn-Air Company
3035 Shadeland
Indianapolis, IN 46226–0901
www.jennair.com

Johnsonite Inc.
16910 Munn Road
Chagrin Falls, OH 44023
www.johnsonite.com

Kaylien
8520 Railroad Avenue
Santee, CA 92071

Kentucky Wood Floors Inc.
P.O. Box 33276
Louisville, KY 40232
www.kentuckywood.com

KitchenAid
701 Main Street
St. Joseph, MI 49085
www.KitchenDesigners.com

Knape & Vogt Manufacturing Co.
2700 Oak Industrial Drive N. E.
Grand Rapids, MI 49505
www.kv.com

Kohler Company
444 Highland Drive
Kohler, WI 53044
www.kohlerco.com

Koroseal Wallcoverings
3875 Embassy Parkway
Fairlawn, OH 44333
www.koroseal.com

Kroin Inc.
180 Fawcett Street
Cambridge, MA 02138

LCN Closers
P.O. Box 100
Princeton, IL 61656

Lees Modular Carpets
3330 W. Friendly Avenue
Greensboro, NC 27410
www.burlington.ind.com\lees.html

Leggett & Platt, Inc. Fiber Cushion Products
P.O. Box 758
Villa Rica, GA 30180–9858

Jack Lenor Larsen Inc.
41 East 11th Street
New York, NY 10003

J.M. Lynne Co., Inc.
P.O. Box 101
Smithtown, NY 11787
www.jmlynne.com

MacLock
8111 LBJ Freeway, Suite 285
Dallas, TX 75251
www.maclock.com

Mannington Commercial
P.O. Box 30
Salem, NJ 08079
www.mannington.com

Marble Institute of America Inc.
30 Eden Alley, #201
Columbus, OH 43215
www.marble-institute.com

Marlite
P.O. Box 250
Dover, OH 44622
www.marlite.com

Marvel Industries
P.O. Box 997
Richmond, IN 47375–0997

MDC Wallcoverings
1200 Arthur Avenue
Elk Grove, IL 60007

Memphis Hardwood Flooring Co.
1551 Thomas Street
Memphis, TN 38107

Merida Meridian Inc.
P.O. Box 1071
Syracuse, NY 13201-1071

Moen Incorporated
25300 Al Moen Drive
North Olmsted, OH 44070
www.moen.com

Benjamin Moore & Co.
51 Chestnut Ridge Road
Montvale, NJ 07645–1862
www.benjaminmoore.com

National Association of Home Builders
Builders Guide to Paints & Coatings
$12.50 + $5 s & h
Call (301)249-4000

National Gypsum Co.
2001 Rexford Road
Charlotte, NC 28211
www.national-gypsum.com

National Oak Flooring Manufacturers Association
P.O. Box 3009
Memphis, TN 38173–0009
www.nofma.org

National Products
900 Baxter Avenue
Louisville, KY 40204-0368
www.nationalproducts.com

The National Terrazzo & Mosaic Association, Inc.
3166 Des Plaines Avenue, Suite 121
Des Plaines, IL 60018

National Wood Flooring Association
233 Old Meramec Station Road
Manchester, MO 63021

Natural CORK
1750 Peachtree Street, Suite 305
Atlanta, GA 30309
www.naturalcork.com

Nevamar Corp.
8339 Telegraph Road
Odenton, MD 21113
www.nevamar.com

Nippon Electric Glass America
650 East Devon, Suite 110
Itasca, IL 60143

W. F. Norman Corporation
P.O. Box 323
Nevada, MO 64772

North American Association of Mirror Manufacturers
9005 Congressional Court
Potomac, MD 20854

Novawall Systems Inc.
561 Keystone Avenue, Suite 325
Reno, NV 89503

Nuway Matting Systems Inc.
8 Sagamore Street
Glens Falls, NY 12801
www.nuway.com

Old World Moulding & Finishing Inc.
115 Allen Boulevard
Farmingdale, NY 11735

Paul Decorative Products
810 East 136th Street
Bronx, NY 10454

Pergo
524 New Hope Road
Raleigh, NC 27610
www.pergo.com

PermaGrain Products Inc.
13 West Third Street
Media, PA 19063
www.permagrain.com/home

Pinecrest Inc.
2118 Blaisdell Avenue
Minneapolis, MN 55404–2490
www.pinecrest.com

Pittcon Industries Inc.
6409 Rhode Island Avenue
Riverdale, MD 20737–1098

Pittsburgh Corning Corp.
800 Presque Isle Drive
Pittsburgh, PA 15239
www.pittsburghcorning.com

Porter Paints
Courtaulds Coatings Inc.
P.O. Box 1439
Louisville, KY 40201–1439
www.courtaulds.com

Re-Bath Inc.
1055 S. County Club Drive
Mesa, AZ 85210
www.re-bath.com

Resilient Floor Covering Institute
966 Hungerford Drive, Suite 12B
Rockville, MD 20850

Robbins Hardwood Flooring
4785 Eastern Avenue
Cincinnati, OH 45226
www.robbinsfloor.com

Robern Inc.
7 Wood Avenue
Bristol, PA 19007
www.robern.com

Rockland React Rite
Highway 17 South
Chatom, AL 36518

Roppe Corp.
P.O. Box 1158
Fostoria, OH 44831-1158
www.roppe.com

Russell Range Inc.
229 Ryan Way
South San Francisco, CA 94080-6309
www.russellrange.com

Sargent
P.O. Box 9725
New Haven, CT 06536

Schlage Lock Co.
1915 Jamboree, Suite 165
Colorado Springs, CO 80920
www.schlagelock.com

Schumacher
79 Madison Avenue
New York, NY 10016

L. M. Scofield
6533 Bandini Blvd.
Los Angeles, CA 90040

Seabrook Wallcoverings
1325 Farmville Road
Memphis, TN 38122

Seagrave Coatings Corp.
320 Paterson Plank Road
Carlstadt, NJ 07072

St. Charles of New York
150 East 58th Street
New York, NY 10155

Alison T. Seymour Inc.
5423 W. Marginal Way SW
Seattle, WA 98106

Shanker Industries Inc.
3435 Lawson Blvd.
Oceanside, NJ 11572

Shaw Industries Inc.
P.O. Drawer 2128
Dalton, GA 30722-2128

Sherle Wagner International Inc.
60 East 57th Street
New York, NY 10022

Sherwin-Williams Co.
101 Prospect Avenue N. W.
Cleveland, OH 44115
www.sherwin.com

Speakman Company
P.O. Box 191
Wilmington, DE 19899–0191

Sponge Cushion Inc. (SCI)
P.O. Box 709
Morris, IL 60450

Stanley Hardware Division
Box 1840
New Britain, CT 06050
www.stanleyworks.com

Stark Carpet
979 Third Avenue, 11th Floor
New York, NY 10022

Stone Panels Inc.
1725 Sandy Lake Road
Carrollton, TX 75006

The Structural Slate Co.
P.O. Box 187
Pen Argyl, PA 18072

Style-Mark Inc.
P.O. Box 301
Archbold, OH 43502
www.style-mark.com

Sub-Zero Freezer Co.
P.O. Box 44130
Madison, WI 53711–0130
www.zerofreezer.com

Summitville Tiles Inc.
Summitville, OH 43962
www.summitville.com

Surface Protection Industries International
3360 East Picot
Los Angeles, CA 90023

The Swan Corporation
One City Centre
St. Louis, MO 63101
www.swanstone.com

Syndesis
2908 Colorado Avenue
Santa Monica, CA 90404-3616
www.syndesisinc.com

TacFast Carpet Systems
(800)421-8878
www.3m.com

Tarkett Inc. North America
1139 Lehigh Ave.
Whitehall, PA 18052
www.tarkettna.com

Tasso Wallcoverings
1239 E. Newport Center, Suite 118
Deerfield Beach, FL 33442
www.sweets.com

Terrazzo & Marble Supply Co.
5700 South Hamilton Avenue
Chicago, IL 60636

Thermador
5119 District Boulevard
Los Angeles, CA 90040

Thibaut Wallcoverings
4025 E. Chandler Blvd, Suite 70
Phoenix, AZ 85044

Tile Council of America, Inc.
P.O. Box 1787
Clemson, SC 29633
www.tileusa.org

Tiles Inc.
235 E. Pittsburgh Avenue
Milwaukee, WI 53204

TOPsiders
P.O. Box 428640
Cincinnati, OH 45242
www.topsiders.com

Transwall Corp.
P.O. Box 1930
West Chester, PA 19380

Traulsen & Co., Inc.
4401 Blue Mound Road
Fort Worth, TX 76106
www.traulsen.com

Triarch Industries
4816 Campbell Road
Houston, TX 77041
www.triarchinc.com

Trus Joist MacMillan
P.O. Box 60
Boise, ID 83707
www.TJM.com

U-Line Corp.
8900 North 55th Street
Milwaukee, WI 53223

Universal Industrial Products (Soss Hinge)
One Coreway Drive
Pioneer, OH 43554
www.soss.com

USG Interiors Inc.
P.O. Box 4470
Chicago, IL 60680–4470
www.usg.com

Vasquez Enterprises
811 W. Warner Road
Tempe, AZ 85284

Viking Range Corp.
111 Front Street
Greenwood, MS 38930
www.viking-range.com

Viracon Privacy Glass
P.O. Box 248
Owatonna, MN 55060
www.viracon.com

VPI Floor Products
P.O. Box 451
Sheboygan, WI 53082
www.dataplysnet.com/vpi

Wausau Tile Inc.
P.O. Box 1520
Wausau, WI 54402–1520
www.wausautile.com

Weiser Lock
6700 Weiser Lock Drive
Tuscon, AZ 85746
www.weiserlock.com

Whirlpool Home Appliances
www.whirlpoolappliances.com

Willamette Industries, Inc.
P.O. Box 907
Albany, OR 97321
www.wii.com

Wilsonart International
P.O. Box 6110
Temple, TX 7653-6110
www.wilsonart.com

Wood-Mode Inc.
One Second Street
Kreamer, PA 17833
www.wood-mode.com

Yale Security Inc.
P.O. Box 25288
Charlotte, NC 28229–8010
www.yalesecurity.com

Wm. Zinsser & Co.
480 Frelinghuysen Avenue
Newark, NJ 07114
www.zinsser.com

Index